Apartheid and the Archbishop

by the same author

MEDITATION FOR A YOUNG BOY CONFIRMED

CRY, THE BELOVED COUNTRY

TOO LATE THE PHALAROPE

DEBBIE GO HOME

KONTAKION FOR YOU DEPARTED

HOFMEYR

ALAN PATON

Apartheid and the Archbishop

THE LIFE AND TIMES OF
GEOFFREY CLAYTON
ARCHBISHOP OF CAPE TOWN

JONATHAN CAPE
THIRTY BEDFORD SQUARE LONDON

FIRST PUBLISHED IN GREAT BRITAIN 1974

JONATHAN CAPE LTD,
30 BEDFORD SQUARE, LONDON WCI

ISBN 0 224 00994 X

PRINTED IN GREAT BRITAIN BY
LOWE AND BRYDONE (PRINTERS) LTD
THETFORD, NORFOLK
BOUND BY G. AND J. KITCAT LTD, LONDON

To David Russell, Priest

Contents

	List of Illustrations	ix
	Select Bibliography	xi
	Acknowledgements	xiii
1	Wanted: A Bishop	1
2	Rugby and Cambridge	5
3	Little St. Mary's	14
4	Vicar of Chesterfield	22
5	Geoffrey Johannesburg	36
6	A Strange Society	43
7	Interfering with the World	49
8	'We are governed and we like it'	55
9	A Missionary Church	64
10	Clayton and His Priests	74
11	War	83
12	The Diocese and the War	90
13	The New Order	100
14	The Nature of Hope	106
15	Church and Nation	113
16	A Magnificent Chapter	123
17	Something for Your Comfort	129
18	'Do the next right thing'	140
19	The Diffident Saint	151
20	Visit to Lambeth	161

21	'My heart is turned to water'	171
22	To Bishopscourt	178
23	The Fierce Laws	187
24	Enter Verwoerd	201
25	Assault on the Franchise	211
26	Assault on Protest	224
27	Assault on the Schools	232
28	The Destruction of Sophiatown	246
29	'No time to be lost'	262
30	'We cannot obey this law'	275
31	Verwoerd Bows to the Wind	283
32	'Let us be thankful'	289
	Appendix	293
	Notes to Sources	295
	Index	304

List of Illustrations

BETWEEN PAGES 144 AND 145

1 G. H. Clayton, G. A. B. Newenham, the Bishop of Derby (Pearce), R. P. R. Carpenter and D. B. Harris in 1927 (Photo: H. J. Morgan, Chesterfield)

2 At the Church Bazaar in Chesterfield, October 1928, Archdeacon Clayton with Lady Shentall, the Mayor, R. P. R. Carpenter and Princess Marie Louise (Photo: *Derbyshire Times*)

3 On the same occasion, with the Duchess of Devonshire (Photo: *Derbyshire Times*)

4 After his consecration in St. Paul's Cathedral, London, as Bishop of Johannesburg, May 1934 (Photo: Associated Press, London)

5 The Revd. Michael Scott, passive-resister in Durban, July 1947 (Photo: *Daily News*, Durban)

6 Father Trevor Huddleston, C.R., with children from his mission nursery school (Photo: Constance Stuart, Chestertown, Maryland)

7 As Bishop of Johannesburg in January 1949, after his election as Archbishop of Cape Town but before his enthronement (Photo: *Cape Argus*)

8 With Bishops Peacey, Paget and Reeves at the consecration of Ambrose Reeves as Bishop of Johannesburg, August 1949 (Photo: *Cape Argus*)

BETWEEN PAGES 176 AND 177

9 At St. George's Orphanage, near Cape Town, August 1955 (Photo: Photo-Hausmann, Cape Town)

10 At Episcopal Synod, November 1955, Clayton presiding over the Bishops of (clockwise from left foreground) St. Helena (Turner), Kimberley and Kuruman (Boys), Natal (Inman), Zululand (Trapp), Pretoria (Taylor), Grahamstown (Cullen), St. John's (Evans), Lebombo (Beevor, at back), Damaraland (Vincent), George (Hunter), Basutoland (Maund), Johannesburg (Reeves) (Photo: *Cape Times*)

11 The Bishop of Matabeleland (Hughes) and the Archbishops of Central Africa (Paget), Cape Town, and Canterbury (Fisher) at the Cathedral of St. Mary and All Saints, Salisbury, Rhodesia, during the inauguration of the Province of Central Africa in May 1955 (Photo: *Rhodesia Herald*)

12 The Most Revd. Dr. G. H. Clayton, Archbishop of Cape Town (Photo: E. Bieber, Cape Town)

13 The Revd. R. W. F. Cowdry in 1957 (Photo: *Cape Argus*)

14 The Right Revd. Robert Selby Taylor, then Archbishop-designate, at 'Bishopscourt' in February 1964 (Photo: *Cape Times*)

15 Memorial brass in the parish church of Chesterfield (Photo: R. Wilsher, A.R.P.S., Chesterfield)

Select Bibliography

Ballinger (Margaret), *From Union to Apartheid: A Trek to Isolation*, Juta, Cape Town, Praeger, New York, and Bailey Brothers and Swinfen, London, 1969

Brookes (E. H.) and C. de B. Webb, *A History of Natal*, Natal University Press, Pietermaritzburg, 1965

Clayton (Sir Francis), *The Claytons: Since 1800 A.D.*, private circulation, 1955

Clayton (Geoffrey Hare), *The Citizen and His Right of Association*, Civil Rights League, Cape Town, 1957

Clayton (Geoffrey Hare), *Christian Unity: An Anglican View* (Peter Ainslie Memorial Lecture), Rhodes University College, Grahamstown, 1949

Clayton (Geoffrey Hare), 'The Church in South Africa', a chapter in R. B. Lloyd, *The Church of England, 1900–1965*, S.C.M. Press, London, 1966

Clayton (Geoffrey Hare), *Where We Stand: Archbishop Clayton's Charges 1948–57, chiefly relating to Church and State in South Africa*, ed. C. T. Wood, Oxford University Press, Cape Town, London and New York, 1960

Clayton (Geoffrey Hare), *Yea and Nay*, A.R. Mowbray, London, 1933, 1938

Clayton papers, Library of the University of the Witwatersrand, Johannesburg

Hellmann (Ellen), ed., *Handbook on Race Relations in South Africa*, Oxford University Press for South African Institute of Race Relations, Cape Town, London and New York, 1949

Huddleston (Trevor), *Naught for Your Comfort*, Hardingham and Donaldson, Johannesburg, for Collins, London, 1956

Keppel-Jones (Arthur), *When Smuts Goes: A History of South Africa from 1952 to 2010 first published in 2015*, African Bookman, Cape Town, 1947

Lewis (Cecil) and G. E. Edwards, eds., *Historical Records of the Church of the Province of South Africa*, S.P.C.K., London, 1934

Malan (D. F.), *Afrikaner-volkseenheid en my Ervarings op die Pad Daarheen*, Nasionale Boekhandel, Cape Town, 1959

Mosley (Nicholas), *The Life of Raymond Raynes*, Faith Press, London, 1961

Paton (Alan), *Hofmeyr*, Oxford University Press, Cape Town and London, 1964; abridged ed., Charles Scribner's Sons Publishers, New York, 1956, and O.U.P., Cape Town and London, 1971

Scott, (Michael), *A Time to Speak*, Faber and Faber, London, 1958

Sundkler (B. G. M.), *Bantu Prophets in South Africa*, Lutterworth Press, London, 1948, Oxford University Press, London, for International African Institute, 1961

Survey of Race Relations in South Africa (annually since 1951-2), South African Institute of Race Relations, Johannesburg

Walker (Eric), *A History of Southern Africa*, Longmans, London, 3rd ed. 1957

Wilson (Monica) and L. M. Thompson, *Oxford History of South Africa*, vols. 1 and 2, Clarendon Press, Oxford, 1969 and 1971

Acknowledgements

I wish to express my thanks to all those who helped me to make this book. They must pardon me if I do not set down all their names. Some lent me letters and papers, some helped me with opinions and judgements and recollections and stories, some helped me to gather the material. Of these last I should like to mention three, Miss Julie Wells, an American student at the University of the Witwatersrand, Miss Fenella Robins, a teacher at the Kloof High School, and the late Arthur Blaxall, retired priest.

I am indebted to the library and librarians of the University of the Witwatersrand, and the University of Natal in Durban, the library and librarians of the Natal Society, Pietermaritzburg, and to those of our newspapers who gave me access to their files.

I must give special thanks to my readers, who enabled me to correct errors and to reconsider judgements, but cannot be held responsible for any errors or misjudgements remaining. They were:

In Johannesburg: The Revd. Dick Yates; the Revd. Canon Redvers Rouse; Mr. Jonathan Paton; Dr. Beyers Naude; Mr. Fred van Wyk.

In Natal: The Right Revd. Vernon Inman, Bishop of Natal; the Revd. Dr. Edgar Brookes; the Revd. Canon Paddy Goldie; Mr. Tony Morphet.

In the Cape Province: The Most Revd. Robert Selby Taylor, Archbishop of Cape Town; Bishop Roy Cowdry of Port Elizabeth; Dr. David Welsh; Mr. Gerald Abernethy; Mrs. Dorothy Cleminshaw.

In England: The Right Revd. Trevor Huddleston, Bishop of Stepney; the Revd. Michael Scott; the Revd. Donald Harris; the late Revd. Claude Handford; the Revd. Gonville ffrench-Beytagh.

I am indebted also to those who provided the illustrations and who are named on pages ix and x.

ALAN PATON

Apartheid and the Archbishop

1

Wanted: A Bishop

In 1933 the diocese of Johannesburg was looking for a new bishop to replace the Right Revd. Arthur Baillie Lumsdaine Karney. He had been ill, and had taken a long time to recover. Because of his illness, or for some other reason, he was ready to move on. He had been in charge of the diocese from 1922, but in September 1933 he announced that he had been offered the suffragan-bishopric of Southampton, England, and would accept it.

He was following a well-established tradition. At that time all except one of the South African bishops, of that branch of the Anglican communion known as the Church of the Province of South Africa, had been imported from Britain, and it was generally understood that after a term 'in the colonies', or less offensively, 'abroad', they would return 'home' either to retire there, or to resume their service to the Church of England.

The leaving of England in the first place could be thoroughly justified. The Anglican communion was world-wide, and one could serve as well in one part of it as in any other. What irritated many South Africans, and angered others, was that after this term of service in a world-wide church, one returned 'home'. At one time this use of the word was common, not only amongst British-born South Africans, but amongst their South-African-born children, even sometimes their grandchildren. But in 1933 this particular use was declining, partly because the South-African-born of British descent were beginning to find it ridiculous, partly because the Nationalist Afrikaner found it offensive. Hertzog's Nationalist Party had come into power in 1924, and resented any suggestion that South Africa was inferior to England. The calling of England 'home' by born South Africans was to them monstrous. They were angered by the use of the words 'colony' and 'colonials', and by the expression 'going out to South Africa'. They even objected to the use of the word 'overseas' when it applied only to travel from Britain to other countries.

There was amongst Nationalist Afrikaners a distrust of *die Engelse Kerk*, the English church. This dated back to the early 1800s, when Britain had annexed the Cape, and had introduced laws and regulations which gave servants and slaves new rights over and against their masters. British missionaries (and others) flouted the traditions of the white inhabitants, notably the colour-bar. The final straw was the emancipation of the slaves, not so much that it was done, but rather the way in which it was done; to take but one example, compensation for emancipated slaves was paid in London, and unscrupulous middlemen went about the Cape buying up claims at a fraction of their worth. The result of all this, of the introduction to the Cape Colony of a new and alien mode of thought and action, led in 1836 to the famous migration that became known as the Great Trek.

This dislike of *die Engelse Kerk*, of the flouting of custom by foreign missionaries, and of the changing of laws by British administrators, was still alive in 1933. Nationalist Afrikaners felt that it was becoming intolerable that a church now calling itself the Church of the Province of South Africa should continue to import its bishops from Britain, men who knew nothing about the customs and traditions of white South Africa, men who were mostly from those extremely condescending universities of Oxford and Cambridge, who seldom made any attempt to learn Afrikaans, and who ignored the colour-bar in the life of the church. We shall see later that in fact the church both ignored and conformed to this particular white tradition. To make it worse, these Anglican bishops often delivered powerful attacks on South African laws and customs in their sermons and charges, and it was the practice of the English-language newspapers to give great prominence to these pronouncements, and often to support them editorially.

This intense suspicion, even hatred, of the Church of the Province, did not leave untouched its own white members, most of whom were English-speaking. There were some of course who preferred bishops from Britain, and did not in the least mind if they went 'home' when they felt they had done their stint. But there were others who did not want bishops from Britain at all; they wanted them chosen from the ranks of the South-African-born priests, who 'understood the country'. Between these extremes there was a large body of white Anglicans, who, while they did not object to importing bishops from England, objected when they went 'home'. There grew up a saying that the trouble with the Church of the Province was not that it had British bishops, but that it had no British bishops' bones.

Bishop Karney was himself aware of these feelings. He wrote in the September issue of *The Watchman* that he felt concerned about being English, coming to South Africa for ten or twelve years, and then leaving; it was time that the country produced its own leaders, though he had no regrets at having spoken out on the 'native question' (this being the simplistic name given by white people in those days to the intense complexity of racial relationships which was the beginning and the end of all politics, is now, but not, we hope, ever shall be).

In his last charge Karney pressed for reforms in 'native policy', a recital of which reads very like a recital of the needs today: more effective constitutional channels of consultation between the white rulers and the non-white ruled, agricultural development of the Reserves, better town locations, simplification of the pass system, more financial support for Native Education, and more secure tenure for African labourers on white farms.*

*Some of these terms may require explanation: [*continued on facing page*

So Karney went 'home', suitably farewelled and thanked, and Dean William Palmer, of the Cathedral of St. Mary, was appointed by the Archbishop of Cape Town to be Vicar-General of the diocese. Palmer was an outstanding preacher, held in high regard. He might even have been thought of as a possible successor. But he himself did not contemplate such a thing. In fact he had already decided to nominate a candidate, and to speak for him with all his formidable powers of persuasion.

The new bishop would be the second Bishop of Johannesburg. In 1922 the diocese of Pretoria had been split in two, the second portion to be called the diocese of Johannesburg. The move was overdue. Pretoria and Johannesburg were very different cities, although only thirty-six miles apart. Pretoria was the administrative capital of the Union of South Africa, the seat of the Governor-General, the site of the great Union Buildings and the official home of the Prime Minister and the members of his cabinet; its atmosphere was quite different from that of Johannesburg, though it was the centre of the iron and steel industry, and destined to grow in industrial importance. Johannesburg was primarily a mining and industrial city, the industrial and financial capital of the Union. Moreover it was four times the size of Pretoria, and substantial parts of it were continually being pulled down and rebuilt.

The first bishop of the new diocese of Johannesburg had been Arthur Karney; the second was now to be chosen by the Elective Assembly of the diocese, consisting of all the licensed priests, one representative of the deacons, and lay representatives elected by the parishes in proportion to the number of adult communicants. The Church of the Province of South Africa was not an established church, and therefore the choice of its bishops lay solely with the clergy and laity, and had nothing to do with the monarch or the government.* Of all the bishops who had come to South Africa from

continued from previous page]

Non-white: Many South Africans want an alternative word to 'non-white' but it is not easy to find. In a country where the rulers are white and the ruled are not, the word 'non-white' is in frequent use, and has become objectionable to people who are not white. One alternative would be 'African, Coloured, and Indian people', but this can become tedious. The other alternative is to use the word 'black' of all people who are not white, and this is acceptable to many of them but not all. At the time of writing the South African Institute of Race Relations has decided to use the word 'black'.

Reserves: Those parts of South Africa (13 per cent of the total area) set aside for African occupation. The population of South Africa (1973) is approximately: African 16¼ million, White 4 million, Coloured 2 million and Indian ¾ million.

Location: A township attached to the white town or city, for African occupation.

Pass System: The complex of laws which controls the movements of all Africans, except within the confines of their Reserves and locations. The *pass* is the document that must be carried.

Native: The word 'Native' will be used only when obligatory, as in the name of some law or department; the word 'Bantu' also. The words 'Black' and 'African' will be preferred.

*The monarch, i.e. the King of Great Britain and Ireland, was represented in South Africa by the Governor-General, the country being in 1933 still a dominion of the British Commonwealth.

Britain, not one was ever reported as having said or thought that the established was preferable to the unestablished church. This might, however, be explained by the fact that the largest church was the Nederduitse Gereformeerde Kerk, the N.G.K., called commonly and erroneously the Dutch Reformed Church, there being two other smaller Dutch Reformed churches.

The Elective Assembly met in the Darragh Hall on 6 December 1933. Dean Palmer then put forward the name of Geoffrey Hare Clayton, the Vicar of Chesterfield, Derbyshire, with a parish church famous for its crooked spire. Palmer did this on the strong recommendation of Bishop Michael Furse, who had been Bishop of Pretoria and now was Bishop of St. Albans in England. Bishop Charles Gore, who died in 1932, had also told Palmer that Clayton would make a mark on the Church of England. Palmer's proposal was seconded by Percy Forbes, Rector of Heidelberg, who said that his favoured candidate had a great intellect and a vile temper, but was the best man for the job. Clayton was otherwise almost unknown, except for those who had heard legends of his intellect, his temper, his dislike of women, his ability to squash the earnest and the pompous, and to laugh heartily, not exactly at their discomfiture, but at something the exact nature of which no one ever really knew.

Several candidates were nominated, one of them by no means unknown. This was Edward Paget, the Bishop of Southern Rhodesia, who before his elevation had been the vigorous and popular rector of the Transvaal parish of Benoni. In fact it was soon clear that it was to be Clayton or Paget, and it was Palmer's persuasiveness, and the magic names of Gore and Furse, that finally caused the Assembly to make Clayton the Bishop-elect of Johannesburg.

Although the Elective Assembly was pledged to secrecy, and although its members were persons who were presumably the very souls of honour, the morning papers published the news of his election some time before his cable of acceptance was received. Prescient tributes were paid by the newspapers, and *The Watchman* of January 1934 published a piece entitled 'The Bishop-elect', by G.T.C., a friend of thirteen years standing. According to G.T.C. the new bishop was known for his spirituality, a large and pastoral heart, sound learning, sanctified commonsense, and a strong sense of humour.

'He is not a "party" man, but could be classified as a Liberal Catholic of the Cambridge school. The Master of Corpus,* the chief influence in this school, is one of his greatest friends.

'He has the deepest mistrust of all "hot air", "uplift", and mere words. He is an enemy to all pomposity and is skilled at pricking bubbles.'

G.T.C. adds, almost as though this were the plum, 'He has been very popular with Rotarians at Chesterfield.'

This is a good picture, but it omits two things. These were the greatness and the childishness. It was these that made Clayton such an extraordinary being.

*Sir Will Spens.

2

Rugby and Cambridge

Geoffrey Hare Clayton was born in Leicester, England, on 12 December 1884, in the vicarage of St. Margaret's. His father, Lewis Clayton, had been vicar of Leicester since 1875, and much later, in 1903, become Bishop-Suffragan of Leicester. This post he resigned so that it might be given to a younger and more vigorous man, Norman Lang, brother of the Archbishop of York. He then accepted the lesser position of Assistant Bishop of Peterborough.

Bishop Clayton was a gentle and quiet man, and was regarded by many as a saint; he was elected chairman of the school management committee largely because of the support given to him by the Nonconformists, whose respect he retained throughout his long and unselfish life. His wife, born Katherine Hare, was a woman of force and drive, who was made a Commander of the British Empire for her services to the town and diocese of Peterborough, and was made a Freeman of the City in 1927.[1]

The Claytons had four children, Lewis born in 1872, Harold in 1874, Katherine in 1877, and seven years later, Geoffrey. The small boy was not beautiful; he had a great head and small feet and striking eyes, which though not protuberant, were certainly prominent. He was left a great deal to himself, partly because of his age, and partly because of the busy lives of his parents. He had two invisible playmates, 'Mr. Billy Goat' and 'Mr. Bunny', who were not animals but men. At the age of 4 he married a woman called 'Katherine Nobody', who looked after King's Cross Station at night. At 6 he was reading *The Times* parliamentary reports, and conducting his own services, reading the lessons and preaching the sermon. Some well-intentioned persons urged Mrs. Clayton to stop him from doing so, but she was a sensible woman and refused.

It was a remarkable family. Duty was something not to be argued about; it was simply done. The discipline was firm, and probably was maintained more by the mother than the father. Character was more important than money, position, success, or pleasure. In fact the development of character was the whole purpose of life upon the earth, not merely a parents' purpose, but the purpose of God the Creator. That was why He created man, and it was for that purpose that He gave men life. The family was in fact ruled by God, in the most straightforward and practical and Anglican way. The

Clayton children never felt any desire to rebel against their parents' religion, because it was devoid of cant and hypocrisy. Their parents' love was deep and unquestioned, though not demonstrative. After the bishop's death in 1917, Katherine Clayton wrote a memoir of the most formal kind, revealing nothing of the intimacies of family life. Her son, Geoffrey, of whom she was extremely proud, is once referred to, but not by name; he is called the Dean of Peterhouse. Her husband is called Mr. or Bishop Clayton.

The influence of this home on the small boy Geoffrey was profound, though no doubt other mysterious factors must have been at work also, for his childhood was, so far as we know, without jealousies, hurts, and frustrations. Unknown to any person, here was developing a character of the most extraordinary kind, self-contained, not in the sense of being uncommunicative, but complete in itself, yet preparing, even at that early age to be the servant of others.

In later years Geoffrey Clayton was to believe that his total lack of interest in women as women was manifested in his earliest years. As a proof of this, he often told Roy Cowdry, who was his chaplain at 'Bishopscourt', the home of the Archbishop of Cape Town, a story of his childhood. How old he was at the time, one does not know, but he was still young enough to be taken out in a push-chair by a maid. On one of these expeditions, a lady smiled at him and said, 'Good morning, Geoffrey.' Geoffrey asked, 'Who is that?', to which the maid replied, 'That, Master Geoffrey, is your mother.'

Another story which he often told to Cowdry was that on another occasion when he was being pushed along, he asked the maid, 'Why do you do this?,' to which she replied, 'Master Geoffrey, it is my duty and I will.' This story amused him to the end of his life.

Although Geoffrey was the youngest of the family, to him were given the greatest intellectual gifts. His elder brother Lewis is barely mentioned in Sir Francis Clayton's small book *The Claytons*; according to Venn's Alumni, Lewis Hare Clayton went to Marlborough, and to Clare College in 1891, where he took a Third Class in the Mathematical Tripos in 1894. His second brother Harold was educated at Marlborough and Pembroke College, Cambridge, where he took a First Class Classical Tripos. Their education was almost certainly provided for by scholarships, because the family was by no means wealthy. Harold entered the Indian Civil Service, and became Burma Financial Commissioner. He was a devout churchman, and on retirement became secretary of the Church of England Men's Society. One other interest he had in common with his younger brother, and that was an appetite for stories of murder and detection. Geoffrey's sister Katherine married in her middle thirties the Revd. Robert Roberts, and wrote a private memoir of her youngest brother, which I was not able to discover.

It was Geoffrey who was destined to be the pride of the family. At the age of 10 he went to Hurst Court Preparatory School in the small village of Ore, near Hastings, and at 13 won the top scholarship to Rugby. His mother may have kept his Rugby school reports but only two have been discovered, these amongst his own papers. The first was for the Advent Term of 1901; he was in Form VIa, and his age is given as 17 years and no months, the average age of the form being 18 years and one month. He was placed eighth out of eighteen, and W.G. Nicholl comments, '. . . this report is most encouraging. It looks as if your son would hold his own with any of them in a year's time'. It would appear from this, and from the report for the Trinity Term in 1903, which also placed him in Form VIa, that he had repeated this final year, though for what reason one cannot discover. His age is now 18 years and five months, the average being 17 years and eleven months. He is now placed second out of twenty-one. He is an excellent translator of Latin, and in History is always clear and to the point. Although he is no athlete, he is head of Michell House. His headmaster, H. A. James, who later became President of St. John's College, Oxford, writes that 'his university career cannot but be successful and honourable'. And that 'his high character and power of work will make him a useful man'.

One of the strong influences on the young Clayton was his tutor, Robert Whitelaw. Clayton thought him to be the most gifted teacher he had ever met, and did him the singular honour of having his portrait in his various studies, including his last at 'Bishopscourt'. Clayton always remembered that during his last days at Rugby, when he returned from Cambridge with an open scholarship to Pembroke in his pocket, Whitelaw had said to him, 'Well, Clayton, how did you deceive the authorities at Cambridge?'[2]

Whitelaw taught the form called 'The Twenty', the class immediately below the Lower Sixth. He was a great classical scholar and a poet, and sometimes on Sunday evenings he would read from Wordsworth, Tennyson, and Browning, holding his hearers spellbound. Claude Handford, who was later to be one of Clayton's curates at Chesterfield, writes 'perhaps there was a somewhat submerged poetical streak in G.H.C.', for Clayton was spellbound also.[3] It was possible that a few years later Father Figgis of the Community of the Resurrection could spellbind him too, but he and Whitelaw might well have been the only two who ever performed this remarkable feat. It seems likely that when Clayton was at St. Mary's the Less, certainly when he was at Chesterfield, he had ceased to be capable of becoming spellbound. In fact he was spellbinding others, and doing it in that curious way of his, just by the odd method of being what he was, with no tricks or graces. One thing is certain, his poetical streak remained a streak. He was much later, in the last year of his life, to give his clergy an astonishing address on George Herbert, whose writing he obviously regarded highly, no doubt because of its deep religious feeling, but no doubt also because that feeling was expressed in language of such beauty. In his own writing and speaking the poetic flight was absent. He did not have much poetry in him, but he knew when others did. And what is more, he quoted them often.

Geoffrey won two exhibitions on leaving Rugby, a General Exhibition and a Classical one. He had won prizes for Latin Prose, English Literature, Divinity, and a Reading Prize. This gift of reading he was to be able to use all his life. Unlike many great readers, he used none of the techniques of the great actor. He did not use gestures, whether of hands or face. His gift lay almost wholly in his magnificent voice, which he controlled perfectly, and if one were to add 'with consummate art', one would have to add that the art appeared, not to be concealed, but to be totally unconscious. Something in him responded deeply and naturally to the words that he was reading, and this happened most naturally when he was reading the great passages of the Bible, or saying the Prayer of Humble Access, which he seemed always to create anew.

In September 1904, the young Clayton proceeded to Pembroke College, Cambridge, where his brother Harold had been before him.* I have not been able to discover what he did between July 1903 and September 1904. Perhaps he stayed at home and read and studied, not being considered mature enough to go to Cambridge. He later wrote, on his application form for ordination, in answer to the question 'How long have you been desirous of taking Holy Orders?' the following answer: 'I have never seriously contemplated doing anything else, though at times I have been doubtful. I made up my mind fairly definitely in 1903–1904.'

One supposes therefore that he made up his mind before going to Cambridge. But it is also clear that Cambridge confirmed him very powerfully in his decision. His friends were all Anglicans and practising Christians. He himself was greatly influenced by the Mission to Undergraduates of Fathers Frere and Bull from the Community of the Resurrection, and before it was over he had made his first confession.[4] Many years later, in 1948, when he was elected Archbishop of Cape Town, John How, Bishop of Glasgow and Galloway, Primus of the Scottish (Episcopal) Church, wrote to him commenting on 'that little group of people at Cambridge' who were now in places of responsibility and strategic posts – the Deans of Winchester, York, Exeter, Chichester; the Bishop of Ely, the Primus of the Scottish Church, 'and NOW the Archbishop of Cape Town'. Bishop How wrote of the group as being 'largely centred on H.L. Pass'. Pass was a converted Jew and later became principal of Chichester Theological College, where Michael Scott studied in 1929.

This 'little group of people' belonged to the University Church Society, which Clayton helped to found in 1905, largely as a counterblast to the agnostic influences at the university. John How was a source of strength to the society. Other prominent members were Will Spens later Master of Corpus, Milner-White of King's, who later became Dean of York, Wynn, who became Bishop of Ely, and E.G. Selwyn, later Dean of Winchester, and editor of *Theology* for many years. S. H. Clarke, who when he later became headmaster of St. John's College, Johannesburg, was to be closely associated with Clayton, first met him in 1912. Clarke was at Trinity, and as an undergraduate became secretary of the Cambridge Church Society, thus meeting this extraordinary group of men, many of them then college chap-

*One must note that Clayton's most famous contemporary at Rugby was William Temple, later Archbishop of Canterbury. In his obituary tribute to Clayton in *The Meteor* of 21 June 1957, Sir Will Spens wrote that of all his Rugby contemporaries, these two gave 'the most notable service in their generation'.

lains. Their influence on students was considerable, not only in their own colleges, but in their contributions to the Church of Great St. Mary's. One of their greatest achievements was the Mission to the University in March 1913, conducted by Bishop Maud of Kensington and Father Frere of the C.R. They filled Great St. Mary's, including the galleries, every night for a week, and had a tremendous impact on the university. In this Mission, the other influential university society, the Cambridge Inter-Collegiate Christian Union, C.I.C.C.U., took no part, this being the reaction of the Evangelicals to the Anglo–Catholics, a cleavage which existed within the Church of England itself.

Clarke described Clayton's religion in this way. According to von Hügel there were three elements of religion, the catholic–sacramental–social, the liberal–rational–intellectual, and the evangelical–biblical–mystical. The pre-1914 Roman Catholics stressed the first, the Inges and the Barneses the second, and C.I.C.C.U. the third. But Clayton's group, and Clayton himself, maintained all three to the full. It was this that was to be the mark of Clayton's religion throughout his life.

A more humble member of this distinguished group was Bernard Hepworth, affectionately known in many parts of England and South Africa as Father Thomas, and now living in retirement at the Irene Homes near Pretoria. He was two years junior to Clayton, and spent a holiday with the Clayton family at Peterborough, being impressed by the saintliness of the bishop and the formidability of his wife, who, says Father Thomas, 'wore the trousers'.

Hepworth learned a great deal from his friend. The young Clayton, who had little of the mystic in him, had nevertheless a great sense of the being and majesty of God, which was to remain undiminished throughout his life, and was to be a source of strength to many people. In ordinary conversation he could be jovial, petulant, trenchant, witty and gossipy, sometimes waspishly so. But when he spoke of God, his voice and demeanour would change; he would sometimes close his eyes, and speak with emotional force which was not less intense for being controlled. One would never apply to him the epithets pious, earnest, or intense, yet here was a young man who had given himself and his extraordinary gifts to God, and who would tell others, perhaps again with closed eyes, that they should do the same – that being the only way in which a man could live a full and purposeful life.

Clayton was not vouchsafed visions. In fact he was extremely sceptical about them, but he did not dismiss them as impossible, and would respect the visions of others if he believed they had been given them. As for himself, God worked in him in quite a different fashion. One performed one's religious duties, one prayed and read and studied the scriptures, one received the sacraments, and after that, satisfied that one's talents had been dedicated to the service of God, one got on with one's work, using one's sense and intelligence, without undue fussing about the direction in which one was being led by the Spirit. He was sceptical of the honesty and sensibleness of those who were continually receiving 'guidance', and could not conceal his impatience of and his distaste for their messages.

He was academically brilliant in the same disciplined way. Flamboyance he never had, though he – probably more so in later life – suffered few detectable inhibitions. He could laugh outrageously, sprawling on the floor or the settee in most inelegant fashion, but one was not expected to join in; whether he did not care, or whether it never occurred to him, one does not know, but he would never think to inquire, 'Do you know what I'm laughing at?'

His intellectual gifts were considerable, but one could doubt whether he had a mind of great originality. Even in his early twenties, he was rather showing signs of that judgement and wisdom which were to make him pre-eminent amongst men, and for which he prayed his whole life long. So much did these qualities grow in him that he could preside with an unquestioned authority over men who were as gifted as he.

He was not attracted by extreme dogmatism, yet he himself held tremendous dogmas, and these were of course the affirmations of the Creed. He already held strongly the view that he was to hold throughout his life, that Christian morality was based on Christian doctrine, and that if the doctrine lost its hold, the morality would do likewise.

He was dogmatic about marriage, divorce and the practice of contraception, but not about gambling and drinking, though he would have been opposed to any immoderation, One conventional criticism of gambling he did not hold with at all. He was at a meeting where one of the speakers said that his strongest reason for opposing gambling was that you 'got something for nothing'. Clayton's comment was brief and devastating. 'I should like to remind the previous speaker that the essence of the gospel is that you *do* get something for nothing.'[5] Though opposed to immoderation, he loved his food and ate immoderately and not elegantly. Certainly he was an immoderate smoker. At what time he became so, I do not know, but in later years he smoked continuously. He would talk – which was another of his less moderate habits – with a cigarette dangling from the corner of his mouth, spilling ash over his stock and clothes. He smoked a pipe also, in those intervals when he was not sleeping or eating or smoking cigarettes. During Lent he gave it up, to the despair of his friends and subordinates, because it increased his irritability. He became more approachable on Sundays, because he smoked from the conclusion of Mass until midnight. He was also unable to smoke at synods and similar gatherings; when he was in the chair, it was this abstention which was reported to make him more formidable than usual.

Donald Harris, who was his curate in Chesterfield from 1927 to 1931, records that Clayton could often be seen in Lent sitting at his desk, writing, with the end of his handkerchief in his mouth. In those days he had three curates, and he would have them to supper on Sundays, and was very affable because he could smoke. But on Wednesdays he went to their Clergy House for lunch, and very often did not manage to say a single word. Harris wrote forty years later:

'I can't remember now whether any of us dared to speak. This kind of thing taught me the meaning of ambivalence.'[6]

He had no objection in principle to strong language, though its incessant use he would have found tedious; obscene language he would never use. Strong language was to be used on appropriate occasions, and those were when life, and on occasions even inanimate nature, were offering intolerable frustrations. Even when he became an archbishop, guests at 'Bishopscourt' would hear these outbursts. Edward Paget, Archbishop of Central Africa, was writing in the house, and his wife Rosemary was sitting in the garden, when they heard furious 'damns' and 'blasts' coming from Clayton's bedroom, where he had been laid up for a week by an attack of gout which had virtually crippled him. They concluded that he must have been getting better.

His sexual code was strict, almost puritanical, although he at least once permitted himself a naughty joke (to be told later), in a company where it could not have been misconstrued. It was true that he was not attracted by women. In fact he was afraid of them, though he came to know and value some women as persons; these were invariably those who worked for the Church and for good causes. This fear was no doubt the consequence of the impersonality of his upbringing. During his childhood his mother had been immersed in public activities, and during his boyhood and young manhood he had been at preparatory school, public school, and university. He found great enjoyment in the company of men and boys, and on one occasion later was to refer to this as his 'nature'. His 'nature', like everything except his eating, his smoking, and his irritability, was fully controlled. He liked a 'rough house', even in his mature years, but he indulged in it only with those who were close to him. This mastery of himself helped him to give advice and strength to others. He said once in a confirmation address:

'There may come a time when you are very greatly tempted, when this will be the one thing you want to do more than anything else, when your whole being will cry out, "I want to do this". But you must *never, never, never* give in.'[7]

Clayton was severe in judgement of any sexual irregularity, more specially if a person of authority and responsibility were involved, and most if it were a priest. Yet even in these years of his early twenties, he would never have withheld his charity or his help from anyone who was repentant.

In fact his knowledge, and still more his understanding, of the gospel story and its teaching were profound. On that firm foundation, laid beyond doubt in his parents' home, he built his theology and his religion. The University Church Society helped in this building, but the major influence in his life at that time was Father John Neville Figgis, who had been Rector of Marnhall in Dorset from 1902 to 1907, and in 1907 had entered the Community of the Resurrection. He delivered the Hulsean lectures at Cambridge in the year 1908–9, setting out his religion and theology. He was then 42 years old, and a preacher of renown.

One of Figgis's themes, perhaps the principal one, is that, if one is a believing Christian, as distinct from a Christian moralist or humanist, one believes in certain tremendous mysteries. One believes that God became man, was born of a virgin, was crucified, dead, and buried, and that he rose again. If Christians discard belief in the miraculous birth of Our Lord, then 'it is all up with Christianity'. For the birth carries with it 'the whole supernatural structure'. Christ's rising is less a wonder than his dying, 'if He be who He is'. 'Faith like all trust is an act of the will, which decides to take *risks*; and so wherever it is tried, it must involve *courage*.'

Figgis is therefore intensely hostile to any attempt to rationalise Christian belief, to make it acceptable to intellectuals, to establish the being of God by argument. Such attempts cannot succeed, 'the only deity thus attainable being a creature of the reason'. Figgis speaks of the obsession of scientific uniformity or rational categories. Mystery saves us from a world of cast iron; miracle saves us from the 'slavery of the mind to its own creations, from that superstition of the logical process, which is willing in its blindness to treat the real life of struggle and hope and joy as mere illusion'. He rejects the Roman doctrine of transubstantiation, not because of the truth enshrined in it, but because it is an attempt to rationalise a mystery. So also does he reject 'coarse analogies' of the Atonement.

Figgis has another reason for rejecting the claims of science to explain the universe, and to exalt the *what* and *how* and *when* and be contemptuous of the *why*; and that is because the inner life, with its conviction of freedom and choice, cannot bear any relationship to an exact, rationalistic, explainable world. We must not confuse God with His creation. Only so can we escape from the 'iron chain of cause and effect'. He says, 'it is in the abysmal depth of personality that we find the final and fatal foe of mere intellectualism'. He argues that if one experiences the presence of God in the Eucharist, one is not so dependent on *the factual truth of the story*. He criticises the Protestants who ignore and neglect the continued presence of Christ's spirit in the Church and the sacraments.

Figgis discusses the current attitude towards sin. If this is to be adopted, then Christianity as a religion of deliverance is past. There is no good news, there are no captives to be set free. He criticises those who despise sacramental confession, which is to many the 'only reasonable hope of overcoming temptation'. Sin is real. It was real to St. Paul, St. Augustine, Pascal, Pusey, Bunyan. He himself confesses to a great sense of sin and says, 'I cannot roll it off except at the foot of the Cross.'

One last thing we must note, for it also influenced the young man who first heard Figgis addressing ordinands at a meeting at Westcott House in 1908. Figgis did not suggest that we do not live in this world, but he criticises those who spend their lives 'denouncing social injustice and denouncing nothing else'. Clayton was always wary of those who denounced social injustice because of his suspicion that, for some of them, social justice had taken the place of religion. With others he questioned the wisdom and the efficacy of their actions. Though he himself was to concern himself more and more with social justice, and though like Figgis he resisted the advent of the omnicompetent state', that did not make him necessarily more at ease with those who did likewise. It was not their concern that he objected to, but their methods, which were unlike his own; yet most of the people he disapproved of could hardly have used his methods, which were available only to those who occupied positions of high authority.

More than forty years later, in 1951, Clayton wrote to the Revd. Brian Wormald, who was contemplating a life of Figgis. Clayton regarded Figgis's sermon 'A Plea for Other-Worldliness', delivered at Cambridge on 10 November 1907, as the best that he had ever heard, and acknowledged that Figgis's preaching had exercised a great influence on him. Even in his undergraduate days, Clayton recognised that Figgis was capable of 'rhetorical exaggeration'. Clayton could himself never have declared that the human spirit had turned 'from the middle-aged prose of the 19th century to the poetry of the child'. Nor that it was willing to be led 'up the mountain of purification till it sees once more the rose of glory and the dance of the saints'.

There was another thing that greatly impressed the young Clayton, and that was Figgis's statement that 'to others faith is the bright serenity of unclouded vision; to me it is the angel of an agony, the boon of hourly and daily conflict'. Clayton wrote to Wormald, 'It was because this was so, and obviously so, that many of us who lived among those who denied and despised the Christian Faith, found him so bracing a teacher.' He concluded his letter: 'I owe him so much that I am glad to have the chance of telling someone else what I do owe him.'

One concludes by noting that the influence of Figgis, amongst others, made Clayton an Anglo–Catholic. In his application for ordination he had stated that he communicated 'fairly regularly'. It may well be that he now began to attend Mass daily. He had also begun the practice of making his confession. Throughout his life his faith made him as a rock that was never removed out of its place. If he had doubts and suffered depressions, he seldom revealed them. Indeed he resisted them with all the strength of an extraordinary will, by making himself faithful in prayer, meditation, study, and attendance at the Mass. For he had decided to take upon himself the duty of a shepherd of souls. Therefore one resisted all doubt and depression, and one encouraged and comforted those who suffered from them.

His irritability, his damns and his blasts, his gossip, were continuously there, and could be seen and heard by anyone who came into relatively intimate contact with him. It was only as one grew in understanding of him that one realised that his faithfulness to his purpose was continuously there also. These other things were excrescences on the oak.

3

Little St. Mary's

In 1906 Clayton took First Class Honours in the Classical Tripos Part One, in 1907 First Class Honours in the Theological Tripos, winning the George Williams Prize for Theology, and in 1908 he graduated Bachelor of Arts.[1] One must conclude that he was thought to need little further theological and pastoral training, for he began and concluded his studies at Cuddesdon in 1908, which college he said in his application for ordination, he hoped to attend 'for the long vacation term at least'. At the end of the year he was ordained deacon, and returned to Cambridge as Chaplain and Fellow of Peterhouse. His great-uncle, Professor John Westlake, Q.C., presumably a man of distinction, regarded the whole business as a waste of superlative gifts.

His opinion was not shared by his great-nephew. Clayton had been ordained as a shepherd of souls, and there could be for him no greater vocation. He was fully alive to the assaults on faith of scientific belief, humanism, and hedonism. His influence on young men was considerable, largely because of his certitude, his intelligence, and his lack of all conventional piety.

It was unusual for a man to be invited to join the staff of a college while still a B.A. and still *in statu pupillari.* Almost sixty years later, the Right Revd. H. A. Cullen, then Bishop of Grahamstown, commented on this in an obituary tribute.[2] On the one hand Clayton was thought to merit the appointment; on the other, the autocratic Master of Peterhouse thought it improper for such a youngster to be a member of the High Table, and did not invite him. It was equally improper for a don to join the B.A.s' table, so Clayton made his modest way to eating houses in the town. This roused the Master of Pembroke to wrath, and Clayton was therefore invited to join the High Table at his old college. This absurd situation he accepted with tolerance, and, one may be sure, with some kind of irreverent mirth.

When Cullen was reading for his own Theological Tripos, he made his 'eager way' to a lecture by the young don on the Epistle to the Galatians. 'There for the first time I listened to the incisive utterance, bringing the most profound teaching to us almost in words of one syllable.'

So this stupendous gift was acquired young. A man of Clayton's education must have had a considerable vocabulary. But he wanted to teach, and he wanted people to understand what he was teaching. Therefore he – deliberately, or of necessity, because that was essential to his teaching – jettisoned the greater portion of his stock of words, and as far as one knows never used them again, or to put it more accurately, never used them again in speech or writing. In public addresses and synodal charges he used a slightly larger vocabulary than he permitted himself in sermons.

This simplicity in preaching was to prove a special boon when he went to South Africa, because he was not only able to talk simply to the Cape Coloured church people whose main language was Afrikaans, but he was also a great help to interpreters into Zulu, Xhosa, and Sotho, because they had no difficulty in translating the simple words and the short clean sentences. Clayton had yet one more gift when he was using an interpreter: he not only avoided the use of difficult words, but he avoided the use of difficult idioms, and the use of metaphors and similes drawn from an environment of which his hearers knew nothing. It was this use of simple words that made argument with him so difficult, for it is a common debater's trick to give to less simple language a meaning never intended by the speaker. The trouble with Clayton's arguments was that you knew what they meant, and you knew that you could not make them mean something else.

At the end of 1909 Clayton was priested in Ely Cathedral, his father and mother being there to see it. He then was appointed Dean of Peterhouse, which increased his responsibilities. As Chaplain he had been responsible for the spiritual welfare of the college, or of those of its undergraduates who were willing to use his ministrations. But now as Dean he was responsible for the moral welfare of all, and had to deal with questions of behaviour and discipline. This may well have been the time when he began to offer his probably daily petition for wisdom. He was then a man of 25 years of age.

It is difficult to do justice to these years of his life, because one knows almost nothing about them. He was Dean from 1910 to 1920, but his term was interrupted by the First World War, when he was appointed Chaplain to the Forces. Of these years he left almost no record. It would not be right to say that he kept no papers during his life, but he did not keep the ones which would be helpful to a biographer.

But then of course he did not want a biography. He must have realised in his later years that someone might want to write his life. He told Cowdry that he did not think there was enough material for a full-length biography, but in large measure he himself had seen to it that there was not. He often expressed the hope to Cowdry that no one would try to write his life.

There was something else as well. When he moved from one place to another, he put the first out of his mind. Memories he had many and would tell them to Dick Yates, his first chaplain in Johannesburg, to Cowdry, his second chaplain in Cape Town, and to anyone else he seized hold of, for he did seize hold of people, and would not let them go till one and two in the morning. He received letters from some of those who remembered his six years at St. Mary's the Less, Cambridge, and his nine years at Chesterfield. These were full of regret and nostalgia, but there is no record that he ever replied in like vein. If he had a new job, he gave his whole mind to it, and forgot the old. This characteristic of his would make difficulties for any biographer.

On 15 November 1914, at the age of 29, Clayton was appointed Chaplain to the Forces, Fourth Class. He was sent to Malta where there were many military hospitals. He had time only to care for those who were in danger of dying, and this was his first experience of suffering and death. What is more, it was the first time in his life that he had come into close touch with men of a class quite different from his own, men who spoke with the diverse accents of the East End of London, and the West Country and the North, men who had had to go to work as boys, and hard work too, who did not read books or discuss philosophy and religion. Whether Clayton ever had any snobbery in him is doubtful. He had too deep an understanding of the gospel. But now he decided that his vocation demanded of him that he should not stay in the sheltered walls of Peterhouse.

From Malta Clayton went to Palestine as chaplain to the 5th Cavalry Division, and was also chaplain to the Imperial Camel Corps. His father died in June of 1917, and he was given leave to visit his mother. In March 1918 he was in Cambridge and was instituted Vicar of St. Mary's the Less. On 7 April he presided at a parochial church meeting. He later returned to Palestine, and was in Allenby's advance on Damascus in September 1918. Allenby outran his supplies in what was otherwise a military masterpiece; there was no medicine for the sick or dying, and many soldiers died in Aleppo, of wounds and of malaria contracted in the valley of the Jordan. It was a terrible experience, but it was not the horror of war that impressed itself on Clayton, but rather the heroism of men who had found a cause greater than themselves. For him there were things more terrible than war. Injustice and contempt were two of them, and most terrible of all was to lose one's soul. In the brilliant drive that put the Turks out of the war, Clayton must have acquitted himself well, for Allenby mentioned him in dispatches.

He returned to Cambridge shortly before Easter 1919, and took up his work as vicar.[3] The previous incumbent had been at Little St. Mary's for twenty-five years, and the parish needed an infusion of purpose and strength. Those the new vicar had. He could not be satisfactorily described as exuberant, dynamic, or energetic, because these adjectives did not do justice to the controlled power of his will. He soon showed himself to be, in spite of his lack of experience, a superb parish priest. His first act was to form a parochial church council, for although he had this tremendous power of will, he was a firm believer in democratic government, and the distribution of power and responsibility. The struggle in him between this belief in democracy and his own will was to last throughout his life, and each had its own triumphs, some of them of high entertainment value, with either a triumphant Clayton obviously embarrassed by his own victoriousness, or a defeated Clayton glowering angrily at the stupidity of the democratic will.

The heart of the spiritual life of Little St. Mary's was the Eucharist. At Great St. Mary's, which was 'low church', the vicar was an evangelical and an eloquent preacher, and some wit said, 'The trouble with Cambridge religion is that it's either all Mass or all gas.'[4]

Dr. Arthur L. Peck, librarian of Christ's College, Cambridge, was one of his servers. At the age of 17½, he went on Passion Sunday, 1920, to Little St. Mary's with two of his schoolfriends to the sung Eucharist, and to see and hear these new things, especially the use of incense, six candles on the altar, the *English Hymnal* instead of *Hymns Ancient and Modern*, and the vigorous preaching of the vicar, who at the end of the Easter term of 1920 was to give up the Deanship of Peterhouse to devote himself to the work of the parish. Peck was used to a 'low church', where there was no cross on the altar, but the impact made on him by Little St. Mary's and its vicar was immediate. His parents did not object when he transferred his allegiance, and he became one of Clayton's servers. There were some twenty-four of them, of all sorts and conditions, and a number of them later became priests. Clayton took them on cycling expeditions, but the biggest venture was a trip to the English Lakes, where they stayed at Seathwaite, Borrowdale, the wettest place in England. 'We had great walks every day . . . with magnificent roast joints at night when we got back.' Clayton introduced Peck to his first drink of rum at Dungeon Ghyll, during a walk on a drenching day.

The picture of Clayton at 35 is unquestionably a picture of the man who later became Bishop of Johannesburg and Archbishop of Cape Town. There is the same tremendous reading of the lessons, the same tremendous laughter, except that in later years Clayton rolled about on the settee rather than on the floor. There was also the use of the alphabet, in this instance, to determine the place for his next holiday, a practice which he had just begun. The first time he would choose a county beginning with A, then with B and so on. It is probable that he had already started the extraordinary habit of keeping his books in alphabetical order also, and of reading a newly published book and then an old one drawn from the shelves in its due season.

Peck accompanied him on two of these alphabetical holidays, which were given over to walking, reading, eating, and sleeping, and a daily attendance at the Mass. The first was in Buckinghamshire, and the second was in Derbyshire, where they stayed at the Church Hotel in Edale.

It was at Edale that Clayton looked at himself in a mirror over the fireplace and said, 'I don't think I'm a very handsome sight.' Peck writes very sensibly, 'No doubt this was true, but no one would ever have thought of it.' In fact they might have thought something else, that Clayton's ugliness went unnoticed because of the vitality and mobility of his face, and because of his frequent laughter. Donald Harris, one of his curates at Chesterfield, wrote of him: 'I sometimes thought his countenance was so odd, if not ugly, as to be quite beautiful.'[5] The great head, the great brow, the prominent grey eyes, the fleshy but not gross lips, were not to be forgotten. When he was deeply moved, or was about to flay someone alive, or was about to thunder at a foolish synod, the right-hand corner of his lower lip would go down. When Father Killick of Yeoville, Johannesburg, was dying of a painful cancer, which was breaking his bones one after the other, Clayton, then Bishop of Johannesburg, visited him daily. After one of these visits he spoke to Dick Yates, his first chaplain in Johannesburg, and the corner of his lip came down as he related that Killick had said to him, 'I hope this won't last much longer, for if it does, I shall begin to be sorry for myself, and that would be a very bad thing.' It was his substitute for weeping.

Was Clayton sensitive about his appearance, which grew more ungainly as he grew older because of his immense increase in girth? Was he, as some supposed, undemonstrative and reserved because he was sensitive about his figure, which some people thought comic or grotesque? He did not like touching anybody, except in rough and tumble, and nobody would have dared to touch him. But that may have been because, knowing his nature, he had made it a rule. Nor could he be called reserved, if that adjective is used in its normally understood sense. He could be rollicking and outrageous, but he could never have been described as a withdrawn man.* He could become cold and remote when he was delivering a rebuke, but he was far better known for his petulance. Even after the edification of the daily Mass he was unapproachable. What the Mass did for his soul, the breakfast did for his temper. If one knew the ropes, one did not speak to him at breakfast unless spoken to. Some thought this scandalous, that a priest and a bishop should be so irritable after he had celebrated and communicated. As archbishop he was less irritable, due to the passage of time and the growth of grace, but even then he could damn and blast. The truth was that this scandalous defect endeared him to innumerable people, and most of all to his clergy, who learned that beneath this childishness there was a kind of holiness. No one, however, would have dared to suggest that to him.

One cannot suppose that Clayton's figure, with that great head and body on its short legs and small feet, and his inimitable gait, were the sources of concealed distress to him. That he thought he was ugly, we know. But he could joke about it. Once in South Africa he was called two-faced, which caused him to remark, 'Do you think if I had been given two faces, I would have chosen this one?'[6]

One thing is certain, that his strange gait and strange appearance were no hindrance to his work as a priest. Under him the parish and church of St. Mary's the Less came to vigorous life. It was in every true sense of the word an evangelical parish and church, and it made the conventional distinction between Catholic and Evangelical seem unreal. Yet Clayton himself used these distinctions. In fact there could be said to be three parties in the Church of England, the Anglo-Catholic, the Moderate, and the Evangelical. Clayton was heart and soul an Anglo-Catholic. His theology was the theology of the 'Great Church' as it was on the eve of the year A.D. 1054, when Pope Leo IX excommunicated Michael Cerularius the Patriarch of Constantinople, an event which was the precursor of many others which were to lead to the

*Roger Lloyd, in his excellent chapter on South Africa in *The Church of England, 1900–1965*, calls Clayton a 'quiet, withdrawn man'. He certainly was not. He could be taciturn if he wished to, even morose.

fragmentation of Christianity. It should not be supposed, as it often has been, that Anglo–Catholicism was a move back to the Roman Catholic Church. In fact the Anglo–Catholics believed that they had preserved the original Catholic faith, and that the Roman Catholics had in many ways departed from it, as for example in adopting the dogma of the Infallibility of the Pope. This belief cannot be easily dismissed as arrogant, because in our time it is shared by many Roman Catholics.

Therefore while the Anglo–Catholics earnestly desired the reunion of Christendom, they were not prepared to achieve it at the expense of what they considered to be the true faith, true not because they believed it, but true in the sense that it was the faith of the Great Church as it was in A.D. 1054, a faith the formulations of which in the Nicene Creed had been acceptable to the whole Christian Church. There had been heresies no doubt, but they were not to be compared to the divisions that later rent the Church into many pieces.

The Anglo–Catholics further believed that if there were to be a reunion of Christendom, the Church of England, and not merely its Anglo–Catholics, was in a strategic position to bring it about. Therefore the conflict and distrust within their own Anglican Communion distressed them. It must be admitted that the Evangelical distrust of the Anglo–Catholics was not solely theological. One of the strange things about Anglo–Catholicism, with its firm Nicenian faith and its emphasis on the Eucharist as the central act of Christian faith, was that it also attached great importance to accretions such as magnificent vestments, rich music, incense, and lace. These things frightened the Evangelicals out of their wits, for they saw them as certain proofs that the Anglo–Catholics were hellbent for Rome. Some of the Evangelicals would not enter a church where a cross was displayed. It was not difficult for a nervous outsider to believe that, for the Anglo–Catholics, dressing up had taken the place of religion.

Vigorous though the spiritual and parochial life of St. Mary's the Less might be, some of the messages and addresses to the Anglo–Catholic Congresses of those days were very gloomy. For the Church of England was confronted not only by its own disunity and by the disunity of Christendom, it was confronted also by the growing irreligion of England. Though not much more than a decade earlier Figgis had declared that the enemies of Christianity were no longer unbelief, materialism, and agnosticism, but rather other religions, that was not the prevailing view of the Congress of 1920.

The Bishop of Salisbury, in his opening sermon to the Anglo–Catholic Congress, referred to the widening gulf between State and Church, an example of which was the changing attitude of Parliament towards divorce; but the darkest cloud of all was the indifference and immorality of post-war England. A. E. Taylor, Professor of Philosophy at the University of St. Andrews, declared that 'as far as our mere human foresight can discern, the fate of our Christianity is visibly hanging in the balance'. But according to him its enemies were not other religions; they were the growing beliefs that there is no plan or purpose in the Universe, no wisdom higher than our own, that death ends all and there cannot be a spiritual history of man, that there is no real distinction between good and bad, and that humility and gentleness are signs of weakness while pride and self-will are the real virtues. The Right Revd. W. L. Vyvyan, Bishop of Zululand, also sounded a sombre note, declaring that missions were on the brink of serious disaster, because of the shortage of priests and money. Too many young priests were marrying; they should abstain until they were certain they would not be called to the religious life in some of the monastic communities.

What were the differences between those days and ours? The challenges to faith are the same now as they were then, except that they are now greater. Figgis is seen to have been quite wrong in one respect. It is not other religions that are a challenge to the Christian faith, except in so far as some now turn to the East because they cannot find what they seek in the West. It is rather the belief that the great story on which Christianity is founded is simply not true, that nothing is true that cannot be seen, touched, weighed, and proved. Some turn to myth, believing that myth is essential to the wellbeing of man, but they steer clear of myth blended with or buttressed by dogma. Figgis is, however, right in another essential respect, that the Christian religion is primarily a faith and a mystery, and only secondarily a system of dogmatic belief. That does not mean he entertained no dogmatic beliefs. He stood or fell by the historical truth of the conception, birth, death and resurrection.

One unpleasant lesson is to be learned from the ecumenism of those days, and that is that the desire for reunion has grown as the power of the Church has declined. Reunion should have happened then. Just as Hitler in the beginning picked off his enemies one by one, so did unbelief pick off its enemies one by one, and do tremendous damage before its foes could decide to stand together.

It was Clayton himself who at the 1920 Congress had to deal with the question of reunion with other Christian bodies. There can be no question but that he believed that the work of the Holy Spirit was hindered 'where the Body of Christ is rent and torn', and by that he meant that the healing of these wounds 'must ultimately involve corporate union'. But Anglo–Catholics could not contemplate a reunion which was false 'to the underlying principles of Catholic order'.

He outlined Dr. A. C. Headlam's recently published scheme for reunion.[7] One of the points made by Headlam was that if two religious bodies united, there would be no further laying on of hands, 'for that has already been done'. Clayton could not accept the validity of such laying on of hands, unless it had been done by a bishop. But he was prepared to compromise. He said, 'I cannot see that any act of formal recognition or formal refusal of recognition of each other's orders is necessary. Let us not look back, but forward'. He would be willing to submit himself to conditional re-ordination if that would heal the wounds of Christendom.

What did he mean by 'conditional re-ordination'? Was he going to say under his breath, 'I am doing this for Christendom, but in fact I am already ordained'? In these theological doldrums the ship of reunion was to lie becalmed for at least another fifty years. But until reunion came, Clayton would not agree to intercommunion or the exchange of pulpits. He was throughout his life to form fraternal relationships with leaders of other churches, and he might attend their synods, but never their churches.

Yet it would be wrong to suppose that he was lukewarm. He was a stickler for order, as much as any Presbyterian. And he was not only critical of, but almost hostile to, those who under the influence of goodwill and brotherly love would have taken bold steps into the future. Yet he was prepared, if the Nonconformists demanded it, to take bold steps himself. He said, 'If Nonconformists object to the Establishment, then let it go! Let endowments go! Let everything go that belongs only to this earth.'

It is easy now to be wise and critical. Clayton was to live to see the enemies of faith much stronger than they were in the 1920s. He had only one weapon with which to fight them, and that was his own faith formed by dogma and reason. This weapon he used to such purpose that he became a father in God to countless people, not least those of St. Mary's the Less.

But it was time for Clayton to move on. In September 1924, a man of 39, he accepted from the Bishop of Southwell the benefice of Chesterfield. 'It meant many sad hearts when we had to let him go.'[8]

4

Vicar of Chesterfield

Cambridge is one of the most beautiful cities and Chesterfield is not. They were in those days much the same size, with populations of the order of 60,000. Chesterfield was a very dirty industrial and mining town, though not without history. The most famous building is the Church of St. Mary's and All Saints, the church to which Clayton was now coming. It belongs mainly to the Decorated Period, roughly between 1300 and 1375, and has a wooden spire covered with lead, 230 feet high. This is the famous 'crooked spire', and many people go to Chesterfield for the sole purpose of seeing it.

On 14 July 1924 the Vicar of Chesterfield, the Revd. Canon Francis L. Shaw, left to become Vicar of Ashbourne. The Revd. E. Linley, who was the senior priest in Chesterfield, was in bad health and unable to do much work. The care of the parish and its three churches fell on the shoulders of the Revd. Claude Handford[1] and his assistant the Revd. Dick Carpenter, who was then only a deacon.*

It was not until September that Clayton was offered the benefice, and Handford and Carpenter, following the usual practice, offered to make way for any curates that the new vicar might wish to bring. Clayton did not accept the offer, but asked Handford to come and spend the night with him at 16 Fitzwilliam Street. Handford, an old Rugbeian, was delighted to find that Clayton was also one, and to see in the study the portrait of his old housemaster Robert Whitelaw, the teacher whose reading had had such a profound effect on many of his scholars.

Clayton was taking to Chesterfield the Revd. George Dymond as his senior curate. Dymond, though inclined to be prim and proper, was a holder of the Military Cross. When the Second World War broke out he was with Clayton in the diocese of Johannesburg and moved a pacifist motion in Synod beginning with the words, 'I may appear to be somewhat of a sissy, but the facts do not bear out that impression'. Dymond was devoted to Clayton and could say so. Clayton was devoted to Dymond and could not. Clayton also asked Handford and later Carpenter to stay on. He and Handford talked into the small hours about Chesterfield and all its work. Clayton intended to alter some things, and told Handford of the great

*A deacon is one who has been accepted into Holy Orders. He is usually 'priested' a year later.

importance that he attached to the use of servers, whom, amongst other things, he regarded as potential recruits for the priesthood. Handford wrote, 'He secured my admiration from the first meeting'. But he was not keen on one of the new vicar's ambitions, that all the clergy should live together at the Vicarage. He and Carpenter lived next door in the Clergy House and preferred to maintain their independence. They must have put up a determined resistance, for Clayton was a difficult man to oppose, and it was not until after they had both left Chesterfield that the vicar closed the Clergy House and had all his clergy living with him at the Vicarage, where they improved their souls by taking part in the rigid spiritual discipline which the vicar imposed upon himself, and learning to endure his fits of irritability and his habit of talking until one or two in the morning, which he could do with no ill effect, but which some of them could not. He wrote a humble letter 'To the People of Chesterfield Parish Church', in which he said that he could not hope to be to them what Canon Shaw had been. He asked for their prayers, that he might be given 'strength, wisdom and love, to do my work among you in the spirit and power of Christ'. Secondly, he asked them to show him forbearance and charity if he should make mistakes. 'May God bless you all.'[2]

The induction took place on 30 December. It was a magnificent affair. There were thirty clergy present in the procession, including Bishop Hoskyns in cope and mitre. The bishop preached a sermon, using as text the first verse of Isaiah 61, the same which Jesus read in the synagogue at Nazareth:

'The Spirit of the Lord God is upon me; because the Lord hath anointed me to preach good tidings unto the meek; he hath sent me to bind up the broken-hearted, to proclaim liberty to the captives, and the opening of the prison to them that are bound.'

The bishop could not have chosen words of greater import for his new vicar, for Clayton in his unmystical way believed with all his heart that the Spirit of the Lord God was upon him, that God had anointed him and had sent him to help the broken-hearted and the captives and the bound. Was that not what the Gospel was about? The new vicar was going to be irritable and sometimes rude, and jealous of his curates, and deeply hurt when one of them decided to get married, but the great words of the prophet would have brought him to his feet, or to his knees, in an instant, for that was what his life, all life, was about.

It was said sometimes that Clayton was not musical. That was not altogether true. He had his favourite hymns and he could bellow them with great force. In my days in Johannesburg I often heard him sing, 'It is very meet, right, and our bounden duty', and 'Come, Holy Ghost, our souls inspire', and he certainly sang them as they ought to be sung. At Chesterfield it was he who was responsible for the introduction of a sung Evensong, with the plainsong from Briggs and Frere, with or without an organ accompaniment. Sometimes 600 people would attend on a weekday evening. He was not, to use the phrase, 'fond of music', and did not play recordings in his vicarage or bishop's house, and sit listening to them. But even in this he was perverse. Donald Harris kept a piano in his room and formed the impression that in some way Clayton was jealous of it. Harris wrote: 'Sometimes he would sit for quite an hour at my piano, playing with one finger and preventing me from getting anything else done. I always thought he did it to annoy.'[3]

In 1927 the new diocese of Derby was taken out of the diocese of Southwell, and Dr. Edmund Pearce, one-time master of Corpus, Cambridge, became the first bishop. He made Clayton his examining chaplain, and in 1928 made him Archdeacon of Chesterfield. Clayton made an inordinate fuss getting into his gaiters and expected Harris to do them up for him. In the parish magazine of October 1928, Clayton wrote with humble wit:

'The work of an Archdeacon is rather mysterious to anyone who has not been one. It is to me wholly mysterious at the moment . . . In the Middle Ages it was a recognised subject of disputation in the schools as to whether an Archdeacon could be saved. We in Chesterfield have proof of the possibility of at any rate one Archdeacon being saved, because we know Archdeacon Crosse. But it seems too much to hope for two of them in succession.'

Clayton's impact on Chesterfield was tremendous. He had not been there two months when the ailing Ernest Linley died, on 23 February. He had no relatives, and his friends were his colleagues and parishioners, so Clayton decided at once to give him a priest's funeral with full Catholic rites. Clayton and Carpenter sang the Ninetieth Psalm to plainsong, including those words:

'The days of our years are threescore and ten; and though men be so strong that they come to fourscore years: yet is their strength then but labour and sorrow; so soon passeth it away, and we are gone.'

Clayton asked Handford to sing the Solemn Requiem Mass, as he had known and worked with Linley. Dymond played the organ, which he could do with great effect, and incense was used for the first time since the Reformation (so Handford thought). This was followed by Absolutions of the Dead, and procession with the choir through the streets to the cemetery. It was something of a kind that Chesterfield had never seen before, and people asked, 'Could anybody have a funeral like that?' Thus Clayton began within a few weeks of his arrival to demonstrate the beauty of full Catholic rites.

Soon after this he attacked the 'scandal' of baptisms, the slackness of godparents, and the absence of fathers from the christening of the children. It was the wish of many parents to bring their children to be 'done under the crooked spire', though that was to be the limit of their participation in the parish life; and what is more, the 'doing' was as often as not, part of the Saturday evening shopping, as much notice being given to the priest as was given to the shopkeeper. The number of children was enormous: Handford, when he was a deacon, and one of a staff of five, baptised 383 children in one year. In October 1925 the vicar laid it down that no child would be baptised without three days' notice, and that those bringing children should produce a paper previously obtained from the Vicarage. Carpenter, being the most burly of the curates, was given the job of doorkeeper, and was told by an angry woman, 'You won't get any more from our spot then', to which he replied, 'Madam, that is the idea.' Gradually the fuss died away, and it became known that the new vicar was a man for order and discipline.

Not only that. It became known that he was a great preacher, and could be understood by all but the very young. He was also thought to be a good teacher, not only through his sermons but through his monthly letters. There were in his sermons and his letters the clarity, the authority, the lack of all tricks, histrionics, and unctuousness, that were to characterise his speaking and writing to the end of his life. His reputation grew immense, and this was not only amongst the laity. His curates, who had to endure his moods at Vicarage and Clergy House, were spellbound by his preaching. And not only by his preaching, but also by his deep sense of his pastoral duty, and the conviction that he had been anointed to preach good tidings. Again some thought the coexistence of his bad temper and his extraordinary preaching indicated a kind of hypocrisy. Donald Harris was wiser, and called it an ambivalence.

Clayton certainly fascinated his curates, and they would boast of him to others, as schoolboys do of a headmaster. He had virtually four kinds of recreations. Probably the most popular of all was talking. Another was light as opposed to heavy reading. Another was to thumb through *Crockford's Clerical Directory*, and to make promotions of priests from one post to another. He would say to his curates, 'I have just appointed X to Truro and Y to Argyll and the Isles', and he was delighted when on occasions he was right. A fourth recreation was to do the crossword puzzle in *The Times*. If he failed to discover a clue, he would set his curates to find it after lunch. They received a halfpenny per clue up to two clues; after that the money went to the Missionary Fund.

The number of anecdotes was legion, but D. B. Harris – and Clayton himself – had a special liking for the story of the commercial traveller who found himself with Clayton in a train. The traveller was a great talker, but Clayton did not respond. The traveller touched him on the knee, and Clayton shook his head and pointed to his ears to show that he was deaf. The traveller said, 'You should have been drowned when you were a pup.' This moved Clayton to gales of laughter and conversation began.

During Clayton's first Lent, he preached a sermon on the Prodigal Son which made a deep impression on his congregation, particularly the young. It was one of his persistent themes that, though sin separates us from God, penitence is always met by forgiveness and restoration. That was the Christian sequence, sin, separation, repentance, forgiveness, and restoration. This power to forgive and restore had been given by our Lord to the apostles, and it was still the power of the Church. By the sacrament of confession, one's sins could be forgiven, one's separation could be ended. The worst thing that one could do was, because of an unnecessary feeling of shame, to remain thus separated. Some of the Chesterfield boys came to

Handford and told him that they had been discussing the sermon at work, not only amongst themselves, but with the men also, and they wanted now to begin the practice of confession.

There was a feeling amongst many in the parish that the Holy Spirit was at work in Chesterfield. This is of course an extraordinary feeling to have, and it must be admitted that it is unusual. It is much more common to be loyal, faithful, quiet, and unexcited. It was this sense of the working of the Holy Spirit that enabled Clayton to make changes in the parish life that in other parishes would have been resisted for years, that would have caused bitter dissension, and very often heart-break for the would-be reformer.

Clayton lost no time in making the Mass the main service of Sunday. There had been for years a Parish Communion at 9.30 a.m. and Matins at 11 a.m. On 19 April 1925 the last full Matins at 11 a.m. was held, and on the following Sunday Matins was begun at 10.45 a.m. and was taken only as far as the Benedictus, during the singing of which the priest came to the altar, and the Sung Eucharist began. After the Nicene Creed Clayton preached a sermon explaining the new order of service, and this was printed in the parish magazine, Clayton making it clear – as he always did on such occasions – that this was the wish of the churchwardens, not his own.

He explained to his congregation, which often contained a thousand worshippers, that if one wished to celebrate the Holy Communion 'with the accessories of music and dignity', it was difficult to do so unless it were done at this hour. He then set himself to meet two objections.

The first was that some people were very attached to the service of Morning Prayer. Therefore the chief portion of that service was to precede the service of Holy Communion. He sympathised with these people, but changes were inevitable. He reminded them that some of them would remember the days when a very different service was held. He did not say so, but he was referring to the days when Holy Communion was celebrated only four times a year, the vicar wore a black gown, and the sermons often lasted an hour, and were usually against Popery![4] Clayton was sure that no one would wish to return to that.

The second objection of some parishioners was this. The new eleven o'clock service was a Eucharist, and one could not communicate at it if one had already eaten. They felt it was asking too much of many of them to expect that they should abstain from food and drink until after midday. Clayton's reply to this was that he did not expect people to communicate at this grand Sung Eucharist if they had already taken food, whether liquid or solid. But he told them, they could already have communicated at 7, 8, or 9.30 a.m., and they could then come to the Sung Eucharist, 'not this time with the purpose of Communion but rather with the purpose of worshipping God through Jesus Christ our Lord, and joining in the presentation before the Father of the Sacrifice once made on Calvary'. He explained further that the Holy Communion was so rich a service, and had so many aspects, 'that it is a help to some people to separate them'.

So Clayton instituted the grand Sung Eucharist at which only those who had fasted could communicate; this was an 'ancient and very valuable rule of the Church'. There can be no doubt that he believed this, but he was not to believe it later, and when he became a bishop he was to refuse a dispensation to an ailing priest on the grounds that there was no rule to give a dispensation from.[5]

Only a rare worshipper would today attend Communion twice, once to communicate, once to witness again the presentation of the sacrifice. Ordinary worshippers like myself go to Communion to communicate. There is no hint in the story of the Last Supper that it might be made into a rite in which one did not take the bread and the wine. Yet that was the Anglo-Catholic practice of those days. Later in Johannesburg Clayton conformed to other customs, other ways.

There may have been several reasons why it worked at Chesterfield, but one was undoubtedly the formidability of the vicar. He made it clear that all should remain even if they were not going to communicate. He was particularly concerned that there should be no exodus after the sermon. When the time came, he glared down the church, and no one went out!

There seems to have been very little opposition to the changes introduced by the new vicar. On the subject of the centrality of the Mass there was no opposition at all. He introduced the regular use of incense, writing in the parish magazine of May 1926 that it was 'the most scriptural of all possible adjuncts to worship'. He wrote of ceremonial, that it 'does something to make up for the deficiencies of words'. He wrote again in the issue of January 1927, explaining the importance of the use of vestments. Their use was ordered by the Ornaments Rubric and was not due to the eccentric opinion of a prejudiced vicar. He adds in typical fashion: 'I must apologise for writing at such lengths as I have done on the question of clothes. As a matter of fact they interest me very little' – which indeed was very true.

There were no doubt observers who imagined that the new vicar was introducing a great many unnecessary, unimportant and, in some cases, offensive changes, offensive because they smacked of Popery, which King Henry the Eighth was supposed to have smashed once and for all. There were more of these observers without than within. The worshippers of St. Mary's and All Saints, who listened to their vicar's sermons and read his letters, could not doubt the strength and depth of his devotion. In the parish magazine of June 1927 he wrote to them:

'First comes Whit Sunday, the day on which we thank God for sending His Holy Spirit upon those who were to form His Church. On Whit Sunday will you try to remember the day of your Confirmation, when God gave His Holy Spirit to you? And will you ask yourselves whether you have used that Gift as you might have done? The Holy Spirit is the Spirit of Love, and the Spirit of Power. Have you lived as one who possessed this Spirit? Have you always tried to think and speak well of other people? Has your religious life been marked by a Spirit of Power – power which could conquer sins and influence others? If not, this Whitsuntide remember that you can do these things if you will; for the Holy Spirit is within you if you will only use Him.'

One might criticise the vicar for this or that, and he might do things that one did not regard as essential, but of the essentials he had a profound understanding. In the magazine of January 1927 he wrote of criticisms made of the church and the clergy:

'. . . one criticism that has reached us is worthy of record. It is that we are not intellectual and pay too much attention to the poor. I only wish this was true. We should be following the highest possible precedent.'

Meanwhile Clayton had much other work to do. In 1926 he was made a Rural Dean, and in 1927 Examining Chaplain to the Bishop of Derby. In that year he raised a considerable amount of money for the restoration of the crooked spire, and for the strengthening of the tower which supported it and another amount for the newly created diocese of Derby. When he was appointed to Chesterfield by the Bishop of Southwell, he had been charged with the task of building a new church for the parish of St. Augustine, a rapidly growing part of the town, which was separated from Chesterfield in 1926.

A great four-day bazaar was held in 1928 to raise money for the new parish, the new diocese, and the restoration of the tower and spire. Seven thousand roses were used to decorate the twenty stalls, which were in the Market Hall, the Corn Exchange, and the Assembly Rooms. On Monday, 22 October 1928, Her Highness Princess Marie Louise arrived in Chesterfield, and was met by the Duke and Duchess of Devonshire, who were to be her hosts at 'Chatsworth'. After she had opened the bazaar on the Tuesday, she was photographed on leaving the Market Hall with all the dignitaries. Clayton rather dominates the scene, with his powerful face, his great brow and bald head. He is looking calm and confident, and indeed handsome; he had no belly then, and is holding a shining topper in his left hand. (See plates 2 and 3.)

The four days were full of speeches, compliments and jokes. Although Princess Marie Louise had opened the bazaar on Tuesday, the Duchess of Devonshire opened it again on Wednesday. The treasurer announced that £700 had been taken on Tuesday, but some stalls were holding back so that they could make as good a show on Wednesday. (Laughter.) The Duchess called this very subtle. (Laughter.) The Archdeacon, intending to propose a vote of thanks, started off by saying, 'I do want to propose this toast . . .' at which there was great laughter. On the third day the Mayor, Miss Violet Markham, opened the bazaar again, wearing deep-red velvet and a red hat. She said they could not have the tower of the parish church tumbling down, and therefore they must get on with the job. She finally brought down the house. She said:

'I am glad that Mr. Clayton's duties as chaplain have not broken him down morally, spiritually and physically. The care of such a conscience as mine and the care of my morals must have been a most serious task for him. I am glad that he is sitting up smiling at the end of such a troublesome experience as he must have undergone with the first woman in the Mayoral chair.'

It was a famous bazaar, and the total amount made was £1,618, an enormous sum in those days.

It meant that in 1928 the vicarage of St. Augustine was built, and in 1929 the foundation stone of the new church was laid. When Clayton was praised for his contribution, he replied that all he had done was not to prevent the church being built.[6]

In that same year, in the month of October, the Rector of Liverpool, the Revd. John How, the same who had worked with Clayton in the Cambridge University Church Society, came with others to hold a parochial mission. Clayton wrote of it:

'There is, I think, not one of the departments of our Church life which has not felt the quickening power of the Holy Spirit. Everyone, or almost everyone, seemed ready to take a step forward in his or her religious life. There was no excitement. There were no thrills – except on the one occasion when Father How nearly broke the pulpit.'

There were now five priests in the parish. Harris had left in 1932 to go to Clayton's old parish of St. Mary's the Less. It was Clayton himself who had told Harris about the vacancy and, after Harris had accepted it, had said that he could not do without him. Harris's last few months at Chesterfield were made constrained by this, and once he had left, Clayton took no further interest in him. This was another of the baffling characteristics of Clayton's nature, but Harris's view of it was certainly charitable. He wrote: 'I don't think there was any illwill about it – it fitted in with an odd kind of discipline he imposed on himself to do with personal relations.'[7]

This personal ruthlessness, which was to abate with the passage of years, alienated surprisingly few people. His servers were at times terrified of him. If he appeared morose when he arrived at some church, the warning would go round. Yet the lives of many of them were given direction and purpose by him. When he left Chesterfield in 1934, the fourteen priests who had served under him there and in Cambridge wrote to him testifying to the privilege that had been theirs, wished him good luck in the name of the Lord, and made him a gift of vestments for the Mass.[8]

George Dymond, who left Chesterfield in 1927, wrote fifteen years later to Clayton: 'It would be an exaggeration to say that actually from the very first day I saw you (walking across the Quad at Haileybury to visit Willie Lloyd) you have been the strongest formative influence in my life, but it has been so at least from the days of the reading-party at Cley-next-the-Sea.'[9]

Dick Carpenter, who left Chesterfield in 1930, wrote to thank Clayton for all he had been to him and had done for him, and said, 'You have taught me more than I can at present realise.' He added that many times people in Chesterfield had praised Clayton's work, and they said these things to Carpenter because they could not say them to the vicar himself. George Martineau, who left Chesterfield in 1933, wrote: 'You have been absolutely marvellous to me and what I've learnt these last three years with your help and guidance is perfectly astounding.'[10]

One assumes that people could not express their thanks and praise to the vicar because he was in some way unapproachable. Parishioners asked for their recollections thirty-four years after he had left Chesterfield were of the opinion that this was due to shyness, and to the fact that he had had no experience of life in industrial towns, nor of the people who lived in them. When he visited Chesterfield in 1948, those who had known him were struck by his confidence and friendliness. It seems strange that he was to acquire these after the age of 50, but it seems to be true that he did.[11]

Of women he still seemed almost to be afraid. When Harris's sister came to stay, Clayton greeted her with 'How-do-you-do, how-do-you-do. When are you going?' He could be extremely rude to women, and this rudeness not only disguised his embarrassment, but was caused by it. Florence Blaxall, whom he appointed president of the Church Women's Society in Johannesburg in 1940, declares that he was even ruder to shy women than he was to others. She tells the story of a missionary woman who suddenly encountered Clayton in his Johannesburg garden, and blurted out, 'Your geraniums are very fine this year,' to which he replied, 'My what!' and marched off, leaving her desolated. Florence Blaxall was able to see the man behind the rudeness. For her Clayton was the first archbishop who had thought to improve the quarters of his servants at 'Bishopscourt', and to give his head gardener and his wife, who was also his housekeeper, their own bathroom. And Clayton was able in this instance to see the person behind the woman, for Florence Blaxall was no ordinary woman; the work of herself and her husband Arthur for the church, and for the blind and the deaf, is one of the finest achievements of Christianity in Southern Africa.

Two other women for whom he had a high regard were Nan Chignell and Dorothy Kirby, who helped him to raise considerable amounts of money for clergy pensions, which in those days of the 1940s were unspeakable.

Another exception was Violet Markham, the Mayor of Chesterfield, whose chaplain, he said often, he was so proud to be. And Lady Baring, now Lady Howick, was another. When Sir Evelyn Baring was made Governor of Kenya, Clayton invited himself to Nairobi for the last holiday of his life, and wanted nothing better than to drive out into the country with his hostess and talk to her. Another woman for whom he had a high regard was Miss Doris Syfret, a forceful and faithful churchwoman in the diocese of Cape Town. That there were other exceptions we may be sure, and they would doubtless all be women of character. Clayton did not want the reputation of having a *dislike* for women, but it seems certain that in some strange way he feared them. When he grew older, he was able to joke about it. In Johannesburg a daring woman at some parish affair asked him, 'Is it true, my Lord, that you are a woman-hater?' He went off into one of those great laughs that set his belly quivering, and said, 'No, it's not true. The trouble is I can't tell one from the other.'

The nine years of Clayton's great ministry at Chesterfield were drawing to an end. Towards the end of 1933 he received a letter from William Palmer, Dean of Johannesburg and Vicar-General of the diocese, asking whether he would allow his name to go forward as a candidate for the bishopric, which had become vacant because of the resignation of Bishop Karney.

Clayton was then approaching the age of 49, and the Prime Minister had not thought to ask him to accept a bishopric. It was said that Clayton did not belong to the 'Lambeth clique', and that he was too much of an Anglo–Catholic. For another thing, he was not uncritical of the fact that the Church of England was an established Church, and that its bishops and archbishops were appointed by the monarch after consultation with the Prime Minister. Of one thing he was extremely critical, and that was the right of Parliament to approve or reject any revisions that the Church might wish to make of the prayer book.

In 1927 the Bishops of the Church of England had submitted to Parliament a Revision of the Prayer Book of 1662. This was passed by a large majority in the House of Lords, and rejected by a small majority in the House of Commons. Of those M.P.s who rejected the Revision, some came from Scotland, Wales, and Northern Ireland, in which the revision would not be used. One of the English M.P.s who rejected it was by faith a Parsee. If the vote had been limited to English M.P.s the Revision would have been accepted.* Clayton wrote, 'If this is involved in Establishment, the sooner we are disestablished the better.'[12]

Clayton might therefore have had several reasons for wishing to go to a Province which was governed synodically. He was in every way fitted to be a bishop, because of his intellectual powers and spiritual authority. And what is more, it was natural that he should want to be one.

One may speculate as to what might have happened had the letter from Johannesburg not arrived, and had the Prime Minister continued to overlook him. Could it have embittered him? It seems improbable. It is hard to imagine a man of his stature harbouring bitterness. He was ambitious, but he was first a shepherd of souls, and his duty was to heal the bitterness of others. That was throughout his life the first and overwhelming consideration.

He wrote to Dean Palmer and told him that he was willing for his name to be put forward as a candidate for the See of Johannesburg, and on 6 December 1933 he received the cable informing him that he had been elected.

There was much pride and much regret in Chesterfield when it was announced that the vicar was to become a bishop, and in such a far-off country. The name Johannesburg was by no means unknown, though the city was not yet as old as Clayton himself. Everyone knew that it was the centre of the richest gold mines in the world.

Clayton's mother was never to know that her son was to become a bishop. In 1933 she was living in London, in Eccleston Square, and she no doubt

*In 1928 the Bishops submitted a second Revision, which they hoped would be accepted by the House of Commons, but it also was rejected. Incidentally Clayton disapproved strongly of the 1928 version, and was not grieved when it was rejected. The Bishops then adopted the course of officially adhering to the 1662 version, but allowing changes consistent with the second Revision.

knew that he was to be nominated for the bishopric of Johannesburg. She died on 10 November at the age of 90, a commanding figure to the last. There is much evidence that she was extremely proud of the most notable of her four children, but there is very little evidence that they saw much of each other. Indeed people in Chesterfield were often surprised to hear that their vicar had any relatives at all. It was a strange family, all of them, father, mother, and four children, devoted to the Church, upright, charitable, public-spirited, but revealing little of their regard for one another. That family affection was strong, there could be no doubt, but it was not something to be shown, not even amongst themselves. There is no record that Clayton spent any part of his alphabetical holidays in Eccleston Square.

Nor did Clayton at that time keep evidences of affection, such as letters. It is true that he kept the remarkable letters that he received from his curates, also that from his bishop, Edmund Pearce, who, expressing his heartfelt gratitude, signed himself 'Yours, if I may so say, affectionately'.[13] Violet Minns, worshipper at St. Mary's the Less, and mother of Clayton's godson Anthony, wrote to wish him Godspeed, and said that she did not think any of his friends had followed his whole wonderful career with more loving interest than she. She signed herself 'Your affectionate friend'.[14]

As Clayton grew older, he found it easier to show affection. The relationship between his clergy and himself became stronger and warmer. Their affection for him was often made evident; his for them was shown in less direct ways, perhaps in some speech or sermon. In his last letter to his parish he wrote:

'During the time that I have been Vicar I have been supremely fortunate in my colleagues. I do not believe that any Church in the country has been better served by its assistant clergy.'[15]

He was to feel thus about his clergy all his life. One can hardly suppose that he encountered the most wonderful clergy wherever he went. The fact that they proved so wonderful must have in large part been due to himself. Nor must it be forgotten that they were an extension of himself. He resented criticisms of them as he resented criticism of the church, because it was an implicit criticism of himself. Here again he was ambivalent. Anyone who had sat up with him till two in the morning, and listened to him gossiping about his clergy, in a manner which could sometimes border on the malicious, would have been astonished to have heard his tributes to them.

He felt this same pride in the parish of Chesterfield and its church. He thought there was something 'particularly inspiring' in the way in which the people held the church in such affection.[16] He was in fact annoyed that it should be known for its crooked spire, because its real beauty was in its interior, which revealed itself gradually to the worshippers, who found more in it every day they worshipped in it. By that Clayton probably meant no more than that he had grown very fond of the church. He was not known then, and was not to be known later, for his appreciation of that kind of beauty, nor for the beauty of tree and hill and mountain and valley. One of his curates, M. H. R. Synge, described the vicarage garden as a desert, but said that the vicar was oblivious to it. Even about those other kinds of beauty that he understood, he was not notably articulate. There is no doubt that he found great beauty in Catholic worship, and in the great passages of Scripture, and in the English language, but one most easily grasped this when he celebrated, or read the lesson, or preached a sermon. In fact it was the opinion of some, including Donald Harris, that it was the Revd. T. Dilworth-Harrison, his successor, who brought out the hidden beauties of the parish church. Clayton himself, preaching in Chesterfield parish church on Sunday, 26 September 1948, during his visit to the Lambeth Conference of that year, used these words: 'I cannot begin to speak here today without a word about the joy* of coming once more to this parish where I spent ten happy years, and ministering once more in this glorious church, to which so much has been done to make it beautiful since I last saw it.'[17]

One may conclude that Clayton's appreciation of beauty was austere and not concerned with details. One could in no circumstances imagine him gazing into the heart of a flower, or lingering over the beauty of some illuminated text. A church was much more likely to be beautiful to him because of what was done in it than for anything it possessed.

On 2 April 1934 Clayton resigned his living. The parish had presented him with a pastoral staff, eucharistic vestments, travelling cope, and mitre. On 12 February he had been presented also with a resolution inscribed on vellum, paying high tribute to his teaching, his organising ability, his high sense of duty.[18] Extraordinary tributes were paid to him. The Vicar's Warden, Alderman W. H. Edmunds, said of the cope and mitre and staff: 'When he is invested in the mitre and cope which it has been our privilege to provide him, and he raises his pastoral staff which it is also our privilege to give him, to bestow a blessing on his flock there, Coloured and White, we in Chesterfield will feel that we participate in that blessing.'[19]

Another alderman said he had been told that the Vicar was 'a Communist, a Socialist, a Conservative, and everything'. This lack of political partisanship would be his great strength in South Africa.[20]

It was to be expected that after all this praise Clayton's reply would contain some understatement. He said: 'During the past nine years there is one thing for which I might take some credit, and that is that I have been extraordinarily skilful in getting out of the way and enabling other people to do a good work.'[21]

On his last Sunday in Chesterfield, Easter Day, 1934, he preached at High Mass and Solemn Evensong to tremendous congregations. The writer in the parish magazine for May says:

'Thus ends the ministry in Chesterfield of a Vicar and Archdeacon whose real greatness it would be difficult to overestimate. There were many sad hearts on Easter Day, though we are all proud to think that we in Chesterfield have had the privilege of being ministered to by such a man for nearly ten years.'

In 1933, urged on by clergy and people, he had agreed with A. R. Mow-

* In his script he first wrote 'pleasure'.

bray & Co., of London and Oxford, to publish a book of ten sermons, to be called *Yea and Nay*. The first four sermons constitute the *Yea*; they are affirmations of the duties of discipleship. The next six sermons constituted the *Nay*, and formed a Lenten course dealing with six excuses offered by people for their weakness, faithlessness, and negligence. These ten sermons were of their own kind superb. If one accepts the Christ of the gospels as the historic Christ, and founds one's faith on that certitude, then these are the exhortations of a great shepherd of souls. They are not sermons for doubters and seekers, unless such doubters and seekers are looking for certitude in someone else. Their language is also superb, simple, clear, direct, without ornamentation except that of humour.* Clayton is very witty on the reasons for becoming a Roman Catholic.

'I have heard of a man who, because he was not given some office which he wanted, announced that he preferred to become a Roman Catholic. I even knew someone once who did become a Roman Catholic because her vicar failed to recognise her in the street. If you believe that the Pope is infallible, you ought to become a Roman Catholic, but not otherwise. And the short-sightedness of your vicar or his disagreement with you about your fitness for particular work does not make the Pope infallible.'[22]

The duties of a disciple are fourfold. One is to bear witness by his life; if we go to church, then we either witness for our Lord or against him. The second is to endure. Clayton never excluded the possibility that a Christian, living a quiet and orderly life, might suddenly be called upon to endure martyrdom. He told his hearers of Bishop Polycarp, who, when given the choice of denying Christ or being burned at the stake, spoke the immortal words, 'Eighty and six years have I served Him, and He has done me no wrong. How can I blaspheme my King who saved me?' Clayton added that if the Church had grown soft it was because Christians believed less firmly than they had. 'I think it is because the Figure of Jesus Christ has less reality for us than for our ancestors.'

Personal holiness was another duty of the disciple. But one did not attain it by concentrating one's attention on one's sins. 'We shall do more good in our prayers by not praying very much about them, but mainly praying that we may learn to love God better.'

The last duty was loyalty to Christ, the Church, and the Truth. The Church is not to be identified with any minister; ministers often obscure the beauty and glory of the church. But if we turn our backs on the Church, we are turning our backs on Christ; for the Church is the body of Christ.

In his Lenten course, Clayton dealt with Christian excuses. One was, 'We are all going the same way'; Clayton told his congregation, 'You can't be both a Churchman and a Nonconformist.' Another was, 'A man must live', meaning that Christian ethics were really inapplicable to life. And again 'I have never done anyone any harm'; but a good soldier is not a man who does nobody any harm.

*In one paragraph chosen at random, there are 98 words, 80 of one syllable, 14 of two, 3 of three, 1 of four.

'It's human nature' is an excuse for unchastity and impurity. And 'Everybody does it' is no slogan for those who are called to be the light of the world. And lastly, 'I'm all right as I am', yet Christ said, 'Be ye therefore perfect, as your Father in heaven is perfect.'

It is hardly to be wondered at that Clayton was regarded as a great teacher by humble folk. It was said of him then, and was to be said again later, that he did not preach to the intellectuals. That was in a way true, but it was because of his belief in the nature of faith. One can speak of 'teaching the faith', but in another sense faith is the gift of grace, and one must become as a little child. There can be no doubt that the formidable Vicar of Chesterfield, now to become a bishop, approached God as a child. One had only to hear him say the Prayer of Humble Access to know that.

The people of Chesterfield let him go with sorrow. Their affection for him had grown with the years, but they would have hesitated to approach him. The nature of their love for him and of his for them, was a Christian mystery.

5

Geoffrey Johannesburg

When a priest is appointed (as in England) or elected (as in South Africa) to be a bishop, he goes through a service of consecration, in which he answers questions asked of him by the archbishop, and makes certain vows. He is already vested with rochet or alb, but now he puts on the rest of his vestments. He then kneels down, and the *Veni, Creator Spiritus* – 'Come, Holy Ghost, our souls inspire' – is sung over him, the archbishop beginning and all others responding. Round him are standing the archbishop and all bishops present, and after a prayer is said for him, the archbishop and the bishops lay their hands on his head, he still kneeling.

It is the belief of the Churches of the Anglican Communion that through this laying on of hands by the bishops, the new bishop receives the Holy Spirit. This is the promise of Jesus, who after his resurrection breathed on his disciples so that they might receive the Spirit, and gave them power to remit sins. The bishops are the heirs of the apostles, who by the laying on of their hands impart the Spirit to others.[1] This belief in the continuity of the apostolic ministry to this very day is one of the central dogmas of the Churches of the Anglican Communion, and of course of others, amongst whom are the Roman Catholic and the Orthodox Churches.

The doctrine of the apostolic succession suffered much damage at the hands of the Reformation. Luther rejected the dogma that a laying on of hands could confer supernatural power, and Calvin considered episcopacy to be unscriptural. Groups that broke away from the Church of England, such as the Methodists, were insulted by the assumption that their ministers had no access to the Spirit, while liberal theologians and laymen found it hard to believe that Jesus intended to found an hierarchical organisation. It is in fact the doctrine of the apostolic succession that has been one of the biggest stumbling-blocks in the way of Christian reunion, and it was certainly not explicit in the Nicene Creed. But whatever the case may be, the consecration of a bishop, with the laying on of hands, is one of the most solemn and spectacular ceremonies of the Church.

The Watchman, the monthly magazine of the diocese of Johannesburg, announced in March 1934 that the bishop-elect would have preferred to be consecrated in Johannesburg 'amongst his own people', but that the Most Revd. Francis Phelps, the Archbishop of Cape Town, had asked for the consecration to take place in England, as he would be there at that time.

Therefore, on 1 May 1934, in the famous London Cathedral of St. Paul's, Clayton was consecrated bishop by the Most Revd. Cosmo Gordon Lang, the Archbishop of Canterbury. With him were consecrated the Revd. John William Charles Wand, Fellow and Dean of Oriel College, Oxford, as Archbishop of Brisbane, and the Venerable Francis Whitfield Dankes, Vicar of St. Andrew and St. Catherine, Plymouth, as Bishop-Suffragan of that city. Twenty-eight bishops took part in the consecration, including three from the Province of South Africa, these being the Archbishop of Cape Town, the Bishop of Grahamstown, and the Bishop of Southern Rhodesia, the same Edward Paget who had been a candidate for Johannesburg at the same time as Clayton.

Before the laying on of hands, the choir sang those words from Isaiah:

'The Spirit of the Lord is upon me, because He hath anointed me to preach the Gospel to the poor; He hath sent me to heal the broken-hearted, to preach deliverance to the captives and recovering of sight to the blind, to preach the acceptable year of the Lord; to give unto them that mourn a garland for ashes, the oil of joy for mourning, the garment of praise for the spirit of heaviness; that they might be called trees of righteousness, the planting of the Lord, that He might be glorified. For as the earth bringeth forth her bud, and as the garden causeth the things that are sown in it to spring forth; so the Lord God will cause righteousness and praise to spring forth before all the nations. The Spirit of the Lord is upon me, because He hath anointed me to preach the Gospel.'

It was the kind of language that Clayton understood, even though he could not have written it. It was poetry devoid of all trick or ornament. But above all he believed that he himself, with all the faults of his humanity, was being anointed by the Lord to perform these tremendous tasks in the diocese of Johannesburg.

Clayton had asked his second curate, Michael Synge, to go with him to South Africa as his chaplain, but Synge was planning to get married, which made him unacceptable. Synge told Yates that he had been invited, and Yates replied, 'I wish he'd ask me', which wish was granted.

Yates had counted himself lucky to be asked to Chesterfield in 1933, at the age of 28. He had already served five years in Derbyshire, and the reputation of the Vicar and Archdeacon stood high amongst the clergy of the diocese, both for his fierceness and his genius for training curates. Luckily for the writer of this book, Yates had both a deep regard for Clayton and keen powers of observation. The bad temper he knew well and endured it often, but he never had any doubt of the dedication and the strange holiness. He observed that Clayton was undeniably pleased with the stir his elevation had caused in Chesterfield, though he poked fun at it. He was delighted to be a bishop; he was incapable of boasting, but could not conceal his pleasure.

He prepared seriously for his task. He studied the Constitution and Canons of the Church of the Province of South Africa, and the Rules and

Regulations of the Diocese of Johannesburg. He read what he could find of the history of the Church in South Africa, and read the history of South Africa itself. Somewhere he found the recently published report of the Poor White Commission, and studied that too. His gift of acquiring knowledge was very considerable, and when he arrived at Cape Town with Yates on the *Windsor Castle* in May, he knew more about the country than most newcomers would know, and a good deal more than many of the people who lived in it. All he had to do now was to see the physical land, Table Mountain, the vineyards and orchards of the Western Province, the semi-desert of the Karoo, and the mine dumps of Johannesburg, though how he wedded land and history in his mind is beyond my powers to explain, because I need to see a country before I can really understand what happened in it. Redvers Rouse, who in 1934 was Rector of Potchefstroom in the Transvaal, and in 1938 was made Archdeacon of Native Missions, used to exploit Clayton's imperviousness to scenery.[2] Many of the missions were in the Western Transvaal, which is in the main a flat tract of country, largely grassland and treeless except for areas of acacia, considerable portions being cultivable and producing good crops of maize. Rouse was fond and proud of this featureless expanse, and would boast about it, comparing its unparalleled beauty with that uninteresting kind of country which is full of mountains, kloofs, rivers, forests, and waterfalls. He soon found that praise of this waste was wholly unintelligible to Clayton, with whom by then he had formed a firm friendship which permitted him, and very few others, to mock him gently. He would be driving his bishop through this bare terrain, and would cry out in wonderment at its beauty. Clayton would lift his eyes from his book, for he read a great deal while being driven, and having regarded the scene with distaste, would return to his reading, but Rouse would regain his attention by exclaiming at the miracle of a solitary eucalyptus breaking the line of the flat horizon. Clayton, always ready with a retort, was baffled, because he had no language of scenery at all, and with a snort he would return to his book.

Rouse first saw the new bishop at Potchefstroom station. Clayton had not stayed in Cape Town, partly because the archbishop was still in England, and partly because he was anxious to get to his job. The train, nearly at the end of its long three-day journey, entered the Transvaal at Fourteen Streams, and at Bloemhof he was welcomed by the rector, H. R. Higgs, and at Klerksdorp by the rector, Spencer Watson. Not long after that he was met by Rouse at Potchefstroom, accompanied by the missionary, Ned Paterson, who had brought an African choir to sing to the new bishop. Rouse found Clayton without coat and collar, and introduced himself. Clayton was obviously taken back, even annoyed, to think that he must come out into the publicity of the platform and be sung to. He fled somewhere or other, and emerged, having put on collar and coat, and was then very genial to all concerned. When the train had gone, Rouse said to Paterson, 'We've got a blighter on our hands.' One can but pay tribute to Rouse's perception.

On 24 May 1934 Clayton was enthroned in St. Mary's Cathedral,

Johannesburg. This was the first ceremony of its kind in the cathedral. When Bishop Karney was enthroned in 1922, St. Mary's had not been built. Clayton's enthronement was a tremendous occasion, and was attended by the mayors and mayoresses of Johannesburg, Pretoria, and nine other towns of the Transvaal,* as well as the members of the Johannesburg City Council. H. R. Raikes, principal of the University of the Witwatersrand, was there, and the deans of the faculties, as well as the masters of St. John's College, a church school, and many old Johannians. The Revd. J. Bruce Gardiner represented the Presbyterian Church, and the Revd. A. S. Clegg the Methodists; the Revd. James Gray, the oldest Presbyterian minister in the Transvaal, was also present. Led by the first processional cross of the cathedral came the layreaders, sub-deacons, and clergy, and led by the second, the canons of the cathedral, representatives of the Church of Sweden and the Holy Orthodox Eastern Church, the Chief Rabbi the Most Reverend Dr. Isidore, the Archdeacon of Johannesburg (the Venerable Robert Urquhart), the Archdeacon of Native Missions (the Venerable W. F. Hill, C.R.), the Bishop of Pretoria (the Right Revd. Wilfrid Parker) and many Pretoria clergy.

After the members of the procession had taken up their positions, the dean and the archdeacons went to the closed west doors of the cathedral. Outside, the bishop, whose arrival had been made known to the congregation by a fanfare from the buglers of St. John's College, was waiting, accompanied by his chaplains, the chancellor, the registrar, the bursar, the churchwardens of the cathedral, and the verger carrying the cathedral mace. The bishop knocked three times on the closed doors with the pastoral staff given to him by the parishioners of Chesterfield. The doors were opened, and the bishop entered and presented to the dean of the cathedral his mandate, saying:

'We, Geoffrey, by Divine permission, Bishop of Johannesburg, do seek entrance into the Cathedral Church of St. Mary, and that we may be inducted, installed, and enthroned, as Bishop of Johannesburg, with all the rights thereunto belonging, according to this mandate of the Dean of the Church of the Province of South Africa.'

The dean accepted the mandate, and the bishop was conducted to the chancel, to the singing of the 121st Psalm, 'I will lift up mine eyes unto the hills', and the 122nd, 'I was glad when they said unto me: we will go into the house of the Lord'. When the psalms were ended, the staff was laid on the communion table, and the bishop knelt at the entrance to the sanctuary, while the Invocation and the Lord's Prayer were said, and the collect 'Prevent us, O Lord, in all our doings with thy most gracious favour'.

Then the Deed of Collation was read, and the bishop, standing at the table and laying his right hand on the Book of the Gospels, declared that he would 'respect, maintain, and defend the rights, privileges, and liberties of the Diocese . . . not lording it over God's heritage, but showing myself in

*Benoni, Boksburg, Springs, Roodepoort–Maraisburg, Randfontein, Potchefstroom, Nigel, Brakpan, and Ermelo.

all things an example to the flock'.

The dean then conducted the bishop to the throne, placing the pastoral staff in his hand, and saying the words:

'By the authority committed to me, I enthrone thee, Right Reverend Father in God, in the Episcopal Chair of this Cathedral Church. . . . In the name of the Lord Jesus, the Great Shepherd and Bishop of Souls, receive this Pastoral Staff, the emblem of thy authority as Bishop.'

Prayers were now said for the enthroned bishop, followed by an anthem from the choir, and the congregational singing of 'Our Blest Redeemer', after which the bishop was conducted to the pulpit, where he delivered his first sermon in his diocese.

Clayton first gave thanks to his brethren of the clergy and laity for all the prayers that had been offered for him since his election. It had been his wish to be consecrated in Johannesburg, but the powers that be had decided that he should be consecrated in England. But that did not matter. He was a bishop not of the Church of the Province but of the Holy Catholic Church of Christ. During his consecration he had promised to pay all due honour and deference to the Archbishop of Canterbury and all due reverence and obedience to the Archbishop of Cape Town. These two promises illustrated the unbreakable link which bound the Church of the Province to the mother Church of England.

He took his text from I Corinthians: 'Ye are the Body of Christ.'

'I am a stranger here and I know but little of the conditions of life in this place. But it seems to me that, all the world over, men are confronted by difficulties that they do not know how to solve, and I think that all these problems in the last resort come down to the question of personal relationships: how in the world today men are to live together and so to live together that there may be peace and not war, mutual trust instead of mutual contempt. We are Christians, and so we believe that the solution to all the problems of life is to be found in Christ.'[3]

A collection was taken for the new church to be built in the tremendous new African township of Orlando, and after the bishop had blessed the congregation, the procession left the cathedral, and the enthronement service was at an end.

So Clayton's reign began. He received good wishes from numberless people, both in South Africa and in England. The Mayor of Johannesburg gave him a civic reception in the Selborne Hall, to meet the leaders in commerce, industry, and public life, and of the university and religious bodies. Clayton received an especially warm welcome from the African people of his diocese, and an address which gave indications of things to come.

'Your Lordship will find yourself floating in space like a football between two rival parties. Europeans with adverse views to Christianising African races will oppose your schemes which tend to their advancement, and the Africans who are anti-white will not welcome you as friend, pastor, and Father-in-God on account of the suspicion due to injustice on the part of the European folk.'

The address ended: 'We do pray that God, who has appointed you Bishop over the Black Masses of this land, will give you the power and wisdom without which no Bishop can shelter his flock and drive the sheep to a haven of salvation.'

Dr. Horton Davies, who quotes this address in his article 'The Most Reverend Geoffrey Clayton', adds these words: 'That petition was splendidly answered and even Africans embittered by their frustration who came to scoff remained to pray.'[4]

There was much truth in these words. It might have been possible for Clayton to eschew political partisanship in Chesterfield. During the coal strike of 1925 he kept the regard of both parties in the dispute. He taught his parishioners that, as they lived closer to God, they would begin to see things as God sees them, which means as they really are. But he offered no solution of the dispute. Again in 1931, speaking of the financial crisis, he urged his people not to grumble at the Government. It was the people who had put it into power, and if it called on them to make sacrifices, they must make them willingly.

But politics in South Africa are very different. For one thing, the Government is put into power by the white electorate, which represents one-fifth of the people, and it is to be expected that it will rule in their interest. Problems of racial discrimination and racial injustice abound, and the Christian cannot keep silent about them. Yet they are the very stuff of politics. Therefore in no country in the world is more loudly heard the cry, 'Keep politics out of religion'.

Into this controversial world the new bishop had now entered. We shall learn through what clear eyes he saw it. There was no perfume in the world that could hide from him the smell of injustice. And no power that would deter him from denouncing it. For he recognised only one ultimate power, that of Him who had anointed him, and sent him to heal the broken-hearted.

So Geoffrey Johannesburg was now 'amongst his own people'. So far as is known to me, he never again used the word 'home' when he spoke of England. At some point he began to speak of South Africa as 'our country', and travelled on a South African passport. He never learned to speak Afrikaans, and he excused himself by saying, first that he was no good at languages anyway, secondly that if he *did* learn a language, it would have to be Zulu or Sesotho. By many Afrikaners he was regarded as just another English bishop, who would come 'out' to South Africa and condemn everything, and then would go back 'home' when he felt like it. That would have been a bad judgement. In a real sense he was not an Englishman, just as in the same sense he never became a South African. On the other hand it would have been quite wrong to call him 'a man of the world'. He was not an internationalist or a cosmopolitan. He was a product of Rugby, Cambridge, England, his home and his Church. For his Church he had a deep reverence, but the others were accidents. He would never have referred, unless there was some point to be made, to the fact that he had been at Rugby or Cambridge. He was once invited to Simonstown to lunch, at which was present a naval surgeon who was an old Rugbeian, and was looking forward to meeting the Great Man. When the surgeon was introduced, he stuck his thumb behind his tie and pushed it out saying, 'I believe we wear the same tie, sir.' The archbishop looked at him without enthusiasm. 'Never use them', he said, and moved on.[5]

6

A Strange Society

Clayton entered on his work as Bishop of Johannesburg with humility, authority and gusto. In his first letter to the diocese he wrote: 'My duty at present is to learn, and to keep as quiet as I can till I have been able to form some ideas of the needs and prospects of the Diocese as a whole.'

He enjoyed being a bishop. At Chesterfield he had had at one time four curates and three sisters for the work of the parish. Now he had ninety priests and deacons, about twelve catechists and perhaps a hundred voluntary sub-catechists. There were five women workers including the redoubtable Dorothy Maud, sister of Sir John Maud (later Baron Redcliffe Maud), British High Commissioner for Basutoland, Bechuanaland, and Swaziland. There were three white church schools, St. John's, St. Mary's, and St. Dunstan's. There were over thirty African schools, and the number was growing. One of Clayton's first tasks after his election was to look for a new headmaster for St. John's College to replace Father Runge of the Community of the Resurrection, which had run the school since 1905 and was now withdrawing from it to devote its attention to the missionary needs of Johannesburg, with its rapidly growing African population, its vigorous and exciting and lawless townships, with their almost overwhelming challenge to any person who was trying to lead a Christian life. In the white suburbs, both rich and poor, there were challenges also, but in Sophiatown, Newclare, Western Native Township, Alexandra, and the new township of Orlando, the challenges were crude and blatant. One learned the facts of life when one was a child. One might grow up good but never innocent. It was of this vital, raw, violent and ugly city that Trevor Huddleston could write when he had to leave it, 'Look thy last on all things lovely'. If there was one thing that moved him more than any other, it was to find faith and goodness and love in the midst of carelessness and evil.

The wonder of it moved Clayton too, though in a very different way. Huddleston could wash a black boy's feet and kiss them. Clayton could not. If Huddleston did it, he was not kissing the feet of one particular boy, but the feet of the humble and poor. Clayton would have understood that, though he would not have done it. Clayton's work as an army chaplain had taught him that there was another world outside the colleges of Cambridge. Now as Bishop of Johannesburg he entered yet another, where old black men and women entered the churches on their knees, where there was a humility of worship that has in large measure been lost by Western Christianity, where men and women actually *abased* themselves in the presence of God, where they would acknowledge, sometimes by gesture and sometimes by exclamation, the truth of some word spoken by the preacher, where they in fact forgot themselves and became as little children. Who understood that better than he, for had he not been preaching for twenty-five years that only thus could one enter the Kingdom of Heaven?

Clayton would probably not have said to anyone – if he did, I never heard of it – that he was moved by the wonder of such humility. He was not given to expressing wonder. But it was noticeable that he was far more patient with the weaknesses and the odd customs of black people. During the most reverent service possible, children would almost continually be leaving the church to relieve their needs, and others, having relieved them, be continually re-entering it. Mothers would take out a breast to feed a crying babe. At certain seasons of the year the coughing was incessant, but the bishop would seldom show the irritation that he would unfailingly have shown in any church in the white suburbs of Johannesburg.

It was a strange society to which Clayton had come in 1934, and he was quick to realise its complexity. Long before the advent of the Afrikaner Nationalist Government in 1948, the customs and the laws concerning colour and race in South Africa were many and were often burdensome. The word *apartheid* had not yet become part of the international vocabulary, but the thing existed. The African people, who constituted about 70 per cent of the population, owned about 13 per cent of the land, this land being called the Reserves (now the Homelands). A few of them owned land in 'white' areas. These later came to be known as the 'black spots', and were finally to be eliminated by the Nationalist Government, which prohibited any purchase by an African of land in a 'white' area. The average *per capita* black income could be conservatively estimated at one-tenth of the average white income. All industry, mining, commerce, were in white hands, with a few exceptions. These were mainly Indian shopkeepers and budding industrialists, and were to be found mainly in Natal. Education was compulsory for white children, but not for others. In fact, if it had not been for the churches, amongst them the Church of the Province of South Africa, there would have been almost no African education. Apart from those benefits which could be called spiritual, education was the superlative gift that the Christian churches brought to the black people of South Africa. The diocese of Johannesburg was extremely active in the field of African education, the work in the city and its environs being the responsibility of the Community of the Resurrection, and the work in the smaller towns and in the countryside being the direct responsibility of the diocese itself.

All political power in the Union of South Africa, of which the Transvaal was the richest and most populous province, was in the hands of the all-white Parliament in Cape Town. At the time of the creation of the Union in 1910, the Cape Province had been allowed to retain its own franchise, which gave the parliamentary vote to certain qualified African and Coloured men (but not women), and allowed them to stand for election to the Cape Provincial Council. These provisions could only be altered by a two-thirds majority of both Houses of Parliament sitting together. However no person not white could be elected to the central Parliament of the Union of South Africa.

One of the consequences of vesting all political power in an all-white parliament was that the other population groups of the country had no say in the way they were governed. One of the most cruel of these consequences was the control that Parliament exercised over the movement of people from place to place. There was little work to be had in the Reserves, so that the attraction of the cities, with their bright lights and excitements, with their industries, their great shops and buildings wanting office-workers, tea-makers, and lift attendants, their white builders wanting labour, was irresistible. But the white authorities, although they wanted the black man, did not want his wife and children. That is not to say that there were not tens of thousands of black families already in the cities, but the ever-increasing flood of immigrants began to frighten the Government and the city councils. In Cape Town, the Government, afraid of another Johannesburg, prohibited the entry of black women and children. While there were large numbers of urbanised African families, they too were losing, year by year, more and more of their rights to remain in the white cities, and stayed there on sufferance. The rigid application of the policies of apartheid and separate development led to the vast extension of migratory labour, whereby the employer has access to black labour, but the labourer is cut off from his wife and children. These too were things that the new bishop would have to learn about.

As for the practice of racial segregation in the social sphere, it was almost complete. But in 1934 it was much less rigid than it is today. In certain church circles, in left-inclined political movements, amongst the members of the South African Institute of Race Relations, and in other liberal circles such as existed amongst both teachers and students at the universities, there was a movement away from social segregation. This movement could only take place in a very restricted way, primarily because white and black people lived in separate areas, and travelling between them was always difficult; also because the desire for such communication was largely limited to the more highly educated and more affluent of both communities. Friendship between the less affluent of both communities was almost non-existent. Furthermore, the Nationalists, under General Hertzog, which at the time of Clayton's arrival were about to fuse with the South African Party under General Smuts, the new party to be called the United Party, were actively hostile to social and friendly relationships between white and black. In 1927 the Nationalist Government had prohibited sexual intercourse between white and African, and in 1934 many ex-Nationalists in the new United Party were pressing for legislation to prohibit sexual intercourse between whites and Indian and Coloured people as well, and to prohibit intermarriage between whites and any other persons.[1] At the time of writing, these laws are still in force, and the law against interracial sexual intercourse, the Immorality Act, has brought great suffering to many people. It can therefore be said that interracial relationships, excluding those in industry, commerce, and with servants in a white home, either took place openly and legally, or surreptitiously and illegally. In between these two extremes there was a vast sea of non-communication. It can be said that the white, black, coloured and Indian groups lived almost totally separate lives. Well-meaning groups of white women listened with horror and pain when a black woman addressed them, and told them what life was like in Sophiatown, Orlando and Alexandra Township.

This was the world into which Clayton had come. This was the world in which the Church of the Province, indeed all churches were set. St. James counselled the Christian to keep himself 'unspotted from the world', but it cannot be done. All that one can do is never to give up trying, so that there is a continual tension between what one is and what one aspires to be. The Church of the Province was a South African church and carried within itself all the tensions and all the corruptions, and was continually confronted by the challenge of its Lord that His Church, which was so much a creature of the world, should be its light also. It was the Church of Christ, but it was also the Church of the Province of South Africa. It being of South Africa, the colour-bar entered into every part of its life; being of Christ it strove to break down the walls of partition.

Although the Church of the Province had more African adherents than white, its bishops in 1934 were all white, and were all British except one. It was not until 1960 that the Revd. Alpheus Zulu was made Suffragan-Bishop of the diocese of St. John's which is in fact the Transkei. It was not until 1966 that he was elected Bishop of Zululand. In 1934 only one African priest in the whole Province had attained the rank of Canon. This was Canon Andreas Rakale, mission priest at Springs, appointed by Bishop Karney. The stipends of African priests were one-third or even a smaller fraction of those of white priests. White priests were in charge of black work, but no black priest was in charge of white work.* The only black full-time workers to be found in the diocesan offices in Johannesburg were cleaners and tea-makers. No black priest was on the staff of the cathedral which served the whole diocese. The diocesan monthly, *The Watchman*, never, as far as I know, carried anything written by an African. It must be said quite frankly that the differences in educational qualifications of white priests and black priests were considerable, and that black priests did not speak with the same confidence and facility in synods or any other mixed gatherings. Black and

*This is still true in 1973, with some important exceptions. The Right Revd. Fortescue Makhetha is Suffragan-Bishop of Lesotho (since 1967). The Right Revd. Alpheus Zulu is Bishop of Zululand, which has a fair number of white Anglicans. The Right Revd. E. A. Sobukwe is Suffragan-Bishop of St. John's, which also has a number of white Anglicans. The new Suffragan-Bishop of Cape Town is a coloured priest, Canon George Swartz. The Revd. David Russell, a white priest, serves under the Revd. James Gawe, an African priest, at King William's Town, in the diocese of Grahamstown.

white seldom worshipped together because residentially they were so completely separated, and because they worshipped in different languages. They worshipped together in the cathedral on diocesan occasions, such as Synod Sundays, and on these occasions the presence of so many black people in the heart of white Johannesburg was a source of wonderment, and sometimes irritation, to many of the passers-by. The Community of the Resurrection did its best to involve white Anglicans in work and worship in black areas, but they would have found it impossible to do the opposite, except when there were special white parish occasions such as a Race Relations Sunday.

It must also be noted that there was a binding rule on all Anglican priests and churches to accept any person who wished to worship or communicate, no matter what his colour or his race. Yet Trevor Huddleston in his book *Naught for Your Comfort*, which was received with anger and coldness by many white South Africans, relates the story of the young priest who suggested to his church council that he should hold a monthly Mass at five-thirty in the morning for the benefit of black domestic servants; half his council resigned in protest.[2] Huddleston denied that geographical and linguistic difficulties were the basic causes of the separation within the Church of the Province; according to him, the causes were prejudice and fear. And he felt strongly that for the sake of the Church, particularly for the sake of the future of Christianity in Africa, no time must be lost in removing these causes of division.

There are a few more things to be said about the influence of considerations of race and colour on the church life of South Africa. The Dutch Reformed churches of South Africa. of which there are three, the largest of which is the Nederduitse Gereformeerde Kerk, almost never made common cause with the other main churches when moral issues involving politics were raised. There were three main causes for this. The first was the Dutch Reformed view of racial separation, which was first claimed to be scriptural but, as theological criticism progressively weakened the claim, was then said to be the will of God for a country of such diverse races and colours. The second reason why common cause was never made was that the relationship of the Dutch Reformed churches to the Government was quite different from that of the Anglicans and others. Most of the members of the ruling party and the Cabinet were Dutch Reformed churchmen, and one could make direct representations to them; it has therefore become a kind of conservative dogma that a true Christian does not protest publicly. The third reason is as important as any, and that is the great difficulty in finding any common ground between the Dutch Reformed churches and any church which recognises its Catholic origins. For example, the gulf between Dutch Reformed Calvinism and Roman Catholicism seems unbridgeable, and the important N.G.K. journal, *Die Kerkbode*, to this day warns its readers against the *Roomse gevaar*, the 'Roman danger'. It would almost seem as though Dutch Reformed Calvinist man and Catholic man in South Africa are two different creatures with different and irreconcilable ways of looking at man and the world. This incompatibility makes it difficult for

Dutch Reformed churchmen to work with Catholics and Anglicans; they also find it difficult to work with Methodists, Congregationalists and Presbyterians, and most unpalatable of all for them, with their fellow Calvinists in other countries of the world, who have reluctantly turned away from them.

This incompatibility was cloaked for Clayton in 1934, because of the political reconciliation between Hertzog and Smuts. It would be safe to say that Smuts received his support largely from non-Calvinists, and from Calvinists who were less rigid in their religious and racial views. So it happened that in the August of his first year, when Clayton was being welcomed at a social by the Anglicans of Lichtenburg, a small town in the eastern Transvaal, he was also welcomed by the Revd. J. F. Hugo of the N.G.K., who expressed pleasure that the diocese of Johannesburg was getting such an able man, and referred also to the desirability of Church union. Clayton expressed his thanks, and regretted that he could not reply to Mr. Hugo in his own language.

Yet another thing Clayton had to learn, and that is that there were a large number of African independent churches, and that the number increased yearly. There were several hundreds in his time, and today there are said to be over two thousand. Dr. Bengt Sundkler, who made a study of the separatist churches, did not lay the blame for this proliferation directly at the door of the policy of racial separation, and the doctrine of 'no equality in Church and State' as laid down in the constitution of the South African (Transvaal) Republic. He wrote:

'The problem [of secession] arises when the more repressive view tacitly or openly becomes dominating in churches which, in principle are equalitarian and liberal, but which by "practical necessity" – consideration for the race-conscious White membership of a particular church – have to conform to a general segregation policy within the church.'[3]

Clayton was to have direct experience of this. The movement called the Order of Ethiopia, which was at first a secession from the Methodist Church and then later sought inclusion in the Church of the Province, raised difficult problems. The members of the Order wanted freedom from white domination, but at the same time did not wish to break the apostolic succession. The Order was to be, to this very day, a continual reminder of the failure of the Church to be true to its own professions in matters of race and colour.

These three things Clayton realised quickly – the corruption of the Church by the colour-bar, the great gulf between the Dutch Reformed churches and the others, and the challenge of the separatists to the more orthodox churches. But he did not agonise over them. He certainly did not agonise over the first as Huddleston did. He applied his mind to trying to understand what he could do in the circumstances. He might well have prayed the prayer of Reinhold Niebuhr: 'God grant me the serenity to accept the things I cannot change, courage to change the things I can, and the wisdom to know the difference.' He was not given to agonising.

7

Interfering with the World

Synod Sunday, 1934. A cathedral packed by people of all races, black and white and coloured. Some are very rich, and some very poor. There are many black people, as many as white, and though every part of the cathedral is open to them, and though they could pack the floor if they wanted to, and take all the best pews, they tend to congregate upstairs in the galleries.

A great procession accompanied by tremendous music from the new organ. The first crucifer, the choir, the sub-deacons, the clergy, the canons of the cathedral, the archdeacons, the dean, and then, preceded by the second crucifer and a pair of servers, the new bishop, Geoffrey Johannesburg. Because the bishop is carrying the crozier, his chaplain walks behind him.

Geoffrey Johannesburg enters with that indescribable gait, as of a top-heavy ship rolling its way through the sea. He is carrying the crozier, that is, the pastoral staff given to him by the people of Chesterfield. His mitre is set back on his head, so that nothing is concealed of his enormous brow. He does not look ahead of him, and he certainly does not cast his eyes modestly on the ground. He looks to left and to right of him, not with short sharp movements, but in such a way as to match his roll. People turn to look at him, but he does not look at them, nor is he looking to see if the cathedral is full. He merely looks as though he owns it all. He looks like a Prince of the Church, and he looks as though he knows that he is, but not arrogantly. The last thing that would occur to one would be to think that he was ugly.

The air is expectant. Many of these people have not heard him before. Perhaps the only thing they know is that one must not cough or shuffle while he is preaching. The first service of Synod is the Eucharist. Clayton has done this – how many times before? Perhaps nearly ten thousand? But he does it as though it were new. The great resounding voice, full of a passion that is not passionate because it is so controlled, rings out through the cathedral, giving to some of the passages of the Eucharist a hitherto unrevealed majesty. It is all quite overwhelming. When it is over, people will go to breakfast, at home or in the hotels near the cathedral. The Victoria Hotel looks like a synod itself.

After breakfast the air is still expectant. Soon everyone will return to the cathedral, the great procession will be held all over again, the bishop will roll down the aisle, with something on his lips which is not quite a smile and is certainly not a scowl. That will come later, when someone coughs. This morning the people of the diocese will hear their first charge from the new bishop. It will be his first charge also, but he will deliver it as though he has been delivering charges all his life. It will be delivered with supreme clarity and great authority, and the manner of it will remind some of what was said of Jesus, that he taught as one having authority, and not as the scribes.

There is silence as he climbs his way into the pulpit. He puts the papers of the charge on the lectern. He then glares over the top of his glasses at the packed congregation. Having cowed them all, he delivers his charge.

Clayton divided his first charge into two parts.[1] The first dealt with the Church and the duties of the churchman. It was in fact a call for greater devotion. He made it clear that the Church of the Province, while accepting the faith and doctrine of the Church of England, was not bound by the decision of any tribunals other than its own. The first duty of the churchman was to worship God, not because he would receive help or comfort, or inspiration, but because God claims his worship. And it was when he gave with no thought of receiving, that he would receive.

Clayton reminded his clergy that there should be a daily celebration of Holy Communion, and that they were obliged to say morning and evening prayer daily. But this was to be no formal obedience; there had to be a 'background of earnest and persevering prayer'. The worship of God had the first claim on every Sunday; otherwise Sunday was free. He spoke, as he had spoken often in Cambridge and Chesterfield, and was to speak again in Cape Town, of the dangers that beset the Christian faith, and he quoted one of his favourite passages, written by Bishop Joseph Butler in 1736, on the faith:

'Nothing remains but to set it up as a principal subject of mirth and ridicule, as it were by way of reprisals, for its having so long interrupted the pleasures of the world.'

He returned to another of his favourite themes, and that is that the faith must be brought into relation with knowledge. That did not mean changing the faith, but it meant seeing it in new contexts, and that involved thinking. In particular it was a duty of the clergy to think and read and study. He told another favourite story, of Dr. Hook the Vicar of Leeds, who rose at five, studied from six to nine, gave the rest of the day to the parish, and spent one or two hours in prayer and meditation at about midnight. He made a dead church into 'one of the liveliest congregations in England'.

Clayton made his first public pronouncement on race, not in the context of politics, but in the context of Christian doctrine and duty. First quoting St. Paul, 'Ye are all one in Christ Jesus', he said:

'But that does not mean that the Jew is the same as the Greek, and the male the same as the female. Neither is the European the same as the African. It is not that one is better than the other. When each race is brought to its perfection, I believe the difference will persist. We are not going to be all alike in Heaven, if by God's grace we attain to our final consummation and bliss. But we all alike have an equal right to our membership in the Church of God.'

He made an important statement. 'I do not think that means we should normally worship together. I believe that that would be disastrous to the spiritual development of the African. But special occasions should be sought.' And he gave two injunctions. He told his white listeners that their privileged position imposed great duties upon them, because their African fellow-churchmen were poor. He told his African listeners to beware of suspicion and fear; in spite of all our prejudices we were trying to create a spirit of unity.

These sentiments and opinions would have been found acceptable by the great majority of the white Christians in South Africa. It almost seemed to be a statement of racial immutability, and a foreshadowing of the doctrine of separate development, that is the official policy of the present day. Is any race ever brought to its perfection? Cannot only persons be brought to perfection, through the grace of God and the working of the Holy Spirit? Can one see anywhere signs of a race having been brought to perfection, or of a race in the process of coming to perfection? Is it not an impossible goal, which, when pursued in a multiracial society by a ruling race, can cause great suffering to those races who are ruled?

Yet it would be foolish to pass judgement on Clayton's first charge, and on a charge made in 1934. No one foresaw at that time that it would one day be the avowed policy of the Government of South Africa to bring each race, if not to perfection, then certainly to independence and self-realisation. Nor did anyone foresee that the methods that would be used to implement this policy would be condemned at this time or at that, by nearly all the South African churches except the Dutch Reformed. Nor that it became daily clearer, to all but those people who were fully committed to the policy, that in the first instance it was unrealisable, and that in the second any attempts to realise it must always be characterised by harshness and injustice.

That is why Clayton, the first part of whose first charge would have been acceptable to so many white South Africans, was later himself to have become more and more unacceptable, so much so that, when he died, in the high office of the Archbishop of Cape Town, not one representative of the Government attended his funeral. Why should that have been? The answer to that question is to be found in the second part of his charge, though there must have been very few who could have seen the shape of things to come.

Clayton dealt with the twofold duty of the Church, that of dealing with individual souls, and that of making society more Christian. It is the theme which in its controversial aspect obsesses many white South African Christians. The controversy is endless, between those who believe that the Church should confine itself to the care of souls, and those who believe that the Church cannot discharge its duty towards souls unless it concerns itself with the kind of society in which souls live. The first group, whom we may call the pietists, regard any concern with society as dabbling in politics. The second group, whom we may call the activists, reject any kind of

Christianity which does not concern itself with man in the world, and with social, racial, and economic questions; and would regard the keeping of politics out of religion as being just as bad, and as impossible, as keeping religion out of politics. There is no solution to this controversy. Like so many conflicts, it expresses a dualism in man himself, or, in its extreme form, an incompatibility between two types of man. The extreme pietist regards the activist as aggressive, strife-loving and destructive, and as being, wittingly or unwittingly, a supporter of Communism. The extreme activist regards the pietist as smug, reactionary, and cowardly. Clayton was to have to deal with the problem of the twofold duty of the Church, and with the problem posed by the pietists and the activists, for the rest of his life. But one thing he made clear. The Church would not be able to discharge its duty towards souls unless South Africa produced more of her own clergy. And here he made a plea that he had made and would make again and again, throughout the whole of his preaching life, to parents, that they should never discourage their sons who felt called to the priestly life. What is more, the parishes must learn to contribute more generously to the Ordination Candidates Fund.

With regard to the second duty, he put the question, *Can the Church have a political policy?* The answer was yes and no. It could demand that the holder of any government post should be incorruptible. It could remind governments that their duty was to give every man the opportunity to develop to his utmost. He quoted Newman:

'The Church was formed for the express purpose of interfering, or (as irreligious people will say) meddling with the world... And if they [Christians] can do nothing else, at least they can suffer for the truth, and remind men of it, by inflicting upon them the task of persecution.'

He went on to say:

'I may think that the methods of some of my fellow-churchmen are calculated to produce the opposite result from that which both they and I desire. But I recognise that, as long as they honestly believe that their proposals will bring Society more into accordance with the will of God, they have every right to make these proposals and to remain members, and honoured members, of the Church.'

He added that that was why the Church could not have a detailed policy. He then concluded:

'But I would end this charge, already far too long, by reminding you that in the last resort the world can only become better by the people in it becoming better, and in that matter the wisest and most useful thing we can do is to begin with ourselves.'

Newman's assertion that the Church was formed for the express purpose of interfering with the world was not likely to be acceptable to a very large number of white South Africans. It was true that many churchmen, of whatever churches, would have felt that it was the duty of the Church to watch closely the doings of the world, its pleasures and its naughtinesses and the lengths of women's dresses. But there was the insinuation in Newman's words, and also in Clayton's charge, that the actions of authority might have to be brought under scrutiny as well. The word *interference* was to many a dangerous word, and the moment it was used it gave the impression that the Church was going to encroach upon the province of another divine institution, the State. To many, Newman's observation was aggressive. The Church should go quietly and decently about its business. It was true it had a monitory duty towards the State, but it was not a thing to be talked about. The possibility that the Church would exercise this function, or that it would ever become necessary for the Church to exercise it, was so remote that discussion of it was either academic or impertinent.

In fact the Dutch Reformed churches had never approved of the tendency of the Church of the Province and its bishops to criticise South African custom and legislation, not only because the bishops were almost always British-born, but because of the dogma that had grown up that the Church must not protest publicly against the actions of the State. Some of the critics of the Dutch Reformed churches asserted that they would have protested soon enough had the power of the State been wielded by a government that flouted the customs of racial separation. That assertion was only partly true. When General Smuts defeated General Hertzog in Parliament in 1939 over the question of declaring war on Germany, the Dutch Reformed churches were overwhelmingly opposed to the decision, but *Die Kerkbode*, the official organ of the big N.G.K., maintained a cold but correct attitude towards the new government.

In the year 1934 the Coalition Government, with its tremendous majority, was planning the alteration of the Cape franchise, which granted a qualified right to vote to both African and Coloured people.* There were various proposals, some to abolish the African franchise altogether, some to offer Africans a separate form of representation by white persons of their own choice. In November 1934 the Synod of the diocese of Johannesburg, a day or two after the bishop's first charge, passed unanimously the following resolution:

'Synod expresses its conviction that the only true solution of the Native question is the Christian basis of the *ultimate* right of individuals and nations to full citizenship.'

William Palmer, the Dean, urged upon Synod the strongest opposition to modification of the Cape Native franchise, and urged also that any experiment of special representation should be tried for ten years before the alteration of the actual franchise was considered.

Clayton therefore inherited a synod which was already concerning itself with legislation. Nor was the Synod of the diocese of Johannesburg the only synod which did so. It had become a characteristic of the Church of the Province to consider itself a kind of watchdog over all legislation which

*This coalition gave way to a fusion, and the United Party was formed in 1934 (see chapter 6). One of the reasons why General Hertzog entered this fusion was that only thus could he secure the two-thirds majority of both Houses sitting together, which was necessary to alter the entrenched Cape franchise.

concerned the African, Coloured, and Indian people. This was in general regarded with disapproval by the Dutch Reformed churches, with irritation by politicians, and with anger by extreme Afrikaner Nationalists, not only on the grounds that the Church was encroaching on the concerns of the State, but that the protest and criticism of legislation was led by clerics who had not been born in South Africa, who with few exceptions could not speak Afrikaans, and who in any event would eventually go 'home'. This was by no means the attitude of General Smuts, who reacted to criticism, and even to vituperation, with extraordinary tolerance. He had had long experience of the attitude of bishops and synods towards legislation that they considered discriminatory and unjust. Yet when Smuts met the newly arrived bishop at some function in Johannesburg he said, 'The Church you represent in this country is a minority Church. But don't forget that your Church carries great prestige, and I hope you will speak out to us boldly and clearly, and your words will carry great weight.'[2] There is an apocryphal story that Smuts once said of Clayton's judgements that they were the only ones that he feared. Be that as it may, these two extraordinary men saw little of each other.

Clayton had said in his charge that he thought some of his fellow-churchmen unwise in their choice of methods. Who they were and what they did, I have not been able to discover. But it was something that he was to say again in the course of his twenty-two years in South Africa, though only once again, so far as I know, publicly.

It could be said that Clayton found for himself a synthesis between pietism and activism, and that is why his moral and spiritual authority was hardly ever questioned by his fellow-churchmen. However, it will be seen later that he was more easily irritated by activists than by pietists. He was irritated by priests whose words and actions received more than usual publicity. Above all was he irritated, and sometimes angered, by any person, priest or layman, whom he thought to be trying to use the Church for some social or political end. Sometimes he thought this of any person who was nearer to the activist end of the spectrum than he was. In later years it was to bring him into conflict with some of his fellow-churchmen, notably Trevor Huddleston, Michael Scott, and Ambrose Reeves.

8

'We are governed and we like it'

Clayton had now been in Johannesburg for six months. He had already met all his clergy, and had indeed visited most of them. He had familiarised himself with the Diocesan Works of Mercy, and had met some remarkable and redoubtable women. He had, after consulting the school council, appointed the Revd. Sydney Herbert Clarke as headmaster of St. John's College, Johannesburg. He was the Official Visitor to St. John's, and to all the other church schools of the diocese. He also as bishop of the diocese licensed the priests of the Community of the Resurrection, which at their Priory of St. Peter in the white suburb of Rosettenville had created an extraordinary establishment, a seminary for the training of African clergy, a high school of excellent standard for African boys and girls (most of whom lived at the Priory), a chapel for the monks and a church of striking architecture, a library and a refectory, and accommodation for the monks and for guests. The atmosphere was that of industry, devotion, piety and peace. Tribulation was yet to come.

Now that the Community was relinquishing its control of St. John's College, it was expanding its mission work in the African townships of Johannesburg. Father Raymond Raynes, who had been a master at St. John's, now took charge of the Community's work in the township of Sophiatown, where the new church of Christ the King was nearing completion. There was a school there too, and a house that had been built by Dorothy Maud, and named by her 'Ekutuleni', the place of peace. The habited figures of monks and sisters were to be seen everywhere. In these townships of crime and violence, they were held in great respect, and their white members would be the only people of their colour who would dare to venture out at night.*

Outside the city, in the wide open spaces of the western and southern

*There have been very few cases of the use of violence against the members of these orders, even where they went abroad into most dangerous places. In 1952, during an African riot in East London, a white nun was burned to death in her car, and it was rumoured that some bystanders ate portions of her flesh. Such an event is never forgotten, and is cited as an example of African savagery, which would not even spare a woman whose life had been devoted to service in the townships. But it was one of the tragic exceptions. Another example of the use of violence was the murder in 1942 of Father Wall in his room at Rosettenville, but the motive appeared to be robbery.

Transvaal the work of the diocese was extensive. The white population was almost entirely Afrikaans-speaking, so that the Anglican congregations in the towns were small, but the missions to the African people, mostly workers in small-town commerce and industry, domestic servants, farm-labourers, and a few teachers, were extremely active.

Over this empire Clayton now reigned, and had already established an authority that could only be described as immense. Of the new order Dean Palmer said, 'Now we are governed and we find we like it.'[1] This immense authority was further increased by Clayton's first charge. Very few people in the packed cathedral had ever heard anything like it before. With Clayton's coming, the diocese, which had been by no means inactive under Karney, began to pulse with new life. And what made it more exciting was the fascinating personality of the new bishop, the extraordinary figure, the rolling gait, the Homeric laughter, the looks of displeasure, the great reading of great passages.

To sit under him at Synod was something never to be forgotten. For one thing he was a chairman without peer. Palmer found that he liked being governed, and there is no doubt that Synod liked it too. Nor is there any doubt that Clayton liked governing it. For this he had been born. While those sitting under him did so in awe, their awe was tempered by their enthralment. For at one point he would speak with grave authority, and at another, when some speaker expressed some view which he found more than ordinarily stupid, he would put his great head between his hands, and groan inaudibly. He would have no hesitation in ordering a speaker to sit down, or in peremptorily correcting him on some point of order. The person thus treated would often wish that the earth would rise up and swallow him, but it was rare to feel resentment, and that was because of the impersonality of Clayton's rebukes, which were directed not at the speaker but at his offence. It was painful to be thus humiliated, but one could console oneself that one would sooner or later be able to enjoy the humiliation of others. Synod was very like a big class sitting under a formidable master, with all the ingredients of earnestness, jokes, castigations, and scowlings, and a kind of gay enjoyment at seeing such an exhibition of petulance and greatness. That was in the 'thirties. Today, in the 'seventies, many still remember the days when they laughed, trembled, admired, suffered, under the chairmanship of Geoffrey Johannesburg.

When the tea interval arrived, Clayton would say in a light-hearted way, 'Synod adjourns,' light-hearted because he would now be able to smoke. It was noticeable that his voice was always deep and sepulchral when he said on returning, 'Synod resumes.' During the tea interval his great laugh could be heard, and if he was not laughing he would be smiling, the smile of one who was enjoying himself in this gathering of the diocesan family which he ruled with his inimitable mixture of benignity and terror. I think it would be true to say that Synod could do what it liked as long as he liked it too, or was indifferent to it. But if it seemed in danger of doing something which he judged to be wrong or unwise, he would prevent it, not by the use of any uncanonical power, but by the weight of his personality, which he could make overpowering if he wished to. His chosen form of government was tyrannical democracy.

As has been noted earlier, he was much more tolerant of black stupidity and garrulity than white. It can be said that in his whole attitude to black clergy and black lay people, he set a new standard, if not for the Church of of the Province, then at least for the diocese of Johannesburg. With his unlikely background of Rugby, Cambridge and Chesterfield, he walked straight into the hearts of his African people. On one of his white South-African-born priests his influence in these matters was profound. That was Redvers Rouse, then Rector of Potchefstroom.

Rouse was born in Kimberley in 1899, during its siege by the Boers. He matriculated at St. John's College in 1916, and then worked for a year at St. George's, the Anglican Home for Boys in Johannesburg. At the end of 1917 he enlisted for the tail-end of the First World War and, when it was over, persuaded by his old headmaster he went to Mirfield and Leeds University. He was ordained at St. Aidan's, Yeoville, and after two years, when he was 25 years old, Bishop Karney sent him to Bloemhof as Priest-in-Charge of the Western Transvaal. He was not only to minister to the six small congregations of Bloemhof, Christiana, Schweizer-Reneke, Makwassi, Wolmaransstad, and Leeudoringstad, but he was also the missionary responsible for the African work of that whole corner of the Transvaal, mainly amongst the Tswana people. Rouse was to be assisted by Lucas Mothobi, the African catechist.

At first Rouse did nothing about the missionary work. He felt that he must first get to know the white Anglicans of the western Transvaal. Mothobi complained that he did not come to see the African communicants, and said that he must learn Tswana. Mothobi taught him to take the Communion service in Tswana. He then demanded that Rouse should preach to them, but Rouse, who had to minister to white congregations at 7 a.m. complained that he was not really up to preaching at 5 a.m. Mothobi then told him that he must preach to them at Evensong, which was held at 3 p.m.

Mothobi had had little schooling, and he had been a commercial worker with no great wages, but he was highly intelligent and, when nearly 50, had gone to the Priory at Rosettenville for a year's training. He was a true pastor with a hunger for souls. He told Rouse that the people had many troubles, and that they needed Rouse's advice. Rouse said, 'Look what I have to do. When can I do it?' Mothobi said, 'Saturday afternoon.' So Rouse then had to work Saturday afternoons. He said that it was Mothobi who taught him how to use his 'spare time'. He said of Mothobi, 'He was the man who saved my soul.' Mothobi was later ordained, and when Clayton soon after visited the African congregation at Bloemhof, one of the elders said to him, 'We have had a child for a long time [this was Rouse], but now we have a man.'

Rouse's conversion was completed by his new bishop. In 1935 when Rouse was Rector of Potchefstroom, and Assistant Director of Native

Missions, Clayton came down to see if he was doing any work, and stayed at the rectory. There he put on a blanket, and assuming with ease the ferocity of a bear, played on the floor with the Rouse children. Whatever fear the Rouses had had of him, whatever trepidation they had felt about entertaining him, all disappeared. A strange friendship developed between the two men, which, as we have seen earlier, permitted Rouse to take certain liberties, but did not save him from being slapped down in Synod when the bishop felt that the need had arisen.

In spite of the fact that his soul had been saved by Mothobi, Rouse was still a true white South African, with all the weaknesses that particular kind of flesh is heir to. He was used to the paternalism of the mission field. Karney, though he made outspoken pronouncements on race issues, always took his advice from the white missionaries. He himself was no adept in the field of race relations. In fact he found African work a physical strain. The churches were always overcrowded, and there were an overwhelming number of candidates for confirmation. He did his duty in the townships and locations, and left them as soon as it was over. Nor did he like the rawness of Johannesburg. After twelve years of it he was glad to return to England.

Who would have thought that Clayton would have been so different? He would get out of the car with a beaming smile, and pat the children, even if he had grumbled all the way there. After the services he would go into one of the houses and eat the food that had been prepared for him. The people had usually killed a goat for him, and they would usually cook rice, and perhaps cabbages and peas. To get these things they would have to go to town, for these were not their common articles of diet. There would be bread and butter too, and special plates for this tremendous visitor. It was not the kind of food that Clayton was used to, and there were no electric stoves to cook it on. It was the simplest kind of hospitality, but Clayton knew the work and the care that had gone into it, and he responded to it with all the generosity, so often concealed, of his nature. He would never have thought of grumbling, either then or after he had left. He was visiting his people and he never showed anything but gladness for the warmth of their humble affection. He would be smiling, with that same smile that he wore during the tea breaks at Synod, because he was in the bosom of the family of which he was the head. It was not Rugby or Cambridge, but his understanding of the gospel that had prepared him for this day.

Confirmation was for him a solemn occasion, and not only for him but for the church and the child also. He would pray in his chapel at 'Bishop's House' for all those he would soon be confirming. After one such confirmation he asked, 'Where is George Molekane?' 'My Lord, he is in the fields looking after the cattle.' 'Take me to him.' So they took him to George, whom he confirmed kneeling in the fields.

Somewhat different was a confirmation at the rich church school of Michaelhouse, where Ronald Currey was headmaster. Another George was in the sanatorium with a fever, and Clayton went to confirm him there, and talked to him for two or three minutes about the step he was taking. His mother was so moved by this that she pulled a handkerchief out of her bag, scattering the bed with papers. Years after, Currey asked Clayton whether he remembered it. 'Yes,' said Clayton, 'it was the only confirmation I ever did through a barrage of bookies' tickets.'

Under Karney the Bishop's Senate had first been an all-white body consisting of the dean, archdeacon, Director of Native Missions, and six priests. In 1927 four African priests and one African deacon were appointed.[2] This was the position when Clayton arrived.

In 1934 the educational qualifications of white priests and black were very different. Most of the white clergy were university graduates, some of Oxford and Cambridge. Not one of the black clergy of that time was a graduate, and their theological training was not as rigorous. What was more, the proceedings of the Senate were conducted in English. The consequence of all this was that the participation of the black clergy tended to be poor, constrained, and halting.

One of the most favoured arguments of supporters of apartheid in the church is that the black or coloured or Indian churchman will be doomed for ever to remain at this level of participation. The black minister will never become a leader of the integrated church, the black worshipper will sit in the rear pews, the black parishioner will not be elected to the parish council, or if he is, he will remain subordinate and subservient. The supporters of apartheid can with a considerable measure of justice point to the churches that reject apartheid and find there many instances of the very practices they reject, and many indications that integration is resisted by white worshippers. They can point to the white church schools of the anti-apartheid churches, the authorities of which have offered an almost total resistance to the admission of children who are not white.*

This was one of the things that Clayton learned quickly, that the Church of the Province of South Africa was deeply corrupted by the colour-bar. That the colour-bar was deeply entrenched in South African society, was a fact of life. That it is impossible wholly to free a church from the corruption of its society, is another fact of life. The great sin of a church is not that it is corrupted by its society. Its great sin is committed when it does nothing to free itself from that corruption, or when it deceives itself that in fact there is no corruption, that God himself approves of race and colour-bars because He made different races and colours. And if He has done so, there is a presumption that He wants things that way, and approves of measures taken to keep them so.

There can be no shadow of doubt that Clayton needed no instruction in the Christian way of behaving in such a society. Was he to persevere with

*Whether the Government would step in and prevent such admissions if the white church schools changed their policy, was not tested until 1971. The Government refused to allow St. Cyprian's, Cape Town, to admit a Coloured girl. Meanwhile many supporters of the Government continue to taunt the anti-apartheid churches for maintaining an apartheid policy.

the one Bishop's Senate, with its difficult problems of co-operation and participation? Or was he, in the interest of these ends, to create a second Senate which would advise him on these matters relating to the work of the Church amongst the African people? He chose the second course, and created a second Senate, which was largely composed of black priests, and those white priests who were closely concerned with African work.

Rouse attended the first meeting of the new Senate, which was held at 'Bishop's House', probably in 1936. To Rouse it was the final revelation. Some of the black clergy were guests in the house and Clayton was a jovial host, provided one trod warily until he had finished his breakfast. What Rouse was witnessing was something which, though not common today, was still less common in 1936, and that was the sight of a white man who moved without constraint in the company of black people. Rouse was used to the paternalism of the Karney regime (though Karney was by no means the creator of it) under which the white priest was automatically the superior of the black priest, and under which every black priest was supervised by a white one. Clayton had certainly come to a strange society, but he did not intend to incorporate its worst features into the diocese of Johannesburg. One cannot say that he was *determined* not to allow it. He simply did not do it. In his house there could be no suggestion of condescension or patronage. The things he could not do in his Church, he could at least do in his house. Thus Rouse began to shed the chains of prejudice and of the assumptions of superiority, all the things that we white South Africans have kept from our youth up. His eyes were opened, by an African catechist and an English bishop.

Clayton's opinion of Rouse, of his devotion and ability, of his puckish humour and his perverse view that the scenery of the western Transvaal was the finest in the world, grew higher and higher. In 1938 he made him the Archdeacon of Native Missions, and it is appropriate here to tell the story of a journey made by these two to Makwassi. Rouse left the bishop and his chauffeur in Makwassi, and he himself took the train to Bloemhof. When he returned to Makwassi he found that the bishop could not walk. He was suffering considerable pain in the left heel, and it was decided to return to Johannesburg at once. Rouse sat in front with the chauffeur, and put the bishop at the back, where he began to sing in very doleful tones, 'Fight the good fight'.[3]

To this Rouse said, 'Bishop, when you get to Johannesburg, you are going to see a doctor.' Clayton replied, 'Don't talk nonsense, I will not see a doctor. There's nothing wrong with me.' But after some while he again began to sing 'Fight the good fight', to which Rouse again said, 'You are going to see a doctor', to which Clayton again replied that Rouse should stop talking nonsense.

According to Rouse this antiphonal conversation was repeated at least three more times, after which Rouse was ordered to keep quiet, and silence was kept for a space, to be broken by yet another rendering of 'Fight the good fight', followed by Rouse's response, 'You are going to see a doctor.'

Here Clayton introduced a new response, saying, 'What doctor?' Rouse replied. 'My doctor. Doctor Berry.' After a mile or two Clayton asked, 'Who is this Dr. Berry. Is he any good?' Rouse replied, 'Yes, he's very good, and a good churchman', which added information Clayton greeted with a snort as irrelevant. When they were near 'Bishop's House', Clayton observed that he did not think much of Dr. Berry.

At the house he scorned help and started to crawl up the steps, but Rouse would not allow this, and he and the servants performed the by no means easy task of picking him up and putting him to bed. Rouse said, 'I'm going to call Dr. Berry.' Clayton replied, 'Well, it's your own responsibility.' Dr. Berry came, and diagnosed a streptococcal infection of the left heel. When he came out of Clayton's bedroom, he handed the prescription to Rouse, and told him that the bishop wanted him. Clayton gruffly ordered Rouse to bring his diary, and when he had brought it, said, 'Cancel all my engagements for ten days, it's all your fault.'

After ten days Clayton was well enough to return to his desk. Rouse said to him, 'It's thanks to the pills.' Clayton said, 'Rubbish, I mixed them all up and have been taking them all wrong.'

Such was the man for whom Rouse had a regard amounting to veneration.

Clayton could be very petulant, but it would not improve his temper if the other person became intimidated. Under Rouse's sly goading he could enjoy his petulance. He knew he was being goaded, and he rather liked it, because it enabled him to recover from his ill-humour.

Rouse's veneration was not misplaced. It was remarkable that the bishop, coming to this strange society with its manifold and complex problems, should have gone to the heart of it, one could say, *without having to learn.* There was a move on the part of some of the people of the parish of Orange Grove to have contained in the trust deed of their new church a clause forbidding non-white Christians from worshipping in the church. Clayton announced that the diocesan trustees would not agree to it. He added his own opinion. 'I cannot possibly agree to the insertion of a clause in the Trust Deed which would have the effect of excluding in perpetuity the Founder of our Religion from one of the churches built in His honour.'[4]

It was impossible to argue with such a view. It was also impossible to argue with such a bishop. With some other bishop, the parish might have wrangled for months over the issue, and one would have heard the well-known argument that, while the bishop's view was eminently Christian, it just was not practical. And what is more, when the bishop had been a bit longer in the country, he would see it for himself. Luckily for the Church of the Province, Clayton was not that kind of bishop. It must also be recorded that Clayton's ruling left no aftermath. Anglicans – sometimes wryly – began to accept the view that while a thing was eminently practical, it could not be done because it was not Christian.

The year 1935 was notable for the continuous public discussion of General Hertzog's Native Bills. After sitting for five years, the joint select committee submitted its report to Parliament. It proposed to exclude Africans from the franchise in future, but to leave the existing 11,000 African voters as they were. As compensation, black South Africans would be divided into four constituencies, each of which could elect a white representative to the Senate. Further, these four constituencies would each elect three Africans to the new Natives Representative Council, where they would be joined by four nominated Africans, and by five white Chief Native Commissioners without vote, all under the presidency of the Secretary for Native Affairs.

The opposition to these proposals was vigorous, from the Cape Native Voters' Convention, the Presbyterian and Congregational churches, the Cape Methodists, the All-African Native Convention, and from a crowded protest meeting, largely white, held in the Cape Town City Hall under the chairmanship of Sir James Rose Innes, ex-Chief-Justice of the Union of South Africa.

Clayton decided to speak on the Native Bills in his second charge to the diocesan synod on 13 October. He began his charge by condemning the 'crime of Italy', the invasion by Mussolini of the country then known as Abyssinia. Some might not agree with him, but he believed that it was the duty of a bishop to express his opinion about 'matters of general religious concern even if they are wider than the affairs of his own particular diocese'.[5]

On that principle he proposed to speak about the Native Bills, which 'are going to affect closely many of our own clergy and laity'. He first spoke about the Native Land Bill, by which 15,500,000 acres would be added to the existing 22,000,000 acres of Reserve land, and which would also enable the Government to eliminate squatters and to reduce the number of African labour tenants on white farms. 'Speaking with some diffidence, I should say that these objectives are not objectionable.' But he warned that Africans were being too much left to the mercy of administrative action, without the protection of the Courts. 'I venture to think that we ought to watch very carefully the growth of the power of the Executive over the individual. Let us beware of the Totalitarian State.'

He then went on to condemn the Representation of Natives Bill. He said that the idea that there are European affairs and Native affairs wholly separable is an absurdity.* The Church had in fact shown a better way, 'and this has not meant a complete breakdown of what I may perhaps call segregation'. Clayton condemned the notion that all Africans should live under chiefs.

In the second part of his charge he declared that the mission schools must remain under the control of the missions, and he was here referring to the recurrent threat to place all African education under the direct control of the Government, a threat that he was to live to see carried out. He condemned the policy of using most of the available money to build residential hostels for white children already at school, when many African children had no schools at all.

Clayton's second charge differed from his first in one important respect.

*In 1935 'European' and 'Native' were the usual adjectives. Today it is 'White' and 'African', or 'White' and 'Black'; or in Government circles, 'White' and 'Bantu'.

In his first he had considered the possibility that ultimately each race in South Africa might be brought to its own perfection. In his second he regarded the notion that European affairs and Native affairs were wholly separable as absurd. I am not suggesting that he had gone from one extreme to another; that would be a most improbable thing for him to do. But it appears that he had decided that no policy of separate development could ever succeed. Certainly he had no wish to pursue such a policy in the Church. But he was to grow more and more critical – not so much of the theories of separate development, but of the methods by which it was to be achieved in the State.

The effect of the second charge was to reinforce the impact of the first. To many of his clergy and people he was the spiritual leader for whom they had been looking. To his African clergy and people he was the champion of their cause. One thing was beyond doubt, that he had no time for the comfortable notion that religion could be divorced from politics.

9

A Missionary Church

In South Africa white Christians have widely differing views on the missionary work of the churches. There are some who do not believe in it at all, being of the opinion that it 'spoils the natives', gives them ideas above their station, and turns their thoughts to white collars instead of honest labour. Amongst these critics are some who dislike the missionaries themselves, considering them to be agitators who do not 'understand the country', and who have set themselves the task of destroying the colour-bar, and of undermining law and order. This bias is stronger amongst Afrikaans-speaking than English-speaking people, and for this reason: until 1820, when the first British settlers arrived, the only Britishers in the Cape Colony were administrators, officials, traders and missionaries. It was therefore the Afrikaans-speaking people, called then the Dutch, and particularly those who had trekked into the interior, who had to witness the challenging of local customs by missionaries from the various countries of Europe.

The names of Johannes van der Kemp and his colleague John Read of the London Missionary Society are still held in detestation by many Afrikaners, not only because they championed the cause of Hottentot and slave but because they married Hottentot women. However, it is the name of Dr. John Philip which is most often remembered. He was sent from England by the London Missionary Society to superintend all its missions, and was a man of great force of character. It is not our task to describe his career here, but we may note that he came to the conclusion that only under some system of racial separation would the Hottentot enjoy any freedom or justice. He was opposed to their dispersion as labourers amongst the white farms. Nor is it our task to decide which of the complaints of missionaries against farmers, and farmers against missionaries, were justified. It is sufficient to note that the farmers' primary concern was to get labour, and that the missionaries' primary concern was to win souls. The farmers were hostile to the establishment of large mission stations, where, they declared, the Hottentots led idle and useless lives. Their interests and those of the missionaries were in many instances irreconcilable.

There is also a segment of the white population of South Africa that champions and supports missionary work, not only because of the command of Jesus that the gospel should be preached to all nations, but because they earnestly desire that others should know the joy of the faith that has been given to them.

There is yet another group of white South Africans that supports missionary work because it believes it is a good thing, that it makes people lead better and more useful lives, that it helps to control crime, lawlessness, drunkenness, and prostitution. Members of this group believe also that it leads to better racial understanding, and staves off racial conflict.

Clayton, though he no doubt believed this also, was scathing of those who made this their justification of missionary work. He belonged to those who wanted the gospel to be preached and the joy of the faith to be shared.

Soon after his arrival in Johannesburg he appealed for support for mission work. He wrote in *The Watchman*:

'We all have our own opinions about Native policy, and these opinions are not all the same. But every Christian, because he is a Christian, must desire that men of all races should be brought into the Christian Church.'

He went on to tell his readers of his amazement that the amount of money contributed by the European parishes to the Native Mission Fund was only £25, and told them that since his arrival some five months earlier, he had confirmed 1,300 African candidates.[1]

For him a Church that was not a missionary Church was not a Christian Church. Nor could the white members of the Church be indifferent to its mission work. Their actions must show their belief that 'baptism makes us all children of God, and, therefore, brothers'. Each churchmember, and by that he was referring particularly to white members, must take an interest in the work in his own neighbourhood, and offer to help. Because of this insistence of his, maintained till his death, more white churchmembers began to concern themselves with the missionary work, and the contribution of white Anglicans to the Native Mission Fund began to increase.[2] Other problems were beginning to make themselves clear to him. One was that the white Anglicans of his diocese tended to look on all African work as missionary, with an unspoken assumption that it was the black man who needed to be converted, not the white. Another problem with which he was going to deal was the long-established custom that the work of a black priest must always be under the supervision of a white one.

A third problem was the gross disparity between white and black stipends. It must be said at once that Clayton did not concern himself as much about this as did his successors. But he lived in the days before black consciousness had come on to the scene. Clayton *did* concern himself about the lowness of black stipends, and supported strongly Rouse's efforts to raise them. According to Rouse, black stipends were increased by seventy per cent during the fourteen years of Clayton's Johannesburg episcopate.

In spite of this increase, the disparity remained gross. During those fourteen years white stipends rose also, though not by seventy per cent. The average white stipend was three and more times as great as the average black stipend. Today almost every diocese in the Province is committed to the eventual equalisation of stipends. One reason for this is obviously the moral one. But there is another reason of a most disturbing kind, and that is that for some black priests the difference in stipend has so embittered them that the spiritual quality of their work and lives declines. This was not so in Clayton's day. He and Rouse agreed that the goal of equalisation would not be pursued. One of Clayton's reasons was that an equalised stipend would in many cases make the African priest the richest man in his community, and Clayton did not think that was a good thing for a priest to be.

Yet even though Clayton did not contemplate the equalisation of stipends he expected a great deal of his African priests, more perhaps than a South-African-born bishop would have done at that time. It was because he expected a great deal that he was given a great deal. In that wisdom for which he prayed daily, he knew a truth hidden from many a white South African, that if one's human instruments are weak, and you believe that they can be stronger, then they will become stronger. But believe that they are useless, and they will become useless. Because of this wisdom he was, surprisingly enough, amazingly tolerant of the weaknesses of his instruments, and under his guidance they would almost always become better. One of his African priests wrote of him much later:

'I have been always thinking that the bishop was my true Father in the true sense of the word, because I take it I am the least of them all, yet he used to make me feel as though I was somebody, surely.'[3]

It was before Clayton's arrival that there had begun a steady streaming of Tswana people into the Anglican Church. In 1928 Father Francis Hill of the Community of the Resurrection, who was Archdeacon of Native Missions, felt that he could no longer cope with the demand for more churches, more priests, more money. Father Osmund Victor, also of the Community, was the Director of Native Missions but, though a wonderful priest, was no organiser. In 1932 Bishop Karney had appointed Rouse Rector of Potchefstroom, and made him Assistant-Director of Native Missions, and it was at Potchefstroom that Rouse and Paterson had gone to greet their new bishop on his way to Johannesburg in 1934.

In 1938 when Father Francis Hill retired from the Archdeaconry of Native Missions Clayton had appointed Rouse to succeed him. It was the beginning of a period of great expansion in the life of the diocese, and of great change in the status of the African clergy. Bishop Karney insisted that African clergy must treat white clergy with respect, and was himself almost like a military commander in respect of the first. It is improbable that he ever asked an African priest for counsel. Each year before Synod there was held a Diocesan Missionary Conference, whose members were the bishop, the Director of Native Missions, the Archdeacon of Native Missions, all white priests in charge of Native missions, all African clergy, all the catechists,[3] and certain representatives of the African laity. The main purpose of the Conference was to elect twelve African laymen to be missionary representatives at Synod.

Rouse, whose inherited South African prejudices were steadily breaking down, was extremely critical of the Missionary Conference. Many of the issues discussed were trivial. How could a catechist get from A to B if he had no bicycle? Rouse was extremely critical of the fact that African work was a subdepartment supervised by white priests, and that there existed unhealthy relationships between white superiors and black subordinates. He, who had gone as a missionary to work with Lucas Mothobi, used to say that it was Mothobi who had turned him into a missionary. Who was he, a young man of 26, to tell Mothobi how he should behave?

Rouse therefore gave whole-hearted support to Clayton's reforms of the African work of the Church. In the first place, wherever possible all African priests had to become incumbents; that is to say they were to be the priests-in-charge in their own districts. In the second place, each mission district had to elect a church council and to appoint church officers; in other words, the mission districts were to become parishes. Lastly, each mission district was to elect its own representatives to Synod; no longer would this be the duty of the Missionary Conference.

The effect on the African clergy was considerable. There is no way of measuring what effect this reorganisation had on their own work as priests, but there can be no doubt that it increased their veneration and affection for their bishop. He was given the Tswana name of *Kgomo e e tlhabang*, which means 'the ox that worries with his horns'.[4]

There was yet another thing that added to his stature. In September 1937 there occurred one of those events which plunge all lovers of peace and concord into the depths of despair, which evoke in many white people feelings of hatred towards black people and create deep resentment amongst many Africans. It so happened that the South African Police conducted a raid on the large African location of the growing industrial town of Vereeniging, some thirty miles from Johannesburg. These raids were usually conducted to discover the brewers of illicit liquor, but were usually accompanied by the examination of pass documents, the arrest of people living in Vereeniging illegally, and not infrequently the finding of stolen property. The raids were usually conducted on Sundays or holidays, and this further inflamed the tempers of those who lived in the locations. There was no question of politeness or ceremony. The raids had to be carried out quickly and without warning.

On this nineteenth day of September the anger of the people was so aroused that some of them attacked the raiders, killing one black and two white policemen. There were angry protest-meetings in white Vereeniging and other parts of the Transvaal, demanding drastic action, air demonstrations above the location, and the dropping of tear-bombs till the guilty surrendered. The followers of Dr. Malan, the leader of the Purified Nationalist Party, called for a ban on communism, and on 'the liberalist doctrine of equality between black and white'.[5] The attorney defending some of those accused of the murders asked for the protection of the court. General Hertzog said there was a deep-rooted hostility, perhaps organised, of black towards white, and General Smuts suggested that misguided friends of the blacks put grievances into their heads. However, a commission of enquiry found otherwise, namely that the municipal administration was defective, and the police methods were harsh. It is a weakness of South African white politicians that they too easily suppose black men's grievances to be invented by agitators, and spend their energies in trying to silence the second rather than in trying to redress the first.

One of the wisest utterances, in a time when so many utterances were unwise, was made by Clayton in his fourth charge to Synod. He expressed sympathy for the families of the policemen who were killed. What was at fault was the system of law that suppressed the African people, although this never justified violence. He said with great emphasis that justice must be done to those who were accused of this grave offence.

'Guilty people must be punished. But they must have a fair trial. And every man is innocent until he has been proven guilty. Anything less than this simply reduces us to a state of barbarism, inconsistent not only with Christianity, but with anything that can be called civilisation, whether European or otherwise.'

One can hardly exaggerate the steadying power of a strong, sane voice at a time when emotions of anger, fear, resentment and despair cloud the judgement. One often hears at times like these the remark, 'This has set back the cause for twenty years.' When loud voices are clamouring for a justice which closely resembles vengeance, it is hard to keep up one's courage. The people of the diocese fell more and more under the spell of their extraordinary bishop.

He concluded his charge by declaring that no barrier might be put in the way of any persons – and he was referring particularly to African people – which would prevent them from becoming the best that they had it in them to be. No solution of the 'Native question' could be tolerable to a Christian which did not satisfy the test.*

'The only thing that really matters to a Christian is personality: that everyone should have a chance of being the best that he can be. Always and everywhere persons are more important than things. For when God wanted to give His best, His supreme gift to man, He gave not a thing but a person; and Jesus was born in Bethlehem.'[6]

Though Clayton never adopted the unthinking view that missionary work was African work, yet he had a special concern for the work of the African missions. Again and again he urged white Anglicans to give more generously to mission work. He must have gladdened Rouse's heart by writing, 'I don't think there is anything quite like the Anglican Church in the Western Transvaal.'[7] In that month, he had dedicated three new mission churches, at Newclare, Driefontein, and Lichtenburg. He was full of praise for the people

*I remind readers that in 1937 the term 'Native question' was used to describe the whole problem of race relations. In retaliation some African speakers called it the 'White question'. However the phrase was slowly dropping out of favour. As far as I can discover, Clayton stopped using it at about this time, though he continued to use the word 'Native'. He also used the words 'African' and 'Native African'. He seemed to adopt no rule to use only 'African'.

of these congregations, who had themselves raised most of the money and provided most of the labour. Hardly a month passed when he did not bless some foundation stone, or dedicate or consecrate some new church-building.*

A very important part of the work of the diocese was missionary education. We have already seen that the stake of the Church in what was called Native Education was very considerable. The attitudes of white South Africans towards the mission schools were very much the same as their attitudes towards missions and missionaries. The attitude of white farmers towards the schools was on the whole of indifference, sometimes of hostility, though some farmers were notable exceptions, and encouraged the education of their labourers' children.

The education of an African child cost approximately one-tenth of that of his white counterpart.† Rural school-buildings were often no more than sheds. The salaries of African teachers were about one-third or one-quarter of white salaries. Worst of all perhaps, more than half of the African children of schoolgoing age were not at school at all, and of those that *were*, a very small percentage would reach Standard Six. In 1935 only 0.6 per cent of pupils proceeded beyond Standard Six. The majority of children who had been to school had not gone further than Standard Two.[8] The only comforting thing that a churchman could say about African education was that if it had not been for the churches there would have been hardly any education at all.‡

There were two ever-present fears in the missionary churches. They exercised a considerable measure of control over the methods and content of African education. This control was a source of deep grievance to Afrikaner Nationalists. Another source of grievance was that the administrative control of African education was in the hands of the education departments of the four provinces, the Transvaal, Orange Free State, Cape, and Natal, whereas the Nationalists wished it to be controlled by the central Department of Native Affairs. In other words they wanted African education controlled, not by educationists but by the department which carried out the racial policies of the Government. Their uneasiness was understandable, for the four education departments could be expected to be more sympathetic to the educational aspirations of the African people than could any department of Native Affairs. The churches therefore feared, first, the gradual transfer of whatever control they exercised to the education departments, but second, which they would have thought disastrous, the transfer of all control of African education to the Department of Native Affairs, which they thought was concerned much more with the maintenance of

*A new church-building is consecrated if there is no debt on it, and provided the land belongs to the Church; otherwise it is dedicated.

†The fraction is today still smaller.

‡Eleven years later, in June 1946 there were 4,567 'Native' schools. Of these 4,335 were government-aided, that is, they were established and run by private agencies, the overwhelming majority of which were the church missions. See Hellmann, *Handbook on Race Relations in South Africa*, p. 364.

white authority than with the educational and spiritual welfare of the African people.

Under General Hertzog, and his Deputy Prime Minister General Smuts, these fears were reasonably moderate. But there was always the fear behind all fears, that Dr. Malan's Nationalists might one day gain control, and make African education a tool for the preservation of white supremacy. It is hard for us to realise that as far back as 1935, when the Nationalists held only 19 seats in a lower house of 160, this fear was always present. Their speeches were full of threats and promises of what they would do when they came to power. One of the things that they promised to do was to exercise a rigid control over all African schools, and over the methods and content of African education, which had become a means of spreading dangerous views of justice and equality, most of them implanted by missionaries from other countries who had no interest in maintaining South Africa's 'traditional way of life'.

A minor threat to missionary schools is mentioned by *The Watchman* of June 1936. The Transvaal Department of Education had issued new regulations for the schools. All fees were to be paid in advance, there were to be no more than fifty children in a class, and only children over 7 would be admitted. Clayton appealed for money to enable the diocese to build new classrooms, and to build nursery schools for children too young to be admitted. In many homes in the townships both parents were absent all day. Sometimes the mother was away for a week or more at a time, in the servant's quarters of some white home. Therefore the need for more school accommodation was urgent.

Later in 1936 the Report of the Interdepartmental Committee on Native Education was published.[9] It may be summarised as follows:

1. The most important recommendation was that the control of Native Education should be transferred from the Provincial Councils to the Union Government.
2. The administration of Native Education was 'to be dissociated from the Native Affairs Department (including the Native Affairs Commission)' and was to be placed with the Union Education Department.
3. The financing of Native Education was to become the responsibility of the Union Government, and a Native Education Fund was to be created under a National Board of Native Education under the Minister of Education.
4. A special Department of Native Education was to be created under a Union Director of Native Education.
5. 'There are weighty considerations in favour of retaining the direct influence of the missionaries in a South African system of Native Education.'

These were the most important of the recommendations. Although the churches were not enthusiastic about the transfer of control to the State, they were relieved of a heavy burden of anxiety by the proposal that the State would exercise control through its Union Education Department, and that missionary influence was acknowledged and valued. The Union Education Department was held in respect and, what was more, J. H. Hofmeyr was the Minister of Education.

The other recommendations flowed from those above. Briefly some of them were:

6. Wherever possible, local school committees should be formed.
7. There should be no bar to the appointment of qualified and competent Native Ministers as managers of schools.
8. The Government should provide funds for capital expenditure, i.e. on buildings.
9. The Director should have the power to close down any school where the teaching was 'against the interests of the State'.
10. Primary education, up to and including Standard Six, should be free.
11. The Government should pay half the cost of all books up to and including Standard Two.
12. In view of the practical difficulties the Committee did not recommend compulsory education, but the principle was accepted, and should be applied in favourable areas.
13. 'The Committee, therefore, feels it will not be quite honest to avoid stating clearly that a full liberal philosophy is not at present applicable to Native Education.'
14. Lastly the aim of education is defined. It is 'the effective organisation of the Native's experiences so that his tendencies and powers may develop in a manner satisfactory to himself and to the community in which he lives, by the growth of socially desirable knowledge, attitudes, and skill'.[10] *

Clayton asked his people to support these proposals, and asked them all to read the report for themselves; he did this not only in *The Watchman* of September 1936, but in his charge in November. A day or two later Synod itself carried a motion of support for the recommendations, and hoped they would soon be embodied in legislation.[11] This was again evidence, not only of the deep concern of the diocese for African education, but of the fear that the Department of Native Affairs would take it over, that religious education would disappear or be allowed to continue on sufferance, and that African education would be re-designed to meet the needs of a people doomed for ever to occupy a subordinate position. The attitudes of the Nationalist Party and the Church of the Province to African education were in fact wholly incompatible. This unchanging cry of the Nationalists was that the Anglican missionaries and others were making black Englishmen. Their complaint was justified in so far as some of the subjects taught, notably history and literature, were much more relevant to Europe than Africa. But the truth is that many Nationalists also resented the fact that missionary education was intended to prepare the African child for a better and fuller life. Sometimes

*Twenty-seven years later proposals 10 and 11 have not been implemented. One can only remark that the standard of African education in 1973 is poor. This is not a criticism of administrators and teachers, but of a white Parliament that is indifferent.

they expressed this resentment openly, sometimes they concealed it behind the argument that it was cruel and unChristian to arouse in black children expectations that never could be fulfilled. This incompatibility, until now unresolved, cuts deep into South African life. We shall learn more about it as we continue the story of Geoffrey Clayton.

In 1937 a proposal was made by the Transvaal Department of Education that all African schools should be amalgamated under the control of the Department, and that religious instruction should be given according to an official syllabus. Clayton declared himself wholly opposed to this. He would prefer the practice of the Orange Free State, where the schools allowed the churches access to their own children. At the diocesan Missionary Conference of that year he called on all churches to resist the proposed amalgamation. Only the Church could teach the faith of the Church.[12] Later, in his fourth charge, he returned to the theme. He declared that non-denominational teaching had little value because it could only teach stories, not religion. 'I am not prepared to agree to the spending of Church money on schools where the faith of the Church is not going to be taught.'[13] In December, writing in *The Watchman*, he referred to the Report of the Native Affairs Commission for 1936, which referred contemptuously to the proposals of the Interdepartmental Committee on Native Education.

The Native Affairs Commission was a statutory body, appointed by the Minister of Native Affairs, whose duty it was to advise the Minister on all matters of 'Native Policy'. At the end of 1937 four of its five members were drawn from Parliament, and the criticism was made that, far from advising the Government, it *was* the Government. It was not surprising that this political body had little sympathy for the proposals of the Interdepartmental Committee, in that it was at that very moment trying to persuade the Government to hand over to itself all the Native Poll Tax, together with the control of Native Education and all other services.

Referring to the Report of the Native Affairs Commission, Clayton wrote with what we see now to have been unfounded optimism:

'I should be loath to describe the Native Affairs Commission as an enemy. But, as an unrepentant liberal, I can only hope that the Commission will produce more Reports of the same nature. Nothing could be more valuable for the strengthening of the Liberal cause.'[14]

He added that it was obvious that the Native Affairs Commission was not meeting the needs of the Witwatersrand, and that it was not sympathetic to the cause of African education.

Thus Clayton was being drawn more and more deeply into South African politics, and his bearing of himself makes seem all the more foolish the shallow pietism that wanted politics kept out of religion, and priests kept out of politics. For the Church had schools and homes, and built its missions in the heart of the African townships, and shared with its African people their material as well as their spiritual aspirations. It is little wonder that Heaton Nicholls, the chairman of the Native Affairs Commission, was angered by such interference. He asked:

'What is the difference between a communist protagonist who believes that human happiness can be better furthered if people will only adopt his tenets and the bishops who go around the country telling the natives that if they will only join together and agitate sufficiently and believe that Parliament is animated by the worst possible repressive intentions they will be the happier for it?'[15]

Was he referring to Clayton? If he was, could any account of the work and words of a man have been a greater travesty? Here are Clayton's own words:

'If she [the Church] thinks, as I do, the colour-bar unChristian, she ought to try and get it altered. But in the meantime she has to try to help those living under the restrictions of the colour-bar to live Christian lives.'[16]

When he thought it was time to pass judgement, he passed it. When he thought he had a public duty, he performed it. He joined the Johannesburg Housing Utility Company, which was a non-profit organisation aimed at the betterment of slums. He commented on the abdication of King Edward VIII in order to marry Mrs. Simpson, and on the moral responsibility of Christians in public life, but he did it briefly, quoting General Hertzog with approval, 'If your father or your mother does what is wrong, you do not discuss it in public.' He deplored the institution of municipal beerhalls for Africans, preferring the more natural and traditional practice of home-brewing. He, like Jan Hofmeyr, the liberal Minister of Education, declared that if white South Africans regarded Africans as wards, then they must prepare them to grow up; trusteeship for a child differed greatly from trusteeship for a lunatic. He and Synod scored one notable victory: when they protested against the holding of military displays on Good Friday, they received a reply from Colonel George Brink, informing them that he had ordered their cessation. So he continued faithfully in his endeavour 'to make the outward order of society more in accordance with the will of God'.

He had another triumph too. In spite of the threats that hung over missionary education, from the Nationalists and the Native Affairs Commission, he was able to announce that 'one of the finest Native schools in South Africa' was to be built in Sophiatown, with money given by an anonymous member of the Church.

10

Clayton and His Priests

Towards the end of 1937, the Most Revd. Francis Phelps, Archbishop of Cape Town, decided that he would resign; he was 74, and he died the following year. The Archbishop of Cape Town is the Metropolitan of the Church of the Province of South Africa. He is chosen by a body known as the Elective Assembly of the diocese of Cape Town, and therefore, and strangely, not by the Province itself. There is a safeguard, however, and that is that while the Elective Assembly is sitting, the Bench of Bishops also assembles in Cape Town, and it must approve of the candidate proposed by the Assembly.

Clayton had now been four years in South Africa. He was comparatively unknown in the diocese of Cape Town. He was held by the retiring archbishop in high regard and deep affection, but the retiring archbishop takes no part in the election.* Nevertheless Clayton's name was put forward as a candidate for the archbishopric. He proved to be unacceptable; his great qualities were ignored, and he was rejected because of his overbearingness, his irritability, and his attitude towards women.[1]

Instead the Elective Assembly decided on John Russell Darbyshire, Bishop of Glasgow and Galloway. Darbyshire was a man of 59, both musician and composer, of a temperament delicate rather than robust, unmarried, with an unmarried sister who looked after him and in some measure certainly ruled him. The true inwardness of such relationships can never be fully understood by those outside them, if indeed by those within. But it seems that one would be justified in saying that the new archbishop was inclined to effeminacy. It was commonly said of him that his behaviour on social occasions depended on whether his sister was present or not.

When Darbyshire died in 1948, Clayton paid high tribute to him. He said of him in his fifteenth charge to the Johannesburg Synod of 1948:

*There is a mystifying letter from Archbishop Phelps dated 22 October 1937, amongst the few that Clayton did not destroy. An extract from it reads as follows:

'I cannot thank you enough for all you did on my behalf. And especially for having kept me up to the mark (save the mark!). You made it as easy for me as any one could, and your care for me was most helpful and encouraging. I am so glad I was able to go through with it all, and it is a joy to me now (and will be) to look back on an unforgettable experience. Bless you and all you have done and will do. Ever yours affectionately.'

I did not include this in the main b dy of the book, because I could not find out what it meant. But it shows clearly that Phelps had a high regard for Clayton.

'A talented musician, he had all the charm and all the sensitiveness of the artist, and a wonderful power of sympathy and understanding for all who found life difficult. Despite the cares of his great office, he never ceased to be a Pastor, and to the end he retained the greatest gift of the pastor, the love of souls.'

This was definitely a case of *de mortuis nil nisi bonum*. One may suppose that it was only on occasions such as this that Clayton permitted himself to temper the truth. His estimate of his archbishop cannot be regarded as high. It was Clayton's custom on Christmas Day to entertain his unmarried clergy to lunch. Always temperate, he allowed himself a moderate licence on Christmas Day. These gatherings were decidedly jolly, and his clergy were permitted to take liberties with their bishop which they would never have taken on any other occasion. At one of these lunches in Johannesburg, one of his younger men said to him, 'My Lord, when you get married, will you have the Archbishop as your best man?', to which the bishop, with a great snort, said, 'Bridesmaid!' This was followed of course by a great bout of laughter, in which all joined.

Darbyshire must have known that he did not receive from the Bishop of Johannesburg the esteem and affection that Phelps had enjoyed. When Gerald Abernethy, who still is the Secretary of the diocese of Cape Town and Secretary of the whole Province, and has been so since 1939, was preparing for a meeting of the Synod of Bishops in the boardroom of Church House, he asked Darbyshire how he should arrange the seating. The archbishop replied, 'Arrange it how you like, so long as the Bishop of Johannesburg doesn't sit opposite me.'

There is the story too of Clayton's dog, 'Peter'. Clayton was not really fond of dogs, and paid them little attention, but he chose to keep at 'Bishop's House', Johannesburg, this tremendous dog Peter, a cross between a bull mastiff and a Great Dane. This dog, though reputed to be harmless, was nevertheless awesome, and had the terrifying habit of approaching one from in front or behind, rearing up on its hind legs and putting its paws on one's shoulders. It was quite possible for a person thus embraced to fall to the ground, wondering what terrible fate awaited him. And indeed this is what happened to the archbishop in the grounds of 'Bishop's House'. He fell to the ground and cried out in a panic. The one story is that Clayton was present, and called out in boisterous glee, 'Eat him up, Peter!' The other story is that a servant rushed to Clayton in the house and said, 'My Lord, Peter is eating the Archbishop', to which Clayton replied, 'Good! Good!' It was a strange defect in him, to be so indifferent to this particular fear in others. He was by no means without fear himself. He was the most nervous pedestrian, and when crossing the street with a companion was quite capable of clutching onto him, in something like a panic, if the traffic suddenly appeared menacing. It is interesting to speculate what he would have done had his companion been a woman.*

*I myself had an experience with Peter. I went to stay at 'Bishop's House', and was unpacking my suitcase when Peter jumped on me from behind. As a rule I am not afraid

Was Clayton disappointed when a man not his equal in personality or intellect was elected archbishop? Whether he was chagrined, one cannot say. But he certainly regretted that he was not chosen. In 1948 he said to Edward Langmore, in whose church of St. Anne's, Maitland, he preached the last sermon of his life, 'I should have been here nine years ago. I could have done something.' There were others who were of the same opinion. The menace of Hitler and Nazism lay heavily over Europe and mankind, and it seemed as though the world was on the brink of war. For that reason, as well as others, Anglicans would have been glad to see a man of Clayton's stature as the head of the Church. But history may well say otherwise. He was to be chosen archbishop at a time much more necessitous, and his fourteen years in Johannesburg were to provide the right apprenticeship.

It is appropriate here to say more of the relations between Clayton and his clergy. It would be quite wrong to suppose that Clayton did not, or could not, give to and receive from his married clergy the same affection as he gave to and received from his single priests. He might have thought, he might even have said, with St. Paul, 'It is a good thing if they stay as I am myself', but he would never have regarded marriage as an escape from fornication, as St. Paul appears to do. He received from many of his married clergy the warmest affection; Redvers Rouse was only one example. But with his unmarried clergy he was like a boy amongst the boys, or perhaps more like a prefect amongst the boys.

When he gave them a lunch at Christmas, the wine was not for the stomach's sake. He once told a lunch table of ordinands, for whom he had presented 'Gluttony' as the theme for discussion, that drinking became gluttony only when one began to cease to distinguish between good and evil. Drunkenness in itself was not gluttony.[2] He had no time for puritanism in regard to drinking, and regarded good drink as a gift from the Creator. If temperance meant abstinence, he would have nothing to do with it. He was very impatient with priests who continually complained of the drunkenness and worthlessness of so many of their parishioners. When the Revd. George Swartz* was sent to St. Helena Bay by Archbishop Clayton, he could have been disheartened by his predecessor's tales of the drunkenness and immorality of the community, but Clayton had said to him, 'Bring people to God and don't hammer at their sins. When they are in God, all will be well.' On one occasion Clayton was wearied beyond endurance by a priest who told him tales of the drunkenness of his people, and he burst out, 'As a matter of principle I get drunk every Christmas', and spent the next minute or two roaring with laughter at the priest's bewilderment.

There were four unmarried priests who were especially close to Clayton.

of dogs, but this assault unnerved me. I drove him off, but he came at me again. I decided to put him out of the room and shut the door. As I was doing this, the bishop passed, and said affably, 'I see you don't like dogs.' Having made this totally unjustified observation, he did not stop for me to offer any explanation. I used to wonder what he would have done if Peter had frightened a child.

*Now Suffragan-Bishop of Cape Town.

One was George Dymond, who had written him that remarkable letter when he left Chesterfield, and whom Clayton had brought to Johannesburg in 1934 to become the Rector of St. Mary's, Jeppe. Another was Dick Yates, who came out with him to Johannesburg, and served him as chaplain from 1934–7, and again from 1945–8. A third was Roy Cowdry, who came out to Cape Town as archbishop's chaplain in 1950 and stayed with him till his death. A fourth was Gonville Aubie ffrench-Beytagh, who came under his spell in 1936, and despite rebuffs, insults, and imprecations is under it to this very day.* Of Yates and Cowdry we shall learn more later. Now is the time to relate the story of Gonville Aubie ffrench-Beytagh.

Ffrench-Beytagh has had what one can only call an unusual career. He was born in the French settlement in Shanghai in 1912. He went to school in England and New Zealand, and in 1933 went to South Africa on the Chinese quota. He used in fact to claim that he was Chinese. In Johannesburg he found work with Holman Brothers, Loveday Street, purveyors of mining materials. He was an agnostic, and had no time for the Church, but said daily the Collect for the Nineteenth Sunday after Trinity:

'O God, forasmuch as without thee we are not able to please thee: Mercifully grant, that thy Holy Spirit may in all things direct and rule our hearts; through Jesus Christ our Lord. Amen.'

He had promised an old governess to do this, and he kept his promise, but he declared that it was not religion. Nevertheless in 1935 he joined the movement called Toc H, which, although not a religious organisation, has as its objective the service of all in need and opens and closes its meetings with the lighting of a lamp and a prayer, these prayers being essentially Christian. The pledge which members take is ethical rather than theological, but the whole purpose of the movement, in addition to the service of the world, is to bring men and women nearer to God. One does not have to be an avowed Christian to join it, but there is a clear hope and intention that one will become one.

It was in Toc H that ffrench-Beytagh met the Revd. Tom Savage, the full-time padre of Toc H Southern Africa, Ronald Anderson, who later became a full-time staff worker, and Alan Paton, principal of Diepkloof Reformatory.† At that time ffrench-Beytagh had thoughts of marrying, and he conceived the strange notion that if he had sons, he would like them to resemble these three gentlemen, if not immediately, then certainly later on.

Ffrench-Beytagh was at that time 23 years old, and was as irreverent a young man as could be found in Johannesburg. He was good at deflating

* To Yates, Cowdry, and ffrench-Beytagh this biographer owes much. Dymond has died. Yates became Archdeacon in the diocese of Johannesburg and has now returned to England. Cowdry became Suffragan-Bishop of Cape Town in 1958 and is now Rector of St. Cuthbert's, Port Elizabeth. Ffrench-Beytagh was Dean of St. Mary's Cathedral, Johannesburg. In 1972 he was tried on charges of subversion, and found guilty by the Supreme Court, Transvaal Division. The Appeal Court reversed this verdict and he left immediately for England.

†Tom Savage eventually became Bishop of Zululand. Ronald Anderson devoted the greater part of his life to Toc H.

pomp and pretension, affected a deep cynicism, and despised conventional dress. Behind this protective façade was quite another person, who knew that one's life is wasted if it is not used in the service of others, who if he had any sons wanted them to be a certain kind of persons, and who, when it was time for prayers, shed his irreverence. What happened next, though startling, was not out of pattern.

One day in 1936, late at night, he was walking through the Braamfontein subway on his way home. In the subway, he was set upon by thugs, who knocked him on the head, broke his jaw, and left him for dead. When he came to himself in a bed in the Johannesburg General Hospital, the first person he saw was the writer of this biography.* His injuries were very serious, and his long stay in the hospital gave him abundant time to reflect on the nature and destiny of man, and the nature and lack of destiny of himself. When he recovered, he went to live at 'The Mark', a home for men which Toc H had established in Saratoga Avenue, Doornfontein, under the leadership of Tom Savage. When men went to live at 'The Mark', they were required, not only to make of it a Christian family, but also an instrument of service to the community. Ffrench-Beytagh felt insulted because Savage told him he wanted him to come, but that he would have to attend prayers. He felt insulted because Savage had required him to do something that he had intended to do anyway.

Meanwhile the joint influence of the Holy Spirit and the thugs in the Braamfontein subway was working hard on his soul, an organ which he had supposed not to exist. Finally, after some time in 'The Mark', he wrote to Clayton, saying that he was thinking of being ordained, and asking what he must do. Combining his new earnestness with his old irreverence, he communicated his thoughts by means of a postcard. Dick Yates telephoned him at Holman's, and asked him to meet the bishop outside the cathedral after evensong.

Ffrench-Beytagh went to this meeting with much trepidation. After a while the bishop came out and said to him, 'You must wait a bit, some lunatic wants to see me.' After he had presumably seen the lunatic, he came out again, and took him in his car to 'Bishop's House'.† There he sat ffrench-Beytagh down, and said to him, 'Why do you want to become a priest?' Ffrench-Beytagh replied to this, 'I don't want to be one, but I feel I've got to be one.' The bishop apparently thought that this was a promising beginning, and said he would write to ffrench-Beytagh's employer. This made the candidate for the priesthood nervous, because his employer had once reprimanded him for using bad language. However, all turned out well, and ffrench-Beytagh, assisted financially by the bishop of the diocese, set off for St. Paul's Theological College in Grahamstown, where he was later to be told by the Warden that he was by far the most muddle-headed student that he had ever encountered. So began between Clayton and ffrench-Beytagh a relationship of a most extraordinary kind, of affection on the one side and

*I had forgotten this till he reminded me of it. It apparently impressed him.

†He had a driver. As far as I know, he never drove a car in his life.

affectionate veneration on the other.

The veneration was nevertheless put to severe tests. Clayton spent several holidays with ffrench-Beytagh, and was jolly, morose, insulting, and inspiring by turns. He had given up the alphabetical holidays, because somehow they do not work in South Africa. Usually they went in Clayton's car, and ffrench-Beytagh drove under a barrage of criticism that was lifted only when Clayton took a nap or had some interesting matter to discuss. When Clayton was archbishop, ffrench-Beytagh flew from Johannesburg to the Cape, and they drove to Plettenberg Bay where they spent some days, beginning the day with Matins and Holy Communion, eating, talking, reading, walking in the afternoon, and sometimes quarrelling. On one of these occasions Clayton was in an exceptionally bad temper, and it was tacitly agreed that they should walk separately. When ffrench-Beytagh returned, Clayton asked where he had been. Ffrench-Beytagh told him that he had been walking on the beach, and had seen the coloured fishermen standing patiently in the rain, and had felt sorry for them. Clayton exploded and said, 'The coloured fishermen are the happiest people in the world.' Ffrench-Beytagh said, 'I'm sorry, sir, but I only thought . . .' Clayton interrupted him and said, 'The trouble with you is that it is only what *you* think that matters.' But he gave ffrench-Beytagh wine for dinner, which was unusual.

Of such incidents ffrench-Beytagh said, 'I must have liked it, because I went back for more.' In spite of these displays of petulance, Clayton remained for him, not only the greatest man of his life, but a priestly example to be emulated with all one's powers. Their trust in each other was unlimited. When ffrench-Beytagh had become the Rector of St. Boniface in Germiston, and had transformed the life of that parish, winning the affection and souls of boys and girls, and young men and women, by the sincerity of an uncompromising religion wearing a cloak of irreverence, some indignant parishioner wrote to Clayton complaining that the rector had women in the house. Clayton, as he always did in such cases, sent the complaint to ffrench-Beytagh and wrote, 'What do I say?' Ffrench-Beytagh wrote back and said, 'Tell her (or him) I always send them away before breakfast.' Which ended the matter.

Clayton did not keep many letters, but he kept one written by Mr. D. J. Mills of Germiston, to say that the town was blessed to have such a priest as Father ffrench-Beytagh. He wrote, 'The Church is now a sanctuary in the lives of hundreds as never before,' and again 'Many young men and boys have had their lives deepened by him.' There were young women and girls too, and ffrench-Beytagh had thoughts of marrying one of them. He asked Clayton's advice, and Clayton said he ought not to. So he remained single.

There was yet another young man in the diocese on whom Clayton's influence was very considerable. This was Leo Rakale, whose father Andreas was priest-in-charge of St. Andrew's, in the African location of the mining town of Springs. Andreas Rakale became a Christian as a young man, was priested in 1914 by Bishop Furse, and was made a canon by Bishop

Karney. When Clayton came to Johannesburg, young Leo, then a young man of 21, was studying for his matriculation at St. Peter's, Rosettenville, the famous school of the Community of the Resurrection. At that time the young man had, to use his own words, 'given up religion'. His first meeting with the bishop made a great impression on him. Clayton had called at the house, but Canon Rakale had not yet come home, and Leo had to look after him. What he had thought would be a frightening task was no task at all. He too made acquaintance with Clayton's gift of being able to walk straight into the hearts of the humble. There were very few white South Africans, and very few indeed of Clayton's eminence, who could talk without constraint, without false politeness, without condescension, to an African schoolboy, and see him as a young person with his own ideals and aspirations.

Whether Clayton's influence made itself felt then, no one quite knows, but in 1936 young Leo, who had naturally been keenly aware of the presence of this dedicated body of monks at Rosettenville, realised with relief that he could return to religion without becoming a celibate. And he did not want to be a celibate, because he liked being at a school with girls, and was attracted by them. However, he postponed any decision by going off to the exclusive white Anglican school of Michaelhouse, Balgowan, where under the headmastership of Ronald Currey he became assistant librarian and a teacher of the Sesotho language.

But the call would not let him be. He wrote to Clayton from Michaelhouse, saying that he was thinking of entering the priesthood. Clayton replied:

'I am glad you want to be a priest. I am sending you to the College of the Resurrection. This is not a promise to ordain you. But I think it will be all right. Come and see me when you come to Johannesburg.'

Young Rakale met the bishop in the cathedral vestry, but this meeting was nothing like the first. The young man gained the impression that the bishop was trying to bait him or was putting him to some kind of test. He asked the young man, 'Are you clever?', to which Rakale replied, 'I am not.' 'Are you a fool then?' 'I am not.' 'What are you then? Not clever. Not a fool. What are you then?' Clayton then asked him, 'Are you engaged?', to which Rakale replied, 'I am not.' 'I suppose you will be one day.' 'Perhaps.'

The interview was short and baffling. Clayton gave Rakale his blessing, but the young man decided that he would be careful of him in the future.

In 1939 Rakale passed through a crisis. He was in fact resisting the persistent call to celibacy. He was restless and uncertain. He decided that he would become a priest, but hoped that he would find a beautiful girl to be his wife. In 1940 he was ordained deacon.

It seems possible that Clayton knew of the conflict in Rakale's mind. It seems also possible that Clayton wanted the young man to become a monk, and if so, then no doubt he wanted him to enter the Community of the Resurrection, which at that time had no African member. Be that as it may, when Clayton entertained the new deacons at 'Bishop's House', he again asked Rakale, 'Are you engaged?' and Rakale replied, 'I am not.' 'Do you hope to be engaged?' 'I don't know. Probably not.' Clayton said, 'Why?', but Rakale did not reply. Then Clayton asked, 'Are you one of those who despise women?' Again Rakale was completely baffled, but he replied, 'No. On the contrary, I love them.' At that Clayton roared with laughter, and told Rakale that he was sending him to Sophiatown, and that he must take Father Raynes into his confidence about his problems and his future.

In 1941 Rakale was priested, and again Clayton questioned him about marriage and the future, but the young priest was still non-committal. However, he asked Rakale to let him know if he ever thought of taking up the celibate life, and this Rakale promised to do.

In 1942 Rakale went to a retreat at the Priory in Rosettenville. The bishop took it, and the theme was 'The Good Shepherd'. Rakale knew that the hour of decision had come, but he encountered it in a philosophical spirit, saying to himself, 'Well, OK. I'll enter the Community, and if they won't have me, that will be OK too.' He went to tell his decision to Father Raynes, who said he must go and tell the bishop. Rakale was reluctant, because he was afraid of Clayton's probing, but Raynes insisted.

Rakale found Clayton sitting on the stoep of 'Bishop's House', reading the *Star*, making marks and arrows on the paper, against items, Rakale thought, that he would read before he went to bed. This was the Clayton that he had first met, seven years before in his father's house at Springs. He had no doubt that the bishop, in his own way, was overjoyed that something he had wanted and had no doubt prayed about, had come about. His consciousness of this made him feel more relaxed with the bishop than he had felt for years, but he was still wary, because of the questioning that he knew must come. He asked himself, 'How is this cat going to jump out of the bag?' Clayton said to him, 'Don't you feel drawn towards women?' 'I was.' 'Will it not be a strain?' 'It may be, but God will give me grace to bear it.' This answer clearly satisfied Clayton.

Clayton then asked him, 'What does your father feel?' Rakale said, 'All pain and grief.' 'Why is it pain and grief to him?' Rakale said, 'He seemed not to want me to do it. He was expecting in his old age to come and live with me.' Clayton suggested rather that the old canon, who was then approaching the age of 70, had wanted his son to give him a grandson. Clayton said, 'You are going to the Community to test your vocation. It would be no disgrace if you felt that you had not received the call after all. But we would be sorry to lose you.' The bishop gave Rakale his blessing, and dispatched him, as the robbers had dispatched Francis after stripping him, 'singing on his way'.

So Leo Rakale entered on his long and faithful service to the Community and the people it laboured for. As he himself put it, his 'time of withdrawal came to an end'. His veneration for Clayton grew deeper and deeper, although he too could watch him from a distance, and enjoy the scowls and petulances. He enjoyed most seeing Clayton at synod, holding his head in his hands and groaning over the idiocy and perversity of clergy and laity, and suddenly starting up from his chair and saying in that tremendous voice, 'It is now time for me to speak.'

When Rakale had left Sophiatown to go to the Priory for his novitiate, Clayton said to him, 'The people in Sophiatown must miss you.' Rakale said, 'I'm glad that I have left.' 'Why?' Rakale said, 'The parish is growing by leaps and bounds. More and more people are coming to church. The number of servers has trebled. So they are getting on well without me.' Clayton was delighted. He put his hand affectionately on Rakale's shoulder, which was a thing he seldom did to anyone, and beamed and chuckled.

Leo Rakale, C.R., is now a priest on the staff of the Cathedral Church of St. Mary's, Johannesburg. The story of his call to the religious life, and the relationship between himself and Clayton, I do not pretend to comprehend fully. But I find it remarkable, and moving in a way not fully understood, and am glad to set it down here as it was told to me.

Could it be said that Africa, and in particular the African people, helped Clayton to express more easily those affectionate emotions which were undoubtedly part of his nature? He had left Chesterfield with a reputation for formidability rather than benignity. Was he experiencing a warmth in personal relationships hitherto in large measure unknown to him? Was he in receiving love becoming more able to give it? There seems no doubt that this was so.

11

War

The coming to power of Hitler in 1933, which event left hardly a country in the world unaffected, powerfully influenced South Africa. Yet Hitler did not rouse in the Nationalist breast the same anger and fear that he roused in English-speaking South Africa. For one thing many Nationalists admired him. Germany, like the Boers, had been defeated by Britain, and here she was making a comeback. Many of them too sympathised with Hitler's hatred of the Jews. In any case why should South Africa interest herself in the wars of Europe?

Antisemitism flared up in South Africa during Clayton's first years as Bishop of Johannesburg. It was an ugly time for Jews. South Africa had always seemed to them a haven in a cruel world, but now they could not be so sure. Every new arrival of Jewish immigrants, fleeing from Europe while there was yet time, added fuel to the antisemitic flames, which were assiduously fanned by Malan and his Purified Nationalists. Jews could take some comfort from the uncompromising speeches of J. H. Hofmeyr, Minister of Education and the Interior, who denounced intolerance and antisemitism, and from the fact that neither Smuts nor Hertzog spoke contemptuously of Jews. But the comfort was not great, because Hofmeyr, bending before the fierce antisemitic wind, introduced interim immigration regulations in 1936, and promised a new Aliens Bill for 1937.

Outside of the realm of politics there were two great champions of the Jews. One was Clayton himself. Antisemitism was to him not only a moral offence, it was also an extreme vulgarity. A certain Mr. Cohen announced in the advertisement columns that he would seek to change his name to Clayton. A certain Mr. Clayton was incensed by this, and began to organise a petition of protest among the Claytons. He wrote to the bishop and asked for his support. The bishop's reply was unequivocal and typical. His letter has been lost but the gist of it was: 'Certainly not. What better name could he choose?'[1]

The other notable champion was Alfred Hoernlé, professor of philosophy at the University of the Witwatersrand. It could be said that outside politics these were two of the greatest intelligences in South Africa. They were both clear and penetrating thinkers, they both scorned demagogucry, they both wrote and spoke well, and they could recognise injustice no matter how disguised. What is more, they both appeared to be completely fearless in their public utterances. Hoernlé was not a professing Christian, but upheld Christian ethics, especially in the world of political action. He was continually pointing to the conflct between profession and practice in what the white people of South Africa liked to call a Christian society. He, as also Clayton and Hofmeyr, could well have been called the 'conscience of white South Africa'. It was not surprising then that in 1937 Hoernlé and Clayton became foundation members of the new Society of Jews and Christians formed to combat the rising tide of antisemitism. Nor is it surprising that Hoernlé should have been one of the foremost leaders, and Clayton one of the foremost supporters, of the S. A. Institute of Race Relations, founded in 1929.

It goes almost without saying that Clayton and Hoernlé both called themselves liberals. If one did this, one was likely to imperil one's influence on white opinion. White South Africa, and especially white Nationalists, had scant time for liberals. Yet both Clayton and Hoernlé were moral leaders of great influence and authority. Each recognised the other as such.

It must be remembered that Clayton's primary duty was always to the Church. He never failed to support what he thought was a just cause, but this support was more of a lending of his prestige and sometimes his presence. His job was to run the diocese of Johannesburg. In a certain sense his world was the church and the clergy, and to it were admitted a certain number of laymen, and on the periphery, a couple of laywomen. Therefore, while he was fully alive to the menace of Nazism and Hitler, and to the strains that they were causing in South African politics, and while he would not hesitate to discuss the international and the national situations in private, in public he confined himself to condemnation of antisemitism, and to statements on the ethics of war and the immorality of totalitarian government.

He wrote his first statement on war as early as August 1936. According to him there were three attitudes adopted by Christians. The first was that all war, all fighting, all use of physical force, was wrong; therefore for a nation to arm itself was wrong, even if it was in danger of being attacked. The second attitude was that it was permissible to defend oneself in case of attack, but otherwise the use of force was wrong. The third was that it was permissible to fight in defence of treaties, even if oneself were not attacked. Clayton's own view was that it was justifiable to defend oneself against aggression, and therefore one must be prepared. But there was an accompanying duty, and that was to remedy existing injustices amongst nations. He concludes that the state of the world is sad and anxious, but

> Blind unbelief is sure to err
> And scan His work in vain:
> God is his own interpreter
> And He will make it plain.[2]

In 1938 he wrote on world peace, and the sacrifices that alone could make the League of Nations an instrument of peace. The trouble was that the world did not realise the cost of peace.

'As long as each nation is the judge of its own cause, as long as there is no generally representative tribunal, commanding the confidence of the nations as the judiciary of this country commands the confidence of the individual citizens, so long, it seems to me, the abolition of war is impossible. We will the end, but do we will the means?'[3]

In that same year, in his fifth charge to the diocese, Clayton declared that the great principles of Christianity were challenged by the modern totalitarian state. Man's first allegiance is to God, not to any other power. Each individual is an end in himself, no matter what his race, and he matters to God, and he matters for ever. Totalitarianism – and here he was clearly referring to Nazism – challenges the Christian belief that all can live together in justice and peace, whatever the difference in race, culture, and religion – and here he was clearly referring to South Africa as well. Many Christians could not meet the challenges of the totalitarian state because they did not practise these principles. Clayton uttered the often-forgotten truth that the real defence of the Christian against evil is not his ethics, but his belief that the Divine Power works in the world, and that he can be used by it.

He uttered judgements that can still be uttered today: that African taxes were disproportionate to African means; that the pass laws, which sent so many Africans to gaol for trivial offences, should be reformed; that African wages should be raised; that educational opportunity must be increased. Christianity was not irrelevant to the world, but its message would not be heard if it were not proclaimed by the witness of Christians. It was at this synod that Clayton announced that the old Bishop's Fund, which paid for the travels of clergy to more remote areas, was to be renamed the Church Extension Fund, and that a new Bishop's Fund would be created, for the purchase of new sites and for assistance to new parishes. The financial reports before Synod showed that both white and black Anglicans were giving more. That was recognised by all as Clayton's work. In 1932 the contributions from African congregations totalled £4,135. In 1936 they had risen to £5,807.[4] The new Bishop's Fund, announced in October, had passed the £1,000 mark before Christmas.

Meanwhile the man Adolf Hitler continued to dominate the thinking of the world. The strains to which the giant United Party was being subjected were not only due to the unanswered question as to whether South Africa would fight in a war against Hitler. The presence of the liberal J. H. Hofmeyr in Hertzog's cabinet enabled Malan and his small party to exploit the differences between Hofmeyr and Hertzog's conservatives on all race questions. There was more in common between Hertzog's conservatives and Malan than there was between them and Hofmeyr. The conservatives for example wanted legislation against racial intermarriage, to which Hofmeyr would not agree.* The resultant frustration and anger of the conservatives

*The phrase 'racial intermarriage' in South Africa almost always refers to intermarriage between white persons and others.

caused great glee amongst Malan's followers, although they pretended that they were outraged.

But there was a third and powerful factor. The year 1938 was the centenary of the Great Trek, the great migration of Boers from the Cape to the north, in part at least to escape British rule and British missionaries and British equalitarian ideas. The Voortrekkers were the heroes of Afrikanerdom, and their migration was re-enacted in 1938 by the trek of ox-wagons from many points in South Africa to Pretoria in the north, where they met at the site of the mighty Monument to be erected in memory of the founders of the nation. The wagons were met in every town and city by men and women in Voortrekker dress. Prayers were said, meat and *boerewors** were cooked over the fires, nostalgic Afrikaner songs were sung. Old men and women wept, and touched the tents of the wagons, their wooden frames and wheels. Speeches were made of dedication and burning love, and history being what it was, many of these told of past British sins. By and large, English-speaking South Africans felt themselves totally excluded from these celebrations. Those who tried to identify themselves with these emotional events were often rebuffed.

Clayton's view of the celebrations could only be described as highly dispassionate. That was not because he was an Englishman. It was because these manifestations of commemorative fervour were utterly foreign to his nature. At the time of the death of King George V, of the accession of King Edward VIII, followed by the accession and coronation of King George VI, he expressed those sentiments of admiration and loyalty which were deeply felt by so many of the people of Britain, and by many of the English-speaking people of South Africa. But to feel intense pride in being a member of a particular race or nation was something to him incomprehensible, and while this was partly the result of his own temperament, it was also due to the fact that his supreme loyalty was to Christ and the Church.

He therefore was very polite about the Voortrekker celebrations. At his fifth diocesan synod a resolution was moved conveying the fraternal greetings of the diocese to the Dutch Reformed churches on the occasion of the centenary which meant so much to them. This was hotly opposed by the fiery Rector of Potchefstroom, J. R. Cutten. He opposed the sending of fraternal greetings to churches which were hostile to all that the Church of the Province stood for. He gave a vivid account of snubs and slights to which he and his parish had been subjected by the powerful churches and dominees of the extremely Nationalistic town of Potchefstroom. His speech aroused both laughter and uneasiness, laughter because he was what is known as a character, uneasiness because of the publicity that would be given to Cutten's speech at an abnormally sensitive time.

Some other bishop might have shown uneasiness, but Clayton did not. Cutten had a right to speak, and that right was absolute so long as he did not become repetitive, blasphemous, or abusive. Nor would Clayton suppose, as some other bishop might have done, that Cutten represented the Church and should be stopped. He was in fact highly amused by the rector's denun-

*A special South African sausage.

ciations of what 'they' did in Potchefstroom, and of any diocesan attempt to fraternise with 'them'.

When Clayton first arrived in Johannesburg, there is no doubt that he thought of the possibility of forming some sort of relationship with the Dutch Reformed churches and their leading ministers. In his fourth charge to the diocese he used the most explicit language:

'I ask you to consider what it would mean for this country if union could be attained, I mean a definite corporate reunion between ourselves and the Dutch Reformed Church.'[5]

He went on to say that one of the purposes of the coming of Christ was to break down barriers, those between God and man and those between man and man, so that nations could live together in unity in the fellowship of His holy Church. He asked for a greater attempt at understanding and communication with the Dutch Reformed churches especially among the clergy.

On several occasions during his episcopal ministry Clayton held up the Dutch Reformed churches as examples to be followed in the matter of their financial support of missions. Their people gave more generously than the people of the diocese. It sometimes appeared to him that the Church meant more in the life of the Afrikaner than it did in the life of the English-speaking South African.

It would be improper to doubt Clayton's sincerity when he spoke of 'corporate reunion', but one must state that his interest in corporate reunion was highly academic. In the first place he lacked any burning desire to reunite the churches, or to see them reunited. His great love was the Anglican Church, which was holy, catholic, and apostolic. In the second place, he made no attempt to learn the Afrikaans language, and this alone would have made any leadership from him totally impossible. In the third place, he had no sympathy with puritanism whatsoever, and the Dutch Reformed churches were very puritanical. But apart from all these considerations, there was no desire on the part of these churches for reunion.

It must be said again – and it is not pleasant to say it at all – that the gulf between the Dutch Reformed churches and the other churches in South Africa appears to be unbridgeable. In 1937 Clayton had not realised this. This showed no lack of perspicacity on his part. The reason why he had not realised that the gulf was unbridgeable was simply that he had not tried to bridge it.

Clayton's sharp reaction to the call from the Madras Conference of the International Missionary Council of 1938 for joint evangelism shows more clearly than any theoretical pronouncement his aversion to any attempt to jump the gun in the ecumenical movement. Extracts from the statement by the Church of the Province of South Africa, with the framing of which he had a great deal to do, read thus: 'We desire to make it plain that we are not prepared to co-operate in any such way in a common evangelistic effort.' And again: 'Christendom is not reunited, and we are not prepared to act as if it were.' And again: 'Neither are we prepared to say that it is of no consequence to what church a man belongs, provided he belongs to some church.'

And lastly: 'We are glad to co-operate in matters of Moral Witness and Social Welfare.'[6]

In the event the Johannesburg Synod's fraternal message to the Dutch Reformed churches was approved by a great majority, though it did nothing to increase the amount or quality of communication between Anglicans and Dutch Reformed churchmen. Synod closed with a considerable tribute to its bishop, expressing its gratitude for the 'remarkable manner in which he had contributed to combine notable qualities of firmness, patience, and good humour in his management of our proceedings'. At such times the impatience and ill-humour were forgiven and forgotten.

Meanwhile the ever-present threat of war was growing greater. In March 1939 Chamberlain gave a guarantee of assistance to Poland, having lost faith in his Munich statement of 'peace in our time'. Clayton announced his intention of going to the Lambeth Conference of 1940, but of course it was not held. However, the announcement of intention brought him an illuminated address from the African congregation of St. Cyprian's, Johannesburg:

'You came to us from your homeland knowing perhaps little about our aspirations and ambitions, but you immediately came to grips with the multi-racial problems that are to be found in this country. Your voice was raised above the voice of others . . .'[7]

On 1 September 1939 Hitler marched into Poland. On 2 September General Hertzog called a special meeting of the Cabinet, and it became clear that he and five Ministers were for neutrality, while Smuts and six Ministers were for entering the war on the side of Britain. On 4 September Smuts took South Africa into the war, by a vote of 80 to 67.

Just as the white Parliament was divided, so was white South Africa divided. The events of the Anglo–Boer War of 1899–1902 were still too near and painful. The English-speaking people supported Smuts almost to a man. The Afrikaans-speaking people were bitterly divided, but it was a majority that supported Hertzog.

It was an all-white Parliament, representative of one-fifth of the population,* that decided whether the country should go to war. African, Coloured, and Indian people were not consulted. Those who understood what it was all about gave their support to Smuts.

Clayton, having an understanding of the meaning of Hitler as clear as any, and being a loyal subject of the King, who in 1939 was also King of South Africa, threw all his authority as a bishop behind the decision to go to war.

His diocese was to make great sacrifices before it would be over. But one continually recurring threat was for the time removed. The intention of

*This is not entirely accurate, but it is in essence so. In the Parliament that voted 80–67, there were three white M.P.s who represented the African voters of the Cape Province, who in 1936 had been removed to a separate roll. Also there were many white M.P.s especially in the Cape Province, who had a proportion of Coloured voters in their constituencies. In 1939 a fair number of Coloured people exercised the parliamentary franchise.

General Hertzog's government, reiterated in 1939, was to put all African education under the control of the Native Affairs Department, whose primary function was not to educate but to carry out the 'Native policy' of the Government. Now that Smuts was Prime Minister the danger receded immediately. Smuts had only one primary objective, and that was the defeat of Hitler. What was more he did not share the Afrikaner Nationalists' fear of and revulsion from any kind of education for black children that was not controlled by them.

One can only repeat that the contribution of the English-speaking churches to African education had been and still was immense.* For a time it was safe.

*Amongst many exponents of Black Power and Black Consciousness, there is today a fierce reaction against the education of the missionaries. This must be endured, but it should be mentioned that many of these exponents owe their skill and articulateness to missionary schools.

12

The Diocese and the War

Soon after the declaration of war, Clayton preached in St. Mary's Cathedral a sermon entitled 'War and the Christian'. He quoted 'Glory to God in the Highest; peace on earth, goodwill to men' and explained that it was a mistranslation and should rather read, 'Peace on earth among men in whom He is well pleased.' In other words Jesus made no promise of peace except to those who came to God by Him. Nor could there be peace among nations except on the basis of righteousness.

Clayton, speaking with that great moral authority he now possessed, said that although in one sense the war was the crime of one man, it was the actions of the nations of the world that had produced such a man. It was indeed the result of the actions of all men, because all men shared a common responsibility. He said, 'No nation can go into a war with clean hands.'

Yet even if by our own fault we have produced an intolerable situation, and if that intolerable situation can be ended only by the 'horrors of war', then we must go to war.

'As the individual criminal, though society is partly responsible for his being a criminal, must be restrained by society, so a Government which behaves like a criminal in the international sphere must be restrained, if the world is to be a tolerable place in which to live.'

We have already seen that Clayton, so far as is known, had never since his arrival in South Africa referred to England as 'home'. But it is interesting to note that for him it is England, not Britain who is fighting the war.

'We are not an English Church, preaching an English Gospel. We are a South African Province of a Universal Church, preaching the gospel of Christ, which is the same in every land. Yet we and you alike are bound close to England both by our allegiance to the Crown, and by the innumerable ties of kinship and friendship which so many of us have with England. And England has thrown herself into the cause which, not only, I hope, because I am English by birth, I believe to be the cause on the success of which the future of the world depends. South Africa was free to choose her course, and has made her choice.'

But first and foremost we are Christians, 'and as Christians there is no doubt where our sympathies should lie in the matters that are at issue'.[1]

There can be no doubt that in 1939 the great majority of Christians throughout the world thought that the war against Hitler was a righteous war. This was partly because they believed that Hitlerism, Nazism, totalitarianism, and the persecution of the Jews were intolerable evils, and partly because their own governments had gone to war. In South Africa also the majority of Christians were for the war, but white Christians were bitterly divided. In the first place there was the division between the English-speaking churches and the Dutch Reformed churches, but this could be endured because the contact between these two groups of churches was minimal. Most bitter of all was the conflict inside the Dutch Reformed churches, where all those young men who joined the forces were regarded by many as traitors to Afrikanerdom, and were in some instances either forbidden to enter or counselled not to enter churches when in uniform. This conflict divided families also, and separated son from father, sweetheart from sweetheart, and brother from brother.

Clayton was very prompt in enjoining tolerance for all those who did not support the Government and the war effort. In his charge to the diocesan synod of 1939, delivered about a month after the declaration of war, he made it clear that it was not one's bounden duty to have confidence in one's rulers, though he himself had such confidence; but one must obey them, unless one believed that such confidence was disloyalty to God. One must have no hatred, no bitterness, no contempt, for those who did not share one's ideals or even opposed their realisation. This was a difficult attitude to maintain, yet it was just this that was lacking in the totalitarian state.

He spoke of the injunction to turn the other cheek, which has caused so much heart-searching amongst Christians ever since it was given. 'I do not think it is right to apply to a State, which consists of many individuals, the maxims and example which is set to a single individual. I may turn my own cheek; I may not turn yours.'[2]

Clayton was certain that if the Good Samaritan had come on the scene earlier, Jesus would have wanted him to resist the attacker. If he himself were younger, and not a priest, he would go to fight. Yet war is not and cannot be constructive. It may clear away some things which stand in the way of a better order. It cannot establish that order. In such a time penitence and prayer are crucial, including prayer for our enemies.

It is instructive to study another church magazine of this period. This was *Die Kerkbode*, the official weekly periodical of the largest Dutch Reformed Church, the Nederduitse Gereformeerde Kerk. The N.G.K. had by far the largest number of white adherents, commanding as it did the support of over eighty per cent of Afrikaans-speaking Christians. However, the Methodist, Anglican and Roman Catholic churches each had more African adherents than the N.G.K., the Methodist Church almost twice as many. From the point of view of numbers the N.G.K. was very much the biggest of all the churches, and was followed by the Methodists, the Anglicans, and the Roman Catholics in that order.

In the months preceding the declaration of war *Die Kerkbode* clearly regarded Communism and Roman Catholicism as the two great dangers confronting the world and South Africa. It feared the growing moral looseness which the Communists would use to conquer the world. It reported that the number of Communists outside Russia had climbed from 340,000 to 1,200,000 since 1935, and that there were 746,000 members in their youth organisations. A series of articles was running entitled 'The Roman Church Seen from Within', and these attacked the Popes for their evil and worldly lives, the system of indulgences, the veneration of relics, Mariolatry and the confessional. The confessional led many confessors into sin, because some of it was 'so filthy that it cannot be committed to paper'.[3]

On the whole it can be said that *Die Kerkbode* regarded Hitler and Nazism with neutrality if not equanimity. Nazism was not classed with Communism and Roman Catholicism as a menace to righteousness. But *Die Kerkbode* recognised clearly that Nazism was disturbing the unity of Afrikanerdom. Indeed, the recent Day of Repentance, or Day of Humbling, which had been held in all the Afrikaans churches 'was held with the eye on the division and bitterness amongst our people'. But at the foot of the Cross the walls of separation are broken down.[4]

When finally war was declared on 4 September, no reference was made to it in *Die Kerkbode* of 13 September, though that may have been because of printing arrangements. It was mentioned, however, on 20 September, in an editorial which condemned war in general and gave a critical look at 'Western civilisation'. This war was God's instrument, and it is His will and purpose that is being carried out. Afrikaner Christians are called to penitence for they are also part of the world. The war clouds are dark over South Africa, but Christians must take courage, for God is behind and above all. Of the causes of this particular war, nothing was said at all.

In the issue of 27 September, the editorial deals with a happening 'which we cannot pass over in silence'. This was not the war, but the reconciliation which the war had brought about, and which had reunited so great a number of the Afrikaner people, by which was meant the reunion of General Hertzog's wing of the United Party with Dr. Malan's Nationalists. This meant, in other words, the reunion of all anti-Smuts and anti-war Afrikaners.[5] The editorial added that at the moment it could say nothing of the causes which had led to this reconciliation.

These were the characteristics of *Die Kerkbode* during the years of the great world convulsion, namely, the acceptance of the war as a fact, an absolute neutrality in regard to the issues involved, a sustained editorial refusal to accept contentious letters, a scrupulous recognition of the right of the State to use the sword, continual reminders of the dangers of Communism and Roman Catholicism, and studious avoidance of any discussion of Nazism, and finally, a continual castigation of moral looseness, especially sexual. One should not conclude without noting that both the N.G.K. and *Die Kerkbode* regarded it as a duty to supply chaplains to the forces, although the latter made it clear that this should not be interpreted as approval of Government policy.

Thus it was that *Die Kerkbode* refused to accept letters, or permit any discussion, of the meaning of the Swastika,[6] or about Nazism and British–Jewish propaganda – such a discussion could only land *Die Kerkbode* in a storm of controversy.[7] Nor would it accept a letter asking that the Cape Synod of the N.G.K. should ask the Government to make peace with Germany, for that would plunge the paper into politics.[8] On the one hand it published articles by Professor B. B. Keet of Stellenbosch, the very distinguished N.G.K. theologian, and a believer in the rightness of General Smuts's decision. These articles did not discuss Nazism or the war, but they discussed the respective duties of the individual and the State, a subject very popular among Nationalists in 1939. Keet asked, 'What is a righteous cause? Is it to maintain the status quo?' But the implications in his articles were counterbalanced by 'V.D.M.', who in an article on 'Conflicting Ideologies' condemned both modern Democracy and Totalitarianism, and commended Calvinism.[9] At the time of the invasion of Holland when many children were orphaned, the paper published a letter from a correspondent warning against the danger that the Roman Catholic Church would get hold of them.

There was one setback. The reconciliation of Hertzog and Malan, which was in fact the reconciliation of all 'true Afrikaners', fell on evil days. On 6 November 1940 Hertzog, followed by faithful friends, walked out of the Orange Free State Congress of the new Nationalist Party, the Congress having rejected his views on the political rights of the English-speaking. His followers founded the Afrikaner Party. The movement called the *Ossewabrandwag*, the 'Ox-wagon Watch', under the leadership of Hans van Rensburg, grew so powerful that it ignored Malan's Nationalist Party. And sixteen members of Parliament under Oswald Pirow left Malan for the group known as the New Order. Even before these events took place, *Die Kerkbode*, having hailed the reconciliation in September 1939, had to acknowledge two months later that *die twisduiwel*, the 'strife-devil', had returned, and that there was much disunity and bitterness amongst Afrikaners. Nothing was more feared by Nationalist Afrikanerdom than *die twisduiwel*, or its evil work *die broedertwis*, the 'brother-strife', for the future of this tiny nation in a hostile world depended on its unity.

One last evidence can be given from this source of the tremendous cleavage that war had created in the white population of South Africa. On 5 August 1940, *Die Kerkbode* reprinted the opening address by the Revd. William Nicol to the nineteenth Synod of the N.G.K. of the Transvaal. It dealt with Bible-teaching, work among students, the care of the poor (*armesorg*) and gambling and dog-racing. But of the great struggle that was convulsing the world, not one word was said.*

While the war issue was thus dividing the N.G.K., there was only one minor break in the unity of the Church of the Province. It caused intense indignation at the time, but can now be seen to have been comic also.

*Before one leaves the subject of *Die Kerkbode*, one should say that for students of sociology, history, and theology, who are in search of theses, it is a mine of countless riches.

The Rector of Krugersdorp in the diocese of Johannesburg, the Right Revd. Basil Peacey (pronounced Pacy), who had been Bishop of Lebombo on the declaration of war, posted a notice on the church door announcing that the British national anthem 'God Save the King' would not be sung in his church as it was being sung in many of the other Anglican churches in the diocese. This caused great anger in the parish. One of the churchwardens was the Officer Commanding the Witwatersrand Rifles. One of the parishioners was the mayoress of Krugersdorp, who took the notice down from the church door and confronted Peacey with it. Some parishioners now travelled to the nearby town of Randfontein to attend worship, some stopped paying sustentation, some would not allow Peacey to have anything to do with their christenings, weddings, and funerals. The pressure was so great that Peacey agreed to allow the parishioners to sing 'God Save the King' on their knees, which would have made it a prayer and not a national anthem. This did not pacify the parish, least of all those gentlemen who not only wanted to sing it in church, but wanted to sing it standing stiffly to attention.

Peacey, when he was the bachelor Bishop of Lebombo, and was returning to his diocese by ship from Southampton, had had as one of his fellow-passengers a Miss Anna Hofmeyr, daughter of the renowned Senator Willie Hofmeyr, who was what is known as a 'red-hot Nationalist'. His daughter was no less devoted. When she agreed to marry the bishop it was understood between them that she would become an Anglican, that she would remain a Nationalist, that the children would be brought up in both languages, and that they would choose their politics for themselves. Miss Hofmeyr was an extraordinary woman, forthright, uncompromising, and masterful. She opened the bishop's eyes to the long history of suppression and humiliation of the Afrikaner people by the British, to their aspirations of achieving political independence, to the painful years of 1914–18 when General Botha had entered the war on the side of Britain without even consulting Parliament, to the present humiliation still being suffered by the Afrikaners and their language, to the essential justice of the race policies practised by white South Africa, and to the essential justice of the race policies that would be put into effect by the Nationalists when they came into power. The bishop was powerfully influenced by his new political education, and himself became a believer in the righteousness of the Afrikaner cause and in the rightness and justice of Nationalist race policies. Quite apart from that, he was not as masterful as she.

The Krugersdorp congregation and the church funds began to melt away. Clayton, alternating between anger and laughter, summoned Peacey to Johannesburg for consultation. Clayton was in the exasperating position of understanding the logic and morality of Peacey's position, and yet thinking it immeasurably foolish. They would reach some agreement, but after Peacey had reached home he would telephone to say that he could no longer abide by it, and it was supposed by many that his wife had pointed out the impossibilities and inconsistencies of it. The temporary damage done to the work of the Krugersdorp parish was spectacular, and it lasted into 1941. Any personal relationship between Clayton and the Peaceys was destroyed. Probably Peacey did not know that Clayton had offered him a parish against the advice of Dean Palmer. Clayton had said to Palmer, 'How can I leave a fellow-bishop on the street?'[10] In 1941 Peacey was offered the Cape Town parish of Constantia by Archbishop Darbyshire. The fact that Darbyshire had got Peacey moved Clayton to great mirth. Seven years later Clayton went to Cape Town, and got Peacey back again.

Apart from Krugersdorp, the diocese was adapting itself well to the new situation created by the war. At the Diocesan Synod of 1939 Clayton moved 'that this Synod considers that during the period of the war this Diocese should not accept money for its missionary work from England, and directs the Diocesan Finance Board to make provision accordingly'. The resolution was carried unanimously and an organisation to be called 'Friends of Diocesan Missions' was formed to raise money for missionary work. The amount which the diocese received from Britain (it was always said to come from England, and was in fact called the 'English money') was £1,350, and it came through the Society for the Propagation of the Gospel, usually called the S.P.G. It was earmarked for missionary work, and was used to pay the stipends and expenses of white missionaries. Clayton told his diocese that this was an opportunity for white Anglicans to show a greater interest in the mission work in their parishes, and to help the African congregations, many of whose church buildings were in bad condition. He wrote to the S.P.G. giving thanks for the help that had been given for so many years, and said, 'We should be ashamed to receive money from England at the present time.'[11] To this Bishop Hudson replied on 13 June.

'I hope greatly that your generous action has not had the effect of making things too impossibly difficult for you and the flock. All I can say is that your action has inspired folk all over the Church to follow your lead. I think I am right in saying that yours was the first diocese to take the voluntary step that you did.'

He continued: 'I quite see your difficulty about man-power, and the difficulty about filling up places when the chaplains may at any time return. It is true that passages are extremely difficult to get, but if the man-power question is imperative, do please let me know, and there might be something that we could do.'[12]

Clayton's letters to the S.P.G. are interesting. They were written by hand, and as no copies were kept, they often give the same information and make the same points as their predecessors. Sometimes they were sharp in the extreme. n 1935 the S.P.G. had written that it was not happy that the Community of the Resurrection had its own missionary fund and that Dorothy Maud collected extra money in England, and that it might reduce its grant. This made Clayton angry, and in exasperation he put the question several times, 'What do you want me to do?' Canon Waddy, to whom the letter was written, wrote on it, 'Temper! I replied in tone – and tore it up. Sent an acknowledgement.' Clayton's letter was written in April, but by

5 December he had recovered and wrote to Waddy with his usual affability.[13]

Clayton had decided that it was time for the diocese of Johannesburg to be self-supporting. In this he had the full support of Rouse, who had visited England in 1937 and seen the poverty of many of the parishes who were contributing to the funds of the S.P.G. Johannesburg was a rich city, and many of its Anglicans were both rich and influential. In 1940 Clayton was writing to the S.P.G. to 'keep open the possibility' that a grant might be asked for when the war had ended, but he hoped not.[14] In 1941 he wrote that in the year 1940 the diocese had raised the necessary money to replace the grant.[15] In further letters he reiterated the hope that the diocese would not ask again for a grant from the S.P.G.

He also reported on 13 May 1941 that there was a 'great shortage of manpower'. This was because 'one in eight of our European priests are with the South African forces'.[16] By the middle of 1941, South Africa was fully involved in the war. In May 1940 the first of Smuts's troops left for Kenya to drive the Italians out of Africa. The so-called 'phony war' was coming to an end. On the night of 9 May, Hitler's armies invaded Holland and Belgium. On the morning of 15 May they broke through the French lines near Sedan. On 26 May the evacuation of the British forces from Dunkirk had begun. On 10 June Italy declared war on the Allies. On 14 June the Germans entered Paris. The people of the British Commonwealth might have lost heart had it not been for the indomitable spirit and speeches of Winston Churchill.

It is the task of some people, even when their hope is low, to give hope to others. This falls to the lot of all persons who are in positions of authority and responsibility. The Hebrew prophets saw visions of an ineffable future when the present held no hope at all. It is a fact of life that the discharging of the responsibility of giving hope to others keeps hope alive in oneself. And when to a person has also been given a mastery of language, his hope is enabled to burn more brightly than ever, and he is more able to keep it burning in others. Such a gift Churchill possessed.

Clayton considered Churchill to be a great orator, with the gift of raising men and women from the depths of doubt and gloom to the heights of heroism. Churchill had a touch of flamboyance that Clayton had not, something of the actor, a gift of which Clayton was highly suspicious, because of the possibility that the words might be greater than the deeds. But to Churchill's speeches he gave unreserved admiration. It is indeed hard to find that he had admired another speaker as much since the days of Father Figgis, whom, the reader may remember, Clayton thought at times to be guilty of 'rhetorical exaggeration'.

According to S. H. Clarke, the headmaster of St. John's College, who probably knew Clayton's mind as well as anybody, he was in the deepest of gloom during these catastrophic events of 1940, and thought that Britain was done for. One Sunday in that terrible June he told a congregation in the cathedral to beware of 'false patriotism'. The British Empire was not the same as the Kingdom of God; even though the United Kingdom was far from perfect, it had moral standards which had been forsaken in Germany. The message of Easter was that God's will would prevail, but that did not necessarily mean that Britain and her allies would win the war. God 'uses what is not in accordance with His will to fulfil his purpose'. And again, 'we must take long views and not be frightened out of our religion'. All this was true, but it gave little comfort to the congregation, who wanted and needed something more Churchillian.

Things were not made better by the knowledge that many Nationalists wanted the total defeat of Britain. This they would not have regarded as the defeat of South Africa, but only as the defeat of Smuts. On 29 August, when the Battle of Britain was raging, General Hertzog moved that the country should immediately make peace with Germany. Smuts set his followers cheering by saying, 'We are not deserters, we are not hands-uppers.' He recalled that the same arguments had been used against Hertzog and himself forty years earlier, but they had carried on. At this time Smuts's mastery was complete.

It has been noted earlier that Clayton made a clear distinction between the kingdom of this world and the Kingdom of Heaven. It was this that enabled him to pass such grave and weighty judgements on the racial policies of South Africa and the suffering which they caused, because he judged them by standards that might be called eternal. He understood well that the purpose of every racial policy was to ensure Afrikaner survival, but he did not regard the aim as Christian. That there could be such a thing as Christian–nationalism he simply did not believe. Yet none of this alters the fact that the defeat of Britain would have been for him – at first at least – almost unendurable.

Meanwhile the work of the diocese, in spite of the shortage of clergy, was carried on with determination. This shortage was not experienced till towards the end of 1940, owing to what Clayton described as the indifference to spiritual needs by the military authorities, who allowed the first South African troops to go north without chaplains. When the shortage began to be felt, Clayton having allowed six priests to go by the end of 1940, and another two by the end of 1941, the burden of the eucharistic services began to weigh heavily on the clergy, and Clayton asked laymen to take matins and evensong for those congregations without priests.* One looks back with admiration at the building-plans that were carried out during these difficult years. In 1939 new church-buildings were dedicated in the locations of Boksburg and Bethal. In 1940 in August, an Anglican church hut was built at the tremendous camp at Potchefstroom, and Clayton dedicated a new church-building in the Brakpan location. In September two new churches were dedicated, one at Molotistad and the other in the white suburb of Kensington, Johannesburg. In 1941 Clayton dedicated three

*I took evensong regularly at St. Philip's Church, Kliptown, and preached in Afrikaans too, one of the favourite themes being that one's failures should not discourage one from worshipping, this being a special temptation of some of the parishioners.

additions to the Church of Christ the King, Sophiatown, and also a new mission church at Koster in the western Transvaal, the service being attended, in spite of the strains of those days, by a number of Afrikaans-speaking wellwishers, their presence being warmly appreciated by Clayton.[17] In November he dedicated a new church for the coloured people of Kliptown. The financial position of the diocese for the year 1941 was good, but he gave it as his judgement that there was no real turning to religion.[18]

In his charge at the end of that year he gave expression to his pessimism. He said that we were fighting for a chance of building a civilisation based on the dignity and worth of the individual, and this was difficult in the light of the moral chaos of the world. 'At present society is engaged in running violently down a steep place into the sea. And it shows every sign of perishing in the waters.' Yet he gave the only counsel that is possible in such or any circumstances:

'We must always profess more than we can perform, though our efforts must be to bring our performance up to our profession. Every member of the Church can witness and try to follow Christ's way.'[19]

An account of the diocesan building-programme of the early war years must not omit mention of the building of the new 'Bishop's House'. The diocese was heavily criticised for this, but the fact is that the old house was in bad condition and not worth repairing. Clayton went away for most of April 1940 while it was being pulled down. It was announced that his sister Mrs. Katherine Roberts, known as Kitty, who was seven years older than he but now widowed, was coming from England to live with him.

Katherine Roberts was due for a revelation. She had never really lived with her brother at all. He was now 56 years of age, a bishop, a formidable figure, regarded with awe, fear, worship, affection, and sometimes dislike, with a great bald head reported to contain a prodigious brain, and an ability to scowl, blast, laugh, pray, preach, and inspire, all within the compass of the one soul contained in a body that with the years had become heavier and heavier.

Her view of him had never before been so comprehensive. She was to learn the strange nature of what Donald Harris had called Clayton's ambivalence. He could be offensively rude to her, in a way that probably no one had ever been rude to him. She would let him finish and then say to him, 'Geoffrey, be calm.' She once said to him reproachfully, 'Now Geoffrey, I think you're going too far.' When in a fit of irritability he would glare at the ringing telephone and not answer it, she would say, 'Geoffrey, I think you had better answer it.' Clayton had a strong dislike for the telephone. One of the greatest injuries done to him by this pernicious instrument was when he heard an unknown woman say to him, 'Is that you, darling?', to which he replied with commendable asperity, 'I think it highly improbable', and slammed it down.

Florence Blaxall, who was chairman of the Church Women's Society, believed, with others, that Katherine Roberts had helped him to overcome much of his irritability in the pulpit and elsewhere. Whether she decided that it was too much for her, we do not know, but she took advantage of an opportunity rare in those days, and returned to England in February 1943. *The Watchman* hoped for the speedy return of her prisoner-of-war son, and thanked her for the way in which she had entered into the life of the diocese.[20]

The tide of the war could not yet be said to be turning, but no subsequent months were to seem so hopeless as those of the middle of 1940. By the end of that year the Italians had been driven from Egypt, leaving 40,000 prisoners in British hands. When Bardia fell in January, 45,000 more prisoners were taken. On 22 January, Tobruk fell to the Australians, and another 38,000 prisoners were captured. Italy's part in the war in North Africa was virtually over, and by the end of 1941 she had surrendered in East Africa and Ethiopia.

The collapse of the Italians was taken as more or less of a joke, but one could not joke about Rommel. Then on 22 June 1941 came the electrifying news that Hitler had invaded Russia. The threat of invasion that had been hanging over Britain was removed, and she was able to give more of her attention to the Mediterranean. Still more electrifying was the news of 7 December, that Japan had attacked the American fleet at Pearl Harbour, inflicting tremendous loss of ships and men. Churchill wrote in his book, 'So we had won after all!'

Something else was happening too. In the minds of politicians and churchmen, of teachers and students, of airmen, sailors and soldiers, was being born the realisation that there was something wrong with the world and it ought to be made anew. It was odd that it took Hitler and a war to do this to them but there it was. It was a realisation that was felt across the world, on the grand scale in the Atlantic Charter, on a lesser scale in the diocese of Johannesburg.

13

The New Order

As early as October 1940 Clayton declared in the diocesan synod that there would have to be a new order. As we have seen, the name 'New Order' had already been appropriated by Oswald Pirow, who had been one of General Hertzog's favourite Ministers. Pirow was an admirer of Hitler and a believer in authoritarian government. He declared that the days of parliamentary democracy were over, and with sixteen fellow-M.P.s he created the New Order. True to their principles they would not stand for the 1943 elections, and were not heard of again. Had they ever come to power, South Africa would have experienced life under a dictatorship. Africans, Jews, Indians, Coloured people would have fared badly, for Pirow had a contempt for them all. He shared with Hertzog the belief that the white man would rule, apparently for ever, that part of Africa that stretched from Cape Town to the northern border of Kenya. Smuts and Hofmeyr held that belief also, but both came to realise that the Second World War was going to destroy colonialism and the myth of white supremacy.

Clayton's new order was of another kind altogether. He told the congregation in the cathedral on Synod Sunday:

'Our policy is based on fear, fear of economic competition, fear of racial admixture. But fear is a bad foundation for policy. For years the nations kept the peace because they were afraid. Such a peace could not endure, and did not endure, and a Native policy based on fear will collapse.'[1]

Soon after this Clayton, together with Hoernlé and Professor J. L. Gray of the University of the Witwatersrand, addressed the Johannesburg Society of Jews and Christians on 'The Church and the New Order'. His new order was based on the importance of the individual human being. It was not a Utopia or an earthly paradise. The old order was one of starvation in the midst of plenty, of fear and insecurity, and it prevented men from doing what they had in them to do, and caused frustration, unhappiness and crime.

Clayton was of course referring to South Africa. He called it a racialist theocracy which came from the Old Testament, but was inconsistent with the New.* He found it impossible to understand how any person, in a world

*I was not present at this meeting, and cannot help wondering how some of his audience must have reacted to this.

that science had made so small, could aim at racial segregation. He spoke of his own contribution to the new order:

'I believe that no tolerably decent life is possible in this world without a conviction that the destiny of the individual lies beyond the world. No man can live worthily in this world, no man can be a trustworthy member of any government, unless he has learnt to despise the prizes of the world. Because I believe that, I am a Minister of Religion, and am quite sure that the best contribution I can make to the building of a new world is to do my job as well as I can.'[2]

The imperfections of the old order, and especially in South Africa, began to weigh heavily upon him. He reminded his people of one of the central articles of their faith, so often forgotten, so much neglected, so little preached, that the Holy Spirit was active in the world. When people worried too much about the war, they must remember that although they could not tell God what to do, His purpose was a purpose of love. The belief that the Holy Spirit was active should save us from hypocrisy and self-deception, from the lamentably prevalent idea that the 'wounds of Society could be healed . . . by the pretence that there are no wounds to heal'.

Further, 'the guidance of the Holy Spirit should lead us to face realities and to speak the truth, but to speak the truth in love'. I must say that Clayton did not obviously do so. But what he did do was to speak the truth with great authority, with a total absence of vituperation but often a great deal of severity. If that is speaking the truth in love, then he did so speak it.

Whether it was his own initiative, or whether it was the brainchild of the Revd. A. W. Eaton, Rector of Mayfair and editor of *The Watchman*, and a vigorous critic of the old order, or whether the idea was conceived simultaneously in several people's minds, I do not know, but plans were laid to propose at the next synod the establishment of a Diocesan Commission, which was to set itself a task no less than to define what it believed to be the mind of Christ for South Africa. In *The Watchman* of September 1941 Clayton urged the parishes to choose very carefully their representatives for Synod, because Synod might be defining the attitude of the Church to the existing social order, and its hopes for a better one. It would be very important.

Clayton devoted by far the major portion of his eighth charge to the Old Order and the New. 'Today I propose to suggest some things in the life and organisation of this country which seem to be inconsistent with the principles for which we are fighting.' It was not a question of falling below standards. Sometimes there were no standards at all. Johannesburg was a beautiful and sordid city. 'Both the beauty and attractiveness and the sordidness of the underworld seem to me to suffer from the same disease, a lack of moral standards, charmingly disguised in the one case, hideously flaunted in the other.'

The freedom of the individual was rendered nugatory by an economic system which seemed to take more account of profit than of human values, and in the interest of profits it actually hindered the distribution of the fruits of the earth and the products of industry among those who needed them. South Africa was not a democracy, for one of the principles of democracy is 'no taxation without representation'. There would be many problems in giving the vote to all, but the present order was not Christian.

He referred to trusteeship, that political doctrine which like so many other South African doctrines preserved white supremacy while upholding lofty moral principles, the doctrine that the white man was the trustee and the black man the ward, that one would be just and the other be dutiful. It was J. H. Hofmeyr, Smuts's loyal and industrious Minister of Finance and Minister of Education, who while himself upholding the doctrine of trusteeship insisted always on challenging white South Africa with the difficult question, *What happens when the ward grows up?* And undoubtedly the unspoken answer was that he would never grow up. Had it not taken the white man thousands of years? And why should it take the black man any less?

Clayton said that trusteeship was an attractive principle, but it had no solution for poverty and low wages. He said there were three solutions for the question of poverty. The first was to increase wages, a solution which might temporarily reduce profits, but in the long run would create a valuable local market for South African industry. The second solution was to step up charity. The third solution was slavery, to send all Africans back to the Reserves, with provision for the men to come to the towns to work; there would be an abundance of cheap labour for white people, all on white terms, and African family life would be destroyed. 'Here it seems to me that we have the stark alternatives. On the one side profits, on the other side human values. If we choose profits, well, what are we fighting for?'

Clayton then went on to attack the administration of Johannesburg's Native Revenue Account, and to attack the practice of using the profits on the African beerhalls to make up deficits on the Revenue Account. He was in fact attacking the principle, which alas still holds today thirty years later, that African services should be paid for with African money.* Although he did not say so on this occasion, he was using the powerful and incontrovertible argument that the African worker is in the towns in the interests of white people, and that it is he who has helped the white people to become rich, and that it is therefore totally unjust that the cost of his amenities should be charged to the miserable Native Revenue Account.

Clayton said that unfortunately the actions of the Johannesburg City Council reflected general white opinion. 'But it seems to me that we ought to make it clear that there is one section of public opinion that objects to those things, that thinks they are wrong and that they ought to be stopped.'

Africans were being asked to join the army but it was hard to explain to them that South Africa was fighting for the recognition that human values are paramount.[3] The only tolerable future for the Christian to contemplate

*It is the observance of this principle that accounts for the shocking state of African education today. In 1969–70 the cost per African pupil was R16,97; the cost per white pupil was over R200.

is a just one where all can work and live freely. What was the alternative? It was a growth in the sense of frustration, a spreading sullenness and discontent, an ever-increasing friction leading to an ultimate catastrophe. 'I do know that if we don't try to do what is just and right, we shall be destroying our own souls and the souls of many others, and that after all is the worst thing that can befall.'

Clayton concluded that the war was being fought to kill an evil ideal. But our own hands were not clean. We tolerate much that is inconsistent with our aims. Our motto should be that persons are more important than things.

So ended one of the most powerful charges that Clayton had ever delivered. Clayton was neither a socialist nor an anti-capitalist, but he was a devout believer in the monitory duty of the Church towards State and Society. The more militant clergy and laity were delighted, not only those who were reputed to lean towards the left, but those who shared their bishop's belief in the Church's monitory duty. Had Clayton been a lesser man, his charge might well have caused dissatisfaction amongst those of the laity who argued that if it were not for the capitalist with his brains and energy and devotion, many black people would have had no work at all, and these critics might well have complained that Clayton had not even mentioned it. But the truth was that it was almost impossible to argue against him. This was not only because of his unassailable logic, but also because he spoke as one having authority. Nor did anyone call him a political bishop, at least not yet.

One of the consequences of Clayton's charge was that Synod passed a motion requesting the City Council to alter its financial policy in regard to the Africans of Johannesburg. It requested the Council to assist African charities and to make good deficits in the Native Revenue Account from the General Revenue Account, and to use the beerhall profits, not to finance public services, but to provide social and recreational facilities in the townships.

The Revd. A. W. Eaton also moved: 'That this Synod is of the opinion that the Church of this Diocese is . . . urgently called upon to give itself to the task of defining what it believes to be the mind of Christ for this land, and to the effective preaching and teaching of the same. To this end it respectfully asks the Bishop to set up a Commission to achieve this object.'

Eaton said that the members should come from clergy and laity who were actively engaged in trade-unionism, social welfare, race relations, economics, education, civic and political life, medicine, law, and commerce. The Commission would consult with any person who had something to contribute, regardless of his religious beliefs.

The terms of reference would be three. The first was to study the resolutions of the Malvern Conference and the Ten Points Peace Plan, which had been issued by the leaders of the British Churches, including the Cardinal Archbishop of Westminster. The second was to define the next step in the establishment of a new order in South Africa. The third was to submit the plan to the bishop, and then to Synod, within nine months. In accordance with the resolution, it was left to Clayton to appoint the members of the Commission.[4]

The words 'new order' were certainly in the air. As early as 22 May 1940, J. H. Hofmeyr told a crowd of 30,000 attending a solemn service at the Wanderers Ground, Johannesburg: 'Out of the present travail it is inevitable that a new world order will be born. We are starting on a great divide in human affairs. The issue is between a great advance and a great setback for humanity.'[5]

In that same year an unofficial committee under Hoernlé submitted to Smuts a scheme for an education service for soldiers, so that they could better understand why South Africa was in the war, and could maintain their intellectual interests. Smuts thought well of the plan, and told the Army to discuss it with Hofmeyr. Meanwhile Leo Marquard, the founder of the National Union of Students, had already started lectures and discussions at the Military College. Another enthusiast for the plan was E. G. Malherbe, who was later to become Vice-Chancellor and Principal of the University of Natal. The outcome of it all was that in February 1941 the Army Education Service was established, under Malherbe as major, later colonel, and Marquard as second-in-command. The members of the Service challenged the racial laws, customs, and conventions of South Africa and opened the eyes of many to the inconsistency of fighting Hitler abroad and supporting segregation at home. Here too it was a new order that was sought.

Smuts had also declared that there must be a new world order, and had set up the Social and Economic Council to plan security and well-being for all. In January 1942 he declared at a meeting called by the Institute of Race Relations in the Cape Town City Hall that segregation had fallen on evil days. Isolation had gone; in fact the old isolations of South Africa had gone, and gone for ever. He spoke of the neglect of African housing and the lowness of African wages. He declared that there was 'the best feeling between white and black in the new big army we have in the north', and that this was the forerunner of happiness to come.

Even Malan could not escape the fever of new-order-making. On 19 January 1940 he moved a social security motion of a far-reaching nature in Parliament. It called for a 'speedy and radical reconstruction' of the existing order, with 'social security for every individual'. It called for a 'more equitable distribution of the wealth of the country' and the elimination of parasitic economic activities. Finally it called, as it might have been expected to do, for the maintenance of the position of the white race and of white civilisation 'in accordance with the principle of trusteeship'.

We may very well conclude this account by reminding ourselves that Churchill and Roosevelt, four months before the United States entered the war, promised the world in the Atlantic Charter nothing less than freedom from war, want, tyranny, and fear. In those days nothing was too big to dream. That these dreams came largely to nothing, one must confess. That the dreaming itself had its own important function, one must maintain.

There is the saying that where there is no vision, the people perish. That saying would have been wholly acceptable to Clayton, but by 'vision' he would have meant not only some dream of the future but some plan of the present. Whether his own life came to anything, whether society was made any better by his admonitions or judgements, whether it would have made any difference to South Africa if he had never come there, are questions that we shall consider later.

He now turned to the task of setting up the Bishop's Commission. He appointed nine committees with nine convenors, the categories being Education, Industry, Economics, Social Welfare, Native Affairs, Coloured Peoples, Race Relations and Discrimination, Religious Disunity, and State. As chairman of the whole Commission he appointed Advocate D'Arcy Ussher, as secretary the Revd. A. W. Eaton, and as assistant secretary Archdeacon R. P. Y. Rouse.

To himself he allotted the task of general benevolent supervision. This kind of thing he did extremely well. He would appear at a committee meeting, affability itself. He would not obtrude himself, but would sometimes offer his own contribution. One was very conscious of the velvet glove. The iron hand would be felt later, when the whole amorphous mass would have to be given form and coherence. What better iron hand than his?

14

The Nature of Hope

There was yet another important consequence of Clayton's eighth charge to the Johannesburg Synod. It led to a discussion between himself and Hoernlé that is as relevant today as it was in 1941. This discussion was caused by the following passage in the charge:

'Those of us who still believe in what is usually called liberalism, though liberalism may mean many things, some of them good, and some of them in my judgement less good, have been challenged by a great liberal, who, if he will forgive my saying so, has lost hope, to declare what is our long-term policy in Native matters.'

A long-term policy was hard to lay down, because no one could foresee the future, but 'to Christians there are eternal principles of justice, truth and charity. To do justice and to love mercy are always right. To perpetuate injustice is always wrong. . . . "Seek ye first the Kingdom of God and His Righteousness, and all these things shall be added unto you".'

The great liberal was of course Hoernlé, and it was his approach to the question of the new order which caused Clayton to say that he had lost hope. On 20 January 1941 Hoernlé delivered the presidential address to the annual conference of the South African Institute of Race Relations.[1] This was the same conference at which Smuts had said that the policy of segregation had fallen on evil days. Hoernlé made it clear that his address expressed his private thoughts. He was not speaking in the name of the Institute, but speaking as a student of race relations. He referred to the Phelps–Stokes lectures that he had given in May 1939. These had earned him the title of 'pessimist'. 'Hoernlé has no faith. Hoernlé has no confidence in the future.'

'My reply must be uncompromising; I have no use for confidence based on illusion or on ignorance; I have no use for a faith which is unthinking, or which can flourish only in the atmosphere of an intellectual holiday.'

In his lectures he had challenged all professed 'liberals' to consider how their liberal ideals could be applied in a race–caste society. They must not think that the 'assimilationist' way was the only one. He had come to the conclusion that so long as white South Africans remained determined to maintain the present caste society, none of the 'long-range' liberal alternatives* was capable of realisation, and that liberals were therefore compelled to adopt the 'short-range' policy of exploiting trusteeship as far as domination would permit. Only a makeshift policy of trusteeship limited by domination was here and now possible.

Hoernlé was also to argue that total separation into distinct 'areas of liberty' could be considered a general liberal ideal. Hofmeyr rejected this on the grounds that white South Africa would never pay the price for it, and that because of the measure of coercion that would have to be used separation would cease to be a liberal ideal. But in his turn Hofmeyr drew back from social equality. He insisted that one must go forward in faith, not fear.

Hofmeyr was in fact one of the liberals whom Hoernlé was challenging. Hoernlé was impatient with this talk of faith from one who actually drew back from the idea of social equality and yet at the same time wanted social justice.

'I suggest that it is only when men have done their utmost in thinking things out, as an indispensable basis for acting on their principles, that they have the right to leave the outcome in the hands of God, in the faith that there is an over-ruling principle of righteousness at work in the world which shapes all things for the "best", even if that "best" turns out to be very different from the "best" as we conceived it and strove for it.'

Who could say anything truer than that? It contained the implication that some South African liberals at least had not done their utmost in thinking things out, and therefore were not entitled to fall back on faith. Hoernlé himself could not do that, partly because he was not religious in that particular sense. But what was more, he was being compelled by the intransigence of white South Africa to adopt the 'short-range' policy of exploiting trusteeship as far as possible.

Hoernlé concluded his address with these words:

'My argument is at an end. But custom demands a peroration. Let me say then that I do not believe that our caste society will endure indefinitely. If I am a "pessimist" it is not because I regard our caste society as permanent: change will come to it and transform it. But I am a pessimist in that *I deny that there is in our caste society either the will or the vision for planning and effecting this change.* Only complacency or self-delusion could lead us to believe otherwise. The changes which will come will be forced on us by world-forces and world-events over which humanity has little conscious control. Meanwhile I continue to believe in the liberal spirit and try to be its servant to the best of my ability. For, if I may quote the concluding words of my Phelps–Stokes Lectures: "There is no spiritual bridge between the dominant and the dominated other than the bridge built by those who, loving liberty for itself, will not be content until it is enjoyed, not only by themselves, but by all those to whom it is now denied".'

Clayton's assertion that Hoernlé had 'lost hope' was certainly influenced

*Among such 'long-range' liberal alternatives were a non-racial franchise (whether universal or qualified), removal of the colour-bar in industry, and a common political society.

also by Hoernlé's contribution to the symposium on the 'new order' held by the Society of Jews and Christians in December 1940, in which Clayton and Professor J. L. Gray also took part.

Hoernlé was blunt and to the point. 'Have we any reason to believe that as a result of the present war, a 'new order' in the relations between Whites and Blacks will come into being? My own answer to this question is NO.'

A 'new order' would have to make an end of the master-race versus servant-race structure. In theory this could be done in two ways. One would be to extend the franchise to Africans on the same terms on which whites possess it. But more important would be professional and social equality. Would whites agree? The answer again was NO.

The alternative was not segregation but separation, the sorting out of the multi-racial caste society into separate and ultimately self-determining racial groups, each forming its own self-contained society. The Native Reserves formed a small starting-point for such an order. 'But the great obstacle to its realisation is that our White economy is so completely based on cheap Native labour that we shall never freely agree to the economic revolution involved in shifting to a purely White labour system, as in Europe or in Australia.'

Although Hoernlé could see no hope for a 'new order', he believed that progress could be made in education, health, housing, recreation, agriculture, wages and medical and dental training. Such things would keep hope alive, until the caste society was destroyed, not by white leadership within, but by world-events from without, or by the Africans 'taking their fate into their own hands'.

While Hoernlé dealt specifically with the chances for a 'new order' to come into being, and expressed the opinion that they were minimal, Clayton had stated equally bluntly that he did not believe in the possibility of a Utopia or earthly paradise. 'But I do believe profoundly in the value and importance of the individual human being.' He also propounded two possibilities for South Africa. One was segregation, which he regarded as impossible. The other was trusteeship. Why should it not be given its true meaning, 'with a recognition of the fact that trusteeship comes to an end when the ward comes of age'? Was that Clayton's 'hope', the 'hope' that Hoernlé had lost? If it were, it did not seem to justify the use of such strong language.[2]

Hoernlé wrote to Clayton that he did not think the sentence 'who, if he will forgive my saying so, has lost hope' was justified. After congratulating Clayton on his charge and his criticism of the use of beerhall profits, he came to 'the contentious topic of hope', assuming that he was the 'great liberal' referred to. He did not like the adjective 'great'; it made him squirm though he appreciated the compliment.

Was Clayton right to declare, *without qualification*, that he had lost hope? Had not Hoernlé said at the symposium, 'Things like these will continue to happen and to keep hope alive'? Clayton had not replied to his challenge to liberals, who should acknowledge that their limited improvements were possible only because they did not undermine the pillars of the race–caste society. Clayton had been 'sadly unfair' to one who had 'elaborately distinguished between a practicable "short-range" policy for Liberals and insuperable obstacles in the way of a "long-range" policy'. Hoernlé wrote, 'If anything could make me lose hope *altogether*, it would be the experience of being so consistently misinterpreted even by men like yourself.'

Hoernlé quoted D. L. Smit, Secretary for Native Affairs, who had said to him: 'I cannot afford to think ahead: I can act only from day to day, snatching opportunities for Native advancement as they present themselves.' And that, wrote Hoernlé, was Clayton's policy, and his own too.

'Thus, on this "short-range" plane of gaining a point here and protesting against an injustice there, we are all at one, and no question of hope or lack of hope arises.

'That question arises only when one tries to take the "long-range" view which – may I repeat? – means for me asking oneself whether all one's efforts have any effect, indeed are intended to have any effect, on the racial caste structure of our society. Taking this "long-range" view, I report no visible grounds for hope. You refuse to take this long-range view, and so the question of hope on *that* plane does not trouble you. But – is that any sound basis for accusing me of having lost hope altogether?'

Hoernlé ended with a paragraph that showed clearly his respect for Clayton, and defined again, in the briefest possible way, his 'short-range' policy.

'Forgive, please, this overlong diatribe – or, rather, please accept it, not only as my reaction to your references to myself, but as a tribute to the incisive courage with which you have put the case against the flaws in our Municipal Native Policy. For, even if the reforms you ask for (and which have my whole-hearted support) do not alter the racial caste society character of the Union, they will make it a *better* society of that type. And, if I must be a member of a caste society, I would prefer it to be better of its kind rather than worse!'[3]

A few days later Hoernlé and five others wrote to the *Star*, criticising the City Council's reply to Clayton's condemnation of the practice of using African beerhall profits to make up deficits on the Native Revenue Account. The spokesman for the Council had declared that this was only 'fortuitous', but Hoernlé pointed out that in the budget speech for 1941–42, Councillor Corlett had declared that the Native Revenue Account had now become self-supporting. This was because of the beerhall profits, and this had now become official policy, and that could hardly be described as 'fortuitous'.

The spokesman also blamed white public opinion, but Hoernlé asked if the councillors had ever put the position clearly before the public 'as the Bishop has now so courageously done'.

Hoernlé concluded that the policy of a 'self-balancing' Native Revenue Account meant that 'The white ratepayers are encouraged, without knowing what they are doing, to shuffle out of their responsibilities to the poorest of the poor, on whom is cast the whole burden of paying, through another form of indirect taxation, for even the most necessary improvement in their lives'.[4]

Just as Hoernlé had first congratulated Clayton on his charge before objecting to one portion of it, so Clayton congratulated Hoernlé on his letter to the *Star* before replying to his objection. He wrote that he was glad that the City Council had been put on the defensive. His opinion of Councillor Immink, who was responsible for Non-European Affairs, was not high. The African Township Committee, a citizens' watchdog body of which Clayton was a member, had invited Immink to meet them over the Native Revenue Account. Immink accepted the invitation but said he would not have done so had Father Raynes of Sophiatown been present, and added that he understood that Raynes's colleagues did not agree with his trenchant criticisms of the Council. Clayton wrote that he thought it better to say nothing for the moment, but that he then and there determined to range himself publicly behind what Raynes had said, and that he was delighted by Synod's unanimous support for the condemnatory resolution moved and seconded by laymen.

'Now, as to the question of "hope". It has seemed to me that your attitude has changed since I first met you. You used, I thought, to speak and write as one who, though in a minority, thought it worth while to advocate changes in the structure of S.A. society. Now you seem to me to take the line that the structure of S.A. society is fixed, and that all that is possible is ambulance work for the victims of that fixed society.'

Clayton used words to Hoernlé that I do not know him to have used to any other person. It seemed 'absolutely impertinent' for him to criticise Hoernlé. He did not want to seem patronising, for that would be 'the height of insolent absurdity'. Hoernlé was doing more 'than twenty people like myself'.

'Yet I must confess that I said what I did about you in my Charge quite deliberately. Like you, I do not see how any change in the structure of Society is to come. I see no signs of such a change, and yet it seems to me that the criticism and development of ambulance work within the present framework may in itself lead to gradual changes in the framework itself. If Native Education can improve, if the economic position of Natives improves, it seems to me possible that the Walls of Jericho may fall down of themselves.'

Clayton agreed with Hoernlé's quotation from D. L. Smit. He himself could not look forward far. Gates seemed to be barred.

'But yet I can't despair. You may think it sloppy and sentimental of me. But I am disposed to adapt to the Native situation the lines of Clough that Churchill quoted in another connection: "In front the sun mounts slow, how slowly! But westward, see, the land is bright."

'I think the difference between us is one of attitude to life. I am more prepared to allow for the entrance into history of an incalculable factor. When we have done our best, the resources of the universe are not exhausted. Probably if we sat down and argued the thing out, we should find that our real difference was one of religious belief.'[5]

Hoernlé would not accept this last statement. Though he did not accept 'all the details of Christian dogma' he had no hesitation in subscribing to Clayton's phrase 'prepared to allow for the entrance into history of an incalculable factor', and to the statement that 'when we have done our best, the resources of the universe are not exhausted'. For Hoernlé the real difference was not religious belief at all. It lay in the interpretation of the words 'doing our best'. For Clayton it meant applying his principles to given situations, in the hope that by a cumulative process of 'nibbling', a bad system would be transformed into a better. For Hoernlé this was 'not good enough'.

'It is not good enough to meet a false Christian race-philosophy and its corresponding social order by vague generalities *plus* a refusal to draw the outline picture, at least, of the sort of social order which, in our opinion, would be more truly Christian.'

Hoernlé emphasised that when he said 'No hope' he meant to shock people, and especially Christians, into saying, 'We will prove you wrong.' He concluded by writing that Clayton had not caused him pain; sincere and friendly criticism could never cause him pain.[6]

What indeed were these two giants arguing about? They both believed that 'confidence based on illusion or on ignorance' was valueless. They both believed that ambulance work had to be done. They both believed there was an incalculable factor in history. They both believed that 'vague generalities' were not enough, and Clayton's synod was on the point of setting up a Commission to define what it believed to be 'the mind of Christ for this land'. One could hardly suppose that this was done solely because of Hoernlé's challenge. Hoernlé may have had the intention of shocking people into action, but he had said categorically that only world-forces and world-events would do it.

There were at least two differences, but the first was not a fundamental one. Clayton clearly felt that any person of authority and responsibility should be careful in what he said, lest he discourage others. In his letter of 25 October he wrote: 'It has, however, seemed to me that your pessimism about a long-range policy is calculated to discourage some others who may be less strong than yourself.' In other words, there were times when such a person should keep his peace.

The second difference was more important. There can be no doubt that the utterances of the Hebrew prophets moved Clayton deeply. Isaiah had prophesied that the sucking child would play on the hole of the asp, and the weaned child would put his hand on the cockatrice's den, after there had come forth a rod out of the stem of Jesse. But what could that mean? Was that confidence based on illusion? Was Isaiah having an intellectual holiday? The truth is that the apocalyptic vision has held generations of Jews and Christians in thrall, and that it is inseparable from hope, and that it has no intellectual justification whatsoever. It could move Clayton powerfully, but it had nothing to do with this world, there being no earthly paradise. It is both incredible and ineffable. Faith is essentially a journey of the heart. That is not to suggest that Hoernlé had no heart; no one had a heart more brave or warm. But more so than Clayton, he was a man of the mind.

Hoernlé sent the Clayton–Hoernlé letters to D. L. Smit. Smit wrote to him:

'I can never hope to be the philosopher that you are, but I have tried to build up a simple philosophy of my own, which helps to keep me steady when things go wrong.

'I do not think we should worry too much about the future. What matters in life is the present and the amount of good we can achieve in it.

'Concerning the future, I believe that "somehow good will be the final goal of ill", and that is as far as I can let my mind travel just now.'[7]

What Hoernlé thought of the saying 'somehow good will be the final goal of ill', we do not know. He might have smiled at it wistfully. He wrote humbly to Smit: 'I am really grateful to you for telling me the spirit in which you are carrying on your work. If I were in your position, I would hope that my work would be animated by the same spirit.'[8]

In less than two years Hoernlé was dead. One of his last acts was to print and publish an open letter to the white citizens of Johannesburg, protesting against the proposal to remove the inhabitants of the African township of Alexandra, eleven miles from the City Hall, and challenging them to protest also. Though he was not a churchman his funeral service was held in St. Mary's Cathedral. It was conducted by Dean Palmer, and the bishop read the lesson. It was attended by a distinguished congregation of people of all races. There was no sermon, but before the closing prayers the Dean spoke these words:

'I bid you give thanks for the life and example of Alfred Hoernlé; for the inspiration of his teaching, for the wideness of his social service for the subject races of this land, for his indignation at all that was less than just in man's relationship to man, for the witness of a life in which the values of freedom, opportunity and justice for all were consistently set forth.'

After the closing prayers the bishop gave the blessing.

The Watchman of August 1943 wrote: 'The non-Europeans can ill afford to lose such a magnificent servant. For their servant he had always been.' The preface to *Cry, The Beloved Country*, published in 1948, called him 'the prince of Kafferboeties'.* The writer could think of no higher praise than that.

*'Kafferboetie' is an Afrikaans word which means literally 'little brother of the Kaffir'. It is a term of contempt used by a number of white South Africans of any white person who concerns himself with the needs and aspirations and deprivations of black people, to what his fellows regard as an undue and extravagant extent.

15

Church and Nation

The search for the new order continued unabated. In 1942 the South African Association for the Advancement of Science took as its main theme 'Science and Post-War Reconstruction'. In that same month the Christian Council of South Africa, of which the Dutch Reformed churches and the Roman Catholic Church were not members, held a large conference at the University College of Fort Hare on 'Christian Reconstruction'. John Russell Darbyshire, Archbishop of Cape Town, said in his opening address:

'The truth is that behind what are put up as the problems and social wrongs of our day there are disorders and perversions that can only be brought to light in the light of revealed Truth which is enshrined and (as it were) made incarnate in the historic dogmas of the Church, that is, in Christian Theology.'

Unfortunately in the divided state of South African Christianity it was easy to believe that the disorders and perversions were to be found on the other side. It is impossible to effect any reconciliation between those who believe that in Christ all racial barriers are broken down, and those who believe that it is God's will that racial separation should be maintained, and that it can only be done by legislation. To plan together for any reconstruction of South African society while this irreconcilability persists is impossible. There is little comfort in the belief that one must change men before one can change society. Must one change all men? Or only an electoral majority? And meanwhile must society be allowed to run its course unchecked?

The Revd. A. W. Eaton, editor of *The Watchman,* wrote of this conference:

'The issue that confronts us is between Catholicism and Calvinism. When we are capable of an understanding of these two faiths which form our dual ancestry we shall be equipped to see our more immediate problems in their true perspectives. And only then will it be time to call another Conference on reconstruction.'[1]

One might reply to Eaton that it was not an understanding but a reconciliation of these two faiths that was required. In South Africa today this seems impossible, but in the rest of the world Catholicism and Calvinism at least talk to each other. In South Africa they do not. And while each stands identified with views on race and race policy which are fundamentally incompatible, it is hard to see that they ever will be reconciled. Is it religion that divides the white Christians of South Africa, or is it history, or is it something compounded of both? Whatever may be true, it is clear that the conference at Fort Hare found a great measure of unanimity on the problems of the new order, only because the Dutch Reformed churches were not represented.* For some of the delegates the supreme event of the conference was not to be found in any discussion or resolution. It happened when a little old man came to the lectern to conduct the closing service of dedication, and read the passage 'In the beginning was the Word, and the Word was with God, and the Word was God', ending with the words 'And the light shineth in darkness, and the darkness comprehended it not'. Many of his hearers were filled with intense emotion, not so much because of the words, but because of the utter devotion with which they were read, and the humble love with which the book was held in those old, frail hands. The Fort Hare Conference gave no reconciliation, only the sight of a saint. His name was the Revd. A. W. Wilkie, and he had been the principal of the famous missionary school of Lovedale.

Meanwhile the Bishop's Commission was doing its best to comprehend the light, but it soon became clear that the task could not be performed in the nine months allotted to it. At the end of that time the work had scarcely begun, and Advocate D'Arcy Ussher resigned the chairmanship, thus making way for Clayton himself. One might well say that apart from the usual work of the diocese, and apart from the special duties that came into being solely because of the war, such as the provision of chaplains and church-buildings in the various camps, including a chaplain and chapel at the giant military hospital at Baragwanath just eight miles outside Johannesburg, the work of the Bishop's Commission was to Clayton the most important task that the Church could perform in this time of war. What is more, the diocese was performing the task on behalf of the whole Church of the Province, and that made it still more important.

Clayton therefore gave more and more of his time and energy to the Commission, and left his own individual and ineffaceable mark on its work. He wrote that the Church had two missions, the one to try to establish a more Christian social order, the other to care for the individual in the present order.[2] Clayton was one of those Christians who did not at all object to visions, provided one realised that they came true only through hard work in the present. Some people have been described as having their heads in the clouds and their feet firmly planted on the ground. The idea of that great head being in the clouds would have been absurd. It was more likely to have been in those podgy hands, with their owner groaning at the folly of some synod speech or resolution. His character, so clearly revealed in his synodical charges, was equally clear in his attitude towards taking a holiday

*The Revd. J. M. Hofmeyr of Somerset East, the Revd. J. Reyneke of Pretoria, and the Revd. F. J. Berning Malan participated in the conference, but not as representatives. All were held in high esteem by the other churchmen.

in time of war.

'I am not at all happy about going for a holiday in times like these, when naturally one would like to be at one's post, trying to do one's work, but on the whole I have come to the conclusion that I shall not be much use to you next summer unless I get a holiday now.'[3]

His charge to Synod 1942 indicated that the work of the Commission was uppermost in his mind. He reported that the City Council had followed the recommendations of the Synod of 1941, and had eased the burdens placed on the Native Revenue Account, but it should pay increased attention to the demolition of slums and the provision of new housing, and to the lack of schools for African children, all of which had such a grave relevance to the growth of criminality. Yet another factor contributing to crime was the lack of recreational facilities for domestic servants. Here Clayton was touching on an issue, seemingly trivial in itself, but vital to an understanding of the strange nature of South African society. The white suburbs of the towns and cities are full of black servants, who, if they have nothing else to do in their free time, and no place to go, congregate in the streets, and sing, shout, play their guitars and their portable radios, and sometimes become drunk and disorderly. Public-minded white citizens are always clamouring for the provision of recreational facilities, but there is always tremendous opposition from those citizens who live near the sites proposed for these facilities. Some of these citizens are good and considerate employers, but to the questions raised by the existence of say five thousand servants in a white suburb of ten thousand residents, they have no solution. No one is more aware of this than the Nationalist Government. Their solution has been, first to limit the number of servants who may be employed, secondly to limit the number who may sleep on their employers' premises, and thirdly, in some cases to forbid all servants to sleep in the white sections of towns and cities. Thus white complaints are met, white security is ensured, and one can use the argument that African home life is preserved.*

In his charge Clayton appealed for elected African representation on the City Council, for the abolition of the colour-bar in industry, and for a social-security code for all. One must report that today one must still appeal for the same things. The colour-bar in industry greatly impedes the economic growth of the country, and it is generally recognised that there is a perennial struggle between ideology and economics, and that ideology, though grievously wounded, always wins. One needs much money to implement the grandiose schemes of racial separation, and it is the attempt to implement the grandiose schemes of racial separation that make it impossible to get the money.

Here Clayton, so far as I know, introduced for the first time a new phrase, a piece of practical advice that he was to repeat many times during the rest

*This third solution is too simple. The homes of many servants are far distant, and their travelling costs are greatly increased. The only final solution would be for there to be no servants at all, but that would be brought about only by great industrial expansion, which seems unlikely at the moment. See following paragraph.

of his life. First the Christian must get his objectives clear, he must know toward what end he is working. Then he must decide *what is the next step*. Clayton later was to make the advice both practical and moral; he was to say that when you could not see clearly how you would reach your objective, then *you must do the next right thing*. With this advice he was often to encourage those who were disheartened and frustrated, and were in danger of giving up the struggle. On this note he ended his charge.

'And so we plan for the world and for the Church, and we are right to do so, for God would work through us. But if we depend on our own wisdom and our own strength we should quickly despair. But the world is not our world; it is God's world, and the Church is not our Church, it is God's Church. And God is Love.'

One last thing is worth noting. Synod passed a motion in favour of admitting women to Provincial and diocesan synods. Clayton abstained from both comment and vote.[4]

So the work of the Bishop's Commission continued for another year. It had already completed a very important part of its work, and that was, before it turned to the task of defining what it believed to be the mind of Christ for South Africa, to draw up a statement of the fundamentals of Christian faith. This, after an introductory clause A, was contained in clause B of what came to be known as *The Church and the Nation* Report.

Clause B was largely Clayton's own work. To him it was useless to jump into the fight for a better world, armed only with good will. One had to understand clearly one's nature and destiny as a child of the Creator, and therefore one's duty to other men who were one's brothers. A Christian in search of the new order must take realistic account of sin. Neither intellectual enlightenment nor a change in institutions can save society and man without a change of will. It is not part of the Church's mission to plan for the reformation or organisation of society, but it is the duty of Christian men. And it is in that belief that the recommendations of the Commission will be made.

The Commission then turned to consideration of the relationship between Church and State; the ethics of economics and industry; racial segregation; and the task of effective Christian teaching. Most of the members of the Commission, including myself, had never before confronted these questions. They were Christians who lived in the world and yet wished to be faithful to the teaching of the Gospel.*

To yield the idea of a continuing white supremacy was in those days an intensely difficult thing for a white South African to do. In my young days, before the foundation of the National Union of Students, hardly a student attempted to do so. What was called the 'race problem', or worse, the 'native problem', was seldom discussed. As one grew older one clung to the idea that somehow one could maintain white supremacy and yet be just. One had not learned to understand that justice might be the interest of the stronger. One either did not think about these things at all, or one alternated

*Of the original personnel, 31 were white and 2 black.

between moods of pessimism and hope. One loved what was right and good and just, but one did not yet understand that these things could not be had except at the cost of a change in one's whole life and situation. In my twenties and thirties few white South Africans had faced the possibility of radical change except the communists.

One had now to face the realisation that white supremacy and the principles of clause B were irreconcilable. I cannot speak for others, but I must record that being a member of the Bishop's Commission was one of the seminal events of my life, after which I was never the same again.* Whether that was true of other white South Africans like Margaret Ballinger and Redvers Rouse, I could not say. It affected others in yet a different way; the Revd. A. W. Eaton and the Revd. Tom Comber eventually returned to England, having given up hope that the new order would ever be achieved by the peaceful means of persuasion and change of heart. Several laymen, as we shall see later, found certain findings of the Commission unacceptable.

As for myself, having lived for 38 years in the dark, the Commission opened for me a door, and I went through into the light and I shut it against myself, and entered a new country whose very joys and adversities were made resplendent by the light. This conversion can in a way never be complete, because one continues to live in a colour-bar society, and to obey its laws and to benefit by its privileges. If one did not, one might leave the country or spend the rest of one's life in prison. Some can bear it no longer and they go, and there arises an incompatibility between some of them and those who do not go, caused in part by the irreconcilability of the two views, the one that the honourable thing to do is to get out, the other that the honourable thing to do is to stay.

Yet another incompatibility is possible and common. That is between the Christian who finally rejects and opposes the policies of racial separation, and *first* the Christian who supports them, and *second* the Christian who regards them as politics and thinks that the Church should not be involved with them.

The other clauses of the Report *The Church and the Nation* confirmed powerfully the argument that white supremacy and the Gospel are irreconcilable. Clause C dealt with Church and State, and expounded fully in unmistakable Claytonian language, the 2,000-year-old puzzle of the respective claims of God and Caesar. Certainly a Christian must render Caesar's things to Caesar, but he must remember that it is God who declares what belongs to Caesar. The Commission declared that the witness of the Church of the Province was weakened by two factors. The one was that its white members were almost exclusively English-speaking. The other was that it was not made sufficiently clear that Anglicans who were not white were welcome at any altar. The Commission criticised the Nation too, by which

*The seminal events were: a Christian upbringing; joining the Student Christian Association (aged 16); becoming principal of Diepkloof Reformatory (aged 32); joining the South African Institute of Race Relations (aged 33); the Bishop's Commission (aged 38); membership of the Liberal Party of South Africa (aged 51).

it meant white South Africa and its Government.* It was fighting a war for the rights of men, but 'the charge of hypocrisy cannot be avoided if through the laws and customs of this land, these rights are refused to any of its people on account of colour'.

Clause D dealt with economics and industry. The profit motive must be subordinated to human values. Opportunity to acquire and use skills must be given to all. The control of a community's industrial resources by a few is contrary to God's plan. Gross inequalities of income, maintained by racial laws, are condemned. African wages and housing are shocking. There must be a 'gradual removal of the colour-bar' in industry. Governments and local authorities should lead the way in the raising of wages. The system of migratory labour is to be condemned, on grounds of morality and inefficiency.

Clause E dealt with racial segregation. There was no final wrong principle in segregation, only in enforced segregation.† Occupational segregation, later to be called job reservation, is to be condemned. So is educational segregation, though the Report did not condemn separate schools for separate groups, but rather inequality of funds and equipment, and for so many children the absence of schools altogether. The Report condemned territorial and social segregation, and then went on to deal with the most difficult question of all, that of political representation.

The Report favoured:

1. The extension of the Cape franchise for Coloured men to all Coloured men and women throughout the Union.
2. The extension of the Cape franchise for Indian men to all Indian men and women throughout the Union.
3. The extension of the Cape franchise for African men to all African men and women throughout the Union.
4. The increase for the time being in the number (three) of *white* M.P.s, and in the number (four) of *white* Senators, who represented African voters, but the ultimate aim should be
5. A common roll for all citizens, so that through common election, M.P.s should represent *all* qualified voters in the constituencies.‡

The proposals of the Bishop's Commission were for that time revolutionary, but they were very far from breaking the white monopoly of power. The number of Coloured, Indian, and African males who had so far exercised the Cape franchise was a small fraction of the total because of the

*Afrikaner Nationalists never use the word 'nation' in this way. The Afrikaners form a nation, as do the Zulus, Xhosas, Sotho, etc. South Africa is thus a 'multi-national' country. Unfortunately the English-speaking, the Indians, and the Coloured people do not fit well into this grandiose scheme.

†I assume this means you may segregate yourself but not others. And I assume that means on your own property and not in any public amenity. The assertion of 'no final wrong principle' is from a Christian point of view highly debatable.

‡I remind readers that the Cape franchise was extended only to Coloured, Indian, and African *men*, and these had to have certain qualifications of literacy and income not required by white men and women.

educational and financial attainments of their groups. What was more, the Commission did not state specifically that voters on the proposed common roll should elect M.P.s of any race or colour; the implication of the whole Report was that all discrimination based solely on race or colour should go, but this particular implication was not explicitly stated.

Finally, clause F dealt with the necessity, in schools of Church and State, for Christian teaching which could prepare children for this new order, and clause G concluded as follows:

'In making public this Report we are aware that to implement its findings demands first of all a change of heart within the nation. To this end we believe it to be of the utmost importance that the nation be called back to God, and to a whole-hearted obedience to, and love for, Him and His Church. We are convinced that the need to sound clearly this evangelistic note is as great now as it has ever been. We pray that this note will be sounded by all who accept this Report.

Signed on behalf of Synod
✠ GEOFFREY JOHANNESBURG.'

The actual reading, discussion, and adoption of the Report by Synod was an event not easily to be forgotten. There was only one person who could possibly write the Report, and that was the bishop. He therefore retired to the peace of Swaziland, and there, working many hours a day, he produced *The Church and the Nation*. On 15 November 1943, after Clayton had read clause A, the Revd. A. W. Eaton and Archdeacon Rouse presented it to Synod, reading its seven clauses paragraph by paragraph.

There were two main grounds on which such a Report might be criticised. The first would be on the grounds of clarity and style. The second ground of criticism would be that of the principles, judgements, and opinions. It was now known to many if not all members of Synod that the bishop had written the Report. It was recognised that he was a master of the English language, certainly a master of clarity and brevity, and had never been known to make a syntactical error. It would have taken a brave man to criticise the actual language of the Report. However there was such a man, and he was the Revd. Percy Forbes, Rector of Klerksdorp, tall, dark, distinguished-looking, formidable in his own fashion. Though not a great speaker or writer, he was much respected as a scholar, and was in his own way also a master of the English language. If his mastery differed from that of the bishop, it would have lain in the fact that he was more precise, more exact; some might have said that he was more pedantic.

It was soon clear that he intended to subject the language of the Report to the most searching scrutiny, and that he would be quite capable of adding considerably to the length of this particular session. It is well known that a Synod or any other gathering is the worst possible judge as to whether one word or phrase is better than another. However Forbes intended to make Synod decide.

Clayton's first reactions were typical. His always mobile face showed good-humour, tolerance, and amusement. If Forbes's proposed amendment seemed absurd Clayton would scratch his head in puzzlement, and put the proposal with baffled resignation. When it became clear that Forbes was not to be deterred by any of the chairman's reactions, the first faint sign of displeasure showed itself. By this time the members of Synod were agog. They had already realised that they were witnessing a spectacle not often to be seen, and all for nothing. They settled themselves in their seats and prepared to enjoy it.

Clayton now realised that Forbes would not be stopped. He thought – and many others with him – that many of the amendments, if accepted, would add nothing of value to the Report. He thought – and others with him – that his own English was of a reasonably high standard. He realised that his time-table was being disrupted. As the battle proceeded, his look of displeasure became permanent. He put his head in his hands, picked his nose, scowled, even laughed incredulously that a clever man like Forbes could be capable of such absurdities.

It was not Forbes however who precipitated the crisis, though he no doubt did his share in making it inevitable. It was those who wanted the report to have teeth, who wanted not grand moralising but plans for action, who wanted a crusading Church. Some only asked for stronger language and more direct statement. It is impossible now to remember who said what, but amongst those who wanted more action and stronger language were Arthur Blaxall, Tom Comber, Maurice Clack and two newcomers to the diocese, Father Trevor Huddleston and the Revd. Michael Scott.* While such people would welcome the assertion that the Church acknowledges no limits to the sphere of its influence, they wanted more than that. Huddleston and Scott were both men of action, and were both to become well known, if not famous, as 'political priests', winning in general the devotion of the poor and the hostility of the rich.

Such a sentence as 'the charge of hypocrisy cannot be avoided if through the laws and customs of this land, these rights are refused to any of its people on account of colour' was regarded with disfavour by many members of Synod, because it presented as a hypothesis a state of affairs that actually existed. The phrase 'a gradual removal of the colour-bar' came under heavy fire. If the colour-bar were a wrong, then why should the Church ask for its gradual removal? This conflict between idealists and pragmatists is perpetually present in any kind of organisation. To Clayton, the demand for the immediate removal of the colour-bar was absurd. To the idealists it was intolerable that the Church should identify itself with a policy of gradualism.

The conflict went yet deeper. Clause G of the Report contained these words, 'we are aware that to implement its findings demands first of all a

*Blaxall, with his wife Florence, was a great worker for the blind, deaf and dumb; Comber, Rector of St. Mary's, Jeppe; Clack, Priest-in-charge, St. Alban's Coloured Mission; Huddleston, Community of the Resurrection; and Scott, Assistant Priest to Maurice Clack.

change of heart within the nation'. Now what did that mean? Did it not mean that they would never be implemented? Was there no other way of bringing about reform in society? Was the front not wider than that of pure evangelism?

At last Clayton could bear it no longer. He jumped to his feet, obviously under the influence of great emotion. His voice, always powerful, was now tremendous.

'The Church is not here primarily to serve society. Its prime duty is to worship God and obey Him. And if it is God's will that we should serve society in this or that way, then it is our duty to do it. Let us therefore be very careful that it is God's will we are trying to obey, and that we are not merely trying to make the Church do something that we want to be done. And let me make it quite clear that I appointed this Commission because I believed it might be God's will that we should serve our society in this and that way.'[5]

Then with a strange look, compounded of embarrassment and triumph, he sat down. From that moment the reading of the paragraphs and their adoption went swiftly ahead. So far as I remember, even the indomitable Forbes decided to accept the language of the rest of the Report.

So here again was manifested this strange element in Clayton's character. No one asserted more strongly than he the duty of the Church to concern itself with the affairs of nation and society, no one would have been more critical of a Church that confined itself to piety, no one wanted more than he that the Church should be active in the world, but he never fully trusted others who believed in and wanted the same things. It was not their beliefs he distrusted, but the way they set about things. He did not really trust anyone's wisdom except his own. His distrust of Huddleston and Scott was later to amount to an incompatibility. There was yet one other thing that divided them. All three could be critical of the Church, but whereas Clayton adopted an attitude of confession and contrition, the other two could adopt an attitude of accusation. Furthermore Clayton felt their criticisms deeply because in a way he was the Church. Therefore when they criticised the Church they were criticising him, and like most of us, he did not like it.

He was in fact more patient with those who wanted the Church not to go so far and so fast than with those who wanted it to go further and faster. Three important lay members of the Commission could not accept paragraphs 18 and 19 of clause D, entitled 'The Church, Economics and Industry'. These paragraphs read as follows:

'18. The wage situation is complicated by the fact that on the average one third of the total number of natives employed on the gold mines are imported from outside the Union and Protectorates. This has a depressing effect on the wages of all Union natives in all employments. At the same time we suffer in the Union from an under-employment of labour. The alleged shortage of labour is mainly a shortage at low wages.

'19. The system of migratory labour in industrial and urban employment is generally wasteful, being damaging to the natives in the reserves, and leading to a very wasteful use of labour, so that workers are prevented by this system from being worth a higher wage. The amount of such labour should be progressively reduced.

'We do not overlook the fact that this system is the cause of grave moral evils attendant upon the separation of men from their womenfolk, and the grouping of them together in compounds. These evil results in themselves are enough to condemn the system.'

These three members of the Commission were all of them connected with the mining industry, and therefore could not bring themselves to admit the evils of the system of migratory labour. They would have found it still more difficult to accept a paragraph which would have stated boldly that the great wealth of the gold-mining industry came not from gold, but from black men's wages. All three were pillars of the diocese, and when they announced their inability to subscribe to paragraphs D.18 and D.19 Clayton accepted their decision gravely.

Another important layman could not accept paragraph 5 (c) (iv) of clause E, which declared that the ultimate political aim should be a common electoral roll for all qualified citizens, and that the time would come when separate representation would lead to conflict rather than union. His decision was also accepted.

So a mighty labour came to an end. It must be said that thirty years later, in 1973, another Bishop's Commission would produce a report not markedly different from the first. In certain respects, for example the relationship between State and Church, the position has much deteriorated. The State has given itself extraordinary powers over the life and freedom of its citizens, and these powers can be exercised without recourse to the courts of law. Worst of all, the gap between white and black income is as great as ever.

Did the Commission achieve anything? Did Clayton's life achieve anything? These are questions that must later be considered.

16

A Magnificent Chapter

The year 1943 saw the end of a magnificent chapter in the history of the diocese and in the history of its missionary activity in Johannesburg. For in that year two extraordinary people left to return to England. One was Dorothy Maud, who in December left in order to test her vocation in a contemplative order. The other was Raymond Raynes, who left Sophiatown to return to Mirfield, where he would assume the office of the Superior of the world-wide Community of the Resurrection.

Dorothy Maud had, as a vivacious, gifted and attractive woman in her early thirties, offered her services to the Church through the Society for the Propagation of the Gospel, and was willing to go anywhere. Father Osmund Victor of the Community of the Resurrection advised her to go to Africa, and a headmistress in Westmorland promised to pay her salary. Meanwhile Bishop Karney, who was at that time on holiday in England, asked her to go back with him to the diocese of Pretoria, to work in the slums of Johannesburg which at that time formed part of Karney's diocese.

Dorothy Maud was sent to work for Wilfrid Parker, Vicar of St. Cyprian's, later himself to become Bishop of Pretoria. He sent her to Zululand to learn Zulu, and when she returned she took the tram each day from the city to Sophiatown, that tempestuous township of some 50,000 people.

In Sophiatown there was a little tin church, and a minute clinic run by Dr. Mary Tugman and three other woman doctors in the African headmaster's house. Neither Mary Tugman nor Dorothy Maud was trusted. Dorothy Maud visited the locations and townships for five years, and taught in the small Sunday school. It could have broken her heart, but it did not. She said to Parker, 'We must *live* there.' They bought land for a house in Sophiatown. That was legal then, but such transactions are so no longer, for no person of one racial group may now buy land or property in an area designated for another group, nor indeed can any non-black person conduct any activity whatsoever in any black area without official permission, and unless under stringent observation.

Karney said that Dorothy Maud must have at least two companions and a car, and all three turned up in a short time. She needed £4,000 for her house and a club room. Most of the money came from and through her father and mother, though she would always insist, in her emphatic and laughing and unpious way, that it came from God. Indeed when the money ran out, and the builder asked what security she could offer, she answered, 'Heaven', but he told her that wouldn't do for him. A woman then unknown lent her £1,000 and she said to the builder, 'What about Heaven now?' So the house was built, with five bedrooms, a sitting-room, offices, and a chapel.[1] It was called 'Ekutuleni', the Place of Peace. The breakthrough had begun. The clubroom was separate but adjoining, and provided many activities, including boxing taught by Dorothy Maud. There were baptism and confirmation classes, because for her the social gospel and the evangel were one and inseparable. She wanted to bring colour and light into the lives of the people of Sophiatown, and the brightest colour and the most shining light were the knowledge and love of the Lord. She had what is known as a hunger for souls, not so that she might collect them and make them her own, but so that they might be given to the Lord.

In 1929 Princess Alice, wife of the Governor-General the Earl of Athlone, visited the house and planted a tree, and the new hospital, yet to be built, was named after her. It is hard to recapture the atmosphere of those days. Princess Alice and Dorothy Maud, though not exactly of the same rank, spoke the same kind of language, and recognition by the Governor-General and his wife was something to be thankful for. It has all gone. Any Englishwoman of the stature and vigour of Dorothy Maud would always be in danger of being deported. And the field in which she would have to labour would be immensely restricted. All this was yet to happen, and we shall read of it in due course.

In 1930 Dorothy Maud fell ill and took a holiday in England, returning with Margaret Leake, Clare Lawrence, and Winifred Munton. The work continued to expand, but in 1934 occurred a series of events which turned the breakthrough into a torrent. On 24 May 1934 Geoffrey Clayton was enthroned bishop in St. Mary's Cathedral, Johannesburg. One of his first acts was after consultation with St. John's College Council to appoint Sydney Herbert Clarke as headmaster; thus the Community of the Resurrection severed its connection with St. John's. Clayton then asked the Community to take charge of the parish of Sophiatown, and on 13 December Father Raymond Raynes, C.R., was inducted as priest-in-charge. So began the extraordinary partnership of Raynes and Dorothy Maud.[2]

Dorothy Maud's first meeting with Raynes was not promising. He was then teaching at St. John's College and had brought over a team of white boys to box against the club. He took no interest in boxing, but sat in the garden of 'Ekutuleni' and drank tea and smoked black tobacco. He was tall, fair, good-looking, and shy. At St. John's he had the reputation of being a wit and a raconteur, but he gave no sign of that. He was austere, aquiline, and intense. He could not of course frighten Dorothy Maud, who was afraid only of the Lord; but he frightened some of the others. When the boxing was over, he hung about, and she wondered if he had something to say. Mosley writes, '. . . eventually he told her that his father had just died, and how much he minded. Dorothy Maud was probably the first woman he had talked to like this. Her listening, and his father's death, seemed to be some sort of liberation.'[3]

In six years they built three churches, seven schools, three nursery schools, and they had over 6,000 children under their care. They expanded the hospital and built a swimming-bath. They fought for water, lighting, sanitation, roads. They fought for the poor and the persecuted, in courts and police stations and the City Council. According to Mosley, Raynes was the leader, and Dorothy Maud gave him courage. Their gift to the diocese, to Clayton, to the Church and its people, was immeasurable. In 1935 was built the great Church of Christ the King. Its worship was tremendous, its doors always open. It commanded a view of the whole of Sophiatown. Mr. Smith – the ever-ready benefactor – gave it a campanile and a four-faced clock. On Sundays 800 people came to its eleven o'clock mass. When Raynes and Dorothy Maud walked in the streets, they were greeted on all sides, and children ran to hold their hands. Sophiatown had its share of criminals, but they too knew the Father and the Sister, and knew they must not be touched.

It is difficult to assess the part played by Clayton in this tremendous episode. He is mentioned only five times in Mosley's book, but he is always referred to as 'the bishop', and once as 'his bishop', and not once by name. Raynes, with his hooked nose and intense face, was a powerful figure in the synods, second only to Clayton himself. He also spoke with authority, and the bishop always listened to him intently. Africans have some strange gift of naming a person, and they called Raynes 'Kalofo', which means in Sotho a golf stick, 'because he was tall and bent at the top'.[4] The social evils and injustices which Clayton judged with such severity were intimately known to Raynes. He lived with them day after day, with murders, rapes, adulteries, evictions, wrongful arrests, and the callousness of many officials, and when he spoke of them he was listened to with grave attention. But one did not feel that he was easy to approach. Dorothy Maud wrote of him when he left South Africa that in eight and a half years she had never seen him 'impatient with anyone (except the City Council)'.[5] That he was beloved in Sophiatown, no one could doubt. That he was beloved by those who worked with him no one could doubt either. But for the rest he appeared so fierce, he burned with such intensity, that one certainly did not slap him on the back and call him Raymond.

There are no clues left as to the relationship between Clayton and himself. Clayton had passions, but he did not burn. He hated injustice, especially towards the humble, but if it could not be righted tomorrow, then it could not. When in September 1935 Clayton consecrated the Church of Christ the King, he commended it as a pattern for the future African churches. He knew that it was Raynes's design and that the architect had told him that for that money he could design only a garage, to which Raynes had replied that that was what he wanted, 'a huge and holy garage'. But that was what gave Christ the King its sense of tremendous space, with a high altar that could be seen by everyone in the church, and walls that could be covered with every design and colour.

When in 1942 Raynes was told that he was the only nomination for the post of Superior of the World Community, 'he went to his Bishop and said that he was an unsuitable person to be Superior and couldn't he, the Bishop, write and tell them this at Mirfield? The Bishop said No.'[6]

Mosley cites the Report *The Church and the Nation* as showing the effect of 'these ten years' on the white people of Johannesburg, and mentions that Raynes had been an influential member of the Commission, but he does not seem to have understood that Clayton was the driving force behind it. One is tempted to suppose – perhaps wrongly – that between Clayton and Raynes there was a certain incompatibility, not the same as that between Clayton and Huddleston or Reeves or Scott, but certainly the incompatibility of two men of tremendous purpose and almost unshakable will. Perhaps such an incompatibility is inevitable.

Clayton paid Raynes high tribute on his leaving. He wrote:

'The combination in his person of a burning passion for justice with an intense spirituality, has left an indelible impression on all of us who were fortunate enough to count ourselves his friends; and those who remembered what church life at Sophiatown was like nine years ago will appreciate what his ministry has meant to the people of that place.'[7]

One last thing must be said. When Archbishop Clayton died in 1957, having a few minutes earlier written a letter to the Prime Minister to say that he and his bishops would advise all Anglicans not to obey a certain law, there was no mention of his death in *C.R.*, the quarterly review of the Community of the Resurrection. Raynes wrote in *C.R.* no. 218:

'The news from South Africa is grim. New legislation, which allows the Minister of Native Affairs to prevent people of non-European races meeting Europeans, and even attending so-called European churches, is producing a real conflict between Church and State. As the late Archbishop of Cape Town said in his letter to the Minister: "Such things are not Caesar's but God's; and it is not possible for the Church to order or counsel its people to obey such a law".'

But of the death of the man who wrote it, and the manner of his dying, and of his long years of service to the Church of which the Community was a part, and to the country which was always in the Superior's thoughts and prayers, and of the fact that he was Visitor to the C.R. in South Africa, there was not a word. Yet one should remember that Raynes himself had not much more than a year to live. He was eating almost nothing, he was often ill and in pain, he was 'heavy in the heart', gaunt beyond belief, and still burned with some unnameable passion.

And what of the woman Dorothy Maud? Her gift to the diocese and the people was also incomputable. She and Clayton kept their distance from each other. She thought him both shy and alarming, and by no means easy to talk to. Though she kept out of his way, she called him a rock. Like many others, when there was some trouble that she could not cope with, she would go to him, and he would give her his whole attention. She had seen the children jumping and shouting around him, and Clayton looking enormously pleased with himself, though no doubt wondering what he had done to bring it about. When the stone was laid for the new house in Orlando, 'Leseling', the House of Light, Dorothy Maud wanted it laid during a Mass in the open ground, and they erected an altar for it. When the time came for the ceremony, there was a tremendous wind blowing, and Clayton's robes were frequently blown over his face and head. Lady Clarendon, the wife of the new Governor-General went to him and pinned the chasuble to the alb with her diamond brooch, but Clayton paid no attention to her or the wind. His abruptness, his lack of small talk, his booming laughter at who knew what, never for one moment hid from Dorothy Maud his devotion to those same things to which she had given her life. And he of course knew that her price was far above rubies, but in no circumstances would he have made such a ridiculous observation. When she went back to England, he said in Synod in unpoetic language that she had created a new spirit on the European front, had broken down many racial prejudices, and had built up new sympathies.[8]

When Dorothy Maud said farewell at 'Ekutuleni' on 8 December 1943, 'A Layman' wrote in *The Watchman* that one might listen to a great address a few times in a lifetime, but that he had heard one from her, humble and proud, comforting and challenging, simple and magnificent, all in one. Miss Thompson, the headmistress of Kingsmead, called her a great woman, and Miss Maud laughed. Then she spoke too.

'For her theme was two-fold, the Ever-living and Almighty God with Love immeasurable to pour upon the world and Power immeasurable to do it – the African people in immeasurable need and degradation, to be redeemed only by immeasurable Love and Power. She developed this theme, though such description does poor justice to the warm living words, with a grace and a humour and a force for which there is no description. God and the need and lo! something is done. It then occurred to her that she was in some way thought to be responsible for the something that was done, and she laughed.'

And of course she was in some way responsible, for she had given her life and her gifts to be used by this immeasurable Power.

So Clayton lost two of the most devoted and extraordinary people that ever worked in the diocese of Johannesburg. They were not his intimates. Like himself they had given themselves to the work of Christ and the Church. Now they had moved on, and that was that. Such was his way.

So closed the magnificent chapter. No one knew that another equally magnificent was to begin. When Raynes left Sophiatown, he said to his people, in words reminiscent of another departure, 'Do not be sad, I will send a new father to you. Out of all the fathers, I will find one who will look after you.'

When Raynes rang the front doorbell at Mirfield, the door was opened by a young and newly professed monk whom he had not seen before. After a fortnight Raynes told him he was going to Sophiatown. Like Raynes before him, and Moses before Raynes, the young man pleaded his unfitness. But Raynes would not listen to him. His name was Trevor Huddleston. When he was elected Prior of Christ the King he was 29.

Huddleston set sail from Liverpool on 19 July 1943, and reached Cape Town on 6 September on the S.S. *Themistocles*, one of a large convoy. He lost no time in taking the train for Johannesburg. At Kimberley, he heard that Mussolini had fallen, and had his first taste of porridge made from *amabele*, a variety of millet. At Johannesburg he was met by Father Eric Goodall, the Provincial, and Father Stephen Carter. They wanted to take him to Rosettenville, but he wanted to see Sophiatown. It was Thursday morning and there was a school Mass at Christ the King. As he watched the hundreds of children pouring out of the church, he wondered if he would ever know them all. Then he was taken to Clayton, who said to him, 'You are Prior of Christ the King, but in parish work I am your boss.' Huddleston was impatient to begin.

17

Something for Your Comfort

The Report *The Church and the Nation* was published in full in *The Watchman* of January 1944. Clayton called it the answer to the question, Has the Church anything to say or any contribution to make?

He knew it would be criticised from two points of view, the one that the Report went too far, the other that it did not go far enough. He did not mind that. All that he minded was that critics should be clear in their minds why they did not agree.

Reconstruction is in the air, he wrote, and we must do our best to see that it is in accordance with the principles of Christianity. God must be served with our minds as well as our hearts.

The editor, the Revd. A. W. Eaton, called the Commission the Malvern of South Africa.* It was no light task, for 'we were faced with interpreting the Mind of Christ for this, our land, in the knowledge of deep-rooted national and racial and religious prejudice'. He reported that a Continuation Committee had been set up, with the bishop as chairman and Archdeacon Rouse as secretary. The task of the committee would be to disseminate the findings of the Commission, through literature, visits, lectures, sermons, retreats, and by the establishment of a Church and Nation Correspondence Course. Eaton saw the report as a key with which to open up a new era in the diocesan life.

There can be little doubt that from an early age Clayton had believed that the Christian religious life depended for its health and vigour on a personal relationship with the Lord Jesus Christ. It would appear that about this time he felt this more strongly than ever. It was he who had written these words in the Report, 'a change of heart within the nation'. This was to be his Lenten theme for 1944.[1] He wrote that no Christian social programme would be adopted, or if adopted would be found workable, unless there were at any rate a very strong nucleus of people following the Christian way of life. Mass evangelism might help, but the most effective evangelism would be that by Christians of their friends and neighbours. The season of Lent should be used for this preparation.

His emphasis on evangelism was all the greater because he was passing

*This refers to the big church conference at Malvern, England, held in January 1941. The theme was again the New Order.

through moods of pessimism in regard to the apathy and disillusionment which he sensed in South Africa. In how far this judgement was objective and how far not, it would be impossible to discover. Today such moods and opinions are tested by polls, and even some of these are proved to be wide of the mark. Clayton wrote that some who were earlier animated by high ideals were now apathetic, and had given way to cynical fatalism. The war had not touched South Africa enough. He wrote, 'It will leave us worse than it found us.'

The Commission's Report was met not only by apathy, but by disapproval. In November 1943, the Episcopal Synod strongly condemned the colour-bar as being contrary to the teaching of the New Testament, and urged all members of the Church seriously to consider the whole situation in the light of Christ's teaching. 'Layman' writing in *The Watchman* of March 1944 could not understand it. If the Divine Law did not permit discrimination, why did it permit difference? Did the Church stand for total equality, including intermarriage and the franchise? If so, then the black man would eventually take control. 'Layman' simply could not understand what the Church was trying to say, and asked for clarification; 'there is an uneasy feeling that liberalism can be carried too far, and to an extent acceptable to no South African'. By this of course he meant, acceptable to no white South African.

He was replied to by the Revd. H. R. Higgs, who wrote that racial differences were part of the plan of the Creation. Some had some gifts and some had others, but it was not God's plan to exploit these for selfish ends, and that is what discrimination does.

'Layman' was not satisfied with Higgs's reply and asked further questions. If racial characteristics legitimised difference, discrimination, or distinction, and if this differentiation is made on grounds of varying standards of culture and education, should it not be applied to white people also? Are there not individuals of other races in whom the cultural differences have already ceased to exist, and should they not then be admitted to every sphere of life? Is the Church in favour of the franchise and intermarriage for such people? Will the Native vote not eventually swamp the white, and South Africa become a black man's country, or will intermarriage do away with racial differences?

'Layman' was this time answered by the Continuation Committee itself, which argued that the white franchise was historical and it would not be practicable to change it. Yes, for some Africans the cultural differences had disappeared, and they should in principle be admitted to the enfranchised society, but this would isolate them from their own people. There should be equal opportunities in all spheres; social separation would come about naturally, but enforcement by legislation would not work.* In regard to intermarriage, it was not the duty of the Church to encourage or discourage

*Unfortunately to a very large extent it has worked. The proclamation of residential racial 'group areas' has resulted in increasing separation. This is less true of white–Indian relations, it being not forbidden for members of one group to enter the residential

it. The committee concluded by affirming that the future was in the hands of God, and that the Christian must trust that His will is best, and must live by Christian principles at all times.

Clayton approved of these exchanges. They were much to be preferred to apathy. He gave his encouragement to all discussion of the 'Native issue' in *The Watchman*. The correspondence was illuminating. The fears of 'Layman' were not only the fears of white South Africa, they were also the fears of many of the white members of the Anglican Church, not excluding altogether the members of the Continuation Committee. The fear of extending the franchise, of being 'swamped' by black voters, of race mixture, the fear among the less-qualified white workers of being supplanted by black workers, all these were very deep. Some would admit them. Some would not, claiming rather that their main concern was to maintain Christian civilisation and Christian standards. This enabled them to defend discriminatory laws, all of them repressive, some of them inhuman.

Eaton had once written that the issue which confronted South Africa was that between Catholicism and Calvinism. Yet the fact was that there were white members of the Anglican Church whose fears and arguments did not differ greatly from those of the Calvinists. They stood also for white supremacy, though usually not so boldly or baldly. They stood also for the *status quo*. In synods all over South Africa it frequently happened that when discriminatory laws were debated, a majority of the white clergy and a minority of the white laity would join with the overwhelming majority of black clergy and laity in condemning them. One can only suppose that many of the white laity had different values, different interests, and felt they had more to lose.

That is the never-ending struggle of the Christian, to do what he believes to be right, and not what is expedient, convenient, less frightening, more advantageous. In him there should always be a tension between what he is and what he aspires to be. The tension disappears in the hypothetical event that he becomes perfect. It also disappears – or seems to disappear – when he is able to identify what is expedient, convenient, less frightening, more advantageous,with what is right. This is undoubtedly the solution achieved by many white Christians in South Africa, and one hesitates to contend that white Anglicans do not resort to it as much as white Calvinists.*

It certainly was not the solution of the new young Prior of Christ the King. Of course he was not a born South African, he had not been in the country for more than a few months, he was not a businessman, and he owned no shares. Does that help a man to see and speak with more clarity or less? Does that help a man to interpret the mind of Christ for South Africa more authoritatively or less? The questions need not be answered immediately because the young prior's attention was fully engaged. He was

group of the other. But black–white social relations have been severely curtailed. No white person may enter a black residential area without a permit.

*Especially now, when many Calvinists in the Christian Institute have utterly rejected the racial policies of white supremacy. The price they pay is religious and social ostracism.

falling in love, with Sophiatown, with that dirty, wicked, lively, exciting place. He had heard all about it from Raymond Raynes, and was in fact in love with it before he had even seen it.

What sort of man was this young prior? His face was lean and of good colour, his dark hair was cut short, his eyes were black and beautiful. His hands were finely made and expressive, but when he preached he did not indulge in endless and senseless weaving of them. He spoke eloquently and clearly, but the magnetism of his speaking, like that of Clayton, did not depend on tricks. Apart from that, Clayton's speaking and his were not alike at all. Clayton spoke with deliberation and authority, whereas Huddleston was young, vibrant, eager. His first impression of the diocese and its missionary work was very favourable, much more so than it was to become. He clearly revealed that he had fallen in love with Sophiatown and its people by asking the question, 'For what more lovely thing has God created than the smile and laughing eyes of an African child?' In a few months he had seen a beauty that remained for ever hidden from the eyes of many white South Africans.

At the beginning of the century, a certain Mr. Tobiansky bought a large piece of land four and a half miles from the centre of Johannesburg, with the intention of laying it out as a white township. He called it Sophiatown after his wife, and some of the streets he named after his children, Edith, Gerty, Bertha, Toby, and Sol. His dream was never realised. The City Council first decided to establish a sewage-disposal depot near his land, which made it unsaleable to white people. The Council then built 3,000 houses for African workers on ground next to Sophiatown, and called it Western Native Township, surrounding it with a tall and unsightly iron fence, with watchmen at the gates. Sophiatown became saleable again, there being in those days nothing in the law to prevent Tobiansky from selling to Africans, Coloured people, Indians and Chinese. So grew up the lively township to which Huddleston had come.

Then happened, gradually, what has happened in so many South African cities. The white town spread, encircling Western Native Township and Martindale and Newclare and Sophiatown. These places, which had once been remote and unseen, became offensive to white eyes. They were dirty and noisy, criminals lived there, and made sorties into the white suburbs. The danger of rioting was always present, especially after some accident to black pedestrians and passengers. Over and above these things, there was the overwhelming fact that the value of the land had increased many times since Tobiansky bought and sold it. So it happened in the very first year of Huddleston's priorship that the City Council considered a motion to expropriate all land owned by Africans, Coloured people, Indians and Chinese in the western areas of Johannesburg. That would have meant not only the end of Sophiatown, not only the loss by African people of one of the few places in South Africa where they could own their own piece of land. It would also have meant the destruction of the work of Raynes and Dorothy Maud, and of a great part of the missionary work of the Church of the Province. Huddleston himself moved that the Synod of 1944 should deplore this proposal, which was contrary to Christian justice, and his motion received unanimous support. Those were the days when the Johannesburg Synod was powerful, and the proposal was dropped. But the fact that it had been made left the diocese and the Community much disquieted.

In that Synod of 1944, another champion of the voiceless emerged. His name was Michael Scott, and he was 37 years old. His autobiography *A Time to Speak* is sad, beautiful, and pitilessly honest, both with himself and others. All through his life he had been plagued by the 'question'. Though it assumed many forms, it remained substantially the same. Why was God good and the world so full of evil? What did a Christian do in such a situation? Did he stop praying and start doing? He longed for a peace force, with no loyalty to any race or tribe or nation, an army that would not be afraid of breaking laws that are unjust, whose watchwords would be prayer and action. He resolved the question of God and evil in the way of Francis of Assisi, not questioning the wound in the creation but praying to be made the healing instrument of God's peace. Though he longed for an army, he remained solitary, shy, intense in a way all his own, very humble. Though his body rebelled against him, he forced it to go with him into danger, with a bravery all the more wonderful because he was so afraid. People called him an exhibitionist because he appeared to become the professional champion of all just causes, but whereas Huddleston went out into the limelight and the spotlight and the searchlight, partly because he liked being there and partly because only there could he show people what he wanted them to see, Michael Scott went out into the light shyly and fearfully, also because only there could people see what he wanted them to see.

In England he had agreed to become 'attached' to a Communist cell, even though he was aware of Communist ruthlessness, and of their contemptuous belief that religion was an escape from reality. This created, or rather accentuated, the deep conflict within himself, between religion and politics, between thinking and believing, between praying and acting, a strain that eventually drove him to leave England in order to work as a missionary in Korea, which country he never went to, going to Bombay instead, to become the domestic chaplain of the bishop. He hated the contempt of so many Britishers for Indians, and tried to organise a protest against the use of British troops and planes to support those 'cruel effete tyrants', the rulers of the Indian states. He found preaching in the cathedral 'increasingly unbearable', and returned to England 'in a state of spiritual and ethical disintegration'.

In England he spent many weeks in hospital with ileitis, a painful inflammation of a part of the intestine. When he recovered, it was to face the Second World War. His inner conflict continued, because although he wanted to fight he accepted the task of organising Communist groups, only to discover that their purpose was to undermine the confidence that Churchill was inspiring. He collapsed again, but early in 1940 he was able to go to his parents' home in Buckinghamshire, where his mother, seeing his misery, urged him to have a 'heart to heart' talk with his father. To his father he revealed his conflict, and caused the old man much hurt, because to him Communism and the faith were irreconcilable. That night his father suffered a stroke, and lingered for nine years, for which Scott blamed himself.

He became an air-raid warden, then joined the Royal Air Force, but the ileitis put an end to that. Early in 1943 he sailed for South Africa, to take up the post of assistant priest in the Pretoria Native Mission. His Superior disapproved of African trade unions, and his rule was that African priests came to the back door, so Scott applied to Clayton for a post, and was sent to St. Alban's Coloured Mission under Maurice Clack, Scott to become chaplain to the sisters and the orphanage at St. Joseph's Home, Sophiatown.

Scott did not fall in love with places. He loved people, but had difficulty in showing it because of his shyness. But he loved right and justice with all his heart and soul. He wrote about Sophiatown and Johannesburg:

'. . . there is nothing evil about poverty, ignorance, disease and underfeeding. The evil lies over there where the beauty parlours are, and everything is so nice and hygienic, and people buy and sell to one another with little bits of paper, the products which all these people have created with their hands or dug out of the earth.'[2]

And he wrote, presumably in about 1957, 'There is little time to lose.' How many of us have not thought that, in 1937, and 1947, and again in 1967. And shall we still be thinking it in 1977?

It was at Scott's first synod in 1943 that the Report *The Church and the Nation* was presented. He also knew that the Continuation Committee was planning many ways of making its findings known to as many people as possible. Yet that was not enough for him. In 1944 he founded the Campaign for Right and Justice, for which he secured as president retired Judge Krause, an eccentric and fearless Afrikaner. He sought support from all possible quarters, from United Party Cabinet Ministers to the Communist Party. He poured his energy and devotion into the task of organising a National Conference, and was able to do so because of the sympathy and patience of Maurice Clack. He secured four cabinet ministers to preside at four of the Conference sessions. He also invited several bishops, but only five replied to his invitation, regretting they could not attend. He wrote that he 'made the mistake' of announcing prematurely their support in principle, and when they announced publicly that they had not expressed such support, it was a bitter blow to him.

The people whose support he gained were what one might call active and militant, the African and Indian Congresses, the more radical of the Coloured people, and the African Mine Workers Union, which Scott supported and which, to use his own words, he tried to protect from the relentless attacks of the Chamber of Mines.*

*The African Congress was banned in 1960. The Indian Congress, after many years in eclipse, may or may not be (1973) emerging from a decline. The African Mine Workers

The aims of the Campaign were to eliminate profiteering, to achieve the full development of all the industrial and human resources of South Africa, to obtain social services for all races, and to see that the country's obligations to the armed forces and their dependants were carried out. At the conclusion of the National Conference, the Campaign would call for full and direct political representation for all sections of the population, for the abolition of all discriminatory legislation, and for land for the landless. There would also be a call for a minimum wage of £2 a week.

Scott had hoped to bind together all those who earnestly wanted a reform of society but, for one thing, he could not win the support of the redoubtable Dr. Yusuf Dadoo, who saw the Campaign as competing with his own non-European front. Dadoo was a leading Communist, a compelling speaker, untiring and relentless.* The tensions inside the Campaign were many. There was first the difficulty of finding a common basis of action between white liberals on the one hand, and white and black radicals on the other. There was the tension between Communists and churchmen. Even greater was the tension between Communists and ex-Communists, the latter having drawn back in revulsion from the totalitarian brink. And how in pity's name were four United Party cabinet ministers to be drawn into this ménage? It is true, though, that Scott had promised them that at the Conference there would be no talk of a new party.

The Campaign battled on for two years. On 12 August 1946 African goldminers went on strike on the Witwatersrand, and the United Party Government set out ruthlessly to break it. Relations with the Party were further strained when, after the Campaign had exposed the shocking labour conditions at Bethal, and after the United Party had been forced to appoint a commission of enquiry, many of its members joined Dr. Malan and the Nationalists.

The final blow to the Campaign came when it prepared a pamphlet exposing the Broederbond, a secret organisation which was devoted to the cause of preserving Afrikaner supremacy, and which had as its 3,000 members the hard core of Afrikaner Nationalists. Before the pamphlet could be published Scott was visited by two United Party officials with the information that the material used had been lifted from Military Intelligence, and that its use by any other agency could have dangerous consequences. They brought with them a signed statement to this effect from a leading member of the Jewish Board of Deputies who had worked for Military Intelligence in this connection. He also asserted that there were certain members of the Jewish Board who had decided to use the Campaign and also the forthcoming National Conference for the purpose of launching a new political party.

Scott was thus placed in an indefensible position. He had given assurances

Union no longer exists. Such a union would not be illegal, but it cannot be officially registered, and therefore would have no legal standing in terms of relevant labour legislation.

*He finally left South Africa.

to the four cabinet ministers, Messrs. Hofmeyr, Steyn and Waterson and Dr. Gluckman, that there was no intention of forming a new party, and these assurances had been conveyed to the Prime Minister General Smuts, who would otherwise not have allowed his ministers to participate. Scott went to see the leading member of the Jewish Board who had made the signed statement. This gentleman expressed very strongly his belief that not only the publication of the secret information but also the holding of the Conference itself would be very dangerous for the United Party and very advantageous for the Nationalists.

Scott decided that he could not go on with the pamphlet or the Conference. He was outvoted in committee, and resigned from the Campaign, which was then taken over by its Communist members. Scott, however, at no time asserted that there had been collusion between the Communists and certain members of the Jewish Board. Scott wrote, 'In a mood of black despair I resigned from the Campaign I had struggled day and night for two years to build up.'[3] One result of his resignation was that the Campaign never recovered, and eventually collapsed.

He wrote of the Communist Party, 'their support . . . was in a sense the kiss of death'. He felt that they had used him, and when they had no further use for him, they threw him away. Many others had had this experience. Some of them had pondered what appears to be an insoluble puzzle, the strange feeling that at least some Communists do not know whether they want co-operation or not. Some of them had the suspicion that, in the Communist strategy *before the revolution*, there is a time to build a cause with others and a time to destroy it. There seems no doubt that the Communists in Johannesburg, when Scott seemed to be making an impression they had not yet succeeded in making, willingly joined in the Campaign for Right and Justice. Yet they should have known that the idea of a conference attended by them and churchmen and United Party Ministers was ridiculous. Did they know? Or did they hope that this was the beginning of the Revolution? Or did they hope that the destruction of the Campaign would be even more useful? Who can answer these questions? They belong largely to the realm of the irrational.

It would be too much to say that Scott resented the endeavour of the Communists to capture the Campaign. He was not a man for resentment. But he certainly felt they had treated him badly. What they said when he resigned one does not know, but they no doubt spoke scathingly of those weaknesses and indecisions of which Scott himself wrote so humbly and movingly in his autobiography. Surely only the bravest of autobiographers would have written what he wrote, that when he left St. Paul's College, Grahamstown, the warden said to him, 'You have never been able to make up your mind, dear man, and I don't think you ever will.'

It was not only the Communists. Scott wrote, 'I felt betrayed by my own church.' Surely his tactics had not been so much at fault that 'the hierarchy' were justified in their lack of support, if not their open opposition? He mentioned no names, but Clayton was one of them. Here once more, one comes up against the strange quality in Clayton that would not allow him to encourage, and did allow him to criticise, the efforts of this brave and lonely priest who was trying to bring about the changes desired by the Report *The Church and the Nation*. Yet Clayton held aloof from him.

Scott came to the Synod of 1944 hoping to win its support. He had no success. There was a resolution standing in his name, but he made the error of anticipating it in an earlier speech. When finally it came on to the agenda, Synod was nearly over, and Clayton had the excuse to speed up the discussions. He told Synod that it was his intention to complete the business by 6 p.m. and he then with every sign of irritation called Scott to the platform, saying to him, 'I hope you'll not be long, Mr. Scott.' Scott was never a good or confident speaker. His voice was not strong, he had no tricks, and he could not do justice to the drama of injustice. He was extremely nervous, and his nervousness was increased by Clayton's obvious impatience. When he had been speaking for some time, which might have been five or ten minutes, Clayton said to him, 'I hope you won't be much longer, Mr. Scott.' It was indeed almost impossible to continue speaking in the face of such disapproval, and Scott ended ineffectually. His resolution was referred to a Diocesan Social Action Committee which did virtually nothing about it. There were many who sat uncomfortably through this episode. There were times when they enjoyed the slapping down, but this was not one of them. There was something in it that did not square with the Gospel.

There may have been another reason why Clayton regarded the Campaign so coldly. He had already tried to widen the reconstruction front by inspiring the formation of a Christian Social Front, in which Anglicans, Catholics, Presbyterians, Methodists, Baptists, and others were willing to co-operate. The Front held a United Christian Demonstration in the Johannesburg City Hall on 23 May 1944, with Clayton the chief speaker. Persons were more important than things. Things exist for persons, the person exists for God. Man needs the institution of the State to create and enforce order, but it must be an order that ensures the most freedom possible. The State could endanger freedom. It could make its people slaves, as in totalitarianism. In the democratic State there was always the danger of economic tyranny, and again he stressed the need for better wages and working conditions. 'It is an evil thing when a social order deprives people of the opportunity for work, development, education, responsibility and culture, of which they are capable, as now happens in this country.'

Clayton said trenchantly that 'the trouble is that we Christians have never forced the issue. We are frightened.' But he kept aloof from Scott who was forcing the issue. Scott was frightened too, and his actions were therefore the more remarkable, the brave actions of a gentle and diffident man.

In some notes written for Arthur Blaxall twenty-four years later, Scott thought that Clayton had tried in his own strange fashion to make amends to Scott for his treatment of him in the last hour of Synod. Shortly afterwards Clayton was acting, probably for one issue, as editor of *The Watchman* and printed one of Scott's poems, written for a young husband whose wife and newborn child were killed in an air raid while he was away saving a warehouse from the flames.

Of this Scott said, 'I always thought he did that as a sort of apology.' In respect of the piece that he had written for Arthur Blaxall, he wrote that he had thought of heading it 'A Just Beast', but decided that it might not be understood.[4]

This impatience in Clayton towards a young priest who may not have had a monopoly of wisdom but had a great deal of courage, and who was doing these things out of obedience, must be regarded as a defect. One may set against it the message he received from David Rakale, the chairman of the African Clergy and Laymen Association, and from Christian Molefe, the secretary, on the tenth anniversary of his enthronement, 24 May 1944.

The Association gave thanks for the raised status of the African clergy, and for the advancement, 'considered on its own merits', of Africans to the priesthood. The words 'I know my sheep and I am known of mine' had been brought home to the members of the Association in their full meaning, and if proof were needed, it was to be found in each month's copy of *The Watchman.*[5]

Writing to the Society for the Propagation of the Gospel on 13 November 1942, Clayton described the African work of the diocese, still called the Mission Work, although he would have been the first to maintain that white people needed evangelisation as much as any part of the population. He commented on the fact that the Archdeacon of Native Missions, Redvers Rouse, was a South African by birth, and that the two Assistant Directors, Dick Yates and Donald Bailey, were from England. One white priest – the Revd. A. S. Watson – did some mission work; otherwise the rest of the work, except that specifically entrusted to the Community of the Resurrection, was done by twenty-nine African priests, most of whom were incumbents, and were not under any white supervision except that of the bishop, the archdeacon, and the assistant directors. It was his intention to extend the policy; he did not approve of putting African priests under white ones.

When Clayton arrived in 1934, it was the policy of the diocese to put every African priest under the supervision of the white priest in the nearest town or village. White control was thought to ensure orderliness, stability, reliability, punctuality. It was Clayton who realised that black initiative, enterprise, enthusiasm, were stifled by white control, that among black priests who were not inclined to be subservient white control could cause feelings of hurt and resentment that could well destroy the priestly vocation. It was for this recognition that the Association was giving its thanks.

Clayton was in fact more concerned with equalising responsibility and status than with equalising stipends, though it can be argued that one cannot do one without doing the other. Though Rouse too was not in favour of equalising stipends, he was not happy about the stipends themselves. He was Archdeacon of Native Missions, and knew the struggle of black priests to live and buy clothes and educate children. An African had to pay the same price for food as anyone else, unless he and his family lived on a dangerous diet of tea, bread, mealie-meal, and an occasional piece of meat. Rouse visited his priests and was troubled by the difference between their houses and his. He said to Clayton that he thought the stipends should be raised by ten per cent, and Clayton said to him, 'Where's the money?' Rouse said he thought that the black priests would agree to an increase in their parish assessments. Devoted as he was to Clayton, he was troubled by the bishop's indifference. Clayton would always listen, and then he would say, 'It's your job, get on with it.'

Clayton was however very concerned about clergy pensions. After forty years' service beginning in 1916, at 70 a priest would receive £157.10.0 per year. That would first come into effect in 1956. A priest retiring before 1956 might receive from £60 to £162, but in all cases the diocese added something in the region of twenty per cent. The pensions for Africans were one-third of these amounts. The provision for the widows of clergy was £33 per annum if they were white, and £10 if they were not.* Clayton was anxious to do something for those priests who would retire between 1944 and 1956. He asked Nan Chignell, the wife of the much-loved vicar of the wealthy parish of St. George's, Parktown, to collect £2,000 for him. By 1946 the money was spent, and he now summoned Mrs. Dorothy Kirby of the Church Women's Society to what she called the 'amiable presence' and told her that he wanted her to raise £5,000. She was horrified, but he explained that he wanted £500 every year for ten years. When Clayton left Johannesburg for Cape Town she was still collecting the money, but when she visited Cape Town she would go out to see him at 'Bishopscourt' and tell him all the gossip, which would send him into great booms of laughter. She was not afraid of him, nor he of her for some reason. She wrote, eleven years after his death, 'We shall not look upon his like again, I fear.'[6] Taken literally that was true, but she meant something more than that: she was one of the few women who had got behind his formidable guard.

*An economist friend of mine estimates that money could do approximately three times as much in 1942 as it could now in 1973.

18

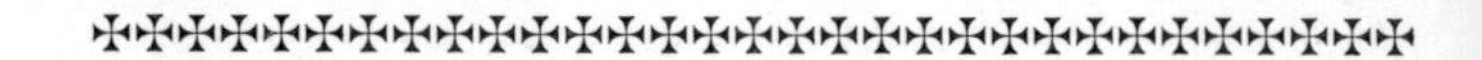

'Do the next right thing'

Towards the end of 1944 it was clear that Hitler and his allies would lose the war. In his eleventh charge Clayton warned against the seeking of revenge, and the creation of another Hitler. People should learn the true lessons of the war, and one of these was that they must rid themselves 'of the idea of a dominant race, with a supposedly divine right to lord it over the other races in the world'.

Clayton, who in 1918 had had to return from the army to civilian life, and knew the difficulties, said that it was the duty of the Church, clergy and laity, to help servicemen to make the transition. The archbishop was preparing a special service for the renewal of marriage vows, and he hoped it would be widely used.

He returned to his urgent theme – the reconstruction of society. In those simple and penetrating phrases of which he was a master, he went to the heart of the problem.

'Only the State can save the individual from economic slavery. Only the State can prevent a group of citizens from holding the whole community to ransom, and that group may be either representative of capital or representative of skilled labour. But woe to the land where the State is in alliance with such a group.'

The Church must put her own house in order. Her own hands were not clean. The diocese must reconsider the stipends and wages that it paid, with reference to the cost of living.

Clayton concluded with a reaffirmation of one of the central truths of the gospel. He said that much harm was done by the wrong use of psychology, that a man does what he does and is what he is because he cannot do and be anything else. The possibility of effort is fundamental to the Christian religion. The grace of God gives to us the chance to break our chains, and to rise above the pressures of the environment.[1]

To Clayton the unpardonable sin was cynicism, the refusal to believe in the sincerity of idealism. If Christian public opinion yielded to the devil's temptation and assumed that nothing that is good could come out of the peace, then Christian opinion would not be doing what God wanted it to do.[2]

This theme was for him most urgent. The achievement of new things must mean a change in the hearts of many. To believe that hearts cannot change, and things cannot be made new, is to give up all hope for the new order.

Clayton's thoughts were remarkably similar to those of William Temple, Archbishop of Canterbury. But Temple, whose leadership was so precious to the Church of England in these times, and indeed to the Anglican Church throughout the world, died on 26 October 1944. Temple had given his full support and encouragement to the Report *The Church and the Nation*, and Clayton paid him extraordinary tribute. He called Temple a man of great intellectual ability and rare spiritual gifts, apparently wholly free from any intellectual or spiritual pride.

'But the fundamental thing about him was his sheer goodness. It was impossible to meet him without being braced and strengthened. I suppose that was the secret of his power of leadership. And, underlying everything else, was a very deep and sincere spiritual life. First and foremost he was a humble simple-minded disciple of our Lord Jesus Christ.'[3]

From Clayton, a tribute indeed. He did not think to mention that Temple and he had been at Rugby together.*

Clayton, so eminent a figure in the Church of the Province of South Africa, was hardly known in the world-wide Anglican Church. There were still those in England who held him in the highest regard, but they were not bishop-makers. There were those, both in England and South Africa, who would have thought him a worthy successor to Temple.

At this time he and Yates and ffrench-Beytagh spent part of their holidays at the Mountain Inn, just north of Louis Trichardt, in the Zoutpansberg mountains. Clayton took both serious and light reading. The light reading was in the form of thrillers; he was able to read them without effort, and with pleasure if they were good. There was always the Bible, which he read and pondered over a great deal. This time he had brought the *Pseudepigrapha* as well, an enormous book containing those writings which were not admitted to the Bible. It was a typical Clayton holiday, private prayers and then the morning Mass, good meals, much reading, a moderate amount of exercise, and a moderate amount of liquor, some wine with dinner, much conversation and laughter, and late to bed. Ffrench-Beytagh made no secret of the fact that he could listen but not contribute to Clayton's conversation, although he could to his gossip. He took a masochistic delight in relating the story of the day when Clayton read aloud the news item which reported the death of a former Archbishop of Cape Town, William Carter, of heart failure. Ffrench-Beytagh, wishing to contribute, said that Carter must have had a weak heart. 'Geoffrey's "*Fool!*" still rings in my ears.'[4]

This holiday was not quite the same as others. Clayton received a cable from *The Times* requesting confirmation of the rumour that he had been offered the See of Canterbury, made vacant by the death of Temple. He

*All those communications between Clayton and the various Archbishops of Canterbury which are kept in the archives of Lambeth, may not be seen until forty years after they were written. If I may quote Clayton (page 176), 'I won't say what I think about it.'

showed the cable to his companions but did not discuss it. But it was clear that he was disturbed, a condition so unusual for him that it was very noticeable to them. It took him a day or two to recover, and to return to the conversation and the laughter.

Had ambition stirred again? He had become Bishop of Johannesburg in 1934, and in 1939, after the death of Archbishop Phelps, Darbyshire had been preferred to him. Well, Darbyshire might be there for a long time yet. Clayton had now been Bishop of Johannesburg for eleven years, and it would have been natural for him to want to be an archbishop. It would seem, however, that he had never contemplated the possibility of becoming the Primate of all England, who could in some ways be regarded as the head of the world Anglican Communion. So far as one knows, the offer was not made to him, but the rumour disturbed him, and one guesses that he thought and prayed about it and then put it from his mind. Perhaps he knew that the work that was waiting for him was also urgent.

The diocesan year 1944–5 was full of events. As Sophiatown had conquered Huddleston, so he in turn conquered it. Raynes had left the people sorrowing, but now they had another man, one would hesitate to say more loving, but less inhibited in love. A Miss K. having attended Mass at Christ the King wrote a letter to the *Star* about the poverty and the coldness of the winter in Sophiatown. The response from the white people of Johannesburg was astonishing. Food, clothes, blankets, poured in. Huddleston wrote that 'the mail was stiff with cheques'. He called a public meeting, and the African Children's Feeding Scheme was born. At that time, in the year 1945, every white schoolchild in the Transvaal was entitled to a free meal per school day, at a cost of sixpence per child per day. But for the African child there had been nothing until J. H. Hofmeyr, Minister of Finance and Education, extended the scheme to African children at a cost of twopence per child per head per day. But Huddleston's scheme applied to all African children, whether at school or not. He wrote to the press criticising the shortcomings of the official African school-feeding scheme, and was commended by Clayton, who added on his own account that such discrimination would not exist if Africans had the vote.[5] Huddleston did not stop at school-feeding. In three years he raised enough money to build an Olympic-sized swimming-bath at Orlando, the first such swimming-bath for Africans in Africa. Not satisfied, he founded what was called, not by him, the 'Huddleston Jazz Band', to add to the myriad noises Sophiatown already possessed. And he already had of course the church of Christ the King. It would have been difficult for an outsider to know which of these things he put first. He never boasted about the church, but he did boast about the jazz band.

What Clayton thought of the young prior, apart from the recognition of his energy and devotion, is one of the secrets of the grave. It is improbable that he would have taken him as a holiday companion. As Huddleston became more and more of a public figure, and more and more the subject of public controversy, Clayton began to withdraw from him. Yet both he and Huddleston were equally convinced of the need for evangelism and a change of heart. Both of them were advocates and defenders of justice. Both were extremely critical of white South Africa and its Government. But for Clayton such actions were to be taken with dignity and propriety, whereas Huddleston, who after all had founded a jazz band, wanted to shock people out of their apathy. 'I wanted to be a gadfly; he did not', Huddleston said to me.

One of Clayton's actions taken with dignity and propriety had not long before come to nothing. With the unanimous support of Synod he went to see General Smuts the Prime Minister about the squalor and misery in which so many of the African workers of Johannesburg had to live. Many of them lived in the shanty towns 'with the rain flooding in through roofs of tin and sacking, in unlit streets stinking of sour mud, waking at four in the morning so that they could appear punctually before employers who expected them to rise out of the filth and shine'.[6] Clayton had already been to the Johannesburg Municipality, whose officials had explained that they could not accept the whole responsibility and bear the whole burden of rehousing; the Government must help. So he went to Smuts, and with justified hope, because Smuts had declared publicly that something must be done about African housing; but Smuts explained to him that the Government could not accept as much of the responsibility and the burden as the Municipality thought it should. Smuts did not even promise to have the position investigated. Presumably Government and Municipality would continue their delicate negotiations indefinitely while people lived in mud and misery. Clayton came away shocked by Smuts's apparent indifference, and said of him and the Municipality, 'They put things before people', which for him was the severest of judgements.[7]

African wages were so low that a rise of a penny in any staple commodity was a blow to struggling people. The bus fare from Alexandra Township to the city was raised by just that amount, and the workers of Alexandra, men and women, old men and old women, physical weaklings and cripples, refused to use the buses and walked to and from the city, twenty or twenty-two miles a day. Those who started work at 7 a.m. would have to rise at 3 a.m. and start walking at 4 a.m. If they finished work at 5 p.m. they would get home at 8 p.m. A great part of the distance was the length of Louis Botha Avenue, lined with comfortable white houses, whose occupants had of necessity to watch the daily march. Some white people were deeply moved by the marching protest, and would come daily with their cars to help the old and crippled, often being warned by the police that they were breaking the law. Others were angered by it and thought it should be ended by force. It is a temptation of white authority to this very day to silence black protest by force. Most of the white people of Johannesburg had no conception of the importance of twopence per day to most African people.

The Alexandra bus boycott, the lowness of African wages, African poverty, the lack of housing, the filthiness of the slums, the misery of the cold and the rain, weighed down heavily on Clayton. He wrote that he was 'greatly perturbed' by the rise in bus fares, and he commended the City

Council for its attempts to break the deadlock, and said they had done much better than the Government departments, which he described in severe terms as 'purely obstructive'.[8] At that time the restrictions in the use of African labour in the building-trade went beyond all reason, and white artisans had the legal monopoly of all building within certain defined areas, which meant, amongst other things, a monopoly of all building for the municipality, whether for white or black people. Thus the cost of municipal housing for low-paid African workers became prohibitive, and such housing was not built. It is the white skilled workers who most strongly resist the entry of black skilled workers into any trade of which they have the monopoly.

Clayton in his efforts to influence the municipality to use black labour for building black houses, had the strong support of Graham Ballenden, the Manager of Native Affairs for the city of Johannesburg. Ballenden was a big man, in more ways than one; at times his geniality concealed his toughness, and at others his toughness concealed his generosity. But neither he nor Clayton could make any headway, and it was clear that Smuts was not willing to antagonise the white workers at this important stage of the war.

The Allied armies, having recovered from their setback in the Ardennes, were driving for the Rhine, which they crossed in March 1945. On 7 May General Alfred Jodl signed the German act of surrender, and on 15 August Japan followed suit. So one of the most terrible decades in the history of man came to an end.

Clayton thought that the surrender of Japan and the end of the war ought to be celebrated. On VJ Day he got his chaplain Dick Yates to ring ffrench-Beytagh, then Rector of Germiston, and ask him to come to Johannesburg. He took the two young men to the Chinese restaurant in Orange Grove, where they had a splendid dinner, good drink, and much talk and laughter. Clayton was an abstemious and highly disciplined drinker, but it was not every day that a world war came to an end, and he intended to celebrate it properly. They therefore had more to drink than usual, and the party was a merry one. On the drive home Yates and ffrench-Beytagh sat in front and, used as they were to Clayton's unpredictabilities, they were astonished when he began singing the music-hall songs of the beginning of the century. They had heard him sing the Mass and 'Come, Holy Ghost, our souls inspire', but they had never heard this. It was what today would be called a happening, and for the two young men it was a happening never to be forgotten.

But when the celebration was over, how was the world to be put right? Not by fear of the atomic bomb, Clayton thought; only when the brotherhood of man and the Fatherhood of God became the motivating forces in men's lives. He dealt with the problems of world peace in his twelfth charge, but it was the peace of South Africa with which he was most concerned, and the problem which troubled him most was that those who spoke in the name of Christ did not speak with one voice. What to him and others seemed to follow directly from the teaching of our Lord, seemed to many of their fellow-Christians to be directly contrary to the will of God. Yet there must

1 G. H. Clayton, G. A. B. Newenham, the Bishop of Derby (Pearce), R. P. R. Carpenter and D. B. Harris in 1927 (Photo: H. J. Morgan, Chesterfield)

2 *(below left)* At the Church Bazaar in Chesterfield, October 1928, with Lady Shentall, the Mayor, R. P. R. Carpenter and Princess Marie Louise (Photo: *Derbyshire Times*)

3 *(below right)* On the same occasion, with the Duchess of Devonshire (Photo: *Derbyshire Times*)

4 *(left)* After his consecration in St. Paul's Cathedral, London, as Bishop of Johannesburg, May 1934 (Photo: Associated Press, London)

5 *(right)* The Revd. Michael Scott, passive-resister in Durban, July 1947 (Photo: *Daily News,* Durban)

6 *(below)* Father Trevor Huddleston, C.R., with children from his mission nursery school (Photo: Constance Stuart, Chestertown, Maryland)

7 As Bishop of Johannesburg in January 1949, after his election as Archbishop of Cape Town but before his enthronement (Photo: *Cape Argus*)

8 With Bishops Peacey, Paget and Reeves at the consecration of Ambrose Reeves as Bishop of Johannesburg, August 1949 (Photo: *Cape Argus*)

be no appeasement. 'We must speak the truth, as we see it. So must they. But we and they must speak the truth in love.'

He returned to his favourite phrase 'Do the next right thing'. And when would one use such a phrase unless at a time when the road to the desired goal was full of obstructions, perhaps had not even yet been built? The crux of the matter, so he said, was that there were two views of life. The first was that God had created certain classes of men to rule, and others to maintain them. The second was that every individual had to grow and fulfil himself, regardless of his race or colour. The second view seemed to be that of the Christian faith.[9]

Why was Clayton's view of the future so sombre? It seems that he had a premonition of the prophetic role that the Church of the Province, with other churches, would have to assume, and that he was beginning to realise clearly the threat which Afrikaner Nationalism would pose to all that the Church stood for, and that the threat would be posed in the name of Christianity itself. It is extraordinary that this threat should have seemed so ominous at a time when the Allies had achieved victory, when Smuts was being fêted everywhere, and above all when Dr. Malan and his Nationalists numbered only 43 in the Lower House, while Smuts's United Party numbered 89, and had the support on the war issue of an additional 18. Yet the apprehensive noted that the United Party had polled 427,000 votes and the Nationalists 338,000.

This apprehension was increased when on 7 September 1945 Smuts's party lost the parliamentary seat of Kimberley, which it had held in 1943 with a substantial majority. A few months later his majority dropped ominously in Caledon. Malan and his followers were full of confidence, and he wrote in his autobiography that he could see rays of the long-awaited dawn.[10] At last a united Afrikanerdom would rule, and Malan promised that apartheid would be enforced in every conceivable sphere of life. He did not specifically mention the churches, though he was to do so later. Between the new order which he promised, and that planned with such industry by the Bishop's Commission, there was hardly a common element.

A considerable amount of hard work had been done by the Continuation Committee of the Bishop's Commission, and speakers had been to almost every white parish in the diocese to make known the Report *The Church and the Nation*. The same attention had not been given to the black parishes, but there was a specifically South African reason for that. The Report was essentially a white report. It called for 'a change of heart', but it was the white heart that had to change. It was only white people who had the power to reform society. Black people might read and hear and approve of the findings of the Commission, but beyond that they were powerless. The most that they could do would be to hope that their white fellow-Christians would achieve the reforms. But in fact their white fellow-Christians did not have great power either. Some of them were very influential in commerce, industry, and mining, but if they had attempted to use their influence to bring about the far-reaching reforms envisaged by the Report, it would have rapidly declined. It was therefore not to be expected that this particular Report would have much better luck than the numerous reports which had been submitted to South African governments for many years.

Clayton and many of his clergy, and especially the members of the Community of the Resurrection, felt strongly the need to evangelise and, so to speak, re-Christianise, the white people of South Africa. That indeed had been the conclusion of the Report. The outcome was the holding of an Evangelistic Conference for lay members of the Church at Randfontein, from 28 September to 1 October 1945, and about eighty attended.

One of the opening addresses of the Conference was disastrous. It was given by Father Christopher Millington, C.R., the principal of St. Peter's School, Rosettenville. The picture that it drew of the future of Christianity held out little hope for any evangelistic campaign. Millington foresaw the withdrawal of Christians into cells and enclaves in a hostile and indifferent world. Clayton was later to call it 'Father Millington's acid realism', but to many of the delegates it was the speech of one without hope. To many of them it was almost a grotesque way to open an evangelistic conference. When Millington sat down, the silence was palpable. The first layman to open the discussion voiced the feelings of many when he not only spoke of his intense disappointment, but criticised Millington for choosing such a theme for such an occasion. They had come there to talk about evangelism, the preaching of the Gospel, which is the good news, yet *this* was what they got. It was indefensible.

Clayton, however, defended it in his twelfth charge.

'Our enthusiasm cannot depend on the expectancy of abolishing the darkness, and no such expectancy can be drawn from the Bible. As the bearer of the truth of man's inability to save himself, even when he invokes God's assistance, the only course that the Church can safely pursue is that pursued by her Master, and that meant crucifixion.'[11]

All this is true, but it does not sound like good news. That one must endure the darkness, even to crucifixion, one knows, or should know, but the blind also see, the lame walk, the lepers are healed, the deaf hear, the dead are raised up, and the poor have the Gospel preached to them. Those speakers who followed Millington tried to redress the balance, and Clayton reported that the enthusiasm of the laymen at the Conference was very promising, although he admitted that their enthusiasm was 'daunted' by the acid realism.

The diocesan evangelical campaign which was launched at the close of the Conference was planned with industry and zeal by the newly established Evangelistic Council. A number of evangelistic study circles were formed, where young people discussed their successes and failures in 'making contact' with others. There were fortnightly lectures on what was called the social gospel, and these dealt with the issues raised by the Report *The Church and the Nation*. In Johannesburg a Christian Fellowship Group was formed, for both playing and praying together, and teams were sent to the parishes. A 'Church and Town Council' was set up to study the affairs of the various

Reef towns and the proceedings of their town councils. The Fellowship also interested itself in Anglican children at boarding-schools, and planned to visit them regularly. Plans were made for the presentation of religious drama. A League of Intercessors was established, and group prayers were held for those whose names had been handed in, by priests, parents, teachers, friends. The programme showed thoroughness and devotion, but it was handicapped from the beginning by the fact that the diocese did not appoint a full-time director, whether priest or lay. The burden of responsibility and organisation fell very largely on the shoulders of T. M. Wurts, an earnest and devout layman, who had neither enough time nor energy to carry out such an ambitious scheme.

The decision of A. W. Eaton, always known as Tubby, to accept the vicarage of St. Peter's, Leicester, England, must be taken as a sign of those times. Eaton had been one of the moving spirits in the Bishop's Commission, and had seen it as 'the key to open up a new era'. He too had preached the urgency of the 'change of heart', and had supported the evangelistic campaign. Therefore the news of his decision to leave was received by many with dismay, even with pain. Clayton, regretting his departure, likened him to Socrates; he was a gadfly stinging people into action. The truth is that Eaton had lost heart for stinging white South Africans into action. *The Church and the Nation* had not yet opened any of the doors into the new era.

It is impossible to criticise any priest or reformer or dreamer who, having given his time and energy to the task of reforming the race–caste society of South Africa, decides that he can no longer go on, that he is wasting the time and the gifts that God has given him, that he does not want his children corrupted, that he wants to live in a freer air. The decision of such a person to leave can arouse pain, anger, envy, despair, in others. Certainly Eaton's decision to leave did nothing to help the evangelistic campaign. What was the point of winning others? So that they too could undertake this fruitless labour, perhaps even worse than that of Sisyphus, who could at least move the stone? Clayton's views on such questions were pungent and succinct, and he expressed them in his fourteenth charge.

'The Church is said to be losing ground among educated Africans because it does not procure for them political reforms. But that is not what the Church is for. The Church exists primarily to preach the gospel of the Lord Jesus Christ . . . Churchmen must do all they can to bring about the reign of justice . . . but the fact remains that the message of the Church is a message about God. People are trying to use God as a means to an end, to say that a man should be a Christian because that would make him moral, or would make him free. It is as though Christ had said, "Blessed are they that see God for they shall be pure in heart." But he didn't. You are to be pure in heart in order that you may see God. . . . The Church does not exist among Africans with a view to securing the vote for African people, or even with a view to securing better housing or better wages, or even better manners.'

Clayton told his hearers that they must not suppose that he was saying that Christians would be doing wrong in trying to secure better conditions. 'That is a cause for which it would be worth while for a man to live and die.'[12] Yet there was no implication in his words that the cause would be successful. The stories of Dorothy Maud, Raynes, Clayton, Huddleston, Scott, are an imperishable part of the history of the Church of the Province, and who would have had them live otherwise? Yet much of their work has been totally destroyed. And what was one to do in a race–caste society that would not change? Clayton repeated the advice, 'Do the next right thing', and added the rider, 'We generally know what that is.'[13]

But it was not just a matter of gritting one's teeth, and doing one's duty without reward. There had to be hope too. St. Paul had written: 'Now to see is no longer to hope: why should a man endure and wait for what he already sees? But if we hope for something we do not yet see, then in waiting for it, we show our endurance.'[14]

Many Christians, and especially priests and ministers, would say that our hope exists because of Christ's resurrection. It is clear that Christian hope is founded 'on some kind of belief', in God's goodness and providence, or in Christ's resurrection, or that the Holy Spirit lives and moves in the world and can use us as His instruments, or that there is a state called heaven and that happiness is to be found there. Yet some people – including some of the young people who sing 'We shall overcome' – have no Christian belief. What reason then have they to sing 'We shall overcome'? Is it a belief perhaps that good will eventually prevail? Or are some people just to be described as 'hopeful' persons with 'hopeful' temperaments? What right had the prophet to prophesy that the wolf would one day dwell with the lamb, or that a day would come when they would not hurt or destroy in all that holy mountain? Yet such a hope kept the courage of the Jews alive through countless trials and tribulations, even unto death.

I should like to conclude this discussion with one last observation, that the Bishop's Commission may have failed to open many doors to the new era, but it opened the eyes of at least one who was blind.

Returning to Clayton himself, one could not possibly imagine him in a state of hopelessness. For one thing he had firm grounds for hope, and for another he had a cause for which he lived and for which he would have been ready to die. Sloth, melancholy, accidie, were as far as one knows quite unknown to him. And perhaps there was yet another thing, that in no circumstances whatever could he have dared to be hopeless, because that would have meant not only the destruction of himself, but the destruction of many others also. If Clayton had come to believe that effort was fruitless, and had returned to England, he would have destroyed the faith of many. And how could he do that, who had vowed to be a shepherd of souls?

But he told the 1946 July reunion of the Evangelistic Council that they must not hope for a large-scale religious revival in the near future, either in England or in South Africa. Yet he saw no reason for defeatism, certainly not in the diocese of Johannesburg. No one who believed in the Resurrection could be disheartened. He persistently sounded the note of hope, and it was needed, for the success of the evangelistic campaign was not spectacular.

The work of the Council, the reunions, and the visits to the parishes, owed a great deal of their persistence to the encouragement of the bishop, but when Clayton left to become Archbishop of Cape Town in January 1949, they gradually came to an end. It was a brave venture that never really left the ground.

Nor was Clayton able to help it leave the ground. His massive self-containedness, the impersonality of his relationship with most people, his distrust of emotion, all these did not equip him for the work of an evangelist. Above all, perhaps, he was not an embodiment of love or lovingness as Temple was. People loved Temple, and wanted to be as like him as some ordinary mortal might be. But of Clayton they stood in awe, and very few, perhaps none, wanted to be like him at all.

After he had become Archbishop, the new Bishop of Johannesburg, Ambrose Reeves, also concerned for the re-Christianisation of white Anglicans, appointed Gonville Aubie ffrench-Beytagh as Missioner to the Diocese. On one of the holidays that ffrench-Beytagh spent with Clayton, they were driving north to Namaqualand, and Clayton said, 'Tell me about the mission.' So ffrench-Beytagh spoke about the mission, its objectives, its results, his travels and experiences, for twenty minutes or more. When he had finished, Clayton was silent for a while, then said, 'Tell me more.' Ffrench-Beytagh was already exhausted; being quizzed by Clayton was for him, with his strong feeling of mental and spiritual inferiority, an ordeal, and he could not think of much more. However, he told Clayton of the methods a missioner uses, the devices, the modulations of the voice, the appeals, the warnings. When he had finished, Clayton was silent for a long time. Then he said, 'I don't think I approve of conversion by gadgets.'

Nor did he. His idea of conversion was a simple one. Conversion was brought about by the witness of the individual Christian, not only in his own personal life but also by his participation in the life and work of his parish church. He did not believe in emotional evangelism. He was indeed wary of all expressions of emotion, though his own emotions were deep and powerful. He was never afraid of the word 'love', nor was he afraid of speaking about love, and as he grew older he grew less and less afraid of showing love.

Love was for him a consecration of the will, an act which he performed daily. All this ffrench-Beytagh understood well; it made the temper and the bullyings seem trivial. When he was at Germiston as a young curate, he was terrified when his bishop presented himself unannounced to make his confession. But he learned later that he need not have troubled himself. Clayton did not go to confession for advice, but for forgiveness.

During a Sacred Synod at Grahamstown, held in either 1947 or 1948, Clayton was asked to speak on evangelism, largely because of the institution of an evangelistic campaign in his diocese. He said, 'I am conscious myself of being singularly devoid of the gifts of an evangelist, and I think that the conclusions we have reached in my diocese are largely negative.'

Clayton spoke of the contemporary situation of the Christian religion.

The first cause of its decline was the influence of humanism and its ideas of inevitable human progress. The second was what Temple had called the 'laboratory mind', which is interested in the *how* but not in the *why*. A third cause was the weakening of belief, for Christian morality depended on Christian doctrine; and again he called the influence of psychology 'morally disastrous' in that many people who found self-control difficult, now found it pernicious. Another cause, and this he called the supreme difficulty, was the lack of any sense of need; even Christ could do nothing with those who had no sense of need.

He concluded:

'No one can bring about a religious revival. Only God can do that. No one can make himself into a prophet. Only God can do that. It may be that He will. But perhaps He won't. If so, there is no reason to despair. It may be that the Church is called to share with her Lord the position of the suffering servant. He was alone upon the Cross. That may be so. Yet we must not forget that Easter followed Good Friday.'[15]

In this very Grahamstown sermon Clayton spoke of 'widespread disillusionment and despair', and this he had been saying almost yearly since 1940. He never failed to add that there was no need for despair, yet he was anxious about the Church and its future. One does not know whether he ever pondered over what Jesus meant by the Church, whether Jesus intended or foresaw that there would be an organisation and a hierarchy, or that the Church would acquire property and possessions. It was unlikely that he pondered over it because he had himself become a member of the Church establishment, and an important member of its hierarchy. And in a way, he himself was the Church. He may have acknowledged the possibility of the decline of the Church, as he was prepared to acknowledge the possibility of the defeat of Britain, but the actuality would have caused him great pain. If the Holy Spirit was alive and moving in the world and the Church declined, did that mean that the Holy Spirit no longer moved in the Church? It is to be noted that from this time forward, often in sermons, and almost invariably in his charges, both to clergy and diocesan synods, he sounded a loud and confident note of encouragement. 'So lift up your hearts. God reigns and God is love.'[16]

19

The Diffident Saint

In 1946 Michael Scott took a step of which Clayton strongly disapproved. He went to Durban, not to join, but to report on the campaign of passive-resistance being waged against the Asiatic Land Tenure and Indian Representation Act. The first purpose of the Act was to freeze all property transactions between white people and Indians, because the white people of Durban were outraged by the 'penetration' of Indians into the white residential areas of Durban. The second purpose of the Act was to give Indians two senators in the Upper House, and three M.P.s in the Lower, all of whom must be white. The Natal and Transvaal Indian Congresses regarded this *quid pro quo* with contempt and showed their resistance to the freezing of property transactions by occupying a piece of municipal wasteland in the centre of Durban. Mobs of white hooligans assaulted the resisters, and set their tents on fire. Therefore it was with apprehension that Scott, who abhorred violence, made his way to Durban.

Scott's heart was with the resisters. Although he had gone as an observer, it was inevitable that he should be arrested for trespass and 'riotous assembly'. He was sentenced to three months' imprisonment. The publication of this news was the first intimation to both his bishop and his rector that he was not in Johannesburg doing the work for which the diocese paid him.

Clayton was unenthusiastically tolerant of Scott's Campaign for Right and Justice, believing that Scott was being used by people for their own ends. He might have been equally unenthusiastically tolerant of Scott's participation in the passive-resistance campaign in Durban, but he disapproved strongly of Scott's leaving of his post without permission. The diocesan secretary, who posted the monthly salary cheques to all priests, consulted the bishop as to what should be done with Scott's cheque, and Clayton ordered that payment should be suspended till Scott returned to Johannesburg.

Clayton's judgement was firm and stern, delivered without anger. He told Scott that he could not continue to hold his licence for a particular piece of work and then leave it for another without permission. He had given instructions that Scott's stipend should be kept for him but he would not do so again. Unless Scott would undertake to abide by these conditions, his licence would be withdrawn.

Scott felt unable to give this assurance. He could not know when he would be called to further action.[1] Accordingly he gave up his post in the parish of St. Albans, but retained the bishop's general licence to preach and celebrate in the diocese when he was invited to do so.

According to Scott, Clayton went further in the Sacred Synod of 1946.* He declared that passive-resistance was incompatible with the Christian faith, and he quoted the saying of Jesus, 'Render unto Caesar the things that are Caesar's, and unto God the things that are God's.' He also quoted St. Paul's statement that the powers that be are ordained of God, and that he who rebels against authority is resisting a divine institution. Yet it was Clayton himself who had earlier declared that it was God alone who could declare what things belonged to Caesar. Nor did he deal with St. Paul's contention that government has no terrors for the well-behaved. Was it not government that had crucified St. Paul's Master, and would it not in due time execute him also?

Rightly or wrongly, Scott felt that this part of the charge was directed against him, and that it did not rank with the best of Clayton's utterances. But Clayton was great and he small, so he kept silent, 'as did everyone else on that particular subject'.[2]

Yet Scott's judgement was merciful. When ten years later Archbishop Clayton decided that he could not enjoin his clergy to obey the notorious 'Church Clause', Scott did not charge him with inconsistency, but wrote feelingly of the great ordeal through which Clayton must have passed before deciding that he could not submit himself 'unto every ordinance of man, even for the Lord's sake'.[3]

I give this account of Clayton's charge with certain reservations. The first is that it is Scott's own account, yet the substance of Clayton's argument is confirmed by Huddleston, in a letter to me dated 14 September 1967. The second is that, although Scott was a truthful man, he was no doubt smarting under Clayton's censure. The third is that Clayton (see page 222) adopted a very different attitude to passive-resistance in 1952. The fourth is that if Clayton had changed his attitude in six years he probably would have said so. The fifth is that Clayton was probably smarting too.

There were of course critics who felt that Clayton had treated Scott harshly. The truth was that their views of the nature and function of the Church were irreconcilable with his. In those days, more so than now, the organisation of the Church's work was relatively rigid. There were no special appointments such as youth advisers, university chaplains, and education directors; the appointment of Dick Yates as curate of St. Cyprian's with special responsibility for domestic servants in the northern suburbs was one of the first such. What is more, Clayton held the strong belief that the work of the Church was done through the parishes. The activities of priests like Michael Scott did not fit into the hierarchical pattern. The idea of witnessing,

*At Sacred Synod, which is a synod of bishop and priests, the bishop gives a charge, but this and other proceedings are not published.

to use Scott's words, 'when or where the Spirit will tell me' was no doubt comprehensible to Clayton. It could hardly not have been. His dilemma, or perhaps one should say Scott's dilemma (because Clayton's mind was hardly a favourable breeding-ground for dilemmas) was the dilemma of many Christians. It is seen in its extreme form when the prophet condemns the priest, and the priest the prophet.

Scott, being now homeless, went to the Blaxalls at 'Ezenzeleni', the famous home of the blind. But he left them too without warning, for the Spirit had called him to 'Tobruk', a shanty town that had grown up on municipal wasteland ten miles from Johannesburg, with shacks built of sackcloth, pieces of wood and linoleum, and old tin cans and between the shacks, muddy and sour-smelling lanes. Scott was invited there by African ex-soldiers, who wanted to establish law and order and social services. He helped to draw up a constitution, and lived there in defiance of the laws of the land, which prohibited any white person from living in a 'native area'. But the gangsters of Tobruk wanted neither law nor order, and terrorised the people, the opposition to them being centred in the Congregational Church of Christ, where Scott lived with the minister, known as the Reverend Theophilus.

Scott was eventually arrested, and fined £5, or fourteen days. He was in these times pale, hungry, gentle, determined, driven on by this relentless Spirit. The gangsters were out to get him. The church was burned down. On 29 April 1947, one thousand police surrounded Tobruk, arrested hundreds of people, and poured thousands of gallons of illicit liquor into the already sodden streets. Scott, pleading in mitigation of sentence when his appeal was heard, concluded his plea by saying: 'If the story of the shantytowns could bring both races face to face with their problem before it is too late to solve it, God will have brought some good out of this evil.'[4] With that strange honesty of his, he wrote that he said these words 'rather pompously'.

Scott was next asked by some Africans to go to Bethal in the Transvaal to investigate the conditions of black farm-labourers in this overwhelmingly Afrikaans-speaking district. Nothing arouses greater anger amongst white farmers than the investigation of their labour affairs by an outsider, a priest of an alien church wearing an alien garb, born in England, a known agitator, a friend of black people, a man who could so degrade himself as to live in the filth of a shantytown. Scott not only investigated, he gave the results to the English-language press. The farmers demanded that he attend a mass-meeting. Fearful but determined, he attended it, but eventually the police called him out for his own safety. One wishes that one could write that as a result of his lonely courage, things have changed markedly for the better, but one cannot.*

Scott now became much sought after by those who had espoused what they believed to be just causes, but needed the strength that seemed to come from this shy, diffident man. Those who disliked him, perhaps because

*It was on 25.10.1944 that the diocesan synod of Johannesburg first warned the Native Affairs Department of the labour conditions in the district of Bethal.

they felt judged by him, regarded him now as a professional 'angry man'. The cause with which he most strongly identified himself was that of the Herero people, 15,000 of whom had fled from South-West Africa to Botswana after Von Trotha had issued his terrible extermination order. Scott met Chief Frederick Mahareu in Botswana, and was sent as an emissary to Chief Hosea Kotako, who had remained in South-West Africa. After his meeting with Hosea, Scott became the spokesman for the Herero people at the United Nations assemblies in New York. He returned to South Africa in 1948, to report to Chief Hosea and to take further statements, meeting everywhere with intense white hostility. When he went to Johannesburg to fly back to New York, he was at the last moment denied permission to take the plane. The authorities demanded his passport, but as they could produce no validating document he refused to part with it and drove secretly into Rhodesia. Back in New York, by a supreme irony, the United States Government restricted his movements to a small area. It was in his own words a 'rather lonely and forlorn fight'. One of the hardest blows he received was a letter from Ambrose Reeves, Bishop of Johannesburg, terminating his general licence on the grounds that he was no longer there. He wrote, 'I could understand his difficulty, but it distressed me at the time.' Finally in 1950 the South African Government declared him to be a prohibited immigrant, and he returned to London to found the Africa Bureau and used it to further yet more of his causes.

So a sad chapter came to an end. Trevor Huddleston wrote these words of Tobruk: 'Father Michael Scott came and lived amongst the people and ministered to them as best he could. To my shame, I did very little to help him. Somehow it took me a long while to wake up, and it is good to be able to apologise publicly now for an apathy I cannot excuse.'[5]

So Huddleston acknowledged generously the selfless courage of a diffident saint. He himself was to reach a crisis in his relations with Clayton in 1956, for reasons both similar and different. Clayton had said of himself that he was not an evangelist. And if he could be called a prophet, and there were good reasons for calling him that, he was not the kind of prophet who lived on locusts and wild honey, or in the sour mud of Tobruk. He was indeed a judge rather than a prophet, and spoke with gravity and authority. When he entered his cathedral, people rose to their feet as they did for a judge when he enters his court, and they listened intently to his judgements.

Administrator, priest, prophet, teacher, evangelist, judge? Can one person be them all? Can one organisation hold them all? Perhaps only under a Temple or a John.

Clayton's failure to appreciate Scott, and his inability to extend to him that pastoral love the strength of which so many of his priests acknowledged, must in no way be allowed to obscure the inspiration of his leadership, nor his concern for the witness of the Church in the world. Most of his chaplains were now back from the war, many of them strongly committed to the building of the new order. One of them, Alpheus Mataboge, who had gone up to Egypt with a contingent of African servicemen, had had to endure many humiliations and inconveniences on the voyage. He was not allowed to use the ship's lounge for the celebration of Mass, but had had to take his service on the open and windy and noisy deck. He wrote his story to the principal Anglican chaplain at Roberts Heights, who in his turn wrote to Clayton saying that he feared much of the story was true. But the war was now over, and Clayton decided not to raise the matter with the authorities.[6] His standing amongst his African priests was very high. His pronouncements on issues which vitally concerned the African people left nothing to desire. No one could ever say of Clayton, 'He rather side-stepped this issue', nor could one ever say, 'He soft-pedalled on that.'

Huddleston's standing amongst his African fellow-priests, his own African church people, and amongst African people of Johannesburg was also high, and his co-operation with his bishop very close. He had come out strongly in favour of the representation of African people on the city and town councils, a proposal which the diocesan synod of 1945 had strongly supported. The resolution had been sent to every city and town council, and to the Transvaal Provincial Council as well. All replies received indicated that the proposal was considered premature, even though it had been in favour of 'indirect' representation, that is, representation of African residents by white councillors.

It was Huddleston's view, and Clayton's also, that it was the duty of the Church to press for such representation. Huddleston argued that the war had been fought for just such a principle, that South Africa was a member of the United Nations, and that the Native Representation Act of 1936 was a sufficient precedent. He warned that the African people were growing increasingly distrustful of plans that the Government made for them.

'It is only a matter of time before this feeling of resentment, suspicion, and deep distrust finds expression in a manner disastrous to all races in this country. The only alternative to such disaster would seem to be to take some definite step *now*, before it is too late, in giving to African people some real responsibility for their own government, some real share in the decisions made concerning them.'[7]

Although Huddleston was fully aware of the pressing need to redress African grievances, he was also opposed to those who tried to exploit them. With Clayton's support, he appealed to the white people of Johannesburg for £3,000 for the establishment of an African weekly newspaper 'to reach our African people with Christian propaganda'. Unless the Church did this, 'our African people will be the victims of that kind of propaganda which is in itself subversive and opposed to Christian principle'. The paper was to be called *The Light*, but the project came to nothing.

That was twenty-six years ago. One can no longer talk about 'our African people', though even more offensive is the phrase 'our Bantu'. The claim that one must protect Africans against subversion would be ridiculed by Africans today. It remains only to note that Huddleston himself was to be forced by circumstances to become what many white people considered subversive, and his 'subversiveness' was to be considered by the most extreme of them as 'opposed to Christian principles'.

An example of what happened to people without representation was the plight of African education, even in 1946. The control of black education, the content of black education, the aim and purpose of black education, were all decided by white authorities. In this year all African schools in the Transvaal, including the mission schools, came under the complete control of the Transvaal Provincial Education Department, but the missionaries could at least be thankful that they had not been handed over to the Native Affairs Department, whose control would have been political not educational, and in whose view the task of African schools would have been to train African children to occupy those stations in life prescribed for them by an all-white Parliament of 153 members, of whom 3 were elected by African voters on the separate roll established in 1936.

Another example of the consequences of non-representation was the African miners' strike of 12 August 1946. African miners earned less than £4 per month, and were now demanding ten shillings a day. Some of the miners marched towards the Johannesburg City Hall, and were driven back with the loss of four lives. Smuts's War Measure No. 145 forbade Africans to strike or to hold meetings on mine property. The Chamber of Mines itself refused to regard the African Mine Workers Union as representative, and would not even reply to the Union's letters. The Natives Representative Council, then in session in Pretoria, asked to go to Johannesburg to see for themselves what was happening, but their request was refused. Therefore even representative bodies were impotent. Councillor Paul Mosaka called the Council a 'toy telephone'. Councillor Selope Thema said bitterly that it was not Hitler who had invented Nazism, but white South Africa.[8]

Eventually the strike was crushed by force. At several mines the police had to drive the miners underground and then drive them up again. Just before Prime Minister General Smuts left for Lake Success, then the headquarters of the new United Nations, he said – as so many lesser men had said before him and so many lesser men have said since – that the strike was not the result of real grievances but was the work of agitators. Even he was unable to concede that a wage of less than £4 per month was something to have a grievance about.*

Smuts left Hofmeyr as Acting Prime Minister, and Clayton and the diocesan synod appealed to him to recognise the African Mine Workers Union.[9] They were asking for the impossible. In no circumstances could Hofmeyr have taken such a revolutionary step. He was in the terrible position of having power to crush disturbances, but no power to remedy their causes.

Clayton in his thirteenth charge roundly condemned the dictatorial handling of the miners' strike. Violence could have been avoided had there

*The argument was used then, and is still used now, that the wage of £4 was only one of the rewards of labour. The others were good food, vermin-free quarters, excellent medical care, and a ration of nutritious millet beer, *utshwala*. These unfortunately could not be shared by a miner's wife and children, who were not allowed to accompany him.

existed proper channels for conciliation. The mine authorities' complaint of outside interference was like the complaint of a lion interrupted when he was about to eat a man for dinner. Some form of machinery for negotiation was urgently needed.

Clayton condemned the housing situation in Johannesburg as being one of the worst in the world, and condemned also those white officials and artisans who would not allow Africans to be trained in building. He condemned also the system of migratory labour, the compound system, and the destruction of African family life. The city of Johannesburg was celebrating its diamond jubilee, but there was much also to be ashamed of.

Clayton concluded by speaking of the centenary of the Church of the Province of South Africa. We could be thankful for the past, but we look mostly to the future. The problems of today were very different – the widespread repudiation of Christian morality, the use of science for purposes of destruction, the danger of population expansion being regarded with mass indifference, the increasing power of a materialist view of man and the world. Meanwhile the Church had not shown a worthwhile alternative. Clayton gave the consolation that the time would come when this disillusionment would bring people back to God. It was not the first time he had given such a consolation. He had given it also to the battling members of the diocesan evangelistic campaign. More than once he had spoken of the spirit of defeatism that brooded over South Africa and the world. That he at times was discouraged, no one can doubt. But he had also that rocklike quality of which Dorothy Maud had spoken. When he made his great utterances, one could forgive him all.

It was at the diocesan synod of 1946 that Huddleston had his first personal taste of Clayton's brand of tyrannical democracy. At that time it was almost impossible to get a berth on a ship, and preference was given to soldiers' wives. Huddleston, after consulting Rouse and getting his approval, tabled a resolution asking for similar privileges for women missionaries. It was his first motion at synod, and he was taken aback when he stood up to move it, to hear the bishop say loudly, 'I intend to oppose this from the Chair!' After Huddleston had finished, Clayton did oppose from the Chair, and said with great force that he did not believe in the 'Church pulling strings'. It hardly needs saying that the motion was defeated by an overwhelming majority. Huddleston waited for Clayton after synod had adjourned, and said, 'My Lord, you have been unfair to me.' Clayton said with great affability, 'Come and have tea with me tomorrow.' Huddleston went, and explained the purity of his motives, whereupon Clayton was 'as nice as pie' but did not apologise.

The diocesan synod of 1946 showed very clearly the difficulties of the problem of defining Christian action in a secular society. It was true that each daily meeting of Parliament was opened with prayer, but it was equally true that to apply Christian ethics to a human society was considered to be impracticable, unrealistic, impossible, and starry-eyed. H. R. Higgs, editor of *The Watchman*, summed up the debates under the title 'Left–Right–Left', and epitomised the conflict by observing that the trend of the Church was away from concern with established congregations towards a dynamic conception of the gospel as a crusade to bring liberty and life to those without them. These two concerns, he wrote, had been labelled the right and the left.

Higgs clearly sympathised with the left, and he described three of the arguments used by the white conservatives in synod as untenable. The first was that Europeans should not espouse the cause of non-Europeans in social and economic matters; in other words, they should not meddle and manufacture grievances. The second was that non-Europeans were not yet fitted to take full advantage of the benefits of education, trade-unionism, and franchise; to this Higgs replied that no group in history had ever been fully fitted beforehand. The third argument was that many Africans had not yet emerged from the tribal state, and that their detribalised brothers must wait till they were freed; Higgs found this the worst argument of all.

So Higgs exposed very lucidly the cleavages in Synod, and therefore the cleavages in South African Anglicanism. It was the cleavage between the conservative and the liberal, the pietist and the activist, the gradualist and the impatient reformer. One must note again that in those days the cleavage between white and black was not articulated. One must note, also again, that Clayton presided over these debates with great tolerance and benevolence towards the arguments that Higgs found untenable, and that he was much less tolerant of reformers' impatience than he was of the conservatives' resistance to change. Yet he himself preached in season and out of it the urgent need for change. This must remain one of the fascinating paradoxes of his extraordinary personality.

Higgs concluded with a compliment to Synod: 'We believe, indeed, that there is no other kind of conclave in the Union where men so single-heartedly, yet forthrightly, so altruistically, speak out their heart and mind and conscience, and are accorded the respect even of their opponents for so doing'.[10] This compliment can hardly be called modest, but it was justifiable. It was a compliment to Clayton too, for it was he who gave to the diocesan synods of Johannesburg their peculiar force and flavour.

In 1947 there were three events which gave Clayton much pleasure. The first was the visit to South Africa of the head of the British Commonwealth, King George VI, and his wife and two daughters. Clayton, like most Englishmen of his time and class, was deeply attached to the Royal House, and was an honoured guest at the mayoral reception in Johannesburg. He did not enjoy the honour of preaching to the royal visitors, but he commended them for having no engagements on Good Friday and Easter Day, and regretted that it was thought necessary for them to attend a race meeting. The second event was his election as an honorary fellow of Peterhouse, the Cambridge college of which he had been made chaplain and fellow nearly forty years before. The third event gave him most pleasure of all. He received a letter from the University itself to ask whether he would accept an honorary degree of Doctor of Divinity; that was an honour indeed.

One has no right to conclude that it was not his own university that first thought of honouring him. But it appears certain that the new Chancellor of the University of Cambridge, Field-Marshal Jan Smuts, who had by virtue of his office a right to nominate candidates for honorary degrees, was responsible for the according of the honour.[11]

Clayton kept the congratulatory letter written to him by the Revd. Bruce Gardiner, formerly the minister of the Presbyterian church of St. George, Johannesburg, and later minister at Alice, the Eastern Province town where the University College of Fort Hare was situated. Gardiner and Clayton had always got on well together; Gardiner had a good mind, and Clayton liked talking theology to him. Gardiner wrote, 'May you be long spared to carry on the work you have been doing so valiantly and may this honour strengthen your heart.'[12]

It is hardly surprising that Clayton condemned so roundly the 'prevailing spirit of defeatism'. 'I see no reason for any kind of defeatism in this country, or at any rate in this diocese.'[13] It is unusual – though it can happen – for a person to fall prey to defeatism when his own work is recognised. It is much easier when the work is not. Another source of cheer was the financial position of the diocese at the end of 1947. For the first time in history there was a surplus, a small one, in the Native Stipend Fund, and that meant that the stipends had been paid in full by the African mission districts themselves. The European Stipend Fund was also in a healthy position. Yet it was disappointing that the Native Missions Central Fund had a deficit greater than the combined surpluses. This was the fund which made a grant to the Community of the Resurrection, and paid the stipends of those European priests who were 'ministering to natives'. That meant one thing and one thing only; that was that white members of the diocese were still not making a generous enough contribution to the fund, and that they were not making good the money that had once come from the Society for the Propagation of the Gospel, which the diocese had yielded at the outbreak of war. What is more, Clayton had more than once assured the Society of his own hope that his diocese would not accept such a grant again.[14]

At this time J. L. Durant, the efficient and industrious secretary of the diocese, reported that, although the white parishes had contributed £2,165 in 1943, this had fallen to £1,836 in 1946, and would in 1947 probably be less. He appealed to church people to make the 1947 Diocesan Gift the biggest ever recorded.[15]

The year 1947 came to its close with another magnificent charge, one of the themes of which was the theoretical structure of the Church of the Province, as contrasted with the reality. Clayton gave expression to his own hope. Although he had defended Millington's 'acid realism' at the opening of the Evangelistic Conference, he was not partial to it himself. Though he did not believe in watering down the medicine and coating the pill, he did not care for acidity.

The New Testament taught that 'the barriers that divided men were to be broken down, had in fact been broken down by the Christ'. What then was the Church of the Province to do 'in a country where the official policy of successive governments is a policy of social segregation, and so far as possible, residential segregation'.* He instanced the racial parallelism practised by the Dutch Reformed churches, and said, 'It seems to me that the system of parallel churches is almost exactly what St. Paul fought against successfully.' He then spoke of the theoretical structure of the Church of the Province.

'Theoretically there is nothing to prevent an African being elected to be bishop of this diocese. Yet in practice the position is not so simple. The African laity accept the ministrations of the European clergy. I do not think the majority of the European laity would accept the ministrations of the African clergy. . . . Very many European parishes are alive to the position and co-operate in every way they can. I believe they will continue to get better. We are trying to do something which is difficult but which is immensely worth while. There has got to be infinite patience and forbearance on both sides. I believe God is leading us along the right road. But all of us, white and black, right wing and left wing, must remember that the wrath of man worketh not the righteousness of God.'

That was in 1947. Today there are signs that the patience and forbearance will not be infinite, and that the Church of the Province of South Africa faces a great crisis, largely because it too is deeply infected by the disease of parallelism, and because the chasm between profession and practice is so vast.

Perhaps one can do no better than end with Clayton's own words. He commended the saying of St. James, which had often brought him courage: 'If any man lack wisdom, let him ask of God, and it shall be given him.'[16]

Wisdom yes, but a bit of pace too.

*The reader should note that this charge was delivered *before* the Nationalist Party came to power in May 1948.

20

Visit to Lambeth

The Lambeth Conference is the gathering of all the bishops of the Anglican Communion throughout the world. It has no legislative powers, as each Province is autonomous. But it was established in 1867 in the hope that its pronouncements might 'serve as safe guides to future action'.[1] Another of its purposes was to strengthen the feeling of unity amongst the Anglican Provinces, in times when communication was infrequent and slow.

Clayton had been going to Lambeth in 1939, but the outbreak of war had put an end to that. Now in 1948 the opportunity came again, and he prepared himself for his first visit to England in fourteen years. The Conference would last from 1 July to the middle of August, but Clayton was going to have a holiday as well of about six months, from the middle of April to the middle of October. That it was a bishop's holiday, we shall see. He announced that he had nominated Dean William Palmer as Vicar-General of the diocese, and he gave his readers in *The Watchman* some facts about the world Anglican Communion. There were 312 dioceses and 20 provinces, and a number of dioceses not in provinces. He wrote of the universality of this Communion, which guards against 'any tendency to tune the Christian Gospel to meet the particular prejudices of particular parts of the world'.[2]

Before he left for England Clayton wrote three articles for *The Watchman*, on marriage and divorce.[3] He said that canon XXIX of the Church of the Province of South Africa declared adherence to the teaching of the Church of England on marriage and divorce. Divorce and separation were recognised, but not remarriage during the life of the divorced spouse. Marriage is a lifelong and indissoluble union. What is the Church to do with someone who marries a divorced person whose spouse is living, or with a divorced person who marries while the spouse is living? 'It is quite untrue to say that the Church treats these people as outcasts. They remain God's children; they remain members of the Church.' But if they break the rules they must subject themselves to discipline. All this teaching, Clayton concluded, is based on Holy Scripture.

Clayton dealt fully with the scriptural evidence. In the Gospel according to St. Matthew, Our Lord is represented as teaching that remarriage is forbidden except in the case of adultery, and then not for the adulterer.[4] In the Gospels according to St. Mark and St. Luke, Our Lord forbids all remarriage.[5] St. Paul taught the indissolubility of marriage.[6] The disciples were shocked by the second teaching, but they would not have been shocked by the first because it was taught by one of the schools of Jewish thought. What then was the Church to do? According to Clayton, 'The Christian Church must be conclusive.' He found it difficult to believe that the account in St. Matthew was accurate, and decided that the 'weight of evidence is enormously in favour' of the view that Jesus taught that there was to be no remarriage unless in the event of the death of one of the spouses.

At that time the views of the Anglican Church in South Africa were inflexible. I was then principal of Diepkloof Reformatory, and lived in a world of broken marriages, vanished husbands and, less often, vanished wives, and homes ruined beyond repair by violence, drunkenness, and incest, and I was unable to hold these inflexible views. I was talking to a group of older African boys at the Priory of Christ the King about Diepkloof Reformatory and its problems. At discussion time one of the boys put the case of an Anglican mother and children who had been deserted by a worthless husband who had brought them all nothing but unhappiness. She was now being asked for in marriage by a decent man, also a member of the congregation of Christ the King. But the priest had told them that for both of them marriage after divorce would be a grave sin, and would result in excommunication. What would the lecturer advise them to do? What a terrible question! The atmosphere in the room was tense. It was clearly a question that had been put before. I said I could not advise them, but I wished with all my heart that they would be able to marry. This answer pleased the audience, but the chairman, who was a priest of the priory, repudiated it emphatically. The cleavage between him and the boys was complete.

So in those days was the cleavage between the clergy and the laity very deep. Many of the laity would have called it putting dogmas before people. This made Clayton extremely angry. This was caused partly by his utter devotion to the teachings of Our Lord, but it was also caused partly by his attitude towards sexual matters. He himself was able to practise abstinence, and one would imagine that by this time it was, and for a long time before that it had been, no struggle to do so. His solution for the deserted wife in Sophiatown would have been an obedient abstinence for life if need be. He not only had little understanding of the sexual nature and needs of men and women, he also had little understanding of the desire of a woman to have a husband who would cherish her and help her to bring up her children. His judgement was absolute. 'For myself I do not see how the Church could go back upon its teaching without treachery to its mission as a witness to the teaching of Our Lord.'[7]

In April Clayton flew to England. This gave Palmer the opportunity to pay him extraordinary tribute.

'. . . we have had as our father in God, one who has been unremitting in his care for all the souls of this great diocese. There are times when I wonder if there is one loose thread in the diocesan organisation. We may truly thank

God that there was given to us fourteen years ago, one with the wide vision of our leader, and the grasp of detail of our administrator.'[8]

In England Clayton was having a real bishop's holiday, preaching everywhere. His sermon at the Church of St. Mary the Virgin in Oxford was out of the ordinary, and was broadcast by the B.B.C. He preached about South Africa, but then changed the subject.

'And now forget about problems and think about people. Some people are congenial to you and others are not. Both are your neighbours. Because you are a Christian, you should love them both on the pattern of Christ's love to you. I do not know how it is with you. I can speak only of myself. I am sure Christ loves me. But I can't believe that Christ likes me – that I am congenial to him. His love for me is never patronage. It is willingness to share with me. And that must be the pattern of my love for others. That need not necessarily be liking. If it is, all the better. But it need not be. And it must never be patronage. We have to put ourselves where other people are, and try to understand them. To put ourselves where they are! Christ did not call to us from Heaven to come to Him. He came to fetch us back.'[9]

Clayton's comparing and contrasting of love and liking had been done before, for example by Dick Sheppard, the beloved and eccentric Vicar of St. Martin-in-the-Fields. When asked by a friend how he could possibly love a certain person, he replied, 'I do more than love him, I positively like him.' If Sheppard was right, love and liking are akin, but liking is stronger. If Clayton was right, they are to be contrasted, in that Christ could love a person whom he did not like. It was in this sense of the word 'love' that Clayton spoke of differing from those Christians who upheld the policies of racial separation. One must differ from them 'in love', and there can be no doubt that Clayton meant something important by it, even though I could never fully comprehend what it was. Of course this particular sermon was exceptional in that Clayton was actually talking about himself, as though he were observing himself with a kind of wry humility and humour, and at the same time saying important things in short sentences and simple words. The sermon reminds one of the story of the Cape Town woman who said to him, 'Your Grace, do you expect to go to heaven?', to which he replied, 'Well, hardly, because if I went there, it wouldn't be heaven, would it?' This was the same Clayton who had said at Chesterfield, sure that his predecessor Archdeacon Crosse would be saved, that he himself would probably not, because it would be too much to expect two archdeacons to be saved in succession.

It was not long after this sermon that there happened in South Africa one of the most momentous events in her history. On 26 May 1948 Smuts fell from power. He lost twenty-five seats to Malan's Nationalist Party and seven seats to Havenga's Afrikaner Party. He was driven from virtually every Afrikaans-speaking country constituency, and lost his own seat at Standerton that he had held for twenty-five years. Malan, supported by Havenga, although 150,000 votes behind, commanded a majority of five in the important Lower House, thanks to the overloading of urban constituencies and the underloading of rural constituencies, a provision approved by Smuts in 1909, and therefore one by which he felt morally bound, although he had been urged by many to abolish the provision before it was too late.*

The jubilation of the Nationalists was boundless. At last the country which the British had stolen from them had been restored. The Afrikaner, his culture, his language, his church, would all come into their own. And the foundation of it all would be the grand policy of apartheid, by which the white people of South Africa would be totally separated from all others in schools, universities, hotels, buses, trains, residential areas, trading-areas, sporting-facilities, beaches, concert halls, cinemas, theatres, circuses, councils, parliaments, and in every other place and on every conceivable occasion, in so far as it could be made possible.

Just as the election result filled the Nationalists with jubilation, so it filled others with fear and gloom. Smuts was beside himself; this was one of the only occasions in his life – perhaps the only one – in which he seemed to lose his massive self-containedness. In just over six months Hofmeyr was dead. All those who had worked so long and so hard to gain a painful inch in the field of race relations looked with anxiety to the future. So did those who loved their Englishry, revered the Royal Family, boasted of the Royal Navy, and were proud of the British Commonwealth. The less militant Indian and Coloured and African people waited with fear to see what would be done to them by the policies of apartheid. And not least fearful were those churchmen who were not Dutch Reformed, those whose churches had great mission enterprises, many of which could not survive without the aid of the State.[10]

None of these fears and apprehensions were groundless. Nationalists had poured contempt and invective on all ventures in the field of race relations. They had threatened to legislate to prevent inter-racial and non-racial undertakings. They had threatened to spend less money on African education, and to make Africans pay more towards it. They fulminated against the universities of Cape Town and the Witwatersrand which admitted a number of students of races other than white. They fulminated against any kind of education which would turn out 'black Englishmen'. They condemned those churches which disregarded the customs and traditions of South Africa, and in their administration and worship ignored God-given race differences. It was useless to point out to them that the Afrikaners themselves were the descendants of Dutch, German, English, Scottish, Irish, French progenitors, and that the Coloured people of South Africa were the descendants of the same progenitors, with the addition of others such as the Khoikhoin and the Malays; such arguments aroused only anger.

It was Dr. Malan himself – on the eve of the election campaign – who stated, 'Churches and Societies which undermine the policy of apartheid and propagate doctrines foreign to the nation will be checked.'[11] Nobody

*It is often argued that if Smuts had abolished the provision, white South Africa would not have embarked on its present collision course. I think this conclusion is questionable.

could have been less prophetic than the editorial writer of *Church News* on 9 June 1948: 'It is unlikely that very many people took the "apartheid" policy very seriously and it is even more unlikely that it will be applied, though some change in the Native Policy may be looked for.'

Meanwhile Clayton continued his bishop's holiday, preaching in Oxford and Cambridge, and in many of the cathedrals. What he thought of the elections, this writer does not know. One may surmise that he discussed them a great deal, but did not agonise about them as many did whom he had left behind. That there would be new and difficult problems to deal with when he returned, no one knew better than he. But there would have been no point in fussing about them now. In any case he was enjoying England and preaching and being a bishop. There were not many preachers of his calibre in England, or anywhere else for that matter. It was almost impossible for him to preach badly. He held his audiences and congregations, not with any tricks nor with those gadgets he had so scathingly referred to, but with that authority, those considered judgements, those reports on his adopted country which somehow rang true, because it was very difficult to believe that this preacher could practise deception or self-deception; and all this delivered in those short sentences and simple words. It would have been very difficult in the course of this busy and satisfying round to have given as much thought to the results of the South African elections as he would have given them in Johannesburg.

For another thing the great day was approaching. Another important South African would be there, and that would be the fallen Prime Minister, who was coming to England in the aeroplane of the new Prime Minister, to receive what was doubtless the greatest honour of his illustrious life, the Chancellorship of the University of Cambridge, where he had graduated brilliantly fifty-four years before. Among Clayton's fellow-graduands were Winston Churchill, Cyril Garbett the Archbishop of York, and yet another South African, Leif Egeland, the High Commissioner in London.

At 11.15 a.m. on the great day Smuts was installed as Chancellor. After that a performance of music was given in his honour in King's College Chapel. Luncheon was held in Trinity College, and the Chancellor proposed the toast of the recipients of Honorary Degrees. Then was performed the ballet 'Dainty Fine Sweet Nymph', composed by Thomas Morley in 1595, the language and sentiments of which were not exactly Claytonian:

Dainty fine sweet Nymph delightful
While the Sun aloft is mounting .
Sit we here our loves re-counting
With sugred gloses
Among these Roses
Fa la la.

Why alas are you so spiteful,
Dainty Nymph? but, O too cruel,
Wilt thou kill thy dearest jewel?

Kill then and bliss me
But first come and kiss me.
Fa la la.

Winston Churchill responded to the toast and after luncheon the procession formed. All Cambridge turned out to see the grand sight, and Garbett said to Clayton, 'They haven't turned out to see us but to see the old man. The people of England will give him anything he wants except the Prime-Ministership.'

At 2.45 p.m. the procession left for the Old Schools, where the honorary graduands signed the Registrary's book. Then it proceeded to the Senate House for the Congregation at 3.15 p.m. The Archbishop of York was presented first, followed by Churchill. The third to be presented was Geoffrey Hare Clayton, Bishop of Johannesburg, otherwise known as Galfridus, Episcopus Johannesburgensis, the Orator of course outlining his career and acclaiming his virtues in Latin, among these being his affability and wealth of knowledge.

So came to a close one of the momentous days of Clayton's life, when his industry, devotion and leadership and his service to the Church were recognised by his own university. His greatest honour in life was to be a bishop, his greatest academic honour to have been made an honorary Doctor of Divinity of Cambridge.[12] Back in Johannesburg Dean Palmer collected some money and presented the bishop with his doctoral robes.

Clayton now returned to his round of sermons and addresses, including a sermon to the University. Then to Lambeth for the Conference, when there occurred another momentous event. On the opening day, 30 July 1948, Archbishop Darbyshire died at the age of 68. He had been Archbishop of Cape Town for ten years. The *Church News* of 14 July called him 'a Father in God, deeply respected, deeply revered, deeply loved . . . Truly a great leader is gone from us.' Bishop Lavis, Coadjutor Bishop of Cape Town, said that his death 'seems at first sight tragedy without relief or mitigation'.

How far were these things true? Certainly, after the first sight had been taken, it was possible to reflect that Darbyshire, who in the opinion of many Anglicans was lacking in strength and decisiveness, was not the man to deal with the problems which would now confront the Church in South Africa. For those in the know it was hard to see how Clayton could again be passed over. In 1948 the chances of appointing an archbishop from England were small. The new Nationalist Government was likely to react vigorously and with hostility to any bishop from abroad who would criticise their policies. What was more, Clayton's renowned irritability was now known to be a minor defect, even endearing him to some, and actually in the process of abatement. His supposed dislike of women was also seen to be more a fear of them, and an embarrassment in their presence which sometimes led him into rude and gauche behaviour, an embarrassment which was also abating. Most of all, he was seen by many to be the man for a dangerous hour.

At Lambeth his reputation climbed yet higher. He was appointed to

Committee No. 1 which had to draw up a statement of the Christian doctrine of Man. Clayton was not the chairman of Committee No. 1. The chairman was J. W. C. Wand, the Bishop of London. Yet the Bishop of Malmesbury, Ivor Watkins, writing on 30 November 1948 to congratulate Clayton on his election as archbishop, used these words: 'We who were privileged to sit under you on committee at Lambeth ...' The Archbishop of Quebec, Philip Carrington, writing for the same purpose on 17 March 1949, recalled Clayton's chairmanship of Committee No. 1.[13] He could conceivably have acted as chairman during the absence of the appointed chairman on the many duties involved in such a conference. There is also the possibility that Committee No. 1 broke up into sub-committees, and that Clayton was chairman of one of them.* However, Bishop Wand, in a letter to Bishop Stradling of Johannesburg, thinks he may have presided over the sub-committee that prepared the second part of the report.

The Lambeth reports from its various committees are not official pronouncements; to have endorsed them all would have been impossible. The procedure was to frame resolutions based on the reports, and if these were approved by the Conference then they became official pronouncements. Yet even then they had no executive force. Only the constitutional authority of the Province could give them that.

What can one do better than give Clayton's own impressions of Lambeth? The Revd. Cyril Tomkinson, Vicar of All Saints', Margaret Street, London, W.1., who had been one of Clayton's curates at Cambridge, asked Clayton to write on Lambeth for his church and parish magazine for October 1948. He himself wrote, 'I would rather have Dr. Clayton's judgements on affairs than those of anyone else in the world.' It is interesting to note the things Clayton thought most worthy of mention in an article consisting of some 1,500 words.

A Christian humanism based on the Christian doctrine of man could not be reconciled with Marxian Communism, but the Conference was not prepared to embark upon an anti-Communist campaign. Was Clayton thinking of Scott when he wrote, 'Many people, possibly muddle-headed people, become Communists because they have a passion for social justice.'

There was no defeatism at Lambeth. 'The Bishops were sure that the tide of faith was coming in, and that there was every reason for confidence and hope. Secondly the Bishops assert that the Church in the Diocese and Parish is the key to the whole situation. With regard to these two points I should like to say how strongly I agree.'

Clayton then devoted nearly half his article to the question of the relations between the Anglican Communion and the new Church of South India, which was an amalgamation of the Congregational, Methodist and Presbyterian Churches, and of four of the dioceses of the Anglican Church of India, Burma and Ceylon: Clayton, like many Anglo-Catholics of his time, believed that the divided Church was a grief to its Founder, but laid down conditions for reunion which made it virtually unrealisable. He believed

*Committee No. 3 had such sub-committees.

that the Anglican Communion held the key to reunion, in that it was part of the Catholic Church, yet had strong links with the Nonconformists. There can be little doubt that he saw reunion in the light of a return to Mother Church, and one of the conditions for that was an acceptance of the doctrine of the apostolic succession, the doctrine that the risen Christ had breathed on the disciples the gift of the Holy Spirit, giving them power to remit sins, and the further doctrine that this gift could only be imparted to others by those to whom it had already been imparted. These doctrines were further enlarged to include the dogma that it was through persons called bishops that these powers were transmitted by the laying on of hands in the rites of consecration, ordination, and confirmation. This was the doctrine of the episcopacy, which was challenged by Luther and completely repudiated by Calvin. Nor can this confinement of the Spirit be accepted by those apostolic sects who believe that the Spirit, like the wind, 'bloweth where it listeth'.

Clayton was immovable on the doctrine of the apostolic succession and the episcopacy, and viewed with great distrust the plans to create a united Church of South India, of whose fourteen bishops seven would be Anglicans and seven would be ministers who had never received the gifts of the Spirit by the laying on of hands. According to Dick Yates, Clayton went to Lambeth debating with himself as to whether he would oppose any recognition of the new Church. At Lambeth he was approached by a number of Anglo-Catholics to take part in a movement of opposition, but, influenced by the knowledge that Temple favoured recognition, he declined.

Clayton explained to readers of Tomkinson's parish magazine those decisions of Lambeth which concerned the Church of South India. Ex-Anglican members of the new Church, clerical or lay, would continue to have Anglican privileges. Non-Anglican ministers of the new Church at the time of amalgamation would not have these privileges, as they had not been episcopally ordained. But the difficult question was the status of those who would be ordained or consecrated after amalgamation. Were they to be regarded as Ministers of the Catholic Church? The majority of members of the Lambeth Conference of 1948 were able to accept the new Church as a living part of the one holy, catholic, and apostolic Church. A minority could not. Clayton believed the members of the minority to be right, though he did not publicly espose their view that only time would tell whether the new Church would be acceptable to the Anglican Communion.

Clayton concluded his article with the statement that if one was a Christian, one's standards really were different from those of one's neighbour. 'I don't think we Bishops adequately meet that need.' Lastly he came away from Lambeth greatly encouraged, confident in the 'belief in the Church as part of the Gospel'.

Lambeth passed many resolutions. It condemned race and colour discrimination. It condemned war as a method of settling disputes, and believed that it was time for nations to yield some of their sovereignty. It recognised the differences between the conservatives and the activists, calling the first those 'who value tradition' and the second those 'who feel most urgently the need for change and reform'; and it declared that 'the fellowship of the Christian community should contain them'. It implored the unhappily married to 'remain steadily faithful to their marriage vows', and confirmed the discretionary power of the bishops to admit to Holy Communion those who have married contrary to the law of the Church, a power which one supposes Clayton would not have exercised unless after much consideration.

It remains to say that the Nonconformist churches resented the resolution on the new Church of South India. To them it represented a harsh and legalistic view, lacking in brotherly love. Their view was expressed by Dr. Nathaniel Micklem, chairman of the Friends of Reunion, who said that 'a real longing for reunion is still confined to the relatively few'.[14] Twenty-four years later this is less true, but the road to reunion certainly winds uphill all the way. As I write, the Church of England, after sixteen years of negotiation, has rejected union with the Methodists. In 1969, 69 per cent voted in favour, yet in 1973, 65 per cent of the General Synod voted for it, but 75 per cent was needed. It is reported that 'the result of the vote was heard in total silence'.[15]

Clayton spent two more months in England after Lambeth was over, doing a great deal of preaching, and visiting his sister Kitty, his brother Harold, and many of his old Cambridge and Chesterfield friends. He had already visited Chesterfield in May for an afternoon, but he went there to preach during the weekend of 25 and 26 September, and received a tremendous welcome. It was on this occasion that he commended his successor, the Revd. T. Dilworth-Harrison, for his work in the beautifying of the church.[16] Part of his sermon he devoted to South Africa, saying that 'the white South African, at any rate if he is of Dutch extraction, has no other home'. He was historically inaccurate – and inaccuracy was rare in him – when he said that the black tribesmen came from the north at about the same time as the Dutch came from the south. Some white South Africans like to believe this, thinking no doubt that it strengthens their right to be in the country, but modern historians – and their findings were not unknown in 1948 – believe that Bantu-speakers had reached as far south as the Transkei by the sixteenth century, and probably much earlier; what is more, Bantu-speakers had lived in the Transvaal in the eleventh century.[17]

Clayton told his Chesterfield congregation that the white people of South Africa had not made much of a success in their attempts to deal with their complex racial situation. One could not see far into the future; one must do 'the next right thing'. He concluded:

'So we can be of good cheer. We don't know what is going to happen. Whatever happens, we are in the hands of God. And not life nor death nor anything else can separate us from the love which is in Christ Jesus our Lord.'[18]

Soon after this he returned to South Africa, and Dean Palmer wrote in *The Watchman* of November: 'The whole diocese rejoices in the presence of the Bishop among us again.' That was true. The Church of the Province was facing the greatest challenge that had ever confronted it, from a Government that found its theology and its practices and its moral pronouncements completely alien, and had announced unequivocally its intention of entrenching racial difference and separation, a course of action that would threaten not only the enterprises of the Church but its spiritual life also. Who better than Clayton to deal with such grave matters?

On 6 July *Die Kerkbode* had published an editorial entitled 'Church and Parliament'. It said: 'We as Church give thanks with humility that the members of our Government are all bearers of Protestant belief and members of the Christian Church.' They must be prayed for. They face tension amongst the racial groups, the complicated race question, and the struggle against alien directions of thought. How one had prayed for Christian leaders! The Church was vitally concerned. More than 30,000 Afrikaners in the big cities belonged to the English churches, and an equally great number to the sects. One had been told that the Church must keep quiet when great problems are discussed in the political sphere. 'The Church must be free to speak, not to say what it wants to, [but to say] "Thus saith the Lord".' *Die Kerkbode* concluded by hoping that Church and Parliament would move still nearer one another.[19]

So *Die Kerkbode* discarded the political neutrality that it had observed so scrupulously during the years of the Second World War. It did not say so in so many words, but this was its own Government. And where did one find the 'alien directions of thought'? Where better than in the letters, sermons, and charges of the Bishop of Johannesburg, who out of the depth of knowledge acquired at Rugby and Cambridge, pontificated about South African affairs in his cathedral?

So Clayton entered the last phase of his life. In December 1948 J. H. Hofmeyr died. For the next eight years it was Clayton who was to be the foremost upholder and defender of Christian liberal principle and practice. Ironically, he was to defend them against the new Christian government, bearers of Protestant belief and members of the Christian Church. He was going to comprehend more fully the vast and seemingly unbridgeable gulf that yawns between South African Calvinism and all the world's other churches.

21

'My heart is turned to water'

On 7 November 1948, Clayton delivered his fifteenth and last charge as Bishop of Johannesburg. After he had paid his respects to the memory of Archbishop Darbyshire, a tribute more formal than warm, he devoted a great deal of his charge to an account of the Lambeth Conference, and in particular to its consideration of the Christian doctrine of Man. He repeated his favourite teaching that the environment in which man lived did not make it easy to lead the Christian life, but by the grace of God it did not make it impossible. Speaking of man's duties to God and neighbour, he said that men must exercise certain rights to be able to perform these duties, and these rights should be secured to them by the State. He then quoted Lambeth Resolution No. 7:

'The Conference declares that among such rights are security of life and person, the right to work, to bring up a family, and to possess personal property; the right to freedom of speech, of discussion and association, and to accurate information; and to full freedom of religious life and practice, and that these rights belong to all men irrespective of race or colour.'

Clayton had returned to a country whose new rulers had an intense fear and hatred of Communism. This was not so much a fear of the methods of totalitarianism, which indeed they soon learned to use themselves. It was rather a fear of the dictatorship of the proletariat, and the South African proletariat was black. To put it in other words, it was a fear of the end of white supremacy. The new rulers promised a relentless attack on Communism and Communists, and the more far-seeing South Africans realised that this attack would also be directed against all non-Communist militant opposition to apartheid, which would be accused of furthering, wittingly or unwittingly, the aims of Communism. Clayton realised this clearly. In his charge he rejected repression as a means of eradicating Communism, and said, 'I think we are in great danger in this country through the failure of public opinion to recognise this.' He said also that the tragedy of South Africa was that in these matters Christian opinion was not united. He concluded with the call which he now never failed to give, to take courage. 'So I commend you to God's love. May He who has begun a great work in you perfect it until the Day of Jesus Christ.'[1]

On 16 November 1948 the Elective Assembly met in Cape Town to choose a new archbishop. The Assembly consists in the first place of all the licensed priests in the diocese of Cape Town, and the chosen candidate must receive a two-thirds majority of the votes cast by them. Before the voting takes place the names are submitted to the Synod of Bishops, which meets in Cape Town at the same time, but in another building. The bishops do not vote at this stage, but may send back comments to the Assembly. The candidate chosen by the clergy must then receive the assent of a two-thirds majority of the lay representatives elected by the parishes for this purpose. Nominations can come from the clergy only.

The new archbishop will be titled the Archbishop of Cape Town, and the Metropolitan of the Church of the Province of South Africa. Because he is the titular head of the Church of the Province, he must receive yet a third endorsement, and that is from the Synod of Bishops. Criticism has often been made that the clergy and laity of the other dioceses have no representation in the Elective Assembly, but no changes have so far been made in the procedure.

At the Elective Assembly of 1948, six candidates were nominated by the clergy. These six names were submitted to the Synod of Bishops, and one of the candidates, himself a bishop, withdrew his name. The Synod of Bishops suggested that it would be unwise to elect a candidate from outside the country, and the clergy accepted this suggestion and reduced the number to four. One of these was Bishop Lavis, the much-loved and respected Coadjutor-Bishop of Cape Town, and it was agreed that his name should be withdrawn on account of his age.

Thus three candidates were left. The first ballot gave a preponderance of votes to the Bishops of Johannesburg and Natal, each of them receiving forty. The Bishop of Natal was Leonard Fisher, brother of the 99th Archbishop of Canterbury. While Clayton was known for his formidability, his great utterances, and his intellectual gifts, Fisher was considered to be a man of saintly life, gentle, compassionate, and loving. The third candidate, Dean Michael Gibbs of Cape Town, then withdrew his name. The second ballot gave Clayton a one-vote lead over the Bishop of Natal, and a third increased the number of votes for Clayton but did not give him the required two-thirds majority. The Assembly then adjourned to the following day.

On 17 November the fourth ballot was held, and Clayton received the required two-thirds majority. His name was then presented to the lay representatives, who also gave him the necessary majority. The result was communicated to the Synod of Bishops, who gave their immediate assent.[2] The whole procedure occupied only a day and a half.

Clayton then went over to present himself to the Elective Assembly presided over by Dean Gibbs. This was not one of the occasions when he was grave and somewhat awe-inspiring. He was smiling, with what one presumes to be joy and satisfaction. He became serious, however, as he went to the altar. The Te Deum was sung, and the Archbishop-elect asked for the prayers of the congregation, and led them in a collect. After he had given his blessing he stood at the door and shook hands with all, again pleased and smiling. After lunch Blaxall saw him in St. George's Street, and had never been greeted so affably, but he understood all when Clayton beamed at him and said, 'I've been elected Archbishop.'

That afternoon the *Cape Argus* welcomed his appointment. 'The importance of the part played in South African life by the Church of the Province may be judged by the frequency and violence of the attacks made on it.' The newspaper commended the Church of the Province for its 'defence of the poor and the weak, and those who have no other champion. . . . His career as Archbishop will call for courage and leadership. No man can better provide these qualities than Bishop Clayton'. No words could have been more apt and true.

The Metropolitan has by no means the powers of a Pope. He summons and presides over Provincial and Episcopal synods. He confirms with his comprovincials the election of bishops of the Province. He hears in his Provincial tribunal appeals from the sentences of diocesan tribunals. He sits in judgement on his brother-bishops if charges are brought against them. Finally he has visitatorial powers over the dioceses of the Province, but he may not interfere with or alter any of their arrangements unless he has the consent of his brother-bishops.

It has been shown that Clayton would not hesitate to use the power of his personality to influence the decisions of synod, and even on occasion by his intervention to compel a synod to draw back from a decision that it was prepared to take, and to take another or none at all. By and large such masterful actions, often accompanied by that well-known look of irritability, were treated as jokes. It should therefore be recorded that Clayton was a stickler for constitutional rule and would never have taken any unconstitutional course, no matter how much the course would have been to his liking. And had a synod ignored his masterful directions – which this writer never saw happen – he would have abided by it, however wrathfully. One other thing should be recorded. Several of the priests in the Elective Assembly consistently opposed Clayton's election as archbishop, and were in the last ballot still voting in the minority. What is more, they made no attempt to conceal their opposition, before, during, and after the election. They were therefore known to a great many people, among whom was Clayton. There is no record whatever that he allowed his knowledge to influence him in any way in his relations with them. Bearing grudges was not one of his failings.

Clayton now returned to Johannesburg for the rest of the year 1948. The news of his election had been received there with mixed feelings. Some rejoiced that he was to lead the whole Province, others grieved that he was leaving Johannesburg.

Clayton was no keeper of letters. He kept almost no newspaper cuttings, and few photographs. One assumes that after a decent lapse of time he destroyed illuminated addresses, gifts of all kinds, tributes, and many letters of congratulation. He kept the menu of the lunch given to the honorary graduates of Cambridge in 1948, and the order of ceremony, and the robes of a Doctor of Divinity. He kept several letters of a tragic nature, from failed priests, and persons in prison and in trouble. He kept one school report from his preparatory school and two reports from Rugby, also his registration as a South African voter, and the order of service of his consecration as bishop in St. Paul's Cathedral on 1 May 1934. He kept his 'Mentioned in Despatches', the distinction accorded him by General Sir Edmund Hynman Allenby on 5 March 1919. Of sermons and addresses, however, he kept many hundreds. He was ordained deacon in 1908 and had been a priest for forty years. Assuming no more than that he preached and spoke three times a week for this period, he had delivered over 6,000 sermons and addresses. Almost all of these had been written by hand; it was not until he went to Cape Town that he had a secretarial staff. It is not necessary to study more than a hundred of these compositions to grasp the essentials of that spare, simple, and unadorned style, its lucidity, at times its depth, its absence of all sentiment and pretension, its lack of poetic expression, at times its wit, at all times its authority; this great spiritual and intellectual power being communicated to paper in a small, sometimes illegible script, strange companion to the voice which at times could be so tremendous. When one writes that the style has at times its depth, this does not mean that he could be shallow. It means only that he would be deep if the occasion called for it, this being the justification also for his wit.

All this noted, there remains one thing to say about his papers. His election as archbishop brought him letters from all over the world. Whether he kept them all, one does not know, but he kept nearly one hundred. Several were from bishops who had been with him at Lambeth, two of whom claimed, as we have seen, to have sat under him.

Geoffrey Fisher, Archbishop of Canterbury, sent his best wishes, and also George Bell, Bishop of Chichester, another man whom Clayton regarded highly. Bell, whose work for Christian reunion had brought him fame, quoted Arnold Toynbee as lamenting in *Civilization on Trial* that the 'extinction of race consciousness is, as it has worked out, an Islamic virtue'. Thomas Hanray, Bishop of Argyll and the Isles, wrote, 'Congratulate you I do not, for it is a thorny throne on which you are to sit.' William Bradfield, Bishop of Bath and Wells, whose wife had been gravely ill during Lambeth, wrote, 'I am more grateful than I can say for all the sympathy and understanding which you gave me during those difficult days in July.'

Frederic Deane, former Bishop of Aberdeen, sent his congratulations. 'I loved your dear old father in my Kettering and Leicester days before I came to Scotland forty years ago, and because of my love for him I came up to London, and helped to lay hands on you at St. Paul's when you were made Bishop.'

It is impossible for any Christian to read without emotion these selfless letters, some from men whose active ministry was over, but whose concern for the Church and their successors continued so devoutly.

Another remarkable letter came from Bishop Ferguson-Davie, then living in retirement in Pietermaritzburg, Natal. He writes that Clayton 'should frequently thank God for the wonderful preparation you have had for the work':

'Your home.
Your Cambridge years, bringing you in constant touch with other bright brains, with youth and with national religious education.
Your parochial experience.
Your 14 years here, enabling you to know our South African problems well.
Your physical and intellectual vigour.'

Clayton's brother Harold, 74 years of age and secretary of the Church of England Men's Society, besides sending his congratulations, wrote, 'I have not been able to find any detective book you are not likely to have read so I have sent you a small thriller of a rather novel type.' Clayton's cousin Frank, Sir Francis Hare Clayton, 79 years of age, and author of the small book *The Claytons*, in which cousin Geoffrey is described as 'a brilliant scholar and organiser', wrote that 'when Archbishop Carter retired he told me he felt sure you would one day succeed him'. Clayton's sister Kitty, who in Johannesburg had on several occasions urged her brother to be calm, prayed that he would be guided with power from on High. She was temporarily in London where she was having her son-in-law 'amputated out' of her will. 'He was only going to have had £10 so he hasn't lost much.'

Sister Margaret Teresa, of the Convent of Wantage, 71 years old, wrote: 'My dear Geoffrey, I am thrilled to the marrow about your Archbishopric . . . . How your dear Mother must rejoice, she must know, I feel sure. . . . To think of that precious little Lord Fauntleroy (I see you so plainly with your curls and your suit, bowing, asking for a dance! aged 6, I think). . . . You would have come across our sisters of course and I am sure you would be very nice and fatherly (but I shall always see you age 6!) . . . . This is I fear a stupid letter, but I *am* stupid, so that's that.'

From within South Africa the tributes were warm and many. What could a priest say more than 'It is with the deepest sorrow that I part with you'?[3] Leo Rakale, that shy young man of 22 who had entertained his bishop twelve years before in his father's home in the Springs African location, and was now a member of the Community of the Resurrection, expressed his 'joy and gratitude to God and to you for championing the cause of all sections of the community, and the cause of the poor and oppressed in particular'. S. H. Clarke, headmaster of St. John's College, wrote in his own controlled fashion, 'From our point of view I am sorry, but hope you will still be able to remember us from time to time.' Clarke, who was thought by many to be a cold, aloof and autocratic man, and who could be terrifying in rebuke, had a great respect for his bishop, who was eleven years older than he, and could at times treat Clarke with considerable brusqueness. Clarke had one controversy with Clayton, and admired the way it was settled. The diocesan clergy used to retreat at St. John's during the school's holiday, and the dates had to be fixed with care so as to cause the least inconvenience to the housekeeper and her staff. In 1947 Archdeacon Urquhart changed the dates, and after protests from the staff Clarke cancelled the offer of the school. Clayton replied to his letter by postcard. 'I note your difficulties and that you can't take us. I won't say what I think about it.'

Clarke told another good story. He and Clayton attended an Old Johannians' dinner, at which the speaker was an old boy who had reached the dizzy heights of Parliament. He told the gathering that his style was cramped because the bishop and the headmaster were present. He then proceeded to tell a 'long and dull and vaguely indecent story'. Clayton said in a low voice to Clarke, 'I could tell a much dirtier story than that, but it would be short and to the point.'[4]

Huddleston sent a telegram reading, 'Community of the Resurrection sends sincere congratulations. Philippians chapter 1 verses 3–6.' These verses read as follows: 'I thank my God upon every remembrance of you, always in every prayer of mine for you, making request with joy, for your fellowship in the gospel from the first day until now; being confident of this very thing, that he which hath begun a good work in you will perform it until the day of Jesus Christ.'

I wrote to him: 'I myself am sure that there is no programme or policy that can by some magic reconcile the respective claims of justice and survival, and that we must learn to do what is right . . . and I believe that you, with no desire to cause antagonism, will teach us what are our duties to God and what are our duties to the state.' That belief was never shaken.

It was to be expected that those who would miss Clayton most of all would be his African clergy and people. It must be regarded as one of his supreme achievements that he so won their love and confidence, and as one of his most fascinating attributes that he who could silence a synod, should have this strange affinity with the poor and humble, and they with him.* The Revd. A. Mabuto, priest-in-charge of St. Michael's, Alexandra Township, wrote to thank him for appointing an African priest as Assistant Director of Native Missions, and for proposing that church leaders in South Africa should come together to shape a united Christian opinion that would be respected throughout the country by all races. R. E. M. Mguli of Johannesburg wrote, 'We can't believe that you would leave us, it is sad, yet we are on the other hand proud of you. . . . I am, my Lord, your son. . . .' The Revd. C. H. P. Nyovane wrote, 'I want to thank you, my Lord, for all you have done and been to me . . . nowhere have I known

*The words 'poor and humble' are now suspect, but they are used here as Jesus used them in the Sermon on the Mount.

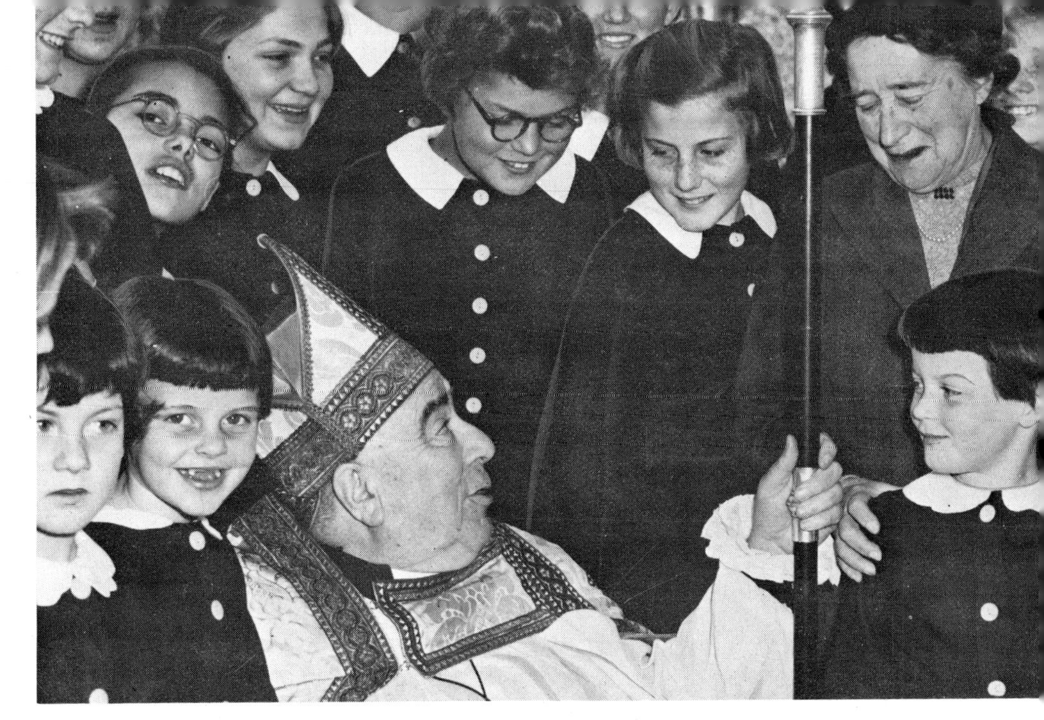

9 At St. George's Orphanage, near Cape Town, August 1955 (Photo: Photo-Hausmann, Cape Town)

10 At Episcopal Synod, November 1955, Clayton presiding over the Bishops of (clockwise from left foreground) St. Helena (Turner), Kimberley and Kuruman (Boys), Natal (Inman), Zululand (Trapp), Pretoria (Taylor), Grahamstown (Cullen), St. John's (Evans), Lebombo (Beevor, at back), Damaraland (Vincent), George (Hunter), Basutoland (Maund), Johannesburg (Reeves) (Photo: *Cape Times*)

11 The Bishop of Matabeleland (Hughes) and the Archbishops of Central Africa (Paget), Cape Town, and Canterbury (Fisher) at the Cathedral of St. Mary and All Saints, Salisbury, Rhodesia, during the inauguration of the Province of Central Africa in May 1955 (Photo: *Rhodesia Herald*)

12 The Most Revd. Dr. G. H. Clayton, Archbishop of Cape Town (Photo: E. Bieber, Cape Town)

13 *(right)* The Revd. R. W. F. Cowdry in 1957 (Photo: *Cape Argus*)

14 *(left)* The Right Revd. Robert Se
Taylor, then Archbishop-designate, at 'Bishopscourt' in February 1964 (Photo: *Cape Times*)

15 Memorial brass in the parish church of Chesterfield (Photo: R. Wilsher, A.R.P.S, Chesterfield)

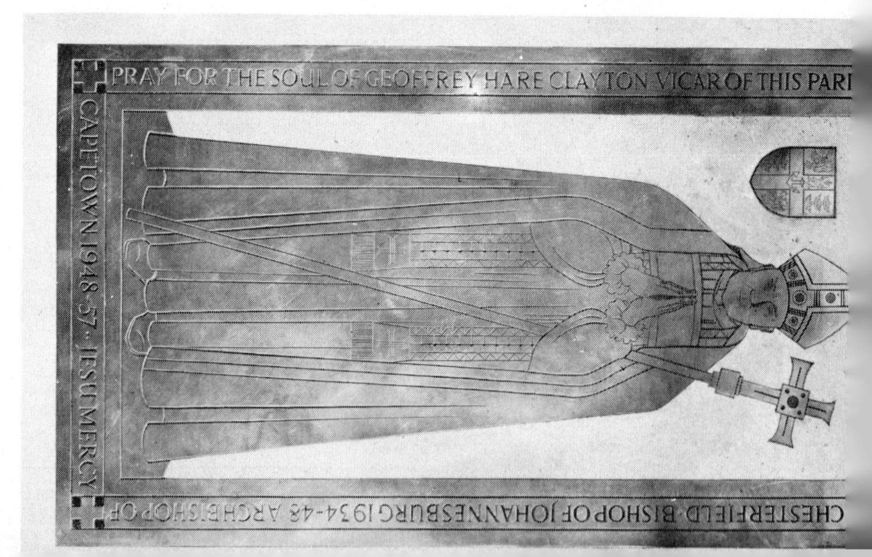

all clergymen irrespective of colour to be standing in the same relation to their Bishop.' M. Kika, secretary of the Order of Ethiopia, wrote, 'We are not surprised to learn of this decision which we think you are fit for . . . Greetings, your humble son . . .' One could write more, but this is enough save for one short passage from a letter from Redvers Rouse to his friend Donald Bailey, Rector of Klerksdorp:

'My heart is turned to water, I cannot think straight and in fact I do not know what to do next. I knew that it had to be and yet I was hoping that it would not happen, and now the thing is fixed. . . .'[5]

Rouse was a man of 49. If any man knew the defects of Clayton's character, it was he. Clayton had once come at him with his fists, between Holy Communion and breakfast, because Rouse was trying to save an Anglican priest whom Clayton wanted to get rid of, and from whom he had received a letter of resignation. After breakfast they transacted their business, both very bad-tempered. But when Rouse was ready to leave, Clayton, with a change of voice, said, 'What's his trouble?' Rouse told him that the man was in debt, and thought, wrongly, that if his resignation was accepted he would get six months' stipend. Clayton said, 'Tell him to come and see me.' The man went to see the bishop and left with his letter of resignation torn up, and the gift of a cheque for the amount of his debts. Rouse said to the writer, 'The change of voice was a kind of apology.'[6]

And now Rouse's heart was turned to water.

There can be no doubt that about this time a considerable change took place in Clayton, what is usually described as a mellowing, but was really more of a ripening, the coming to fruition of a lifetime of consecration. One may not presume to say his election was the cause of it, but it hastened the process. He became more humble, more affectionate, more patient. He became less afraid of women. He became less irritable. He gossiped as much as ever. He damned and blasted on suitable occasions. He had clergy to morning tea, and had sandwiches made for them, and when carried away by his conversation put his elbow in the sandwiches. When he noticed it, he paused momentarily to wipe the mess off his sleeve, then continued his conversation and put his elbow back in the sandwiches.[7] As his Lord had done before him, he increased in wisdom, and in favour with God and man. Or should one say, with God and with some men?[8]

22

To Bishopscourt

It was now time to pack up and leave it all. One of the things that he would miss would be the Johannesburg Zoo. It was one of his relaxations to go there, and to visit the rhinoceros. Some legends say it was the hippopotamus, and some say both. He told one of his Christmas parties that in his next reincarnation he would like to be a rhino, and one of his priests, emboldened no doubt by the wine and the general bonhomie, retorted, 'My Lord, you didn't miss it by much in this one.' Horace Willson, while still an ordinand, stayed with the bishop in December of 1948, waiting for his ordination. They had eaten well, and ended with pancakes and cinnamon and syrup. Willson refused a second helping, and when asked why, said it would be gluttonous. They embarked on a discussion of gluttony, and Clayton recommended to Willson that he ought to study the rhinoceros, 'a powerful beast which never stops eating'. When Clayton had gone to Cape Town, Willson found a wooden rhinoceros in a curio shop, and sent it to him with the definition from the *Oxford English Dictionary*, 'a large, unwieldy quadruped, having . . . a very thick skin'. To this Clayton replied, 'You are quite wrong about the rhino. If you really got to know it, you'll find it quite a sweet animal.'[1]

Saying goodbye to the clergy was not an easy task. As had been the case at Chesterfield, Clayton's opinion of his clergy was very high. That this opinion was deserved, one could not doubt, but as at Chesterfield they were a very part of himself. This was the secret of the tremendous hold that he had on their devotion and affection. On 10 December, he wrote to the members of the secular clergy the following letter:[2]

> My dear Brother,
>
> On December 29th I shall cease to be your Bishop. I write to thank you for your cooperation in the work of the Church during these last years, and for the friendship and forbearance which you have unstintingly given me. Your example and your affection have been an inspiration to me to try to do my best. I ask your pardon for my failures.
>
> It seems to me that the very best way of saying good-bye is that we should say our prayers together. I hope to attend the Retreat at St.

John's College from January 17th. to 21st., which is to be conducted by the Revd. Father Young, S.S.J.E. I venture to hope that you may be at the Retreat also, if it is possible for you.

I ask you to pray for me sometimes, in the very responsible work which will fall upon me, and I commend you to God's love.

Yours sincerely in our blessed Lord,
✠ Geoffrey Johannesburg.

These prayers he asked from many. He knew well the magnitude of the task that he was undertaking. He wrote to Bailey that he was 'very apprehensive about Cape Town'. It is hard to believe, but it must have been true. The first Episcopal Synod over which he had presided had taken an unequivocal stand on the proposals of the new Government to bring to an end the representation of Africans in Parliament by three white M.P.s and four white senators, and to remove coloured voters to a separate roll, allotting them a certain number of M.P.s who must be white. These rights Africans had enjoyed since 1936, and they had been given to them as a compensation for the exclusion of future African voters from the common roll, with the fatal provision that these new rights could be removed by a two-thirds majority of a joint sitting of both Houses of Parliament. As for coloured persons, those who could qualify had been eligible for the common roll of the Cape Colony since 1853, and had in 1910 had their rights confirmed in the Constitution of the new Union of South Africa, with the same fatal provision that these rights could be removed by a two-thirds majority of both Houses sitting together.

It was now the declared intention of the Nationalist Government, first to abolish African representation, and second to change the method of coloured representation.* This was fundamental to the whole policy of apartheid. To this day the great majority of Afrikaner Nationalists react with anger to the suggestion that any persons not white, or any white representative of such persons, should sit in the Parliament of white South Africa. Therefore this declaration of Episcopal Synod of 1948, which condemned these proposals as breaches of trust, must be regarded as an important event. The Church of the Province had in the past often protested against actions of the State. Now it was to find itself opposing, not only actions, but the fundamental philosophy of the rulers of South Africa.

Smuts's fundamental philosophy had always been a mixture of vagueness and benevolence and pragmatism and sometimes indifference, though this last would be avoided when possible. The fundamental philosophy of the Nationalists was going to be spelt out clearly, and its inevitable consequence would be the enactment of innumerable laws enforcing racial separation. Justice would be done to all, but it would be the white Parliament who would say what justice was. Many might suffer and lose their property and have their lives changed, but the goal of separate destinies was so magnificent, and when reached would bring such inde-

*Ultimately coloured representation was abolished also.

scribable happiness, that any suffering or loss would be justified. It was a clear-cut case of the end justifying the means, and it was a proposition acceptable to the Dutch Reformed churches, and abhorrent to most of the others. Perhaps it would be more just to say that the proposition was acceptable to the Dutch Reformed churches provided that the end was racial separation, and that proposition was in its turn justifiable because racial separation was the will of God. To do the will of God was so supreme an end that all men should be willing to endure the employment of any means.

This was the proposition, so holy and so true, that the bishops of this alien Church rejected. To forgive their rejection, or even to tolerate it, was impossible, and indeed disloyalty to God. So the stage was set for a conflict between the State and many of the churches, and Clayton was to be one of the leading actors. Did he realise it? He did and he did not. His whole upbringing, his deep feeling for order, his reverence for St. Paul, made repugnant to him the notion that the Church might have to disobey the State.

Clayton's last letter to the diocese appeared in *The Watchman* of January 1949. He wrote that the responsibilities of being Metropolitan at that particular time were very great, and that he felt in many ways unfitted '. . . but I have been brought up to believe that it is very wrong to shirk responsibilities, though it is foolish to seek them, and I must go and do my best'. There were many things that had not been done; the stipends of the clergy, both European and African, must be raised, and more money was needed for missions, but in the long run God's will would be done.

One unpleasant thing must be recorded. He was hurt, even for a time angered, by the amount subscribed as a present from the white communicants of the diocese. Less was given per capita than by the African communicants. Both gifts he would of course have given to some work of the Church of his own choosing, but he told Rouse that he had actually contemplated handing the white gift back. Of this Huddleston said, 'In some ways he got through to his white laity, in some ways he did not.'

One last tribute was paid him, and it came from Dr. J. B. Webb, one of the oustanding Methodist ministers of the time. 'Never have we needed more surely than now, inspired and wise Christian leadership, and voices that command respectful hearing in the councils of the mighty. The Archbishop-elect possesses these qualities and our rejoicing in his election is tempered only by our sorrow at losing him from Johannesburg.'[3]

So came to an end the great Johannesburg ministry, and he set off for Cape Town, for the beautiful house and trees and garden of 'Bishopscourt'. At that time it overlooked no neighbour, and from the terrace one looked up to the great mountain behind the famous gardens of Kirstenbosch. It was a moot point whether the diocese of Cape Town would be able to persuade Miss Darbyshire to vacate the house in time, and there were delighted rumours that she might be planning to act as companion to the new archbishop as she had done for the old. Sir Herbert Stanley, the ex-Governor of Southern Rhodesia, and now an eminent and much respected layman of the Cape Town diocese, had written to Clayton on 29 November 1948, telling him that Miss Darbyshire was still holding on to 'Bishopscourt', 'on the principle of *veni, vidi, manebo*'.* But at last they had persuaded her to leave the house on New Year's Eve. Stanley asked if it were true that Clayton would like a smaller house; if so, there was a buyer. But public opinion would be against selling it. He set out the situation in his inimitable style, of which it was said that he could begin a sentence at 8 o'clock and finish it at 8.15 without using any unrelated clauses, or forgetting how he had begun.

'Obviously public opinion here would not be likely to applaud the severance of Bishopscourt from the Archbishop, but on the other hand the public is not called upon to undertake the burden, financial and otherwise of maintaining so large a house and grounds on relatively exiguous emoluments of office, and for that reason the opportunity of a potential purchaser might conceivably be deemed worthy of consideration.'

Clayton had to maintain 'Bishopscourt' himself, and pay his staff, including his chaplain, and for this he received the income of the See of Cape Town Endowment Fund, which was just over £4,000 per annum. He told Gerald Abernethy, the Diocesan and Provincial Secretary, that he was broke. After his visit to England in 1955 the diocese gave him a present of £1,600, hoping that he would use it to buy a new car, but instead he had his old Chevrolet completely overhauled. He clearly had resources of his own to be able to give presents to newly ordained priests, to pay the debt of Rouse's man in Johannesburg, to make good the cost of clothes stolen from the home of the Revd. George Swartz of St. Paul's in Bree Street, Cape Town, in 1956, to come to the aid of Maurice Clack when St. Alban's was burgled in 1942, and to make contributions to the upkeep of 'Bishopscourt'. When he died he left an estate valued at just over £12,000 and whether this was inheritance or savings or both, one does not know. One thing is certain, his manner of life was frugal, except perhaps in the matter of smoking.

Although Clayton was not in any easily comprehensible way a lover of beauty, he came to feel for 'Bishopscourt' a strong sense of attachment. It was a double-storied house with spacious rooms and many stairs and passages. Its garden was famous, having been made so by Mrs. Carter, wife of the former archbishop. The Darbyshires were not gardeners, and after the archbishop's death Dean Gibbs asked Mr. and Mrs. Graeme Duncan to look after it. According to the newspaper, 'Dr. Clayton has watched with an approving and appreciative eye while friends filled his flower-beds with bright cannas, phlox, irises, and other delights of the herbaceous border.' This was largely the work of the Duncans, who inspired the head gardener Mr. Charles Ackerman to new efforts, it being hard for a gardener to keep his enthusiasm for his work when no one ever looks at it. There is no doubt that the new archbishop knew that he had a

*I came, I saw, I shall remain.

good garden, that he enjoyed its peacefulness, that he walked about in it, and that he made benevolent remarks to his gardeners. But one may presume to doubt whether his 'approving and appreciative' eye really knew what it was looking at.

On one occasion Archbishop Edward Paget and his wife Rosemary were guests at 'Bishopscourt'. Rosemary Paget had been walking with keen enjoyment in the garden, and when she returned to the house she said to Clayton, 'Your Grace, the garden is beautiful.' Clayton considered for some time, and then said to her with great force, 'I *hate* beauty.' He then went off into one of his belly-shaking laughs, as though he had made some very extraordinary point. When people hear this story, they realise that it is telling something, but they are not quite sure what it is.

Clayton was very fond of the Pagets. One day at the dinner table, Mrs. Paget said to her husband, 'Don't you think it's time that the Archbishop called me Rosemary?' When Paget said, 'Of course,' Clayton, who might well have been embarrassed or even annoyed in his earlier days, approached the proposition with a very judicial air. 'You see,' he said, 'if I called you Rosemary, then I would have to call the Bishop of Grahamstown's wife Natalie, and I'm not sure if I could manage that.' In any event he decided to call them both by their Christian names.

It was very odd, but in some way his elevation to the heights of the archbishopric gave him a kind of *sang-froid* that he had never possessed before. When the Revd. Tom Winter was appointed to the Cathedral staff in 1956, the Archbishop invited him and his wife to dinner. Mrs. Winter was very nervous, having heard fearful stories of Clayton's formidability. Her nervousness was not lessened by an incident at the dinner table. Clayton asked where they would educate their son, and Winter said, 'Not at a church school.' Clayton asked why, and Winter replied, 'We're not getting enough ordinands from them.' Clayton's reply to this was a loud 'Bosh!', which put a damper on further conversation. But after dinner when they had moved to the sitting-room, Clayton patted the settee and said, 'Come and sit down, Mrs. Winter.' They got on famously, and dealt with the subject of women, of whom Clayton said he had many foolish ones in the parish. With great daring Mrs. Winter, excited by the unexpected rapport, said, 'Your Grace, now that you are an Archbishop, are you still pursued by women?' Clayton said, 'Yes, I am, I have been all my life,' and went off into a great bout of laughing. He was beginning to be able to accept his own nature, and to welcome the knowledge that though he was not attracted to women as women, he was getting on with them much more easily as persons. On the farm 'Rietvlei' at Robertson, the Afrikaans-speaking farmer had allowed the diocese to build a small church, which Clayton once visited for a confirmation. The farmer invited him to tea, called him 'My Worship', and asked him why he was not married. Clayton said, 'No one will have me', and went off again into a great fit of laughter. On one occasion during Episcopal Synod, when some of the bishops and their wives were staying at 'Bishopscourt', and lunch was over, he asked their plans for the afternoon. Mrs. Vernon Inman, wife of the Bishop of Natal, said, 'I'm going to bed with a thriller', whereupon Clayton, looking round that impeccable company, said, 'Which one?' That was the only occasion I know of when Clayton made a joke of a sexual nature.

On 2 February 1949 Clayton was enthroned in the Cathedral of St. George, in a ceremony of 'ecclesiastical tradition and colourful pomp'. In the congregation were the Governor-General and Mrs. Brand van Zyl, Sir Evelyn Baring His Majesty's High Commissioner, the Commander-in-Chief of the South Atlantic Vice-Admiral E. D. B. McCarthy, Senator Edgar Brookes, Sir Herbert Stanley, Mrs. Margaret Ballinger, M.P., Mrs. J. G. Carinus wife of the Administrator of the Cape Province, and the Mayor of Cape Town Mr. H. E. Gearing.

The service began with the entry of a procession of seventy-five priests, most of them white, some coloured and African. After prayers Dean Gibbs, accompanied by Coadjutor-Bishop Lavis, the Chapter and church-wardens, went to stand at the closed north-west door. The Archbishop, waiting outside with his chaplains, knocked three times on the door, and as the Dean opened the door the Precentor cried, 'Let the people stand.' The Archbishop then presented the mandate for his enthronement, and after it had been read, the procession moved down the nave. The Archbishop was conducted to his throne near the altar, and the Dean declared him enthroned and handed him the primatial cross, that particular kind of cross which is carried in procession before any primate, archbishop, or metropolitan. The Archbishop then handed over the cross and received the pastoral staff. He then received what is called 'The Homage'; the Dean, Chapter, Chancellor and Registrar knelt in turn and kissed his ring. The Archbishop then preached his first sermon, and the service closed with prayers and the Archbishop's blessing. While the procession left the Cathedral, the congregation sang 'Praise my Soul, the King of Heaven'.

Clayton's first sermon was magnificent. He was now 65, a master of language, who could speak with humility and authority, and who would be equal to any occasion however great. Other notable sermons had been preached in that cathedral, but it is doubtful whether many others had ever been preached with such complete authority. He began his sermon by reading again the collect for the day, and continued with the words 'This is for me a humbling and frightening day'. Because he said it, it must have been true, though it is hard to understand how one who spoke with such authority could possibly be frightened. That he felt humble and humbled, can be understood, for he believed that God had called him to be the head of the Anglican branch of the Christian Church in South Africa, and he knew that he was unworthy.

Clayton first paid tribute to the achievements of his predecessors, Robert Gray the great pioneer, William West Jones the great pastor, William Carter the wise statesman, Francis Phelps the holy man, John Darbyshire the attractive and beloved leader.

'You, my friends, have called me to this office. You called me because you thought it was God's will. I accepted your call because I thought it was God's will. But I know that I have nothing which I can bring to you that can match the gifts of those who have been here before me.'

Did he believe that? One cannot possibly answer such a question. All that one can say is that it was extraordinarily humble and quite untrue. Much truer was the humility of the words that followed soon after.

'For myself, it is my desire and intention to dedicate myself wholly and without reserve to the duties of this office. . . . And yet I know that an offering made to God should be without blemish, and I come all shop-soiled and dusty from the sins and failures of the past, which have, I believe, been forgiven, but which have left their mark. For not even forgiveness can make the past as though it had not been.'

One finds that much easier to believe, that one can come believing oneself shop-soiled to take a high office and humbly dedicate oneself 'without reserve' to its duties. This word 'shop-soiled' he used of himself on at least one other occasion, but it is nevertheless an odd word in his vocabulary, much more odd than 'bosh' or 'blast'. There is another thing one can understand, that the same man who received those letters in Johannesburg – 'It is with the deepest sorrow that I part with you' – could regard himself as shop-soiled, and could acknowledge humbly that he could have made greater use of his gifts had he been more dedicated, yet could at the same time declare that it was his 'desire and intention' to dedicate himself anew. If any man ever understood the moral ascent, it was he.

He said more about dedication. He did not doubt that it was also the intention of his brethren of the clergy and the laity to renew their dedication, conscious of the same hindrances as he. But luckily there was that collect for the day, in which they prayed, not that they might offer themselves, but that Jesus Christ might take them and offer them.

He repeated a theme that had run through forty years of preaching that the world was 'a vale of soul-making' and that each individual matters to God, and matters for ever. 'It follows that the supreme disaster is not the collapse of a civilisation but the ruin of a human soul; and the collapse of a civilisation only matters in so far as it is likely to involve the ruin of human souls.'

He went on to speak of the sin of contempt, so well known in South Africa.

'Our Lord taught us that the worst sin against a human being is to treat him with contempt, and the worst sin against God is to regard any of those he loves with contempt.[4] If the Church is to be true to her Master, she must be especially the friend and champion of the under-privileged.'

Clayton used this last affirmation to pay high tribute to Sidney Lavis, his Coadjutor-Bishop, whom he called 'one known throughout South Africa for his faithful following of our Lord in this matter'.

Clayton ended as always, with words of encouragement, but first he made a joke. 'I can only say that my one desire in this Diocese is that I may be able to encourage and support the parochial clergy, and if I cannot be a shepherd, at least to avoid being a wolf.'

In this first sermon Clayton made no direct reference to South Africa. But he said, 'We know that all that we hold dear is challenged by powerful and determined adversaries.' But Christ reigns. Let Him be thanked that He had called them to his service in these days of crisis. And let them pray that they should be worthy of their Master and go forward without fear. He concluded his sermon with a verse from Chesterton.

From all the easy speeches
  That comfort cruel men,
From all that terror teaches,
  From lies of tongue and pen,
From sale and profanation
  Of honour and the sword,
From sleep and from damnation,
  Deliver us good Lord.

So ended one of the greatest sermons that was ever preached in the Cathedral of St. George. As in Johannesburg, men and women, priests and laity, black and white, knew that a great man had come to shepherd them.[5]

The enthronement was followed by a crowded meeting in the Cape Town City Hall. Bishop Lavis presided, and with him on the platform were Mr. H. E. Gearing the Mayor of Cape Town, Sir Herbert Stanley, the Revd. Stanley Sudbury representing the Cape Peninsula Council of Churches, and Mr. A. Sinton, a member of the Executive Committee of the Cape Provincial Council, representing the Administrator. The new archbishop in his address clearly referred to the challenge of Communism and to the avowed intention of the new Government to destroy it. He said that the only way to meet the challenge to the Christian faith was to think aright and to live better lives than those who challenged it. Suppression in itself was useless, and contrary to the teachings of Christ.

Clayton, having entered the life of his new city as Archbishop and important citizen, also joined the Owl Club. He was by no means a club man. He had been held in high esteem by the Rotarians in Chesterfield, but had joined no club in Johannesburg. It is improbable that he would have been able to accept the modern Rotary custom of calling all one's fellow-members by their first names and being similarly so called. The Owl Club was, and still is, a dining and cultural club. Speakers and musicians or other performers are invited to entertain the members. At some time during the evening the Grand Owl calls on all the members to give the owl cry, 'Tu-whit-tu-whoo, tu-whit-tu-whoo, tu-whit-tu-whoo', and the eyes of a mascot owl in the corner light up while they are doing this, three times.

It must not be supposed that the members of this club were amiable simpletons. Its honorary life members included three Governors-General, a Chief Justice, and a Prime Minister. Amongst its other members were a coadjutor-bishop, a millionaire, several members of Parliament, an ex-Governor of Southern Rhodesia, and now the Archbishop of Cape Town. It was in all probability the ex-Governor, Sir Herbert Stanley, the unrivalled master of the long sentence, who had secured the Archbishop for a member. If such men could call 'Tu-whit-tu-woo' three times while a mascot owl's eyes were flashing, who are we to laugh at it? One can only regret that one was never able to see and hear Clayton and Stanley giving the owl-cry together.

23

The Fierce Laws

Whether one liked it or not – and many Anglicans did not like it – the most important issue that now confronted the Anglican Church, and indeed all other churches, was the issue of race, of racial discrimination, of racial justice, of fashioning a South African society in which justice would be done to all racial groups, or if one preferred to state it otherwise, to all persons of whatever racial group. This was hardly separable from another issue, that of the relation between Church and State, because it had already become clear that the State – which for all but philosophers was the Nationalist Party Government – intended to take to itself immense powers to bring about the separation, social, political, geographic, and otherwise, of each racial group from all others. It was sometimes argued that the problems of South Africa were only apparently racial but were in reality economic, but such a view offered little consolation. And there were Christians – Anglicans amongst them – who complained that race was being made too much of, and was becoming an obsession, and who blinded themselves to the truth that even if it had become for some an obsession, it had become for all the supreme political and moral issue.

Clayton knew all this very well. Luckily for the Church of the Province he was not prone to obsessions, and luckily also, if anyone knew what a moral issue was and what one ought to say about it, he was the man. One must therefore pay attention to those words spoken at his enthronement, 'We know that all we hold dear is challenged by powerful and determined adversaries.' Who were these adversaries? He no doubt meant the Government. But he was now going to learn a truth so far only partially revealed to him, that much that he had held dear was also going to be challenged by the Dutch Reformed churches.

Clayton, though that was not his wish or intention, was going to become known as a political bishop. On 3 December 1948, Hofmeyr died. There was no one in the United Party who could possibly play the role that he had played for eighteen years both inside and outside Parliament. Luckily for justice, there were still Edgar Brookes and Margaret Ballinger and their fellow Native Representatives in the Upper and Lower Houses.[1] Outside Parliament it was inevitable that the new Archbishop of Cape Town should become the national exponent of Christian ethics in politics, or one should rather say, Christian ethics as interpreted by the Anglican and other non-Dutch-Reformed churches. And these ethics were inseparable from, and almost identical with, the issues of racial justice.

Clayton delivered an address entitled 'Christianity and Race' to a summer school organised by the Institute of Race Relations at Mowbray, Cape Town.[2]

Clayton said that he spoke with diffidence; he may have meant that he was not speaking as a scholar steeped in the study of race, but otherwise it is difficult to understand what he was diffident about. He said that so far as he could see, Christianity had never been very interested in the question of race. The ancient distinction between Jew and Gentile was religious rather than racial, and that between Greek and barbarian was cultural rather than racial. 'The teaching of Christianity was that within the Christian Church such barriers were broken down.'

Referring to the word *Kafferboetie* (explained on page 112), Clayton said:

'It has been left to professed Christians in this country to use the word which describes one who treats another man as a brother as a term of contempt. I should like to hear St. Paul's comment on that. And I don't think it is difficult to imagine Christ's comment on it.'

He then attacked the sophistry which seeks to evade the notion of equality by denying that equality can exist, and by adducing numerous examples where it obviously does not exist. Clayton conceded this argument at once. He for one was quite incapable of learning to play or really to appreciate any musical instrument. What Christianity did say was that all men are equally important in the sight of God.

He gave his opinion of many racial generalisations current in South Africa. He did not believe that there was any evidence that one race was capable of rising to greater heights either intellectually or spiritually than another. It seemed to him monstrous to say that a particular race is spoilt if it enters into a new environment. 'It is a temptation to parents to prevent their children growing up and losing their endearing ways. But it is a temptation that has to be resisted. The children must grow up.'*

Clayton concluded, 'Race then is part of God's creation, is according to His will, is good. But racialism is of the devil. That seems to me to sum up the whole matter.' And indeed it does. It remains only to comment that the word *kafferboetie*, though by no means obsolete, has lost a great deal of respectability. In 1972 it could not be used by a Cabinet Minister. In 1949 it could. One must admit at once that change in terminology does not always mean change of heart. Yet one must also remember that it was the utterances and the actions of the Hoernlés and the Hofmeyrs and the Claytons, powerless though they might have seemed at the time, that made at least some white South Africans begin to see that there was something shameful in the way they spoke of others.

The talk about race was inescapable. Visitors to the country, entertained in white South African houses, could not but remark the prevalence of the

*This was in 1949. One could not use such metaphors today.

obsession. Their hosts sometimes talked intelligently and sympathetically of black aspirations, sometimes they defended the firmness and reasonableness of the new Government's policies, sometimes they expressed their confusion and their anxiety for the future. Sometimes – and not seldom – the talk developed into an embarrassing tirade against servants, their idleness and their thieving ways, above all their ingratitude; against rich Indians and their rapacity and poor Indians and their dirtiness; against coloured people and their fecklessness and drunkenness; against Africans and their cruelty and barbarism. And when the visitor was reeling under this bombardment, he would often be astonished – if he were in an English-speaking home – to hear the Afrikaners condemned for their arrogance, their disloyalty to the Royal family, their inability to realise that only the British Navy stood between them and utter destruction. And sometimes – if he were not a Jew – he would hear the Jews slated for their insidious infiltration into every sphere imaginable, especially commerce and industry, and their stranglehold on the University of the Witwatersrand. Whether or not it should be called an obsession, it was certainly prevalent. And perhaps one may say that in a country of so many races, even though one is able to overcome racial prejudice in oneself, even if one no longer sees colour in the face of others, nevertheless politics is race.[1]

To the Afrikaner Nationalist politics was race above all else, and race meant, in 1949, Afrikaner supremacy over all others. It was only in Afrikaner hands that the future would be safe. It was only the true Afrikaner who knew what was best for everybody. He would safeguard his own language, his own culture, his own future, but he would in his wisdom and strength and the certainty of his vocation ensure the identities of all others as well.

That these politics powerfully affected the Dutch Reformed churches goes without saying. Every church in every country is powerfully affected by being where it is. But the country of South Africa, with its seemingly insoluble problems of language and culture and race and colour, with its high standard of white living dependent for its very continuance on a low standard of black living, affects – and that means corrupts – its churches more than most others. The turning of the other cheek, the loving of one's enemies, the willingness to lose the world if one can thus keep one's soul, all these things accord ill with the determination to survive at all costs. The signs of this conflict are to be seen in prayers, sermons, synodal resolutions, and addresses. They are clearly to be seen in *Die Kerkbode*, which had given thanks for at last having a Christian government. It is illuminating to see what was meant by this. On 23 February *Die Kerkbode* urged its readers to 'mobilise for 1949':

'The day is coming when the non-white races and powers will stand mobilised against the white for their supposed rights. So also will the time come that the mobilised powers of unbelief under the leadership of the Prince of Darkness will rise up in bloody strife against the real Christendom. These events summon us as Church today. MOBILISE – MOBILISE

TO THE UTMOST!'

The journal continuously warned against the 'Roman danger' and 'Communism'.[3] It defended stoutly the contention that education could be Christian–National, which meant in effect that true nationalism was compatible if not identical with Christianity. It was the firm belief of the exponents of 'Christian–National Education' that God had intended each person to be a member of a certain race or nation, and that it was therefore the Christian duty of schools to confirm and nurture children in loyalty to that race or nation. Some leading Dutch Reformed churchmen, such as the Revd. William Nicol, himself of Scottish descent, condemned intermarriage between Afrikaners and other white persons, because it robbed children of their God-given destiny.

The attitude of the journal in an article 'Prisons and Natives' showed clearly the inability of many white South Africans to think of race except in terms of master and servant. 'The Bantu is not wholly an asset. There are 100,000 in jail. . . . Just think of the losses caused by the breakages of things, neglect and delay which the master and the mistress must put up with!'

The journal was intensely wary of the new World Council of Churches (the W.C.C.) but nevertheless allowed Dr. G. B. A. Gerdener ample space and opportunity to plead for the Council, and to warn against withdrawing from this world fellowship. The truth was that the W.C.C. had already issued statements on race that could not be reconciled with the views of the Dutch Reformed churches. After Amsterdam* in 1948 Gerdener wrote, 'On this point we shall have to be prepared to walk a very lonely path.'[4] A reader warns that it has already 'leaked out' that socialistic and communistic influences are at work in the innermost circles of the W.C.C.[5] At Evanston* in 1954 the only delegates who openly dissociated themselves from the 'Statement on Race' were those from the South African Dutch Reformed churches. Today the breach appears beyond healing. One reason is that the W.C.C. opposes all racial discrimination in both Church and State. The second reason is that the W.C.C. has made money available to guerilla movements, to be spent on education, alleviation of poverty amongst dependants, and kindred objects. It has also made statements on the justifiable use of violence to upset an unjust order. This is one of the most controversial issues of today. Many theologians agree that the use of violence is sometimes justifiable. The difficulty arises when the violence used results, as violence often does, in massacre and atrocity. These gifts of the W.C.C. have not only finally alienated the South African Dutch Reformed churches. They have placed the other churches in an unenviable position. For how is it possible for any South African Church to announce that it supports help for guerilla movements aiming to destroy the South African Government by arms and terror?

Die Kerkbode's doughty writer of the column 'Uit die Vrystaat' expressed himself very strongly on the subject of the search for unity, in an article

*The first and second meetings of the W.C.C. were held at Amsterdam and Evanston.

entitled 'Unity or Truth'. Unity is not the most important issue, or God would have been tolerant of Beelzebub. Peter and Paul would not have left the synagogue. Luther and Calvin would not have left the Roman Church. Truth and not unity is most important in Christendom. Up to this point the non-N.G.K. reader might agree. But he would be put beyond the pale by the conclusion. 'Awake then Afrikanerdom, which has celebrated the Voortrekker festival, awake for white South Africa and a sound Christendom for our children and their children.'[6]

Nevertheless one must note that *Die Kerkbode*, although it espoused the cause of Christian–National education, was also conscious of the fact that the Church was gathered from all the nations. It reacted angrily to Dr. A. C. Barnard who wrote, 'Our beloved Church has become a Volkskerk.' It replied that any spiritual decline in the Dutch Reformed Church was not because the Church was too near to the people, but because the people were too far from the Scriptures and Christ.[7] These things must be recorded if we are to understand fully the events of Clayton's archbishopric. And it should be recorded that, although the other churches were not tempted to make a God of the People, they, like all churches, like many Christians, had false gods of their own.

When it became clear that the new Government was preparing a series of racially discriminatory laws, a number of church leaders decided early in 1949 to seek an interview with Dr. Malan, the new Prime Minister. They approached the Dutch Reformed churches, who would not join them. Finally Dr. Malan refused to see them. He saw no point in discussing with them a matter on which their two views would be quite irreconcilable. *Church News*, which could be regarded as the Anglican equivalent of *Die Kerkbode*, regretted the decision of the Government to abolish the Natives Representative Council, which had been established in 1936 and had been called by Paul Mosaka the 'toy telephone'.[8] It then had to regret the decision to remove coloured voters to a separate roll.[9] One of Dr. Malan's first acts was to abolish the provision for the representation of Indians by white representatives in Parliament. Thus it was clear that Parliament was to become a purely white body, and that other but separate instruments were to be created for other racial groups. Dr. Malan envisaged political independence for these groups, but none except the most idealistic Nationalists believed it possible.

The Government lost no time in presenting to Parliament a Mixed Marriages Bill, which would make illegal future marriages between white persons and others. Clayton gave it as his opinion that there was no existing evil which would be remedied by the passing of such a law. 'If a European and a non-European are living together without being married and have children, and afterwards come under the influence of the Church, is a priest to advise them to separate at the expense of the children's happiness and security, or for their sake to continue to live in sin?'[10]

In Parliament it was claimed that 'the churches' had asked for the Bill. But Margaret Ballinger, an Anglican, said that her Church had explicitly opposed it, and read them the resolution of the last Episcopal Synod: 'That the Bishops of this Church as a general rule discourage mixed marriages, but they cannot regard such marriages as criminal and would offer the strongest opposition to the introduction of any legislation which would have the effect of making them so.'[11]

The year 1949 was in a sense a year of preparation for those Draconian Acts which were intended to confirm old patterns of segregation and to define new ones, such laws as the Group Areas Act, which was designed to establish separate residential and business areas for all the official groups of South Africans (English-speaking for this purpose being regarded as forming one group with Afrikaans-speaking).

In 1949 the Minister of Labour announced that the Smuts Bill to recognise African trade unions would not be proceeded with. The Minister of Railways announced that all mixed travel would cease. The Minister of Posts and Telegraphs introduced separate counters everywhere; these did not make provision for all the different racial groups to pursue their separate destinies, they merely separated whites from all others. The Prime Minister declared that he was determined to stop the admission of students other than whites to the 'white' universities. The Minister of Native Affairs declared his policy of restoring the tribes and building up the power of the chiefs. The Minister of Education announced that the free midday meal in African schools would no longer be given. These events were merely the forerunners of momentous events to come. But they were enough to move *Die Kerkbode* to call 1949 a '*Genadejaar*', which means a 'Year of Grace', or even a 'Year of Mercy'.[12] Words were beginning to change their meaning.

In this year of grace the new Archbishop was asked to address on 4 November the Synod of the N.G.K. of the Cape, the oldest Church in South Africa, with its famous *Moederkerk*, the Mother Church, with a long tradition of friendliness to other churches. I do not know, but it seems probable that the invitation was the work of Gerdener, and of the Moderator, Dr. A. J. van der Merwe, both of whom liked Clayton, and were determined to prevent the isolation of the N.G.K.

Clayton was introduced by Van der Merwe, who said that there were differences in outlook, temperament and approach between their churches, but there was no reason why there should not be mutual esteem and mutual faith. He hoped that the bonds already existing between the two churches would be further strengthened so that a united front could be established against religious indifference and provocative paganism.

Clayton apologised to the synod for not being able to speak in Afrikaans, but he had come to South Africa in middle age, and also had no facility in learning languages. He said something that he had often said before, that it was one of the great achievements of the Dutch Reformed Church that it had made its people conscious of the obligations of churchmanship. Because of that, the drift from religion was less in South Africa than, he supposed, in any other country.

'I do not believe that it is worthwhile for me to come here unless I am ready to face realities. It is obviously true that there are many matters, including some which at this time are of pressing importance, in which we do not agree with you. Yet you and we alike accept the authority of our Lord Jesus Christ. You and we alike desire above everything else in the world to see the Will of God, as declared through the teachings of our Lord Jesus Christ, done in this country. We differ as to what that Will is. It is the dearest wish of my heart that we should learn to understand one another better. Would it not be worthwhile to try to do so? It is inevitable that we should say things which are widely different. Christian ministers must obey God rather than man, and declare without fear what they believe to be the Will of Christ for their country. We must each give the other credit for sincerity. If we do that, might it not be worthwhile, by a real and sustained effort to think out . . . the implications of the teaching of our common Lord, to see if we could not get closer together in our view of what is His Will for this country? We might continue to differ. But I think we should differ with much less bitterness.

'I bring the greetings of the Church of the Province of South Africa. May He whom we both serve so guide you that your Synod may promote His glory and the good of the people of this land!'[13]

Clayton was thanked for his address by the Revd. G. de C. Murray, minister of the N.G.K. at Three Anchor Bay, who said that Synod endorsed the Archbishop's desire for better understanding. It felt gravely concerned that such different viewpoints should exist, for they could only lead to further misunderstanding.

The reader may remember that in 1937 in his fourth charge to the diocese of Johannesburg, Clayton had asked the congregation to consider what it would mean for South Africa if there were a definite corporate reunion 'between ourselves and the Dutch Reformed Church'.[14] It was now clear that he no longer thought of such a possibility. He said in his address that it was the dearest wish of his heart – and this was unusual language for him – that better understanding could be reached. One may be pardoned for speculating that this 'dearest wish' co-existed with a hard-headed realisation that it was humanly speaking impossible to create an understanding between Christians who believed that God wished for a rigid separation of races in Church and State and those who did not. Especially did it appear impossible when the first group of Christians believed that racial separation in the State should be ordered by legislation, and that such legislation could with all moral justification abolish all existing rights standing in its way.

In this year the Disciples of Christ established the Peter Ainslie Memorial Lectures, in memory of one of their founders, and under the sponsorship of Rhodes University College, now Rhodes University. The lectures had in some way to be concerned with the theme of Christian unity. Clayton was asked to be the first lecturer, and chose for his title 'Christian Unity – an Anglican View'. The lecture was delivered some weeks before the address to the N.G.K. Synod, and was much colder in tone, causing considerable disappointment to all those who were in the 'ecumenical movement', a name of which Clayton said he disapproved because the movement did not include the Church of Rome, which had more than half the Christians of the world. Clayton said in his introduction that his attitude could often be found 'irritating and disappointing' to his hearers, as indeed it was.

Clayton first asked whether there was not in fact Christian unity already. There could only be one Church, and all baptised people are members of the Church. 'The separation of Christians from one another and their subjection to different ecclesiastical governments is a grievous thing – not contemplated in the New Testament, yet they are all members of the new Race'. Talking of division he said, 'Many would say that the remedy for all this is a Federation of Christian Bodies. But I believe it is here in particular that Anglicans differ from many with whom they are associated in the consideration of unity'. Federation would not cure the real evil of disunion. Where there is not the one spirit, it was not right to herd people together into one organisation in the hope that oneness of spirit may grow.

Clayton made it clear that the Anglican Church, though immensely affected by the Reformation, claimed not to be the child of the Reformation.

'She insists that she cannot form part of a new church in which the continuity with the pre-reformation Church is broken. . . . We believe that the bridge must be kept ready for the day when it is wanted, and that if we came down wholeheartedly on the one side or the other, the bridge would be gone. . . . It does not look as though there would ever be a reunion of the whole of Christendom. . . .'

He himself would not approve of a reunion of the 'children of the Reformation'. Some Anglicans looked to one side of the river, some to the other, yet they were conscious of the one spirit in the one body.

'And perhaps that is an indication that reunion is not as impossible as it sometimes seems. . . . Let me put it quite plainly and frankly. I am not prepared that Anglicanism should die for the sake of a reunited Protestant Christendom. . . . I dread a patched-up reunion, a sort of political coalition, a marriage of convenience.'

He did not think that the scandal of division could be healed in South Africa. The 'native sects' were never based on any theological principle or principle of Church government. They were, 'as far as I know quite always' personal in origin and racial in character. His next statement referred clearly to the Dutch Reformed Churches. 'In these days, more than ever before, it has become clear that nothing but disaster can come from the religion of a country being an expression of the national spirit of that country. The reunited Church must be a Catholic Church, not a South African Church.' And he closed that particular paragraph with an epigram that came from the days of Chesterfield, perhaps even earlier. 'It is our business to preach the faith to the people of South Africa, not to preach the faith of the people of South Africa.'

Though his ecumenical hopes were small, he thought that Christians could unite in pressing upon those in authority the Christian approach to the country's problems. He believed that discussions should be inaugurated in 1950, at first private, later perhaps public. He concluded:

'I believe that it is the mission of Anglicanism to be a hindrance within the Reunion Movement, and to prevent a premature and incomplete reunion, which, if it came about, would be partial and limited, and a substitute for that recapitulation of all things in Christ for which the world is waiting, where there cannot be Greek and Jew, Latin and Greek, Roman and Anglican, Methodist and Congregationalist, but Christ is all and in all. Can that ever be? It does not look like it. But man's extremity is God's opportunity, and it is when we come to know that we can do no good thing without Him that he enables us to live according to His will.'[15]

As might be expected, the applause for Clayton's lecture was polite and not sustained. It contrasted strangely with the much warmer address he was going to give to the N.G.K. Synod, a gathering much less ecumenically minded. It seemed to be saying at one moment that reunion looked impossible, and at another that it might be possible. It is my opinion that the lack of finality and clarity, so unusual in his addresses, was due to his lack of enthusiasm for the ecumenical movement. Had he lived to know Pope John he might have thought differently. He certainly had no consuming desire to get closer to the Methodists, Presbyterians and Congregationalists. That some of the reasons were those he put forward, one cannot doubt. But he had others also. Dr. J. B. Webb he could like and understand; he was not given to histrionics and sentimentality. But some of Webb's colleagues – especially when they preached – would have irritated him. He was very much an Anglican bishop.

Yet there seems no doubt that in 1949, because he had become Archbishop, because he had come to the Mother City of South African Dutch Reformed Christianity, because men like Gerdener and Keet were against isolation, he entertained hopes of closer association with their Church. He hoped too that this closer association would mean collaboration in 'pressing upon those in authority' the importance of approaching the country's problems in the spirit of the Gospel.

Clayton, himself no lover of great memorial edifices unless they were cathedrals, wrote sympathetically on the tremendous Voortrekker Monument outside Pretoria, the foundation stone of which had been laid in the centenary celebrations of 1938, and which was now completed. He mentioned two things in the spirit of the Voortrekkers which could 'bring new hope for the future of our land'. They were the spirit of adventure and the strong religious faith. On the matter of the exclusiveness of the Monument, and of the fact that it did not then and does not now evoke a response from any but a fervent Afrikaner heart, he did not comment. It was a tribute of the most formal kind, but it accorded well with his desire for a closer association.[16]

Something happened in the year 1950 to cause Clayton to lose this desire for closer association, or rather to realise that closer association was impossible so long as the Calvinist rulers of South Africa were determined to impose their apartheid ideology upon all people, and so long as they claimed some kind of divine right to order the destinies of all groups of the population.

Perhaps what finally influenced Clayton was that 1950 was a year of fierce laws. There was the Group Areas Act, which Dr. Malan called the 'corner stone of apartheid' and which was to uproot, and still is uprooting hundreds of thousands of people, the vast majority of them not white. The Minister of Justice, C. R. Swart, introduced an Unlawful Organisations Bill, which was to give him power to ban any organisation whatever which he deemed to be furthering the aims of Communism, which was given a definition of such wide range 'that it could cover all political opinions, objectives, and activities which the Government did not like'.[17] The Bill became the Suppression of Communism Act, No. 44 of 1950; it was rushed through in thirty hours, and was used to silence organisations and people, including forty of the leading members of the anti-Communist Liberal Party. The Immorality Act of 1927, which made extra-marital intercourse between whites and Africans a criminal offence, was extended to include intercourse between whites and any other persons. Furthermore Dr. Malan's position was greatly strengthened when South-West Africa was given representation in the South African Parliament by four senators and six M.P.s, thus sending ten more Nationalists to Cape Town. Finally Dr. Malan's only redoubtable opponent in the United Party, General J. C. Smuts, died on 11 September 1950 at his home 'Doornkloof' near Pretoria.

At the end of this fierce year, Clayton delivered a remarkable speech in Cape Town to the Conference of Headmasters and Headmistresses of Private Schools, many of which were Anglican, among these being St. John's and St. Mary's of Johannesburg, Michaelhouse and St. Anne's of Natal, St. Andrew's of Grahamstown, and Bishops, St. Cyprian's and Herschel of Cape Town. He decided to speak on the future of private schools, and because the proceedings were private and his address confidential, he expressed himself on certain controversial matters which he usually avoided, not, we may be sure, because he was afraid of them, but because he had not considered it politic to discuss them in public.

Clayton began with an account of the prophecies of Arthur Keppel-Jones, whose book *When Smuts Goes* had caused such a sensation when it was published in 1948. Keppel-Jones had prophesied the advent of the Nationalists, their manipulation of franchises and constituencies so that they would never lose power, and had foreseen that many who did not agree with them would try to appease them. Clayton believed that the prophecies had come true. He believed that the Nationalists would try to destroy English ideas and English culture, and that the English language would finally disappear. He told his audience that he was a member of the national committee to plan the celebration of the tercentenary of the landing of Jan van Riebeeck, and that he received the minutes of the executive committee which were circulated only in Afrikaans.

Clayton said that 'the ideological background of what is envisaged as the South Africa of the future is Calvinist'. But the private schools stood in the way. The Nationalists did not need private schools; they could get all they wanted in government schools at government expense. The private schools were strongholds of English culture, where the English language is taught and a good deal of 'diluted liberalism'; or they were strongholds of Roman Catholicism. 'I believe that there is no place for them in the South Africa of the future as envisaged by our present rulers.'

In one sense it was true that the private schools should become genuinely South African. In another sense it was untrue, if it meant that the private schools should become assimilated to the government schools. These were two cultures, and each had a clear right to exist.

'At the present time I do not want to see the two cultures which European South Africans have inherited fused into a single culture. . . . Just as I believe that for the English Church to be fused with the Dutch Reformed Church would be utterly wrong, so I believe, though for different reasons, that English schools must be unashamedly English, and English as part of the South Africa of the future. At the moment we need not to assimilate ourselves to the rest, but to be different. Whether in the long run that is going to be possible I don't know. We are in a minority, and increasingly in a minority. We do not have as many children as the Afrikaner, and immigration is in the hands of the Government. Yet the future is never like what we think it is going to be. Don't let us be swallowed up without a struggle.'

Clayton concluded with 'something about religion'. Fundamentally the weakness of the English-speaking section was that it lacked a faith. The Afrikaner did not. Many of the boys and girls who went to the private schools came from homes that had no faith. But we did not want a 'Christian–National Education' of our own. We wanted a Christian education. Otherwise we would make the mistake against which we were protesting. 'Frankly I don't want our English-speaking people to have an English faith. But I don't want them to become Calvinists, because I believe Calvinism is a false interpretation of the Christian faith.' Clayton concluded his address by saying: 'I fear that I have said but little of practical value. But I do believe that the situation is very serious. And I do hope that we are not going to sell the pass.'[18]

This private and confidential address was to have public consequences. It was printed and circulated privately, but after a period of just over three years it fell into the hands of *Die Volksblad*, a Nationalist newspaper. The paper was outraged by it, by the contention that the private schools must be 'unashamedly English', and that Calvinism was a false interpretation of the Christian faith. *Die Kerkbode* could write, as it had written for decades, of the Roman danger, but Calvinism, being 'our own', must not be assailed. What was more, it was justifiable to urge people to be unashamedly Afrikaner, but to urge them to be unashamedly English was clearly racialistic.

J. J. Fouche, Administrator of the Orange Free State, warned that subsidies to English church schools in his province might be stopped if they tried to teach religious dogma with the express purpose of counteracting Calvinism. He had now given instructions to keep an eye on such teaching. If private schools were to cause division on racial lines, the position was very dangerous. However Fouche did agree with Clayton that there should be no assimilation of cultures. Interference with each other's cultures would lead to 'hell on earth'. Each must fight for his own language.[19] To this Clayton replied: 'It is clear the religious teaching in an English Church school must be in accordance with the tenets of the Anglican Communion. It is for that purpose that an English Church school exists. Such teaching is positive teaching. It is not given with the purpose of counteracting any other kind of religious teaching, but with the purpose of instructing Anglicans in the faith of their fathers.'[20]

There were two notable things about Clayton's address. One was that he had stopped wishing 'the dearest wish of his heart', and now realised that a closer understanding with the Dutch Reformed churches had become impossible, and one can only suppose that two and a half years of Nationalist legislation, all approved by those churches, had been responsible for this. The second notable thing was that Clayton's address provoked anger from those Nationalists who had been saying similar things about Roman Catholicism, Afrikaner culture and Afrikaner identity. *Die Burger*[21] came out with the headline 'Schools must be unashamedly English' although it had been saying that other schools must be unashamedly Afrikaner for thirty-five years.

In the month before Clayton had given his private address to the headmasters and headmistresses, he had given his public charge to the Provincial Synod in Cape Town. His theme had been very similar. He did not say that Anglicanism and Calvinism were incompatible, but he did say:

'The Anglican Church is not Calvinist, and for that reason it is likely that the Anglican Church should arrive at a different result when trying to apply its fundamental theological principles to contemporary problems. This produces the impression that the difference is racial; fundamentally I believe the difference is theological.'

One could argue that this statement was an over-simplification, that theology, race, and history are all responsible, and it is in fact my own opinion that the historical factor is the most important, with the proviso that the theological and racial factors are inseparable from it. Indeed in any theological argument put forward by the Dutch Reformed churches, however great an effort were made to keep it purely theological, the racial and historical factors would reveal themselves. The important thing is not to discuss the accuracy of Clayton's statement, but to emphasise his growing realisation that South African Calvinism and Anglicanism were in fact incompatible.

Die Kerkbode devoted its main editorial to consideration of the Provincial Synod and Clayton's charge.[22] It offered no objection whatever to the view that all men should be allowed to develop according to their gifts, nor that there should be fair opportunity for all in trade, the professions, and such like. Nor to the view that people must not be relegated to positions of inferiority on grounds of race. Nor to the call to all members of the Church to examine their race attitudes in the light of the Gospel. But when the Anglican Synod declared itself against all racial differentiation or apartheid, this looked fine on paper, but Synod landed itself in a difficult situation 'because the English Church does not live up to its principles consistently'.

Die Kerkbode reported that there had been discussion of the admission of coloured children to the Anglican schools, and that Bishop Lavis had explained that church schools were not part of the diocesan organisation. Every school, he said, had its own ruling body that must decide. The paper said of this, 'It is this inconsistency in the *practice* which characterises the standpoint of the English Church.'

The N.G.K., continued the editorial, believed in racially separate church organisations. Then coloured and black worshippers would not have to sit at the back, and be condemned to play no part in the management of church affairs. Surely the hundreds of splinter churches were evidence of this urge to self-expression. Therefore the N.G.K. believed in separate development leading to greater independence. 'We remain convinced that as the non-white people understand the true meaning of separate development, as many already do, they will see the advantage to be gained in temporal and spiritual spheres.'

Die Kerkbode said that Archbishop Clayton had ascribed this wide difference of standpoint to the fact that the N.G.K. was Calvinist and the Anglican Church was not. 'Here we willingly acknowledge that he is right.' Calvinists not only bear in mind the *unity* of mankind, but also the *diversity* of nations and races that God had given – each with its own calling and destiny. 'However, enough on this matter. The standpoint of the English Church on race relations does not satisfy us, and it will ultimately not satisfy the coloured people either, because it stands in the way of their independence and is not in their best interests.'

So we see the tragedy of South African Christianity, which no doubt is the tragedy of all Christianity. The N.G.K. was justified in pointing to the inconsistency of Anglican practice, and to the poverty – if one does not use a stronger word – of the argument that the church schools were not really under Church control. The Archbishop was Visitor to many of these schools, and if not that, then at least always an honoured visitor. He could presumably have resigned. But as we have seen, he was always more patient with the conservatives than with the liberals. Twenty-three years after these events, St. Cyprian's School in Cape Town agreed to admit its first coloured pupil and then was forbidden to admit her by the Government under the Group Areas Act. For twenty-three or more years the Government had taunted the church schools for their hypocrisy and cowardice, and then had refused to allow them to make amends.

One can criticise the N.G.K. equally strongly. What has separate development so far brought to the voteless peoples? Much heartbreak certainly, and a few good jobs for some. How long will the N.G.K. endure the dilatoriness and hypocrisy of their Christian government? At the moment it appears they will endure it indefinitely.

Provincial Synod of 1950 resolved to give the full support of the Church of the Province to the Lambeth resolution on racial questions. E. H. Louw, Minister of Economic Affairs, called the resolution hypocritical, on the grounds that the church schools were not open to persons of every race. Clayton replied:'In a country where the colour-bar prevails, it is difficult to be loyal to the New Testament, and we know that we sometimes fail to be so. But that does not mean that we ought to throw over the New Testament. It means that we must try to do better.'[23] That is true of course. We must always try to do better. But the fact was that the church schools refused to do better. It is hard to believe that anyone is trying to do better when he refuses to do better.

The school issue has plagued the Church of the Province to this very day. But emotions aroused by the larger issue of which it is a part have grown more intense of late. In the diocese of Cape Town there has been increasing criticism from coloured priests that their prospects of rising in the hierarchy are small, and that the function of coloured people in Church House was to sweep, and to make tea.* In 1971 the boys of Diocesan College, Rondebosch (Bishops), voted by a large majority to admit the son of the Revd. Clive McBride, a coloured priest of the diocese, but the governing body would not agree. Many young Anglicans repudiated with angry scorn the argument that the church schools are not controlled by the Church, and on that account some of them repudiated the Church also.

That the Anglican Church in South Africa has failed and is still failing in many ways to be true to the teachings of the Gospel, no one can doubt. That the Dutch Reformed churches also have failed, and are still failing in many ways, cannot be doubted either. That may be grievous enough. But what is most grievous is that they cannot even talk to each other about it.

*In 1972 Canon George Swartz, a coloured priest, was appointed Suffragan-Bishop of Cape Town.

24

Enter Verwoerd

It would be wrong to assume that Clayton had become wholly absorbed in public affairs, politics, and questions of race. It would have been quite impossible for him. He had been anointed to preach the Gospel to the poor, to heal the broken-hearted, to preach deliverance to the captives and recovery of sight to the blind; and to preach the acceptable year of the Lord. His whole life was centred about these things. He was first and last a priest, and now an archbishop. He believed that God had called him to be an archbishop, but he also believed that it was a bad choice. It is fascinating to reflect how the mind can hold these two contrary notions. It is also fascinating to reflect that although Clayton had said that it was a bad choice, he acted as though it were a good choice, and ruled his archdiocese with great authority.

It did not take long for Clayton to win the same trust and affection from his clergy as he had enjoyed in Johannesburg. There were exceptions, one of whom was Bishop Peacey, who was now at Constantia and, using the arguments of the Dutch Reformed Church, thought it unChristian for his coloured parishioners to sit at the back. But as he also thought that it was unChristian for them to sit anywhere else, he was now calling for a separate congregation for coloured Anglicans. In other words he had now become an out-and-out supporter of apartheid. The members of the coloured Anglican laity were noted in those days for their extreme respect for priests and especially for archbishops, and Clayton to them was a superhuman being whom they regarded with veneration. This veneration increased every time he spoke out against social evils and against new laws that would push them yet further apart from white people, change the nature of their franchise, separate them in railway coaches, at post office counters, and on the beaches, and try to pull back those who had escaped over the colour line. The coloured people venerated him, but they were afraid of him too, especially churchwardens, servers, and choirboys, who came most into contact with him when he visited the parishes, which visits were often made before he had had breakfast. Choirboys are notoriously naughty, but when Clayton visited the parish church they were totally subdued. Servers trembled most, because they were terrified of making some mistake.

As in Johannesburg it was the clergy who were nearest him. In the drawer of his desk he kept a notebook of their names, parishes, dates of appointment, marital status, families, and so on. He was still a great reader of *Crockford's Clerical Directory*, and his notebook in the drawer at 'Bishopscourt' became a kind of small *Crockford.* He consulted it frequently, praying daily for one of his clergy, and deciding just how much longer such a priest should stay in his parish. There is one good story of this. The archbishop had decided that it was time for the rector of one of his parishes to retire, but could not bring himself to tell him so. Therefore he was gratified when the rector wrote to tell him that he thought it was time to retire. Clayton took the train to the suburban station and was met by the rector's wife, who said, 'My husband has now decided not to retire but to die in harness.' 'That's all right for him', said Clayton, 'but what about the people in the cart?'*

Edward King, now Dean of Cape Town, who had first served in Germiston under ffrench-Beytagh, and then had come to the diocese of Cape Town, first to Robertson and then to Stellenbosch, venerated the Archbishop. So did his wife. When Clayton came to the parish, he stayed with them, and although they were in awe of him they looked forward to his visits. Clayton liked nothing better than to talk to them for hours, mainly about the diocese and the province. He enjoyed his food, but during Lent he did not eat much during the day; however, at dinner-time, so he told them, 'I boa-constrict.'

When travelling with them to different parts of the parish, he would often sing hymns, though tonelessly. On one occasion he tried to recall the words of Mrs. Alexander's tear-jerking hymn 'Within the churchyard, side by side', but was only partly successful. When they were back at the rectory, he called for a hymnbook and sang it to them with exaggerated piety. Four verses will be enough.

p Within the churchyard, side by side
Are many long, low graves;
And some have stones set over them,
On some the green grass waves.

For many a little Christian child,
Woman, and man, lies there;
And we pass near them every time
When we go into prayer.

They cannot hear our footsteps come,
They do not see us pass;
They cannot feel the warm, bright sun
That shines upon the grass.

*There are similar English versions of this story but Clayton improved on them.

cr They do not hear when the great bell
Is ringing overhead;
They cannot rise and come to Church
dim With us, for they are dead.

Archdeacon William Victor Gregorowski was another admirer, though critical. He had been born at Hoopstad in the Orange Free State, had been to St. George's Grammar School, and had worked for the South African Mutual Life Assurance Society for nine years before going to St. Augustine's, Canterbury. He fully supported Clayton's stand on apartheid, but found it very difficult to accept his views on the incompatibility of the two cultures, and thought that they betrayed a strain of anti-Afrikanerism. Gregorowski himself had been brought up in an English-speaking home, but the majority of his relatives were Afrikaners. He told two stories of his archbishop. He was posing with Clayton on the lawn of the rectory at Caledon on the occasion of the celebration of the centenary of the establishment of the church in 1856, and Clayton said to the photographers, 'Some of you tell me to look pleasant, and some to look natural, and I can't do both.' The second story was of one of the few occasions – perhaps the only one – when Clayton had his English corrected. It was at a very full lunch-table at 'Bishopscourt', and the archbishop said, 'I'm allergic to mosquitoes', to which Mrs. Gregorowski replied, 'Why, do you come out in bumps?' Clayton said, 'No, they won't come near me.' Mrs. Gregorowski said, 'But that means they are allergic to you.' Clayton said, 'Ha! Ha! Ha!' and no one said much for some time after that.

The Revd. George Sylvester, now a canon, said that Clayton was a 'great archbishop with a golden heart'. Towards the end of his life Clayton had gone to Hopefield for a confirmation and had stayed for the night with the Sylvesters. On the morning he left he had unexpectedly gone into the front garden, where he picked up the Sylvesters' little son Mark, and kissed him on the cheek and gave him a shilling. This small incident was never to be forgotten. When Clayton stayed with them they were extremely conscious of the fact that he was an archbishop, but not that he was a white one.

Another couple who were devoted to Clayton were the Swartzes: George Swartz became a canon after Clayton's death, and still later, as we have noted, Suffragan-Bishop of Cape Town, the first coloured priest to reach this eminence. Swartz was the priest who suffered considerable loss as a result of a burglary, and who next day received a private cheque from Clayton sufficient to replace all that had been stolen. He told the story of the girl at confirmation who had lost her card, and the priest whispered to Clayton, 'Card lost.' Clayton confirmed her as 'Card Lost', and afterwards said to Swartz, 'I wonder by what name she will be called in heaven.' Just before his death Clayton appointed Swartz to be Rector of St. Helena Bay, where Swartz heard this story. Clayton had gone there for confirmation, and then to Vredenburg, one of the smaller churches of the parish, where the wife of the catechist had made a very handsome cushion for him to kneel on, and had placed it on the chancel steps. But when Clayton reached it 'he sent it flying with a kick', for reasons that no one would have dared to enquire. So in spite of the mellowing, the conflict in Clayton persisted between the greatness and the petulance.

Clayton was now not only the bishop of a diocese, but also the chairman of a bench of bishops. This also he enjoyed immensely, and there appears in this book a photograph of him sitting at the head of the table, with a smile of tremendous geniality and satisfaction. (See plate 10.)

The first newcomer to the bench was Ambrose Reeves, the newly elected Bishop of Johannesburg, who was consecrated in the Cathedral of St. George, Cape Town, on Trinity Sunday 1949. Reeves believed, almost without reservation, that a South African bishop must concern himself with the politics of the country. Apartheid was politics, but it was also wickedness, therefore it was the concern of the Church. But the Church could not hope to deal with it unless it co-operated with non-Church agencies, even when they were not Christian. He went further, and actually took upon himself the task of co-ordinating the work of all those agencies and organisations, such as the trade-unions, the non-racial South African Institute of Race Relations, the African and Indian Congresses, the white Congress of Democrats, the non-racial Liberal Party, and others. Some of those with whom he co-operated were antagonistic to the Church, and regarded Christianity as the opium of the masses. Some were antagonistic to the Liberal Party, and regarded liberalism as an obstacle to revolution. Many, and indeed most, Liberals regarded the Congress of Democrats with the utmost suspicion because of the strong Communist influence inside that organisation, while many members of the Congress Movement regarded the Liberals with contempt, and also with bitter hostility, because the Liberal Party attracted Indian and African members who should in their opinion have rather joined their respective Congresses. The presence of the Liberal Party also caused stresses inside the African and Indian Congresses, which had already formed strong links with the Congress of Democrats. It was this strange assortment that Reeves tried to bind together, with a measure of success that was surprising. But it was this very success that alienated many Anglicans in his diocese, and aroused amongst the extreme right-wing whites a dangerous anger. Reeves and his wife lived under intense strain and anxiety because of the willingness of their opponents to use violence against them, and the strange inability of the police to apprehend them.

It must be said in honesty that Clayton and Reeves never achieved a liking for each other. Reeves was another of the Christian activists to whom Clayton was antipathetic. Clayton not only doubted his wisdom, but he questioned what appeared to him to be an absorption – if not an obsession – with politics. Clayton said on certain occasions, 'No man approves of his successor'; whether this referred to Chesterfield, one does not know, but it certainly referred to Johannesburg.

This antipathy was not extended to the other bishops. Clayton had a great respect for Leonard Fisher, the saintly Bishop of Natal, who had appeared at first to be a formidable candidate for the archbishopric. He had a great liking for Edward Paget, the tall, commanding Bishop of Southern Rhodesia, a preacher of quite a different kind from himself, for Paget had many of the gifts of the actor, and did not hesitate to use them if he thought he could shock Christian people into thought and action. Another bishop in whom Clayton had great confidence was H. A. Cullen, the Bishop of Grahamstown, who as a young man had made his 'eager way' to hear the young don of Peterhouse, who could bring 'the most profound teaching to us almost in words of one syllable'. Clayton was to rely on Cullen a great deal in his last years, and especially on a matter which was beginning to occupy his mind, the question of his retirement.

He was, in 1950, in his sixty-sixth year, and though his health was remarkably good for a man who ate well and took no exercise, he was slowing up physically, and this no doubt had something to do with his excessive weight. He confided to more than one of his bishops his regret that he had come to Cape Town so late. He was thinking particularly of the social and political problems which had suddenly become so formidable, and of the new racial laws many of which he felt bound to oppose. One could not help thinking more of these problems when one was in Cape Town, for this was the seat of legislative power. There is only one thing to be said about Clayton's doubt of his ability to face the problems adequately. It was a doubt entertained by no one else, except perhaps by those few who were nexplicably unable to recognise his strength and wisdom, because they perhaps had been involved in some experience painful to recall, or because they could not sense the greatness behind the petulance.

There were fourteen dioceses in the Province when Clayton became archbishop. These were Cape Town, St. Helena, Damaraland, George, Grahamstown, St. John's, Kimberley–Kuruman, Bloemfontein, Johannesburg, Pretoria, Southern Rhodesia, Lebombo, Zululand and Natal.* Clayton intended to visit them all, and in addition to these journeys he intended to visit the island of Tristan da Cunha, which was one of the parishes of the diocese of St. Helena, but was almost impossible for the bishop to visit. Although he was to find this travelling increasingly arduous, his enjoyment of these visits can only be described as tremendous. Whatever his own self-containedness, whatever his own inability to enter into intimacy, he liked to be met by his own people, and his face would wear an almost beatific expression, except of course on those occasions when it did not.

His first visit was to Paget in Salisbury, made a few months after his enthronement. He visited many places, including the stations of the Community of the Resurrection. In the Cathedral at Salisbury he gave them a sermon to remember. Paget described it all as 'a great success',

*Basutoland became a separate diocese in 1950.

and wrote of the great 'supra-racial celebrations in the Cathedral and at St. John's, Bulawayo, Gwelo and Umtali'. It could only be described as a triumphal tour.[1]

Equally triumphal was his tour of the diocese of St. John's, with its cathedral in Umtata, in February 1950. Clayton himself wrote of this. He 'preached thirteen sermons and talked at eleven receptions. The Bishop must have been terribly tired of listening to me. In fact, when we reached Kokstad he could bear it no longer and fled.' The tour was made more arduous because Clayton had an extremely painful attack of gout, and alighted at East London walking heavily with a stick. The bishop wrote of the occasion when Clayton was presented by church members with a Basotho blanket: 'The Bishop was most kindly given a similar blanket, the colouring and pattern of which roused the Archbishop's envy: but he was entirely satisfied with his own when he was told that he could not have one like the Bishop's as that was only for married men.'[2]

Archdeacon John Alexander King of Kimberley was in charge of All Saints' Mission near Engcobo during Clayton's visit to the diocese of St. John's. He wrote an account of the visit which is not only entertaining, but captures the essence of this great, strange man.[3]

'The Archbishop was due to arrive at the Mission in time for lunch on a Friday. Jean and I had not been married very long and it was her first experience of having to entertain a Prince of the Church. She was fairly nervous, having been told many stories of his misogyny and of the importance he attached to his food. We told her that he didn't mind what he ate so long as there was plenty of food and that it was good solid stuff. Being Friday, we advised her to start off with fish and chips. We also told her that he liked his meals on time. Of course he was late in arriving and was further delayed when he did arrive by a fairly lengthy 'praise' greeting which the local tribal poet insisted on delivering at the entrance to the mission. Geoffrey was very patient over this, but was obviously relieved when it was all over, and when at about a quarter to two he was able to sit down to his fish and chips. But alas they had been frying too long and some of them were very hard – so hard that the Archbishop's top dental plate cracked under the strain. He had no spare plate with him. It was very embarrassing – especially for poor Jean. But he was very restrained and gentle.

'After lunch we had to go into the local village, Engcobo, for a service and reception. The Arch. had with him a new primatial cross, very pretty and made if I remember rightly of some rather brittle material. Bill Reynolds had just come on to the staff as a new deacon and he was detailed off to act as chaplain to the Archbishop. Geoffrey gave him the cross and growled some instructions to him about handling it with great care, which Bill received with a nervous grin – and promptly dropped it. It cracked down the middle. His Grace was not quite so restrained over this disaster, and the vestry was very hushed while he allowed himself the indulgence of a little plain speaking. But it passed off and he was in great form at the reception which followed. We went back to the mission for some sort of evening do with the girls of the Training College, where Geoffrey parked himself in a chair in the middle of the School Hall and held court, with the young ladies and the staff all about him, looking rather like a later Roman Emperor. The mission doctor had tried to mend his plate with sticking-plaster but it didn't hold and in the end he abandoned it and champed his gums. Eventually we went to bed after a final gossip session in the parsonage drawing-room with some of the visiting clergy – Geoffrey slumped in an armchair, dripping cigarette ash over his cassock and discussing Provincial personalities in great detail and with great gusto. We had given him one of the outside rooms of the parsonage, thinking it would be quiet for him. We learned the next morning that the saga of accidents had continued.

'He woke up just after midnight and looked at his watch. It was bright moonlight and he misread 12.30 a.m. for 6 a.m. He was due to say Mass for the Sisters at 6 a.m., so he got up, dressed and hobbled over to their chapel on the other side of the mission compound. I forgot to say that he was suffering a bad attack of gout over this visit. Of course when he got to the Chapel he discovered his mistake and had to hobble back muttering the commination service* to himself. He got back into bed. About 2 o'clock a very belated African priest arrived from one of the outstations and of course chose to investigate the room in which we had put the Archbishop. An hour or so later one of the mission horses chose the open window of his bedroom for a short serenade. The extraordinary thing was that, in telling us of these events the next day, in spite of his reputation for cross-temperedness he seemed with each successive disaster to reach new heights of humour. His reaction to his misadventures certainly endeared him to the present writer and his wife.'

In January 1951 Clayton visited the diocese of Basutoland, now Lesotho, and again had a triumphal tour. In May he sailed by passenger ship to St. Helena, the smallest diocese of the Province, with only four parishes. Of this he wrote that St. Helena was an 'extremely attractive island' and that he would retain the happiest recollections of his visit.[4] He paid visits to Pretoria and Johannesburg but did not tour the dioceses. In the case of Pretoria it might well be that he was beginning to find such tours exhausting. In the case of Johannesburg it was no doubt understandable; it had been his own diocese, and as always happens in such cases, comparisons were made which were odious.

The new bishop's involvement in politics, and his inevitable altering of old practices, and the fact that he did not speak with the same immense authority, were adversely regarded by many. Reeves was a man of considerable determination, and did not readily modify his opinions. After Clayton's death, during the state of emergency declared after Sharpeville in 1960, he – or others – or both he and others – feared that he would be arrested, and he took the fateful decision to seek refuge in Swaziland,

*Commination is a 'recital of Divine threatenings against sinners'.

which was under the British Crown. When he finally returned to Johannesburg, he was deported. It was a step from which his reputation never recovered. To me Bishop Reeves had a deep understanding of the gospel-teaching. This led him to challenge the assumption of a colour-bar society and to expose its cruelties. His piety was suspect because of his activism. The synthesis of the two seems not easily accomplished. Clayton accomplished it in his own way, but he did not approve of the way that Reeves did it. So developed between him and Reeves the same incompatibility that had developed between him and Scott, and was yet to develop between him and Huddleston.

As in Johannesburg, so in Cape Town, Clayton's relations with the clergy were considerably more intimate than with the laity. As in Johannesburg, the clergy formed the inner circle. That is not to say that many laymen in both dioceses had not a warm regard and affection for their bishop. Yet as far as I know, only one layman established a close friendship with him, warm on both sides, and that was Herbert Stanley. Clayton's respect for him was such that he would never have slapped Stanley down in Synod. If Clayton was wise, he thought Stanley wise too; after all they were Brother Owls.

Another person who comes into close personal contact with a bishop is his chaplain. When Clayton was elected archbishop he asked Dick Yates, who was at that time at St. Cyprian's, Johannesburg, living at 'Bishop's House' and acting as chaplain, to go to Cape Town with him. But while he was in Cape Town arranging to take up his new task, Yates decided to get married, and when Clayton returned he told him. Clayton was shocked at the news, and told Yates that he would not have a married chaplain. He was not only shocked, he was hurt as well, and after that did not discuss any of his future plans with Yates. He disapproved of the impending marriage and said so. He made two revealing remarks to Yates. One was, 'I am sorry that I failed to help you.' Yates interpreted this to mean that he felt he had failed to fill the need for companionship which he rightly assumed Yates to feel, which need, obviously, could be filled only by a woman. Yates wrote of this, 'I was grieved for him and quite unable to make any kind of amends.' The other important thing that Clayton said was, 'I am not ashamed of my nature.' He added that it was a gift of God and it was something which he had tried to use in God's service.

So an association which had begun at Chesterfield and had lasted fifteen years, came virtually to an end. Yates venerated Clayton, and he knew all his faults. He also had the gift of observation, for which a biographer is grateful.

The end of this association made possible the beginning of another. In 1949 the vicar of Christchurch, Ealing, died. His curate, Roy Cowdry, a young man of 34, thought it was time for him to move on. It so happened that Michael Gibbs, Dean of Cape Town, was in London, and he telephoned Cowdry to ask whether he would be interested in becoming chaplain to the Archbishop. Cowdry said No, but advised by his suffragan-bishop went to see Gibbs at Princes Risborough in Buckinghamshire. To use his own words, he fell for Gibbs, and agreed to become chaplain knowing little of what was in store for him.

Cowdry arrived in Cape Town on 2 March 1950, and was met at the docks by his archbishop. In the car Clayton asked him what he knew of South Africa, and Cowdry said he had read H. V. Morton's *In Search of South Africa*. At this Clayton grunted, which abashed Cowdry considerably. His premonition that he was in for something was strengthened by the size and beauty of 'Bishopscourt', which overwhelmed him.

Cowdry's task was made more difficult by Clayton's gout, which affected both knees and gave great pain. One of Cowdry's first jobs was to put antiphlogiston plasters on both knees morning and night while the bout lasted, which was from seven to ten days. Clayton was never a good patient. On one occasion he was suffering from some kind of fever, and Cowdry stood over him with the thermometer, but he refused to have his temperature taken. At length Cowdry – who must by this time have recovered from his awe – shouted at him, 'Stop behaving like a great big baby!' Clayton's mouth fell open in astonishment, and Cowdry seized his chance and plunged the thermometer into it.

Let this be the final proof of the strangeness and greatness of this man. In spite of all indications to the contrary, Cowdry came to regard his archbishop as a holy man, albeit an unusual one. Of duty and responsibility he knew a great deal, of idleness and infidelity nothing. He rose early, and spent an hour in the chapel before Matins and Communion, and was always at Evensong if he were at home. Much of his thinking over his sermons, addresses and charges was done in the chapel, and he always went there before going to bed. He had some money of his own and was extremely generous with it. He desired to possess nothing. He owned the bare essentials in dress, and his bedroom was very simply furnished, with a wardrobe, a bed, a bedside table with lamp, and a chair. All his devotional books he kept in the chapel. He did not take long to go to sleep, and after the devotions of the day relaxed with crossword puzzles or tales of crime and detection. He provided his guests with three books, taken from his shelves, where all the books were arranged by authors' names in alphabetical order. Sometimes the three books were totally unreadable, and he would take a mischievous delight in asking his guests how they had enjoyed them. In 1955 he went with Cowdry to Salisbury for the inauguration of the Province of Central Africa and the enthronement of Edward Paget, its first archbishop. Clayton stayed with the Governor of Southern Rhodesia, and Cowdry at an hotel. When Cowdry went to see him, Clayton launched into a bitter complaint. 'I've had to go and buy another pair of shoes. That wretched valet keeps taking mine away to clean them.' This simplicity characterised his life. Cowdry stayed with Clayton till his death, and like Yates he venerated him, knew all his faults, and had the gift of observation.

In this same year of 1950, the year of Smuts's death, there occurred another momentous event, that was to have far-reaching consequences for South Africa, and for the missionary and educational work of the churches. This was the appointment of Dr. Hendrik Frensch Verwoerd to the portfolio of Minister of Native Affairs. This event was to affect profoundly the activities of the last six years of Clayton's life.

In his charge to the Provincial Synod of 1950 Clayton made a clear statement on the nature and duty of the Church of the Province that made conflict with Verwoerd inevitable. Verwoerd was a forceful expounder of the doctrine of racial separation and the great benefits that would flow from it. Clayton affirmed again the multiracial nature of the Church of the Province, but he claimed also that it was the nature of the Church of Christ. It was convenient for many reasons that people of the same race should worship together, but no confirmed member might be excluded from any Anglican congregation. And every Anglican should be prepared to accept the ministrations of any Anglican priest of whatever race. In 1950 Clayton felt impelled to add, 'We have some way to travel before we can get this universally accepted.'

Suffice it to say that these teachings were anathema to Verwoerd. It was offensive to many Nationalists to see mixed congregations pouring out of the Anglican cathedrals – and churches of other denominations – on special days such as Synod Sundays. Such special services usually took place in large church-buildings in white areas. In 1950 one did not foresee that Verwoerd would one day try to prevent the holding of such services by law. Clayton, after those safe and certain beginnings at Rugby and Cambridge, was moving into strange and dangerous waters. Luckily he was not unprepared. Fourteen years of Johannesburg had prepared him.

25

Assault on the Franchise

When Parliament opened in 1951 the Government announced its intention to introduce a Separate Representation of Voters Bill, the purpose of which would be to remove all coloured voters to a separate roll, where they could elect white persons to represent them in Parliament.

Now the difficulty was that by the South Africa Act of 1909 the franchise could be altered only by a two-thirds majority of both Houses sitting together. Such a majority was nowhere in sight. Therefore the Nationalist argument was put forward that, because South Africa, by virtue of the Statute of Westminster and the South African Status Act of 1934, had become a sovereign independent State, she was no longer bound by the franchise entrenchment of 1909, and could in fact alter the franchise by a bare majority. This in fact Parliament proceeded to do.

Early in 1951 Dolf de la Rey, a relative of the famous Boer War general, and 'Sailor' Malan, a most distinguished war pilot, founded the War Veterans' Action Group. The purpose of the Group was to resist the advance of the very totalitarianism against which the veterans had fought, but it not only restricted its membership to white veterans but excluded Coloured and African veterans from its celebration of El Alamein Day. Soon the Group was renamed the Torch Commando, which was determined to protest vigorously against the way in which the Government intended to pass the Voters' Bill by a bare majority. The Torch Commando grew by leaps and bounds to a membership of some 250,000 and seemed to manifest the first real opposition to the racial plans of the Nationalist Government. The Commando first concentrated its spectacular efforts on the coloured vote and, South Africa being what it is, excluded coloured voters from its ranks. But such gross inconsistencies did not prevent a great surging of hope in the coloured people themselves, and indeed in all people who were filled with revulsion by the extreme racial laws which the Government was determined to enact.

The Torch Commando decided to send convoys from as many cities and towns as possible to the city of Cape Town, where a mammoth demonstration would be held. The times were exciting indeed. For nearly three years the opponents of the Government had been almost numbed by the legislative blows dealt by their rulers, and the Torch Commando gave them new hope. Eric Walker the historian wrote of the protest march in Cape Town on 28 May 1951, in which 10,000 ex-servicemen took part, the purpose of the march being to present a petition to the Government against the Separate Representation of Voters Act:

'The Commando's own proceedings were orderly, but those of some of the Coloured Folk who had tagged along behind it in its march were not. These folk, trooping home to the slums of District Six, found themselves faced in Church Square, under the shadow of the Groote Kerk, by teams of young policemen, who had been trained to break up mobs and had been brought in specially from the countryside to show their prowess. They did, and for the second time during this disastrous Session, the Mother City was the scene of scarcely-excusable violence by the guardians of law and order. The police charged without warning, and equally without warning used their truncheons on the heads and other parts of the anatomy of anyone they could get at. It was diligently noised abroad that the crowd had been trying to destroy the Groote Kerk, a rumour well-calculated to induce Nationalists, if inducement were needed, to vote for the virtual disenfranchisement of Coloured Folk.'[1]*

Clayton wrote on the Separate Representation of Voters Bill in *Good Hope* of 14 March. He wrote that Dr. Malan was not necessarily guilty of a breach of faith in that in 1928 he had actually advocated the extension of voting rights to coloured women, yet now in 1951 he intended to alter their status. 'But his change of mind . . . is bound to create a sense of insecurity in the minds of the non-European.' The Church must say boldly that neither a man nor a Government had a right to break a promise. The Revd. J. J. F. van Schoor, M.P. for Zoutpansberg, would not hear of any imputation of breach of faith. The election of 1948 had shown that it was God's will that white supremacy should be maintained.[2] Thus Van Schoor stated, even if over-baldly, what many Nationalists and many Dutch Reformed churchmen believed, that the will of the Nationalist electorate and the will of God were the same. If the Nationalists had lost the election of 1953 – which they did not – it is difficult to know what Van Schoor would have said then.

On 14 May 1951 the Separate Representation of Voters Bill became law. J. G. N. Strauss, who had succeeded General Smuts as leader of the United Party, promised that the Opposition would contest the validity of the Act in the courts. Dr. Malan replied that if the courts declared the Act invalid, they would be undermining the sovereignty of Parliament, and he hoped that such a crisis would not arise.[3] The passing of the Bill caused great gloom, not only among coloured people who had lost their century-old franchise, not only among English people who realised that the constitutional entrenchment of the English language appeared to be now valueless, but also amongst those who were witnessing the embodiment in law of a morality which was to them immoral and unChristian. Appeals were made to Clayton and other church leaders for a national day of prayer. The

*Brookes and Webb, *A History of Natal*, p. 278, records that 164 people were injured on this occasion.

Archbishop was not 'at the moment' convinced that there should be a special day of prayer. It could be very easily understood as a political demonstration. The Church was not against political demonstrations, but it was not its business to organise them. In any event, a Christian should regularly pray for his country.

The tide of new legislation was fast and irresistible. On 11 June the Suppression of Communism Amendment Act further increased the power of the Minister of Justice to act against persons without recourse to the courts. The new Minister of Native Affairs, Senator Hendrik Verwoerd, presented his Bantu Authorities Bill, which would get rid of the Natives Representative Council of 1936, and reinforce all the tribal institutions. At the base of the pyramid would be the chiefs and their councils, and regional councils to co-ordinate and control at least two chiefdoms, and above them territorial councils to co-ordinate and control at least two regional areas. Every African in the cities and towns, whether he had seen his ancestral homeland or not, was deemed to be a citizen of it. His living in the city or town was not a right, but a 'temporary sojourn', even if he, and his father before him, and his grandfather before that, had known no other home. At this time – 1951 – it was estimated that over four and a half million Africans lived outside the Reserves.[4]

Dr. Verwoerd justified the abolition of the Natives Representative Council by quoting the opinions of various of its own members concerning the efficacy of the institution itself. These opinions could hardly be expected to be laudatory, because the Councillors believed their Council to be impotent. It was the white Parliament which remained all-powerful. One supposes that Dr. Verwoerd's use of these arguments showed what is called 'political acumen'. Two threats were posed by the Bantu Authorities Bill. One was that once the authorities were established, there would be no more need for Senator Edgar Brookes, Mrs. Ballinger, and the other white Native Representatives in Parliament. The second was that ultimately African education would be handed over to the Bantu Authorities, and that the African schools established by so many of the missions would be handed over also. The missionaries had traditionally had three great tasks, and that for the better part of two centuries. They were, the establishment of churches, hospitals, and schools. The achievements of the missionaries in the field of African education have been described by many Africans as the crowning work of the churches. The possibility was now strong that Afrikaner Nationalism, for all its devotion to the Christian religion, would destroy all missionary education, because that part of it which was not in the hands of the Dutch Reformed churches was a danger to the continuance of white supremacy, which according to Van Schoor, was the will of God.

On 21 June 1951 the Bill was read for the third time. Verwoerd launched a fierce attack on Communists and agitators who had 'advised' the Natives Representative Council, and when asked by Mrs. Ballinger who they were, said that she was one. That was twenty-one years ago, but today it is still Communists and agitators who are said by the Government to be behind most of South Africa's troubles. It seems they are a hardy breed, but they could not prevent the Bantu Authorities Bill from becoming law.

The Bantu Authorities Act thus attempted to re-establish the tribal structures, and to recreate the 'homelands'. Today the debate centres on the question whether such homelands can ever achieve any measure of viability, or whether they will remain reservoirs of labour for white industry, white commerce, white municipalities. In 1951 much of the debate centred on the threat to the settlement of 1936 which provided for representation of black voters by white representatives in a white Parliament.

The debate was characterised by the thoughtless talk of so many white people who either talked as though black people had no ears, or talked as though they did not think it important whether they had ears or not. The Cape Synod of the N.G.K. passed a resolution to the effect that Africans were not capable of voting. The Port Elizabeth *Evening Post* carried the headline 'D.R.C.: Natives not Capable of Voting'. One speaker said, 'The vote is a privilege which is entrusted only to adults who can use it with responsibility before God.' The Revd. J. A. J. Steenkamp, an N.G.K. missionary, wrote to *Die Kerkbode* to ask whether it was *necessary* to take such resolutions, and whether it was *desirable* to give them to the press so that they could be spread throughout the world. Could they not be taken privately? Steenkamp was distressed for members of the Mission Church. This made life a *lydensweg* for them. *Lydensweg* is a strong word, and can mean the *via dolorosa* of the Christ. Thus there were those inside the Dutch Reformed churches who were made bitterly unhappy by the colour-policies their churches endorsed. But to break away on that account was almost impossible.

When I was principal of the Diepkloof Reformatory, the Sunday preacher once a month was an African minister of the N.G.K., and after the service he would go for refreshment to the vice-principal's house. He entered by the back door, and had his refreshment in the kitchen. The African teachers at the reformatory plagued him with questions that made him deeply unhappy – why did he go to the back door? would he enter Heaven by the back door? when he was in Heaven would he eat in the kitchen? Not only he, but many of his white fellow-churchmen, felt deeply the continual accusations that the colour-policies of the Dutch Reformed churches were unChristian.

Dr. Malan strongly criticised those churches which opposed the policies of the Government, and said that while they had so much to say about politics, 'as far as spiritual work was concerned, they stood far behind the Afrikaans churches'. Clayton quoted these words in his charge delivered to the Cape Diocesan Synod on 7 November 1951. He said that it was a sorry business to count heads, but the Prime Minister's remarks had moved him to examine the latest statistics.

'I think it ought to be publicly stated that the Methodists have more than five times as many African members as the Dutch Reformed churches, and the Anglicans between two and three times as many. It is difficult, therefore, to understand by what right it can be said that, as far as spiritual work is concerned, we stand far behind the Dutch Reformed Churches.'

In this charge Clayton defined the threefold task of the Church, pastoral care, evangelism and social witness.

'The Christian Church owes it to her Lord and to her members that she perform the duty of bearing witness. Whatever there is in the organisation and general set-up of the country which is contrary to the mind of Christ, as we have received and understood it, against that we should make our protest, always remembering that our primary concern is with individual people, that, like our Lord, we should be less interested in systems than in persons, and only interested in systems as they affect persons; that we should condemn anything which makes Christian living unnecessarily difficult, even though it cannot make it impossible, and that we should condemn anything that deprives a man of the rights that belong to him as a human being, or of the opportunity of discharging his duty and making his contribution to the common life of the nation of which he is a part. If that is interfering in politics, then the Christian Church must interfere in politics.'

Clayton again had something to say about the British tradition, which was a subject he had rarely mentioned before the coming to power of the Afrikaner Nationalists.

'If to value the traditions which we have inherited from our fathers is to be a jingo, then I am certainly a jingo, and so, incidentally, is the Prime Minister of this country. But we have met here as the Church of the Province of South Africa.... We do not want our non-European Churchmen to have a British religion.... We claim to stand for the Catholic Faith of Christ, the Faith once for all delivered to the saints. We believe that we can offer men the Christian Faith without what seems to us to be illegitimate developments, whether those developments had their origin at Geneva or at Rome.'

One could not really be much clearer than that. Clayton was equally clear in his concluding remarks about Communism. Though he did not mention the Suppression of Communism Act and its 1951 amendments, he was clearly referring to them.

'... there are many people who are afraid of the spread of Communism in this country. It seems to me that those who are afraid of this are taking the kind of action which is most likely to make their fears come true.... I can imagine no more certain method of forwarding the growth of support for Communism, underground and secret support, than the withholding from individuals of the rights which safeguard their freedom. And one of those rights is access to the courts of law before being found guilty of an offence.'[5]

Meanwhile the magnitude of the threat to the mission schools was becoming clearer. In 1949 the Government had appointed a Commission on Native Education under the chairmanship of Dr. W. W. M. Eiselen. No missionary had been appointed to the Commission, nor any African. Of Dr. Eiselen it could be said that he and Verwoerd were the co-architects of the new policies of separate development, separate cultures, separate homelands, separate destinies. Dr. Eiselen was the son of a German missionary, a man of upright character and blameless life, and he now planned to destroy missionary education.

The report of Eiselen's Commission, published in 1951, made it clear what was in store. Native Education – as it was called – had since 1910 been in the hands of the four provincial administrations. Money was always short, but the relations between the authorities and the missions were in general excellent. Now, however, it was recommended that Native Education which in future was to be styled Bantu Education, should be placed under the control of the Minister of Native Affairs. It was to be suited to the Bantu environment, based on Bantu tribal ethics, and be given through the medium of the Bantu tongues. So would be removed a long-standing grievance against the missionaries, that they taught through the medium of the English language, that they were intent on turning out black Englishmen, that they taught foreign philosophies such as the rights of man in such a way as to give black children ideas above their station, *that they were in fact preparing children to live in a world that did not exist*. Verwoerd made no attempt to conceal his dislike of the mission schools of the non-Dutch-Reformed churches. He said later in Parliament when he was introducing the Bantu Education Bill, which was based on the Eiselen report: 'I want to remind Honourable Members that if the native in South Africa today, in any kind of school in existence, is being taught to expect that he will live his adult life under a policy of equal rights, he is making a big mistake.'

Dr. Verwoerd had the gift of speaking with the outward appearance of complete confidence and assurance. His speeches filled the non-Dutch-Reformed missionaries with tremendous apprehension. He appeared to be a man of unshakable will. In public he appeared smiling and benign, but gave few evidences of wit and humour. He spoke indeed of the advances black people would make under his policies to greater freedom and self-expression, but his prophecies were cold and clinical.

For the next five years Clayton and Verwoerd were not only two of the greatest figures on the South African stage, but each was always conscious of the other. Clayton told Cowdry that he had never before encountered such an alien mind. Verwoerd was conscious of an antagonist who could be neither silenced nor cowed, and who for many reasons, both explicable and inexplicable, opposed this master-plan for the harmonious future of a most complex country. The explicable reasons were obvious to Verwoerd – upbringing, education, a liberal and ornate religion, an extreme, even morbid, concern, not always disinterested, for the welfare of other groups than his own. The inexplicable reason – the existence of which sometimes caused Verwoerd to reveal his rancour in public – was Clayton's total inability to see the justice, the reasonableness, the logicality, the comprehensiveness, of the master-plan.

Verwoerd once told an interviewer that he always slept well because he had no doubt in his mind of the rightness of his plans. Though in his younger days he had been inclined to scepticism, he later became sure that he was God's instrument for South Africa. Indeed it is hard not to hold such a belief if one becomes a leader, and subsequently *the* leader, of the Afrikaner

Nationalist Party. It is closer to the belief of Hitler that he was the instrument of Providence than to the belief of Clayton that he was called to be a shepherd. Both Clayton and Verwoerd believed themselves to be God's instruments. Was not Clayton called a bishop 'by Divine permission' and an archbishop 'by Divine providence'? In what, then, lay the difference between them? It lay precisely in this – that Clayton, with all his faults, was dedicated to the serving of men, and Verwoerd to the ruling of them.

In 1952 the state of African education was shocking. Only one third of African children were in school. Education was – and still is – not compulsory. The drop-out rate was enormous. In 1948 half of the children at school were in the two classes below Standard One. One child in twenty-five of those at school reached Standard Six. One child in a thousand reached matriculation. The amount spent on each white child was £44, on each black child less than £3.

Although the state of African education was so unsatisfactory, there would have been even less of it had it not been for the missionaries. In 1945 in South Africa there were 4,360 mission schools and only 230 government schools. Some of the mission schools were famous – Adams College, Mariannhill, Lovedale, Inanda Seminary, and many others. As the years passed, so the financial contribution of the State increased, and in fact the schools could not have offered what they did without it. In 1952 ninety per cent of African education was still in the hands of the missions. Under Smuts the relations between Government and the missionaries had been good. Hofmeyr, Minister of Education as well as Minister of Finance, had increased the expenditure on African education by small percentages each year. Though the total amount remained paltry, and the expenditure on each African child shocking, the missionaries never regarded the Government with apprehension. Although the pace was slow, the direction was right.

However, there was nothing much that could be done but to await the introduction of Verwoerd's Bantu Education Bill in 1953. Meanwhile in 1952 the preparations for the great tercentenary festival went ahead. It had already been announced that there would be functions and celebrations for all, but that the traditional customs of apartheid would be observed. These traditional customs were much stronger in the rest of South Africa than in the Cape Province. In Cape Town white people and coloured people had been living together in peace for 300 years. The announcement therefore caused great resentment among many white and coloured people, and the call to boycott the functions and celebrations was very strong. Clayton was not only a member of the national committee, but he had been accorded what can only be described as a considerable honour by being asked to be the preacher at the tremendous service to be held on 30 March 1952. The committee planned to hold a national conference on social welfare, which was to be limited to white people only, and there were many threats to boycott this function.

The problem of the boycott is perennial in South Africa. If one is to be a thorough boycotter, one could not travel by train, or have a cup of tea in a restaurant, or go to a cinema, or send one's children to school, or even have any children at all, except illegally. When the New Zealanders at last decided to include Maoris in their teams to visit South Africa, should one have boycotted them because the South African teams remained all-white? Is one to reject the good that might come from a national conference because all the delegates will be white? Should one refuse to donate blood because one's blood will be kept in a segregated container? Clayton wrote: 'Either we must refuse to take part in anything that is organised by the Government, or we must take part in gatherings which meet under conditions which we deplore. It seems to me that it is a mistake to adopt the former course.'[6]

The tercentenary festival could hardly be said to have been a unifying force. It was no doubt only because of Clayton's eminence in the world of the English-speaking churches that he was invited to be a speaker, and an important one. But in general critics of the Government and its policies were not invited to participate. The question was heard on all sides, what is there to celebrate? *Die Kerkbode* asked in an editorial, of Van Riebeeck's coming, 'Was it Disaster or Salvation?' The arrival of the whites, which was it? The answer was, salvation. 'There is in so many cases a loving relationship between whites and coloured, on farms, work places, and in the kitchens.' *Die Kerkbode* wrote that 'separate development would bring happiness to all', and that the white man did not get credit for all he had done. That was true, he did not. In many places, on the day of the tercentenary itself, thousands of people, most of them not white, pledged themselves to launch a campaign of defiance against unjust laws.

Clayton's centenary sermon, delivered on the foreshore to a tremendous and unsegregated gathering, was one of great power, but was hardly likely to please those who felt that the celebrations should be occasions for pride and gratitude. Gregorowski thought it 'lacked outgoingness'. By that he meant that it really was not a celebratory sermon, and such feelings can be understood. The one thing that the sermon did not lack was 'ingoingness'.

Of all the texts that could have been used on such an occasion, Clayton chose 'Forgive us our trespasses as we forgive those who trespass against us'. He admitted it was a strange text, but he had to speak with sincerity because he was a minister of Christ. In the main he believed that these 300 years had been 'for good' rather than 'for evil'. But Christians must not fall into the sin of pride and boastfulness. They must not be content. In the first place they had come to South Africa as Christians, but after 300 years the majority of Africans were not Christians. 'Christianity had been judged by the lives and characters of professing Christians, and so judged, it has not proved attractive.' Secondly, 'the proportion of the total population that had at one time or another served a sentence of imprisonment was colossal, and did not seem to be diminishing'. Lastly, 'This is a gloriously healthy land. But the ravages of tuberculosis among the people of the land are terrible.'

The slogan of the festival was 'We Build a Nation'. That nation had not yet been built. As they looked back over 300 years, there was much they could be glad to remember, and much that it would be well to forget. 'I don't think a nation has really come to birth until men are prepared to die for it.' A nation could not be built on hate and fear, only on love.

Clayton concluded: 'Today we thank God for the past. But we should not dwell on the past. We look to the future. And we dedicate ourselves to the God Who shall make the future better than the past, and out of the varied riches of our traditions shall build up, if we will let Him, a people to his praise.'[7]

'We Build a Nation' was certainly a strange slogan. When an Afrikaner Nationalist speaks of the nation, he is speaking of Afrikanerdom. He is repelled by the notion that he is one of a nation to which belong Jews, Indians, Coloured people, Africans, and English-speaking people. Therefore one can only suppose that during the festival there were two meanings of the word, one exclusive and one not. Clayton was obviously using the one that was not. But what was still more disappointing, especially to South Africans like Gregorowski, was that Clayton's sermon was penitential rather than celebratory. There is one thing more to remember. The British had been in South Africa for only 150 years. Therefore if one looked back over 300 years, and found much that would be well to forget, it looked as though one were repenting of Afrikaner as well as British sins.

The theme of the festival was to build a nation, but Dr. Verwoerd had more or less declared that there were many nations. What was more, some of the leaders of these other nations had embarked on a campaign of civil disobedience. And the leading English-speaking churchman, speaking in the Mother City, had said more or less categorically that there was not all that much to be proud about. It was surely a time to return to the reality of politics.

On 20 March 1952, just before the celebrations began, Strauss's promised appeal to the Appellate Court in Bloemfontein produced the judgement that the Separate Representation of Voters Act was invalid because Parliament had ignored the procedure laid down for securing any alteration in the entrenched clauses. The Court thus held that the Union of South Africa, although she had been declared to be an independent nation by the Statute of Westminster, was still bound by the provisions of the South Africa Act of 1909. The Appellate Court thus reversed a decision made by the Cape Division of the Supreme Court on 25 October 1951, declaring that it was bound by a previous decision of the Appellate Court made in 1937, namely that the Court had no jurisdiction to question procedures adopted by Parliament. Therefore the Appellate Court of 1952 also reversed its own decision of 1937.

Malan's response was immediate. He announced that he would enact a law to put the sovereignty of Parliament beyond challenge. The response of the Torch Commando was immediate also. It held public protest-meetings, those in Johannesburg and Durban being of unprecedented size. In Natal a movement to secede from the Union gained in strength. The Defiance Campaign began to go into action. The Minister of Justice did something which all intelligent political observers had expected; he warned leaders of the Campaign that he would proceed against them under the Suppression of Communism Act. The country was in a turmoil.

Clayton warned his readers in *Good Hope* of the coming of the totalitarian state, should the Appellate Court be unable to declare any Act of Parliament invalid. 'You will not all think as I do. But with this I hope you will agree: that in such a period of strife as lies before us, we as Christian men must have the courage to speak what we believe to be the truth.'[8]

Malan's plan to prevent any further invalidation of Acts of Parliament was ingenious. His Minister of Justice introduced a Bill to create a Court higher even than the Appellate Division, and this new Court was to be Parliament itself, and it was to be called the High Court of Parliament. Therefore if Parliament passed a law and the Appellate Division invalidated it, then the High Court of Parliament would revalidate it. When people heard of the Bill they laughed or cried or cheered or could not believe their ears. The Bill was passed on 21 April 1952. The High Court met in Pretoria on 27 August and revalidated the Separate Representation of Voters Act. On 29 August the Cape Division of the Supreme Court declared the High Court of Parliament Act invalid, in that it contravened the entrenched clauses. The Government appealed to the Appellate Division, which on 14 November confirmed the Cape judgement. What would the Government do next?

These events, though exciting enough, did not distract Clayton from his other duties. On 26 April he preached at High Mass at the Priory, Rosettenville, at the celebration of the diamond jubilee of the Community of the Resurrection, taking as his text, 'There are three that bear witness, the Spirit, the water, and the blood'.

He said he did not think anyone knew what the words meant, but he was going to use them as a peg. He quoted those words which had obviously meant so much to him for the greater part of his life: 'The Spirit of the Lord God is upon me, because the Lord has anointed me to preach the Gospel'. He recalled those faraway days at Cambridge, when Fathers Frere and Bull of the Community had conducted a mission for undergraduates. He had been at Pembroke then, and that was nearly forty-eight years ago. 'I knew it made much difference to me, and I knew that before it was over I had made my first confession.'

One of the members of the Community said to me, 'You must find the sermon that he preached at our jubilee. It was the greatest sermon I ever heard.' Why, what was great about it? The sermon and the words were simple, the texts were not his own. Was it perhaps to sit and listen to this man, and to know that with all his tremendous gifts of mind and spirit, with his mastery of language and of himself, with his great authority, he abased himself in the presence of One whom he believed to have created him, and not only had created him but throughout his life had cared for him, and thought that the greatest thing that had ever happened to him was to have been anointed to preach the Gospel? Yes, no doubt that is what it was.

Back in Cape Town he launched an appeal for £50,000 for the completion of St. George's Cathedral. He appealed again to parents not to hold back their sons who felt drawn to the ministry. He condemned the deprivation of freedom of those who held certain views, but had not been found guilty of an offence. On 7 July he went off for four weeks' holiday, and left Bishop Lavis to write the next letter for *Good Hope*. After thanking his archbishop for his letters month by month, Lavis wrote: 'His Grace's fearless leadership, balanced judgement, and wise counsel have helped us to think rightly and to act rightly towards certain more recent legislative action involving grave moral and social issues.'[10]

After his holiday Clayton visited Grahamstown for the golden jubilee of St. Paul's College, one of the theological schools of the Church of the Province. A highlight of the celebration was a luncheon given in the dining-hall of St. Andrew's College, one of the church schools, in honour of past students of St. Paul's and distinguished guests. It was a good lunch, but teetotal. Clayton had to make a speech, and he began it by saying that he greatly preferred a luncheon where there was plenty to drink and no speeches to one where there were plenty of speeches and no drink. He went on to say, 'When I was first ordained, I made up my mind that no one should ever say, "What a nice young man",' and after a slight pause he added, 'and no one ever did.' There was great laughter, from Clayton and everybody else. He did not believe in ignoring a good joke just because it happened to be his own.[11]

Canon Synge was at that time Warden of St. Paul's College. He was the brother of Michael Synge, who had been one of Clayton's curates at Chesterfield. He himself had visited Chesterfield and knew its redoubtable vicar. He came to South Africa and St. Paul's in 1955. Though he had a great regard for Clayton's mind, and called it 'very deeply rooted', he did not regard him as a great scholar, nor did he think that he had kept abreast of New Testament studies. An archbishop had to keep his feet solidly planted, and he must speak with absolute confidence; therefore perhaps he avoided critical studies of the gospels.

Synge must have been one of the few people to whom Clayton had ever apologised. St. Paul's granted a Licentiate of Theology, but it also conferred an honorary award on those who deserved it, and this was called the A.Th., or Associate of Theology. Clayton had a low opinion of both. At a meeting of the Ordination Candidates Board in Cape Town, the members were discussing the names of people to whom the awards might be made. Clayton, who was in a perverse mood, said, 'Let's give them away.' Soon after that they adjourned for tea, and one of the members of the board spoke to Clayton and told him that he had hurt the feelings of the Warden. On resumption Clayton, referring to his earlier remark, said, 'I should not have said that', which for him was an apology.

Synge had another story about Clayton and Cowdry. Synge was staying with a family in Cape Town, and had an invitation to dine at 'Bishopscourt' at seven o'clock. Cowdry arrived in time to fetch Synge to dinner, but then accepted a sherry from Synge's hostess, and in general dallied. Synge became more and more nervous, and at last suggested that it was time to go, to which Cowdry replied, 'I've had enough of the old man. He's been having a tantrum and stamping his feet at me.' When they got there, they were fifteen minutes late, but to Synge's relief Clayton was affability itself.[12]

South Africa was passing through most anxious times. The Defiance Campaign – which some called the Passive Resistance Campaign – started off in a manner worthy of Gandhi himself. Hundreds of resisters went to prison for breaking apartheid laws, most often by sitting quietly in some place reserved for persons of different race. These acts of defiance were often preceded by prayers and hymns. It just so happened that in the African township of New Brighton near Port Elizabeth, the police arrested two Africans for some offence which had nothing to do with resistance. A riot followed in which eleven persons, four white and seven African, were killed and twenty-seven injured. Further riots broke out in East London and on the Reef. Malan and his Minister of Justice attributed the riots to the unrest caused by the resistance movement, and the Minister promised a new law which would make resistance a very costly course of action. Moroka and other African leaders were arrested, even though they too were distressed by the violent course which events had taken. In Natal the movement for Secession from the Union gathered strength. So the year 1952 came to an uneasy end. It was true that the Bantu Education Bill had not yet been passed, but it was due to lack of time and not to lack of determination on the part of Verwoerd. More fierce laws were promised for 1953.

At the end of 1952 Clayton wrote to the faithful on 'Civil Disobedience'.[13] There was an obligation on every Christian to be a law-abiding citizen. But if a law required him to do something which he believed to be contrary to the will of God, then he must obey God. A Christian could not break a law just because he did not like it. Who was to judge whether a law is just or unjust? Only the man himself; it must be his personal decision.

'The situation at the present time is complicated by the fact that Indian and Native Africans have no effective constitutional method open to them which they can employ to get laws changed which they regard as unjust. This makes it very easy to understand the present civil disobedience movement. I think I understand it, and I cannot see how anyone can avoid having some sympathy with it. And yet I doubt its wisdom.'

He stated his belief that passive-resistance would lead to violence. Yet he would not condemn a man who was led by conscience to take part. However, he believed it wrong to put pressure on men to take part. 'But of course there is one thing about which we ought all to agree, and that is that laws which are unjust ought not to remain on the Statute Book.'

Clayton's letter in *Good Hope* contrasts markedly with Michael Scott's account of his charge to the clergy synod in Johannesburg only six years earlier, the substance of which I recorded with reservations on page 152. Either the record does not do adequate justice to Clayton's charge on that occasion, or he was beginning to revise his attitude towards resistance; or of course, both alternatives might be true. Most Christians draw back from breaking the law. But the laws of South Africa were growing fiercer and fiercer, and many Christians believed them to be unChristian in nature. Therefore it is possible that Clayton was being compelled to think again. This was decidedly not a characteristic of his maturer mind; it was a characteristic of the times.

There were of course many Christians – not all of them Calvinists – who approved of the new laws. They were making possible the building of a new society in which all groups would move harmoniously forward to a just racial order. They were also making possible something essential to this building of a new society, the silencing of those who opposed.

On 19 November 1952 *Die Kerkbode* entitled its first editorial 'Ons Blankes op die Weegskaal', which means 'We Whites in the Balance'. This grave article ends, 'So the colour problem is really a white problem. It is we ourselves who are thrown into the scales.' The article also, referring to a deep-seated fear of so many white people, remarked that if the blacks wiped them out, it would not only be that they were cruel, but that the whites had been unfaithful to their calling.

Grave and sombre words.

26

Assault on Protest

1953 was the year of the first general election that the Nationalists had had to face since their victory of 1948. They were determined to increase their majority. Opponents of the Government were also hopeful, largely because of the militancy of the Torch Commando. The Resistance Campaign continued, but it was not so much the success as the insolence of it that angered the Government. In the short session which always precedes a general election, during which new legislation is cut to a minimum, the Government nevertheless passed two fierce laws, the Public Safety Act and the Criminal Laws Amendment Act. The first gave the Minister power to declare a state of emergency and to suspend 'all save a very few common or statute laws, whenever the country or any part of it was in danger'.[1] The second virtually brought the Resistance Campaign to an end. For a person to sit on a seat designated for persons not of his race might have cost him a fine or a few days in prison; but now to sit on it *by way of protest* might cost him three years or £300 or ten lashes or any two of these, and if he incited others to break laws *by way of protest* it could cost him five years or £500 or ten lashes or any two of these. The law contained the provision that lashes would not be inflicted on persons over 50 years of age.

Many persons and organisations protested against these laws. The Christian Council of South Africa, of which Clayton was the president, sought an interview with the Prime Minister, who was 'unable to grant it'. Clayton as president of the Council then made a statement protesting against the severity of the laws. He declared that the Public Safety Act was a dangerous extension of the principle of government by regulation, and that the Criminal Laws Amendment Act infringed upon the right of citizens and the Church to criticise existing laws.[2] The refusal of the Prime Minister to see the Christian Council delegation was the beginning of a Government practice which is not invariable but is more and more common. The Prime Minister and his colleagues today often decline to meet delegations from organisations which are known to hold contrary views on race policy and state security, no doubt on the grounds that it is a waste of everyone's time.

Writing on the impending elections, Clayton twice gave advice. 'It is right that we should be politicians. But because we are Christians we should be politicians with a difference.'[3] He wrote again that every voter ought to vote, 'even if . . . he is not very anxious to vote for either of the candidates who are standing for his constituency'.[4] In fact he himself was not very anxious to vote, having been disappointed in the attitude of the United Party towards the Public Safety and Criminal Law Amendment Acts, which they had at first condemned and later supported, because, said Minister Eric Louw contemptuously, of the coming elections.

Whether this was true or not, the United Party gained no benefit. In April the Nationalist Party was returned with an increased majority. It increased its number of seats from 85 to 94, while the number of United Party seats dropped from 65 to 57. Opponents of the Government and its racial policies were plunged into gloom, and the Torch Commando, which had been the symbol of hope for many, began to fade away. The Government, elated by its victory, promised to proceed relentlessly with its racial laws.

Clayton wrote on 22 April in *Good Hope* on the matter of civil obedience, and the claims of God and Caesar. It was clearly a theme to which he devoted more and more serious thought. It was not only he; the question of obedience was troubling the minds of those who believed that many of the new laws were unjust and unChristian. Clayton wrote:

'Everyone who regards the New Testament as authoritative is bound to admit the claim of the State to obedience. But it is not an absolute claim . . . we have another King, one Jesus . . . It is as a rule possible to do what our Lord tells us to do, to render unto Caesar the things which are Caesar's, and to God the things which are God's.'

Clayton did not say that it had become impossible to reconcile the two duties. Nevertheless the relations between the Government, or, to put it more accurately, between some members of the Government, and the Church of the Province were not improving. Minister Eric Louw was the sharpest-tongued critic of churchmen, pressmen, university teachers, race-relationers, and other do-gooders who condemned the racial laws. He did not, like Verwoerd, expound the eminent reasonableness of the laws. He much preferred to examine the practices of his critics and expose their inconsistencies. Irritated by the attacks of the Anglican Church, he accused it of hypocrisy in its own actions, particularly in regard to the white church schools, which had never got further than to admit a few Chinese.

Clayton would not accept the charge of hypocrisy. He admitted that the Church had in practice been infected by the racial prejudices in the world about her. 'This does not mean she is hypocritical.' Surely every Christian fell short of the Christian standard.

In regard to the schools he wrote, 'I think myself that it is impossible, if you live in a country where the colour-bar prevails, to act as though it did not prevail.' He discussed the adverse effect of the education of a non-white child at a white school. He went on, 'I think myself that the universities are different. . . . I do not believe it is right to sacrifice a child in order to assert a principle. . . . I regret very much the conditions. . . . I should like these conditions to be altered. But as long as they exist they cannot be ignored.'

In regard to the method of seating in churches, another thing which had been criticised, he wrote that the rule of the Church is that people must be seated regardless of race, but 'neither I nor anyone else can assume that all churchwardens obey this rule in every church'.

Clayton concluded: 'Criticism is a good thing. It makes us examine ourselves to see whether the criticism is true. Perhaps it would be a good thing if some of those who criticise us were a little less resentful of criticism themselves.'[5]

It may have been with some hope of drawing closer that the N.G.K. invited the other churches to join it in a deputation to the Minister of the Interior, asking for the establishment of a Board of Censors to prevent the circulation of immoral literature, and to protect children. The N.G.K. was joined by the other two Dutch Reformed churches, and by the Presbyterians, Methodists and Baptists, but not by the Anglicans. The actual circumstances are not known to the biographer but one could guess that Clayton was not a lover of censorship, and one could guess too that the N.G.K. would be exasperated by a Church which had such emphatic views on the evils of apartheid, but just could not make up its mind on pornography. In 1955, however, the N.G.K. (or rather *Die Kerkbode*) found itself in agreement with the Anglicans on the question of the Wine Festival to be held at Paarl, while most of the other churches were opposed. It was true that the great majority of the wine-farmers were members of the N.G.K., but one must not conclude that this determined the decision of the Church or *Die Kerkbode* to approve the holding of the Wine Festival. The paper opened its columns to many readers who condemned its decision and the debate continued for a few months.[6] The unusual ally was Clayton himself, who, preaching at Paarl on 27 February, refused to join in condemnation of the Festival; wine was God's gift, though it could be abused.

It must not be supposed that the leaders of the N.G.K. were indifferent to the widening gap between themselves and other churches. Keet, Gerdener, and Van der Merwe were men of considerable influence. Although *Die Kerkbode* regarded the election results as *die beskikking van God*, which can be translated as 'God's ordinance', it praised and supported all attempts to create understanding within the churches. One of the things that made such co-operation necessary was the 'Roman danger'. The paper denied strongly the allegations, or rather the suspicion, that the N.G.K. planned to make itself the all-powerful church in South Africa.[7] There was another good reason for co-operation, and that was that the N.G.K. had withdrawn from the Christian Council of South Africa, largely because it found unacceptable the Council's attitude to the policies of racial separation. *Die Kerkbode* approved strongly of the national conference to be called by the N.G.K. mission churches in December 1954. The theme was to be 'The Extension of the Kingdom of God in Multi-racial South Africa'.

There would be sixty representatives of the Federated N.G. churches, forty from about twenty-five non-Afrikaans churches, and some representatives from the two smaller Dutch Reformed churches.[8] This indeed was a bold and imaginative venture, because it was decided to open the conference to delegates of all races. It was in fact an enlargement and extension of the conference of non-Catholic churchmen called by the N.G.K. in November 1953, which had been open to white delegates only. The holding of this earlier conference had itself been criticised by Afrikaner churchmen because the English churches had been invited. *Die Kerkbode* defended their inclusion, on the grounds that when people understood the circumstances, they began to feel sympathy for South Africa's racial policies.[9] The conference revealed great differences of opinion, not only as between Dutch Reformed churchmen and others, but even, though to a much lesser extent, within Dutch Reformed ranks as well. The main debate centred round the Dutch Reformed contention that race differentiation did not mean discrimination, and that discrimination in its turn did not mean the denial of human dignity. It was B. B. Keet from Stellenbosch who told the conference that the real reason for the formation of separate churches and congregations was 'colour-feeling'. In any event it was decided to hold, in December 1954, a conference open to churchmen of all races.[10]

On 23 December 1953 *Die Kerkbode* felt compelled to return to the subject of the conference because the mission policy of the N.G.K. was opposed by some churches and suspected by others. Dutch Reformed churchmen must not be surprised; the policy was very much their own and was intimately connected with their history. It was difficult to accept the claim that the opposition was on *Christian* grounds. Much of it was a reaction to Nazism, and there was no doubt that political propaganda was also mixed up with it.

Clayton gave a wholehearted welcome to the proposal to hold a wider conference, and announced that the Church of the Province had gladly accepted the invitation to take part in it.[11] It is difficult to know what he expected to come of it. Undoubtedly the issue of apartheid and racial separateness would dominate the conference. The Episcopal Synod, meeting in Pretoria under Clayton's chairmanship, had not long before, in October, issued a statement clarifying the attitude of the Church of the Province towards racial discrimination. It was the kind of statement that a loyal Nationalist would have found unacceptable, and that a loyal N.G.K. man would have found difficult to accept 'in love'. The Synod declared that the only morally defensible policy was one which gave to all the fullest opportunity of development. It was indefensible to follow a policy the object of which was to perpetuate inferiority, as was the case in South Africa. This was powerful language, and even J. G. Strijdom, who expected to succeed Dr. Malan as Prime Minister and who stood unashamedly for *baasskap*, which could be badly translated as 'boss-ship' and meant white supremacy, would have hesitated to 'identify baasskap with the perpetuation of inferiority'. But the statement would have been not only offensive but hurtful to N.G.K. men, who would not believe that apartheid was expressly designed to perpetuate inferiority, and who in fact believed the contrary, that it was designed to give separate freedoms to all.

The Episcopal Synod was of opinion that separate freedoms were unattainable, that if racial groups were separated, there could not possibly be full economic and cultural development for all. In fact, the development of the country depended on the co-operation of all, and this was recognised by the political parties.

Synod referred to the Reservation of Separate Amenities Act which the new Parliament had passed on 4 September 1953. This law was passed because Mr. George Lusu, an African who had sat in a white waiting-room at Cape Town station as an act of defiance, was acquitted by the magistrate's court on the grounds that if separate facilities were provided for different groups, they must be substantially equal. The State appealed, first to the Supreme Court, and then to the Appellate Court, and lost both appeals. The situation was serious. If it were allowed to continue, a large number of South African buildings would have had to be reconstructed. Therefore the Act laid down that when separate amenities were provided, the provision could not be declared invalid on the grounds that the amenities were substantially unequal.[12] Synod declared that since the passing of this law, it was no longer legitimate to defend segregation by claiming that it did not infringe the principle of equality.

Synod dealt with the thorny problem of separation in church and school. Because white and black Anglicans usually worshipped in different church-buildings, that did not justify the accusation of segregation. Linguistic and geographical factors were the reason. An African Anglican could worship in any Anglican church and could not be debarred. The Government had not attempted to interfere in this matter.

It was also reasonable that there should be separate schools. So long as the present insistence on social segregation persisted, it would not be in the interests of any child to accustom him or her to an intimacy which would be impossible to continue in post-school life. The bishops greatly desired a change in public opinion that would make it possible for children of different races to be educated together.

The bishops deplored the tendency abroad to isolate South Africa for condemnation in respect of discrimination which was also to be found in other parts of the world. Yet it was their duty to express this world-wide Christian opinion, which they themselves shared in relation to the situation in South Africa, 'and we desire to make it plain that no attempt has been made by those in authority to prevent us from doing so'.[13]

Minister Eric Louw had no difficulty in finding the inconsistencies in these pronouncements. The bishops opposed separation but agreed to separate education in the circumstances. Could it be that they were worried about the drop in revenue which would result if children of well-to-do-parents of races not white were admitted to the church schools?[14]*

It was in this first session of the new Parliament that the Nationalists, full of confidence, through their redoubtable Minister of Native Affairs, Hendrik Verwoerd, introduced the Bantu Education Bill. Many of the things feared by the churches were now to become true. African education was to be taken from the provinces and placed under the Department of Native Affairs. There were to be three types of schools. First, there were to be Bantu Community Schools, controlled by Bantu Authorities and any other tribal or community organisation approved by the Government. Second, there were to be Government Bantu Schools, newly established by the Government or taken over from the provinces. Third, State-aided Bantu Schools were provided for, and these would include the mission schools, but the Minister was required to consult the local Bantu community before granting any aid. As from a date to be laid down, every school was to be registered, this registration being at the discretion of the Minister.

In moving the second reading of the Bill, Verwoerd made clear the extent to which African education would pass under his control. The second and third types of school would disappear gradually in favour of Bantu Community Schools. He said, 'Education must train and teach people in accordance with their opportunities in life, according to the sphere in which they live.' And again, 'Native education should be controlled in such a way that it should be in accord with the policy of the State. . . . Good racial relations cannot exist when the education is given under the control of people who create wrong expectations on the part of the Native himself.' Racial relations 'cannot improve if the result of Native education is the creation of frustrated people'.[15] Frustration in Verwoerd's opinion was not caused by the Group Areas Act, by Race Classification, by Criminal Law Amendments. It was caused by people like Clayton, Reeves, and Huddleston. The last-named called Verwoerd's policy 'Education for Servitude'.[16] Who was right, Verwoerd or he? On 29 September 1953, the Bantu Education Bill became law. Its influence on African education was to be immense. It put more children into the schools, and drastically lowered the quality of their education.

Clayton, delivering his fifth charge to the diocese of Cape Town, spoke with relative calm:

'I want to say a few words about the Bantu Education Act, and the anxiety which has been caused to very many of us by the appointment of a Cape Province Coloured Education Commission. The Bantu Education Act puts Bantu education in the hands of the Native Affairs Department, and like other recent legislation it puts dangerously wide powers in the hands of an individual minister. It makes it possible for him so to use his power as to make Bantu education the kind of education which will only

*Mr. Louw did not make his point clear. The revenue would not drop because the coloured parents were well-to-do, but because white parents might take their children away.

fit people for a permanently inferior position. The Church has always, I think, taken the view that the aim ought to be to give to everybody, whatever his race, the opportunity of development so far as his ability makes development possible.

'There is something peculiarly offensive in educating people to fit them only for an inferior position and then to withhold from them the more responsible positions on the ground that they are not fit for them. There is a very widespread fear that this is the intention. What I want to say is that while I regret that so much power is put into the hands of a particular minister, we have no knowledge that he will use his power with that intention. I don't think we must assume that that will be so. Similarly we have no knowledge what the Commission on Coloured Education in this Province is going to report. I deprecate the assumption that the worst is bound to happen. It may happen. But do not let us make ourselves miserable before it is necessary. I think myself that to expect the worst is to make the worst more likely to occur.'

Clayton went on to say, 'This land is hagridden by fear. Fear is at the bottom of most of the legislation which some of us deplore. But fear is a very bad guide. A great many of the cruel things that are done in the world are done because of fear. Don't let there be any fear in the Church.'

It is noteworthy that his fifth charge was largely concerned with politics, with the growth of the power of the Executive, the Separate Representation of Voters, the Group Areas Act and, as we have seen, the Bantu Education Act. This was not Clayton's choice. Almost every new law had a racial intention, and was a challenge to that kind of Christian morality which was upheld by the non-Dutch-Reformed churches. Clayton was never the political bishop that some of his opponents alleged him to be. He concluded his charge with the words, 'And so we come at last to the real work of the Church. . . . What about the extension of the Gospel? What about the deepening of the spiritual life? The Report of the Committee on Evangelism asks Synod for advice. We must try to give it.' He then gave his own advice. He spoke of the recent Johannesburg crusade and the Bryan Green mission in Durban. He did not disparage them but he was sceptical. He repeated his own belief that the real missionising forces were the parish and the congregation. He concluded, as he always did, with words of encouragement to laity and clergy. To his clergy he said:

'You set out with high ideals. You have often been disappointed. The things you wanted have not happened. Well, there was no promise that they would. There are two great commandments, the love of God and the love of neighbour. Don't try to live on the love of neighbour. . . . It is only the love of God that will save you from growing sour and cynical, or content with secular compensations. You can't live on the love of neighbour. You can live on the love of God.'[17]

1953 was a year of great activity for him, and the calls on his time and energy were incessant. On 12 December he turned 69 years of age. His health was good considering the little care he took of it. He was very heavy, and had to watch where and how he placed his feet. His intellectual powers seemed as great as ever. The mellowing continued. He was gratified when his old college Pembroke made him an Honorary Fellow. One loss affected him. That was the death of William Adolph Palmer, the retired dean of Johannesburg, whom he had appointed only a year earlier as head of the Diocesan Clergy School at Zonnebloem.

Clayton wrote a Christmas message for *Good Hope*:

'In the early days of my ministry as a priest I was Chaplain to a college. . . . Nothing struck me more forcibly than the fact that most of these young men were not on terms of anything like intimacy with their own fathers. Fathers either failed to realise the obvious fact that their sons were growing up or had grown up, or if they did realise they were often inhibited by a sort of shyness from making friends with their own sons. And I doubt whether there has been much change in this matter since that time. . . . It is necessary to make time and to spare attention if a friendship of any kind is to grow. . . . Christmas is an obvious time for remembering this and putting it into practice.'

It is interesting to speculate how much he himself knew of intimacy between father and son, and to speculate what he meant by intimacy. Of one thing we may be sure; it would have been a brand of his own.

27

Assault on the Schools

On 1 January 1954 the Bantu Education Act came into force. It brought about what can only be described as a revolution in African education. Except temporarily in the Cape Province, the Department of Native Affairs took over the control of African education. Verwoerd stated that Bantu Education would stand 'with both feet in the Reserves'. All private schools had now to apply for registration, and he said that this would not be refused unless there were substantial reasons for doing so. But state subsidies to such schools would eventually disappear. If churches wished to run schools entirely at their own expense, that would be permitted if registration had been granted.* In general, mission-buildings outside 'scheduled Native areas' would not be purchased by the Government. In the Assembly on 3 June the Minister stated that the training of African teachers should take place amongst their own people, preferably in the Reserves and homelands, not in white cities. For the same reasons high schools would not be built in urban areas. This statement caused much anxiety to black, urban parents, who had now to face the possibility that their children would have to be sent to the homelands for high-school education; in the first place their education would cost a great deal more, in the second, many of them would be going to an environment unknown to them. It could be seen that Verwoerd was implacably determined that all Africans living in the urban areas should be regarded as 'temporary sojourners'.

In January the South African Institute of Race Relations declared the transfer to be unsound and undesirable. The Cape African Teachers' Association announced its intention to call a national protest-meeting of teachers, but was warned by the Secretary for Native Affairs that such action would be regarded in a very serious light. The Transkeian General Council deplored and noted with dismay the provisions of the Act. The Act was condemned by a joint body representing the African National

*In 1973 there are still schools, mostly Roman Catholic, which continue in spite of receiving no subsidy. On 31.3.1972, there were 391 such Catholic schools with 80,000 pupils. But the Church is finding the financial burden no longer bearable, and may soon capitulate. Letter to me from the Secretary, Education Department, South African Catholic Bishops' Conference, dated 18.12.1972.

Congress, the South African Indian Congress, and the Congress of Democrats. The bishops of the Catholic Church in Southern African decided to make every sacrifice to keep their schools going. The Methodist Church of South Africa decided for financial reasons to relinquish control, but condemned the Act in language as strong as Clayton's, declaring that it aimed 'at conditioning the African people to a predetermined position of subordination'. The General Assembly of the Presbyterian Church of South Africa gave authority to each presbytery to let but not to sell their school-buildings. The Congregational Union of South Africa decided to do the same.[1]

On 24 March the Minister of Finance announced a new plan for financing Bantu Education. At that time it cost £8½ million per annum, of which £6½ million came from general taxation, and £2 million from Native taxes. In future the amount of £6½ million would be pegged and any additional expenditure would have to be met by the African taxpayer.[2] These proposals were heavily criticised on the grounds that the African paid a great deal in the way of general taxation – in fact, when he bought goods, as much as a white buyer; and that it was unChristian to insist that the poor should pay for the services of the poor. On 3 June Verwoerd, speaking in the Assembly, took full responsibility for the new arrangement. 'I support it because I think it is in the best interests of Bantu Education and its control.'[3] He quoted a letter written by an Anglican priest, the Revd. C. W. L. Skey, who wrote to the *Cape Times*:

'Everyone is familiar with Communist practice. The first thing they do is to place all schools under their control so that they may be free to inculcate their foul doctrines into the children. Our rulers are again closely following Communist precedent.'[4]

Such an accusation was sufficient to make Nationalists very angry. Who in the whole wide world did more to stamp out Communism than they? Verwoerd replied, 'Here we have a prominent person . . . who has the insolence,* the astounding temerity, to make the accusation that the Government is busy carrying out a Communistic policy.'[5] He also quoted the Most Revd. G. H. Clayton, Archbishop of Cape Town, whose letter to the *Cape Times* of 25 May the editor had entitled 'Prelate's reference to Nazi technique'. Verwoerd also quoted Clayton as stating in *Church News* that the reason for the taking over of African education 'seems to be not so much that the Church cannot do the job efficiently as that the Government desires to make African education an instrument for forwarding the ideas of a European political party. That is the recognised pattern of a totalitarian State. It is the sort of thing most of us objected to in the Nazi regime of Germany.'[6]

Verwoerd said that he quoted these persons to show that 'it is highly desirable that their hold on Native education should disappear'.[7] He said that the old system, which was largely a mission-school system, had 'tried

**Hansard* uses the word 'brutality' instead of 'insolence'. This is due to the translators' misunderstanding of the meaning of the Afrikaans word *brutaliteit*.

to create an English-speaking Bantu'.[8] He replied to the charge of indoctrination by saying, 'We rather find it is done by our critics who inculcate the spirit of equality, the aim to achieve equality.'[9]

On 18 May 1954 Clayton delivered the presidential address to the biennial meeting of the Christian Council in Bloemfontein. He again defined what he meant by being political; it meant the attempt to promote the study and investigation of the problem of evangelising, and establishing a Christian social order. For this reason he welcomed the December conference called by the Federal Missionary Council of the N.G.K. 'Possibly we shall never reach agreement but we will never agree unless we see where our differences lie.' He dismissed as error the attempt to create a Christian Party; it would stigmatise as unChristian all those who did not support it. He concluded that the preservation of religious freedom required eternal vigilance. Such vigilance was urgently needed.[10]

The Revd. A. H. Jeffree James, a Baptist minister and the secretary of the Protestant Association of South Africa, had by now taken upon himself another kind of vigilance, and that was to study and rebut any utterance by Clayton on the matters of race policy and individual liberty. This was caused partly by his conviction that the Church of the Province was a schismatic church, and partly by the fact that he had come to espouse the policies of the Government, and partly because of his own strange character and temperament; whether these three causes were in fact one and the same cause we shall not inquire. He chided Clayton for not specifying the source of the threat to religious liberty. In his view no single act of Government had infringed religious freedom. The Government continued to subsidise education and other institutions which were completely under denominational control.

So the war of words continued, Verwoerd, Clayton, Louw, Skey, James. And now more and more loudly in the north, Reeves and Huddleston. It would not be true to say that they signified nothing. But the power to do things, to change things, to alter the course of events, remained entire in the hands of the Nationalists, in the hands of the aging but venerated Malan who had brought Afrikanerdom to this present glory, in the hands of Strijdom who would succeed him and who stood unashamedly for white supremacy, and now more and more in the hands of Hendrik Frensch Verwoerd, who had an intense sense of mission and a strange hypnotic power of speech, enabling him to give some of his sternest opponents the eerie and uncomfortable feeling that perhaps he might be right after all. These three were the giants of the Cabinet, although Strijdom had few of the intellectual gifts of the others. Malan would soon go, Strijdom would succeed him and lead for a few years before he died. But Verwoerd was already the master-planner, the architect of a new world, a man utterly certain of the rightness of his intentions, and destined to become the most feared Prime Minister in the history of South Africa.

On 2 August 1954 the Secretary for Native Affairs gave three choices to all African state-aided schools. They could retain their schools and hostels as private *unaided* institutions. They could retain them as *aided* institutions, but the subsidies would be reduced. They could relinquish control to Bantu community organisations.

If control were relinquished, the Department would buy or rent the buildings. It was willing that hostels should remain under mission control for the time being. All recognised churches would be allotted time to give special religious instruction to their own children, provided this was done in the mother tongue. School authorities were asked to make their choices by 31 December 1954.[11]

In Clayton's sixth charge to the diocese of Cape Town, he reminded the congregation that a year earlier he had said that no one had any knowledge as to how the Minister of Native Affairs would use the dangerously wide powers that had been put into his hands. Unfortunately that knowledge was now available, the Minister having outlined his policy in the Senate. 'The purpose of that policy is to remove the influence of Christian missions from the control of Bantu education: what he calls the change-over from mission to community schools; and to train African Natives for such positions as in the view of the present Government ought to be open to them.'

Clayton said there were three conditions which the Church should observe:

'First, the Church must retain the ownership of its buildings if it possibly can, and there does not seem to be any reason why it should not do so. Secondly, in the case of schools which are also used for church purposes, they should not be leased to the Department unless satisfactory arrangements are made for them to continue to be used for church purposes. Thirdly, the Church should not take any part in giving this fantastic "Bantu education". If it does so, it will have to follow a syllabus and a timetable of which it cannot approve.'

Clayton believed that the Church should lease its buildings to the Department.

'. . . I am haunted by the fear that if the number of school buildings available is greatly reduced by refusal of the missions to lease any of their buildings, the result will be the throwing of large numbers of children upon the streets . . . Even a rotten system of education is better than that which young children pick up in the streets, when, as is usually the case, their fathers and mothers have to go to work and cannot supervise them.'

Clayton had another reason for not giving up ownership of the buildings. He said '. . . if, as is obviously more than possible, the new system breaks down, we should have no buildings in which we could take up our work again.'

Clayton announced that the policy he was advocating had the support of all the bishops in the Union with one exception. '. . . in one diocese no schools may be leased to the Department, and the reasons given will command respect.' But that decision affected only 23 schools, whereas in the Cape the Church of the Province controlled 450 African schools.

This one exception was Ambrose Reeves, Bishop of Johannesburg. When Episcopal Synod met at Umtata, in November, the most important item on the agenda was the question of the leasing of church-buildings to the Department. The bishops were in favour of doing so, for the same reasons given by Clayton in his charge. But Reeves suggested that there was still another choice, and that was to keep the buildings and to close the schools. He asked the Archbishop whether the vote was binding. Clayton replied that the matter was so important that he would rule the following day. His ruling was that the decision was not binding.[12] Reeves, acting on behalf of his diocesan synod, then closed the schools. The Community of the Resurrection in the Transvaal and the Society of the Sacred Mission in the Orange Free State decided to do the same.

Reeves found the period before the decision 'excruciating'. Which was the lesser evil, to close the schools and deprive many children of education, or to keep the schools and to teach the Government syllabus, with the possibility that the certificate of registration might be cancelled at any time? Which was the greater good, to keep the children in schools, or to hamper the Government in its plan to train them for their allotted stations? Some people thought that Reeves's decision was doctrinaire. Such people would no doubt have called Clayton's decision pragmatic. Neither adjective was satisfactory. Clayton had said that Reeves's reasons would command respect. But he did not think the decision wise.

Reeves set out his reasons fully, not only in his 1954 charge, but in the liberal–progressive weekly called the *Forum*. He wrote: 'The church has no alternative but to refuse to co-operate in any way in furthering an education policy which violates the principles from which all true education ought to spring, for it proposes to train the great majority of African children for a status in life which has been assigned to them.'

He wrote, '. . . it is a painful decision, particularly as it meant that I found myself at variance with so many other leaders in the Anglican Church'. He quoted Verwoerd's words: 'Until now he has been subjected to a school system which drew him away from his own community, and misled him by showing him the green pastures of European society in which he was not allowed to graze.' Therefore Reeves found it in conscience 'impossible to take any part, however remotely and indirectly, in implementing such a policy, still less to encourage anyone to give money to help the Church retain some measure of control' over its schools. He wrote, 'I dare not take the risk that buildings which have been erected by the money and labour of church people may be used to indoctrinate children with a racial ideology which I am persuaded is clean contrary to the Gospel.' Then Bishop Reeves announced that the Anglican Church in the Southern Transvaal had decided to close all its African schools on 1 April 1955.[13]

So there was the terrible choice – a 'rotten education' or the education of the streets. Who was right – Clayton or Reeves and Huddleston? It was a pity in a way – though it does not matter now – that Clayton used the word 'rotten'. What would one choose to eat – rotten fruit or no fruit at all? The word 'rotten' stuck in Huddleston's throat, and he was never to forget it.

The growing gap between Clayton on the one side, and Reeves and Huddleston on the other was further widened by the fact that the struggle between Government and Church was most intense and most publicised and most spectacular in the city of Johannesburg, and by the further fact that the Government had introduced a Natives Resettlement Bill which would enable it to remove all Africans from Sophiatown, Martindale, Newclare, and Pageview, to the new town of Meadowlands. Meadowlands was not only several miles further from the centre of Johannesburg, but there would be no freehold rights there. The removals would affect 60,000 people, and the Government defended the plan on the grounds that it would constitute a massive and decisive slum clearance.

If the Bill became law, that would be the end of the mission work in Sophiatown. Dorothy Maud's house of 'Ekutuleni' and Raymond Raynes's great church of Christ the King would become monuments of past endeavour in a dreary waste. That no doubt would give Huddleston great pain, but he felt equally deeply the coming destruction of that vital and exciting township of Sophiatown with its shebeens and its boys' clubs, its brothels and its churches. His book *Naught for Your Comfort* was not only a sombre warning to white South Africa; it was also a lament for Sophiatown. Huddleston was himself such an attractive personality, so persuasive in speaking, with a face made alight by inner fire, that he became a compelling public figure. The English-language press and its hardbitten reporters regarded him as a saint and hero, and recorded avidly his deeds and his speeches. Reeves also received a great deal of publicity, and was scathing in his attacks on the Resettlement Bill.

These attacks greatly angered the Nationalists, and especially Dr. Verwoerd. He declared in the Assembly on 22 March 1954 that the resettlement proposals were in the best interests of both Johannesburg and the Natives. The *Star* of 4 March had published an article entitled 'Dr. Verwoerd versus the People', to which he said he would not reply because it was venomous.

'The background to this agitation is that there are certain people, liberalistic cliques, if I may put it that way, who for a considerable time have offered resistance. Unfortunately the leaders of these liberalistic cliques are certain people of the Church, like the Rev. Huddleston, and even the Bishop of Johannesburg, Ambrose Reeves. . . . Most of these people, or practically all of them, are people who have no ordinary interest in these areas, except the Rev. Huddleston.'

Verwoerd said that for years he had sought co-operation with the people, 'and that co-operation was obtained until these outside influences spoiled it'.[14]

Two days later in the Assembly D. J. Potgieter, M.P., attacked Reeves, who had invited the American Bishop Campbell to visit South Africa;

Campbell had returned to America to predict a revolution and to describe the oppression of the Natives under apartheid. Potgieter also attacked Huddleston who was the 'source of all slandering propaganda in the English Church publications and in certain English newspapers overseas'. Huddleston had been described in America as 'the most dedicated man on earth'.[15] Mr. Potgieter clearly thought this outrageous.

On the following day, Mr. Martins, another Nationalist M.P., said that he wished to state emphatically that not one Afrikaans minister had opposed the resettlement of the inhabitants of Sophiatown and other places. Verwoerd rebuked Mrs. Ballinger for saying that 'good Europeans do not mind living next to Natives'. He said that Bishop Reeves lived in Westcliff, Rabbi Rabinowitz in Parktown, the Revd. J. B. Webb on the Berea. 'They are good Europeans, but they live in good European areas.'[16]

In a later speech Dr. Verwoerd said that the Anglican churches were 'not arousing my sympathy by the way in which they are agitating. The people who cause all the difficulty and make the most venomous personal attacks are clergy of that very Church, and now I want to pose the question whether the fact that the Anglican Church owns property worth about £150,000 there is the cause of that agitation. . . . Do the Rev. Ambrose Reeves and the Rev. Huddleston concern themselves about the £150,000 investment and not so much about the soul of the Native?'

> *Mr. Lawrence:* Are you not ashamed of making such an insinuation?
> *Dr. Verwoerd:* No, not at all. I am not ashamed. I am just asking whether they are causing that agitation for that reason.[17]

Reeves and Huddleston were naturally concerned about their property worth £150,000. The buildings had been built with much devotion, and without them one could not have carried on the work of the Church in Sophiatown. Verwoerd said that Reeves and Huddleston 'did not mind vilifying me in a way that is anything but Christian. They went so far as to say that our actions were not those of civilised people'. He also criticised J. B. Webb, but said that, though in opposition, Webb had known how to behave like a man of God, but the other two had not.[18]

So the debate continued, acrimoniously and fruitlessly. Certainly Reeves and Huddleston were sharptongued, much more so than Clayton. They were Christians, and so was Verwoerd. In the name of Christianity and in the interests of it Verwoerd was ready to uproot the people of Sophiatown, Martindale, Newclare and Pageview. In the name of Christianity Reeves and Huddleston protested against it. The chance of reconciliation, of mutual accommodation, of mutual understanding, was exactly nothing.

Perhaps the most bitter invective came from Arthur Barlow, who in 1945 had said, 'I back Mr. Hofmeyr's policy because it is the policy of Christ',[19] who in 1948 had said, 'Hofmeyr must go',[20] and who in 1954 was supporting the Resettlement Bill. He said, 'I have hardly known a single bishop in my Church who has remained in South Africa after he has lost his job. He has left us here to nurse the baby.' He claimed that 'the great fight against the Bill is led by the Bishop of Johannesburg'. He and Huddleston were not playing the game by South Africa when they opposed the Bill.[21]

Clayton added his powerful voice to those who protested against the destruction of Sophiatown, and against the allegation that the Church was concerned about 'investments'. To this protest he added his denunciation of the deplorable housing of coloured people in Cape Town.

'When I, like every other Anglican bishop, was consecrated to be a bishop, these words were said to me: "Hold up the weak, heal the sick, bind up the broken, bring in again the outcasts, seek the lost". That gives every bishop a special responsibility for the poor. How can he dare to be silent when he believes that a wrong is being done to them?'[22]

One more thing that added fuel to the fires of this furious year was the visit to South Africa by the redoubtable Canon John Collins of London. He was a relentless opponent of apartheid, and had through his society 'Christian Action' roused British public opinion. Now Jack Shave, a Durban businessman, invited Collins to come to South Africa as his guest, so that his eyes could be opened to the truth. Alas, Canon Collins was totally unable to see Mr. Shave's truth. His opposition to apartheid was reinforced by his visit, by what he saw and heard and read, by the people he talked to, particularly those who had no say in their own affairs.

Die Kerkbode of 4 August 1954 said editorially that South Africa had many visitors from overseas, and in more than one case they had undertaken to try to change the wrong impressions held abroad. But not so Canon Collins. 'He apparently has not got any wiser, at least as far as we can tell from his irresponsible statements.' The Revd. C. B. Brink, Moderator of the Synod of the N.G.K. of the Southern Transvaal, said that the Collins visit had made things difficult for the multiracial conference to which the N.G.K. had invited Clayton and so many members of other churches. However, the statement by Archbishop Clayton, that neither the Church of England nor the Church of the Province of South Africa accepted any responsibility for Canon Collins, had helped to clear the air, although one would have expected the leaders of the Anglican Church to state openly their disapproval of his actions.

Die Kerkbode was expecting too much. Clayton for example was no admirer of Collins, but he would have agreed with much that he had said, even though he might not have liked the way he said it. Collins called South Africa a 'police state', and said that Communism was not the threat, but white tyranny. Clayton would have agreed with that. Collins called South Africa a 'madhouse', which was a description Clayton might have used privately but not publicly. *Die Kerkbode* charged that Collins moved in liberal circles, and apparently was not interested in the other side. 'This visit has done no one any good – least of all the visitor.'

Two weeks later, F. J. van Wyk* wrote that Collins had met many

*In 1973, Director of the South African Institute of Race Relations.

Afrikaans-speaking people, including Dr. Gerdener and Dr. Keet, Dr. Nicol the Administrator of the Transvaal, and Dr. Eiselen the Secretary of Native Affairs. The editor admitted the error, but replied that although Collins had met these people, he had not listened to them. That was certainly the opinion of Mr. Shave. It was also the opinion of the Revd. P. P. Stander of Dingaanstad – all that Collins had asked him was whether he had voted Nationalist!

The last piece of fat was dropped into the fire by Huddleston himself. One of his African friends, Oliver Tambo, a faithful worshipper at the Church of Christ the King, had just been banned under the Suppression of Communism Act for his activities in the African National Congress. Huddleston was angered by the lack of reaction of Christian South Africa, and of the Church of the Province, to Tambo's banning. His impatience with the Church suddenly boiled over, and he wrote for the *Observer*[23] a piece that is still remembered by those who lived through the events of that strenuous year. He gave it the title 'The Church Sleeps On', and he began it with four lines from Chesterton's 'Ballad of the White Horse'.

> I tell you naught for your comfort,
> Yea, naught for your desire,
> Save that the sky grows darker yet
> And the sea rises higher.

The article sounded a grave warning. What hope was there for the Christian faith, the Church and its missionary work, when white Christians were not true to the fundamental principles of their faith – amongst them love and justice? How could they persuade their African brothers that theirs was a living religion? Had the twenty-fifth hour already struck, and was the battle already lost?

Huddleston quoted a recent circular from the Department of Native Affairs which warned that any Church whose representative criticised the Minister and the policy of the Department could have its mission work closed at three months' notice. It was time for Christians to resist such laws and take the consequences.

Huddleston criticised those churches who were still prepared to negotiate with the Government in the matter of African education. He wrote, 'They are still prepared to believe (or are they?) that some good can come of this great evil.'

He wrote:

'The Church sleeps on. It sleeps on while 60,000 people are moved from their homes in the interest of a fantastic racial theory: it sleeps on while plans are made (and implemented) to transform the education of Africans into a thing called "Native Education" – which will erect a permanent barrier against Western culture reaching the African at all: it sleeps on while a dictatorship is swiftly being created over all Native Affairs in the Union, so that speech and movement and association are no longer free.

'The Church sleeps on – though it occasionally talks in its sleep and expects (or does it?) the Government to listen.'

The day was drawing near when the African Christian would accept no longer the authority of the sleeping Church '*and he will cast it off*'.

What authority would he then accept? It did not much matter whether the Communist or the African Nationalist ideal was to be his goal. It would not be the Christian ideal. Huddleston declared that such a thought was to him unbearable – a burden so heavy on the heart that it could not be borne indefinitely.

'In God's name, cannot the Church bestir itself all over the world and act? Cannot Christians everywhere show their distress in practical ways by so isolating South Africa from contact with all civilised communities that she realises her position and feels some pain in it?'

It is difficult for a writer to conclude successfully such a powerful and prophetic article. The world cries out at him, 'Well, tell us what to do.' Huddleston's last paragraph was anti-climactic.

'*I am pleading for a cultural boycott of South Africa.* I am asking that all those who believe racialism to be sinful or wrong should refuse to encourage it by accepting any engagements to act, to perform as a musical artist or as a ballet dancer – in short, engage in any contracts which would provide entertainment for only one section of the community. True, this will only be a demonstration. But I believe it will be quite an effective one. At least it will give white South Africa an opportunity of tasting the medicine they so freely give to their Black fellow-citizens – the medicine of deprivation and frustration. And at least it will be better – considerably better – than sleeping.'

Clayton was much displeased – Huddleston described him as 'very angry' – by 'The Church Sleeps On'. He wrote to Huddleston strongly disapproving of the idea of asking the churches of the world to express condemnation of things in South Africa. Clayton desired the prayers and the remembrances of the churches of the Anglican Communion, but he had on more than one occasion stated his belief that the Church of the Province and indeed the people of South Africa, must work out their own salvation. He disapproved of boycotts. Although he had already directed that his ashes were to be buried in some place where no colour-bar prevailed, he belonged to clubs where the colour-bar did prevail. Nor did he believe that any cultural boycott of white South Africans would cause them to change what they called their 'traditional way of life'. Indeed their traditional way of life was immune to the displeasure of foreign musical artistes and ballet dancers.

In my opinion, Clayton was even more displeased by Huddleston's use of the words 'The Church'. For Clayton the Church was the creation of Christ, whatever its human manifestation. He could himself, in prayers and addresses, repent of the weakness and lack of devotion of Christians, and of the shortcomings of churchmen and churchwomen. But how could one write of a sleeping Church, when the Holy Spirit was alive and working through it? To him the use of such words was distasteful, and the use of them by a leading churchman was reprehensible.

But there was even another reason. In one particular sense Clayton *was* the Church. He could not have condemned more strongly, and in the name of the Church, the Bantu Education Act, the destruction of Sophiatown, the restriction of people by Ministerial edict. Was this the Church occasionally talking in its sleep, and expecting the Government to listen to it? The writer does not know whether Clayton actually thought these thoughts, but he does know that it would have been very difficult not to think them.

Whatever the truth may be, 'The Church Sleeps On' widened further the gap between the Archbishop and the best-known South African Anglican priest. If Clayton had been less wise, he could have caused a disastrous breach in the Church of the Province, all the more disastrous because African priests and laymen would have been almost solidly behind Huddleston. A minority of white priests and laymen would have been behind him too, but it would have been small. Even amongst his own white brothers in the Community of the Resurrection, there were some who doubted his wisdom, who feared and disliked the almost daily publicity, and who thought their brother was getting too much caught up in the affairs of the world.

One last thing should be said. 'The Church Sleeps On' intensified the anger of the Government against Huddleston. Here was yet another case of an alien priest interfering in the affairs of a country not his own. But now he had taken an unforgiveable step. He had not only blackened its name in the columns of an alien paper; he had sought the interference of its enemies in its own intimate affairs.

Whether the British Broadcasting Corporation felt that there was need or room for another Anglican view, one does not know, but it offered Clayton ten guineas to speak on 'The Apartheid Issue' in its service 'At Home and Abroad'. He accepted the invitation, and spoke on 29 October 1954. In his broadcast Clayton said that he agreed with every word of the Archbishop of Canterbury's recent statement on apartheid. The Europeans of South Africa, in trying to enforce separation by law, seemed to be throwing overboard some of the values of the very civilisation they were trying to preserve.

He condemned the industrial colour-bar, which could only be justified if Africans were not employed in European industry at all; but if they were employed there, then their progress could not be limited.

He condemned the Separate Amenities Act, which laid down that authorities were not obliged to provide equal separate amenities. He condemned the laws forbidding mixed marriages and making sexual intercourse between Europeans and non-Europeans a criminal offence. He said that he believed the Bantu Education Act would perpetuate the master–servant relationship and was more likely to increase than diminish subversive teaching in the schools. He criticised the anti-communist laws which gave the Minister power to silence and restrict any person without right of appeal.

He condemned as a 'most serious blow' the law which gave the Minister of Native Affairs the right to close any church without right of appeal. He said, 'We Anglicans in South Africa need the prayers of our friends in England, and we need help in men and money to deal with the new problems with which we are faced.' But he was not despondent. He deplored the fear that was at the back of South Africa's policies. 'But in the Church there must be not fear but faith. I think there is. In spite of everything our work goes on, and we look forward to the future with confidence.'

He thus in his conclusion implicitly rejected Huddleston's plea for a boycott and explicitly his prophecies of disaster.[24] The nature of his broadcast and the nature of Huddleston's article point clearly to the difference in the natures of the two men. As Huddleston had so honestly put it, he wanted to irritate and Clayton did not.

This bitter year in the history of the non-Dutch-Reformed missionary churches came to an end with the conference of church leaders called by the Cape and Transvaal N.G. Churches. The Moderator of the Transvaal N.G.K., the Revd. C. B. Brink, who was to be the chairman, had with what Clayton called the 'greatest courtesy' invited the unilingual Archbishop of Cape Town to act as joint chairman with him, an invitation which Clayton readily accepted.[25]

The N.G.K. had invited representatives of churches never before invited to such conferences, for example, the African Methodist Episcopal, the Apostolic Faith Mission, the Bantu Methodist, the Bantu Presbyterian, the Plymouth Brethren, and the Disciples of Christ. It was a noteworthy ecumenical and interracial venture, and was held in the Great Hall of the University of the Witwatersrand.

A special part of the hall had been set aside for delegates not white, but a number of white delegates went and sat with them. Tea and coffee were served morning and afternoon, but in separate rooms. Such was the atmosphere of goodwill that this separation was mentioned only twice, once by an African minister who utterly condemned it, and once by a Coloured speaker who called it a triviality, and said it was the blood of Christ and not a cup of tea that united them.

There was no assertion of language rights. The unilingual Archbishop of Cape Town would graciously interrupt a speaker in Afrikaans with the English warning, 'One minute more, sir.' Some Afrikaners displayed the ultimate courtesy of addressing each other in English so that English-speaking and African delegates might understand. The Revd. L. E. Wilkinson, an English-speaking Methodist, delivered half his speech in English and half in Afrikaans. A speaker in Xhosa was translated into English by an Afrikaner. An African minister took devotions and prayed in Nederlands, the language in which he had learned to pray on a Free State farm fifty years before.

Into this sweet dish was introduced the raspberry (or the plum some would think), by Basil Holt of the Disciples of Christ, in a witty and entirely permissible speech. He was replying to an N.G.K. delegate who wished that the word *apartheid* had never been born, and that a better one had. Thereupon Mr. Holt observed that if a polecat were brought into the house, one could call it what one liked, but it would smell just the same. His speech was received not coldly but calmly by a house determined to keep the peace.

The shining example of this determination was the Revd. C. B. Brink, who was a magnificent chairman; he was the brave man who the year before, with grim, strained face, told the great gathering at Evanston that he and his fellow-delegates could not accept the resolution condemning enforced racial separation. Another shining example shone in the background, the Revd. Johan Reynecke of Pretoria, of whose devotion and Christian persistence the conference was in part the child; one observer called it a miracle child, it having been born of a country thought to be barren.

What came of it? Nothing. The delegates came together because something impelled them. They trod delicately because the ice was thin. But the ice was stronger than one thought, and bore up under some occasional fancy-skating. However, most of the delegates avoided fancy-skating, and went round the course with great decorum.

That all the delegates wanted justice in their country, no one could doubt. But some believed it could be achieved only by racial separation, and the others did not. It is hard for Christians to cherish a common end when they are so deeply divided about the means. Yet though the issue of apartheid hung above the gathering like a sword that might in a moment fall and cleave it in two, it also sent the Great Hall into gales of laughter. An African minister announced his intention of speaking about it. However, he stood too far from the microphone, and there were cries, 'We can't hear you', to which he replied spiritedly, 'You will hear me soon enough.' That brought the house down.

So the conference came to its end, with words of warmth, love, hope, and congratulation. Look upon it graciously for its like has not been seen again.[26]

Clayton enjoyed the conference hugely. He knew as well as any that there was a great unreality about it all, but he could enjoy it, and the companionship of Brink, Keet, Gerdener, and Reyneke, and their desire for closer co-operation. But Reeves and Huddleston could not help asking themselves – and others – the unanswerable questions. It is something not easily explained, that Clayton, who knew as well as they that the N.G.K. supported the policies of racial separation, who was attracted as little as they by South African Calvinism, should nevertheless enjoy meeting with those with whom he profoundly disagreed, and whose religion he felt to be in such great degree incompatible with his own. One can only suppose that the goodwill of Brink and others was something to which he attached tremendous importance, that this was 'disagreement in love'. And who is to judge him wrong? One might also suppose that it was a kind of relief to him to be welcomed by Christians whose political and social beliefs he had so forthrightly condemned, even although he had never attacked them personally. This condemnation was reciprocated, and indeed in this very year *Die Kerkbode*, in congratulating the Presbyterian Church of South Africa on its 125th anniversary, wrote, 'The Presbyterian Church is our ally, especially when the Anglicans are always more prominent and, in our opinion, prepare the way for Roman Catholicism.'[27]*

Clayton had not only acted as joint chairman of the conference; he had also been invited to give an opening address. In this he again showed his ambivalent attitude to Christian unity. He said that the divisions of Christendom made the churches look like rival shops competing for the custom of the heathen. He spoke of the danger of building up self-contained church communities uninterested in those outside their communities. South Africa had failed to produce a Christianity sufficiently vital to be stronger to unite than the divergences of race, background, and habit are to divide.

Clayton concluded his address humbly. He gave thanks to the organisers because they had allowed the churches to bring as representatives any of their members of whatever race.[28] On 12 December he returned to Cape Town, where he turned 70. He thought it was time for him to retire.

*The Presbyterian Church had in this very year condemned the Bantu Education Act.

28

The Destruction of Sophiatown

10 February 1955 was the day set for the beginning of the destruction of Sophiatown. On 9 February the Minister of Justice banned all public meetings in the magisterial districts of Johannesburg and Roodepoort for a period of twenty days. Replying to a question the Minister said that he was compelled to take this action when he was informed of the possibility of trouble in Sophiatown. He said that the position was serious, not as a result of resistance from the people to be moved, but as the result of incitement by a number of agitators. 'I was told that the greatest threat came from a group of idle, lawless *tsotsis,** who unfortunately were incited by certain people, who pretend to be responsible people, among others I am sorry to say, certain clergy, and among them Father Huddleston.' The Minister gave details of the 'dangerous situation' caused by Huddleston and the African National Congress. Verwoerd quoted me as having said, 'Apartheid is something which is done by people who have power to those who have not,' and he asked, 'Can there be anything more inciting than this?' This was the stock argument of the Nationalists, that it was not the removals and the destruction of houses, and the restrictive laws that incited people; the inciters were those who condemned such actions.[1]

The threat to destroy Sophiatown had hung over the township for twenty years. In 1953 a group of people under Huddleston as chairman formed the Western Areas Protest Committee. This committee was to co-operate closely with the African National Congress and the Transvaal Indian Congress, to organise the people of the areas, and to educate the white citizens of Johannesburg. On a second front Reeves and the Citizens' Housing League had been attacking the City Council for its failure to build houses. The 'shelters' at Orlando and Moroka were worse than anything in Sophiatown, and there was little likelihood that they would be removed. Some of the houses in Sophiatown were in sound condition; they represented the life savings of their owners. Reeves was away in England at the time, and Huddleston was the spokesman for those who opposed the removals. He was seen everywhere, in the streets, on public platforms, and in the columns of the newspapers. His lean, handsome face, his shining eyes, his expressive hands, became the inspiration for many, and the object of hatred for others. What

*A violent, lawless young man of the townships, usually member of a gang.

right had a man who had been in the country for less than twelve years to pronounce its laws unjust?

A whole fleet of army lorries arrived at dawn on 10 February. A couple of thousand armed police, white and black, were there in case of trouble. The Commissioner of Police patrolled up and down in a radio van, in hourly contact with the Minister in Cape Town. Wherever Huddleston went he was surrounded by black people; his progress was a series of banned meetings, and no sooner had he obeyed the order to move on from one than he was in the middle of another. That day he was not only the most prominent person in Sophiatown. He was the most prominent in South Africa and the news of his identification with the cause of the black people was sent round the world by the newspapermen of many a country.

Huddleston seemed to be full of inexhaustible energy. He said his prayers and his offices, celebrated and communicated, met with committees and led deputations, gave interviews to newspapers, foreign visitors, diplomats, wrote and spoke and persuaded. He knew that Sophiatown had gone but at the same time he could not believe it. He challenged the Ministers of the State to repeat their allegations about him outside the walls of Parliament, but they did not do so. 'Nor did any of my ecclesiastical superiors (the Bishop of Johannesburg was away in England at the time) attempt to come to my defence.'[2] He did not say so, but he meant no doubt that his Archbishop had not done so. Did he mean Raynes also?

Clayton wrote to Raynes saying that he no longer wished to be Visitor to the Community of the Resurrection while Huddleston was the Provincial. This news distressed Huddleston and, when Clayton was in Johannesburg on 13 April on his way to London to preside over the annual meeting of the S.P.G., the Society for the Propagation of the Gospel, Huddleston went to the airport to try to persuade him to withdraw his threat. He said he would try to behave with greater regard for Clayton's feelings, but he made clear to the Archbishop his grief over Sophiatown and the schools. Clayton withdrew his threat, but Huddleston was well aware of the gulf between them.[3] He was made aware of it again when he met the Archbishop of Canterbury, Geoffrey Fisher, at St. Augustine's, Penhalonga, in Southern Rhodesia. Fisher was on his way to assist in the inauguration of the new Province of Central Africa, and he and Huddleston were standing in the small parlour awaiting the guests at a reception. Fisher said to Huddleston, 'You are entirely wrong in the methods you are using to fight this situation. . . . The Christian must never use force . . . must never use the same weapons as his opponents.' A fierce but friendly argument followed, but Huddleston was not convinced.

Nor was he convinced by the statement of Father Cecil Wood, whom Clayton had in 1955 brought back from the South African Church Institute in London to be rector of Hermanus. Wood accepted the offer, despite Clayton's warning that he would have a female choir and a synthetic peal of bells. Father Wood had said that Anglicans made the greatest possible mistake in trying 'to fight his [the Calvinist's] convictions with political weapons'. This belief of Father Wood was shared by both Clayton and Fisher. Clayton had said to Provincial Synod in 1950 that the Anglican and the Dutch Reformed Churches arrived at different results when applying theological principles to contemporary problems. 'This produces the impression that the difference is racial: fundamentally I believe the difference is theological.'

This did not satisfy Huddleston. It made no allowance for the prejudice and fear and self-interest that were the motives for racial policy. He would not try to fight the 'religious convictions' of the Calvinist except by the proclamation of the Catholic faith. But the political weapons of white South Africa, that 'hurt and wound the African every day', must be fought with political weapons, and Christians must use them. Huddleston would no doubt have argued that it was the historical factor, admittedly impossible to separate from the theological and racial factors, that determined contemporary policies. The truth is that Huddleston was not a theologian, or if he was, he had a simple theology that comprehended God's love for man, man's need of God, and man's duty to man. In fact Huddleston burned with zeal, whereas Clayton prayed for wisdom. Huddleston was the passionate advocate, Clayton the judge. Huddleston could be exasperated by Clayton's judiciality, just as Clayton could be exasperated by Huddleston's passion. Through these experiences Huddleston came to a deeper understanding of Michael Scott. But he was lucky; he did not have Scott's diffidence and shyness, and therefore he did not have his loneliness. Both he and Scott burned with the resolve that something must be done. They were exasperated by Clayton's judicial opinion that that particular something would never be done.

In the event all were right, Huddleston and Scott in what they wanted to be done, Clayton in his assessment of what could and could not be done. Without the three of them, their lives and works, the annals of the Church of the Province would have been the poorer. One thing should be added: if anything exasperated Clayton, it was to be urged – and with such urgency! – to do something that he knew he could not do. This is what Huddleston was doing now, and throughout the year of 1955 the gulf between them grew steadily wider.

On 13 April Clayton left for London, where on 26 April he was to preside over the annual meeting of the S.P.G. He appointed Lavis as Vicar-General during his absence.

Just before he left, he wrote a dissertation on how he should behave in England. It was clear that the problem – for problem it was – much exercised his mind. He was living under a government that was highly sensitive to criticism, that was easily angered by criticism from abroad from people who 'did not understand the country', and was made especially angry by South Africans who, having been given passports by the Government, went abroad and criticised its laws and policies. It seems quite clear that Clayton did not wish to anger the Government; it was not that he was personally afraid, but he was anxious not to expose the Church of the Province and its manifold works to any danger.

'I know I shall be expected to make pronouncements about South Africa, for South Africa is news in England, and I have got to speak at a number of meetings. But South Africa is very difficult to describe. It is possible of course to avoid telling lies about it, but even if everything that one says is quite true and every photograph one shows is quite genuine, one can yet give a false impression, for the whole difficulty is the selection of one's material.

'The extreme complacency of the publications of the State Information Office, so far as I have seen them, gives the impression that the Union of South Africa is a kind of earthly paradise for its inhabitants of every group. The accounts given by some of the visitors to this country suggest that the Union of South Africa is a hell on earth. The facts stated on both sides are mainly correct. But, as I say, the difference lies in the way the material is selected. Both are true, but neither is the whole truth.

'It appears to be supposed that there is something wicked about saying anything about South Africa or about the policies of its Governments, past and present, which is in any way critical. This seems to me nonsense and very ill-judged. If people are so touchy about criticism the impression they produce on the outsider is that they have a bad conscience. I should not have thought that was the impression they desired to give. . . .

'My one desire is to give as true an impression as I can. I do not desire to make propaganda for or against either State or Church. But I do know how difficult it is to be fair and therefore I should prefer not to go overseas at all. . . . I don't often write about myself for I do not think it is a very interesting subject, but there are times when it seems right to do so.'[4]

What could have been more judicial than that? And what could have been more relevant than his reference to the supposed wickedness of saying anything critical 'about South Africa or about the policies of its Governments'? And who could have been wider of the mark when he said he was not a very interesting subject? On the contrary, anything that he wrote about himself was bound to be funny or interesting or mordant or all three together.

Clayton's first speech was made on 26 April in Church House at the annual general meeting of the S.P.G. He was not only the main speaker, he was in the chair as well. His speech was restrained and objective, but the newspapers seized on his most provocative utterance: 'I think that all the machinery has been provided so that we could become a police state, if the Government wanted it to happen, in less than a week.' He added that a dangerous amount of power had been placed in the hands of individual Ministers, and people were being deprived of the right to an effective resort to courts of law.

But according to one observer, A. W. Wells, formerly editor of the *Friend* of Bloemfontein, the audience was taken aback by Clayton's objectivity. They were used to hearing stronger stuff. Clayton told them that South Africa spent more on education and health services for Africans than most of her neighbours, that Africans flocked into South Africa from other countries because they could get higher wages there than in their own, that the African townships 'though rather unimaginative in their layout, are really quite good', and that South African Indians refused to go back to India. According to Wells the audience lost some of its 'mystification' when Clayton said: 'And yet it is true that the South African Native has not got freedom of movement in his own land. He has to carry a pass, and is frequently subject to insult.' But back came the 'air of stunned, almost hurt silence' when Clayton said white South Africans were not birds of passage but had no other home.

He told his joke too. He told them he had agreed to visit Basutoland, a country famous for its ponies and their riders, on condition that he would not be required to mount any animal unless it might be a camel or an elephant.[5]

In South Africa he was not obliged to defend the country and its customs. In London he clearly felt such an obligation. The Nationalists and their Press were nevertheless displeased, for all that he had tried to do justice to both sides. In their view there was only one side. Their newspapers impugned Clayton's competence, motives and honesty, and even questioned his intelligence. If their opinions appeared absurd to the outside world, they were not concerned, because they lived in a closed world of their own and did not put out their heads to see or listen.

The *Cape Times* came to Clayton's defence. It described him as a sober, responsible, tolerant and informed clergyman, enjoying by reason of his person and his office the respect of the vast majority of South Africans. It said that he sought 'some sounder foundation to elementary liberty than a childlike faith in the essential goodness of South African politicians'. That put the matter very well.[6]

On 28 April Clayton spoke at a great meeting organised by the S.P.G. in the Albert Hall to celebrate its 254th anniversary. According to Cecil Wood, who was in the vast audience of 6,000, he ambled on to the stage like a cross, shaggy bear, accompanied by a roll of drums and a tremendous ovation. According to A. W. Wells, he dominated the audience, surely and quietly. Wells wrote that he 'told London things it had not heard before'.[7] These obviously were not the things that showed up apartheid in a bad light, because London had heard plenty of these already. Nor was it the extenuating circumstances that Clayton cited to lessen the enormity of white arrogance and injustice, the fact that so many white South Africans had no other home. London if it wished could have heard of them also, through the bulletins of the South African Information Office. What London had not heard before was the stating of these extenuating circumstances by the Archbishop of a Church whose educational work had virtually been destroyed by the Government. If it were possible for *him* to find extenuating circumstances, then even the most implacable opponents of apartheid must pay attention.

Clayton told his audience that what was wrong was not the taking over of the schools, but the decision that 'the African boy would be educated for such a position as the Government thought it right for him to hold – not for such a position as his talents might enable him to hold'.[8] He told his audience of the far-reaching effects of the Bantu Education Act, on both the character and the content of African education, and on the schools of the Church. His judgements were delivered firmly and irrevocably. At the Albert Hall meeting he was, as he had been at other meetings for many years, at the height of his powers.

The great event of the evening was the handing over to Clayton of a cheque for £30,000. This amount had been collected by the S.P.G. through its South African Emergency Fund, 'to help the Anglican Church in the Union to continue its educational work among the Natives'.[9] The money was to be used to 'promote new ways of getting into touch and influencing the African youth now that the opportunities of doing this through the Mission schools had been lost because of the Bantu Education Act'.[10]

On 1 May Clayton preached at Pembroke, his old college. He was again determined to be fair to the white people of South Africa, and again made the misstatement which had already been corrected by historians. He said:

'The Bantu, as the black people are called, arrived from the north about the same time as the Dutch arrived from the south. Between them they practically exterminated the people that were there before them, that is the Bushmen and the Hottentots. The Bantu did more of the extermination than the Europeans.' Clayton told the congregation what Smuts had said to him, '. . . we South Africans want people like you to say boldly and repeatedly what you believe to be true. If you do that you will get a great deal of criticism but you will win everyone's respect.'

Clayton wanted more priests to go from England to South Africa, and he gave them advice.

'But no one ought to come if he can't keep his temper. He must not mind being criticised and abused, and when he is reviled he must not revile again. And he must have a sense of humour, otherwise he will break his heart. If he has a sense of humour, he won't. But if he has courage and faith and if he believes in God, and if he does not take himself too seriously but can laugh, not only at other people but also at himself, he can really help. And in helping he will himself grow and get on with the work which God has given him to do; for by helping others and forgetting about himself he himself grows. He won't finish his work as Our Lord did but he will make progress in his work of growing up into the measure of the stature of the fullness of Christ.'[11]

This was not advice for zealots. It could hardly be reconciled with Huddleston's plea for a cultural boycott of South Africa, nor with the views of those who believed that if the country was forced into isolation its rulers would have the change of heart. It was not the kind of advice that satisfied those who wanted righteousness *now*. But others thought it wise.

The gifts already made by the S.P.G. to the Church of the Province were munificent. But besides all this, the S.P.G. had appealed to the parishes of England, and it was hoped that a sum of £40,000 would be put at the disposal of the bishops without conditions. Of these gifts Clayton said:

'But what we appreciate so very much is that our friends who are of the same Communion as we are have understood that in present circumstances we are having a difficult and anxious time and have given us this money as a mark of their sympathy and confidence to help us to bear our burdens. I do not think that any action could well be more Christian.'[12]

On 13 May Clayton left London for Salisbury in Southern Rhodesia for the inauguration of the new Province of Central Africa. Its new archbishop was to be Edward Paget, who, had Clayton not advised him to the contrary, would have already been living in retirement. Geoffrey Fisher, Archbishop of Canterbury and the senior Archbishop of the world-wide Anglican Communion, had also come for the inauguration. It was a tremendous occasion and, as was to be expected, Clayton preached a tremendous sermon. It was directed to the big question of the moment, and that was whether there was any hope for the success of the new Central African Federation, which had been brought into being without any consultation with the overwhelming majority of the people living in it, and was to last only ten years before it broke up into the three countries which today are Malawi, Zambia, and Rhodesia.* Clayton revealed what was uppermost in his mind: 'Have you any special task of your own? You are a multi-racial province. Christ came to break down barriers. In his name it is for you to create a union of hearts.'[13]

Central Africa is still a multi-racial Anglican province, although its continuance is not assured. The countries of Zambia and Rhodesia observe a hostile neutrality, and there are Zambians, both Anglicans and others, who protest against the close association of their Anglican dioceses with those of Rhodesia. But in 1955 there was still a large measure of optimism, which is well illustrated in a magnificent photograph, taken in the cathedral cloisters, of the three archbishops convulsed with laughter. (Plate 11.)

It was time for Clayton to go back to work, but before he did so he spent a holiday of three weeks with Robert Selby Taylor, Bishop of Pretoria, and now Archbishop of Cape Town. Selby Taylor was a tall, quiet, reserved man of whom Clayton had a high opinion, and whom he would have liked to succeed him at 'Bishopscourt'. Selby Taylor had great respect for his archbishop, and said that this respect was felt by all the bishops, though Reeves must have had reservations. Selby Taylor thought that Clayton towered head and shoulders above them all, in intellect, clarity of mind, and clarity of expression, all gifts, he thought, which stemmed largely from his spiritual life. When he opened an episcopal synod he would read some passage of scripture in his controlled and magnificent voice, and say a few sentences which revealed to those eminent men listening to him a depth of understanding of God and man and man's life which they could only hope one day perhaps to attain.

The holiday was spent first at Peterhouse School with the Snells, then with

*Rhodesia is still Southern Rhodesia in the eyes of the British Government.

the Community of the Resurrection, Penhalonga, a weekend at Zimbabwe, then to the Mountain Inn in the Zoutpansberg, the inside of a week at the Sabi River bungalows, and finally a few days in Pretoria. It was the kind of holiday that Clayton enjoyed, and he gossiped to his heart's content. In particular he made it clear to his companion his attitude to churchmen like Reeves, Huddleston, and Scott. He detested what he took to be exhibitionism. He believed that their judgements were unbalanced, and that they could not see the other side of the question. He himself had a pastoral responsibility for white as well as black, and he believed that Huddleston in particular overlooked this first responsibility. He admitted that he had great difficulty in being patient with Reeves in episcopal synods. He found Reeves incompatible, and on that account he tried to cut himself off as far as possible from the affairs of the diocese of Johannesburg. He felt also that Reeves, Huddleston, and Scott grew too emotional over South Africa. Selby Taylor said that Clayton himself had powerful emotions, but he kept them very highly disciplined, and he was easily irritated by those who did not do the same. Selby Taylor added that it was Clayton's ability to see both sides and to weigh up an entire situation that made it difficult for his critics to fault him. To this I would add that it certainly made it difficult for his Nationalist critics to fault him, so that often they were reduced to saying things about him that were palpably absurd.

But his more activist critics *did* fault him; they did not think it so great a virtue to see both sides of a question. Huddleston said that he had a love–hate relationship with Clayton, 'with love predominating, but hate breaking out because temperamentally we were different, and also because I have no doubt at all I was much too aggressive and even impertinent – but then I was young'.[14]* Whether Reeves expressed much criticism of his archbishop, I do not know; but I can say that such criticism was not expressed to me, even when an opportunity was offered. Of Scott we know that he passed a gentle judgement after Clayton's death, though he would have entitled his biographic piece, 'A Just Beast'.

The few days at the Sabi River bungalows were memorable. They paid several visits to the Kruger National Park, and on one occasion followed a procession of eleven cubs, five lionesses, and the lion himself, for about a mile. Although the rest of the visitors at the bungalows were a little frightened of the Archbishop, and although he was a bit frightened of them, he described for them all the pleasure and excitement in encountering no less than seventeen lions in one pride. Usually the visitors went to bed early, and the two bishops would have the lounge to themselves. Clayton talked incessantly, and about midnight Selby Taylor would say, 'We must go to bed' and if Clayton looked unwilling, he would have to add, 'If we don't go to bed, the staff can't go to bed.' Clayton enjoyed talking much more than he enjoyed reading; in fact Selby Taylor would not have described him as a reader or a student. One qualification should be added to this: of the affairs

*In a subsequent letter he emphasised that the word 'hate' must not be understood in any extreme sense. I suggest that Clayton could exasperate and infuriate him.

of the world, the country, and the Church, few had a knowledge more extensive than his. These were in fact the things that he read and studied; these and the scriptures. They were part of the duty of a priest.[15]

His return to Cape Town was triumphal. A committee under Sir Herbert Stanley had planned a welcome meeting for him in the Drill Hall, and there was to be a presentation to him to celebrate the twenty-fifth anniversary of his consecration in St. Paul's Cathedral, London, on 1 May 1934. Stanley would no doubt have welcomed Clayton and extolled his work in those sonorous and magnificent sentences of his; instead it was Clayton who farewelled Stanley and extolled his work at a memorial service on 8 June. He said of his services to the Church that they could 'hardly be exaggerated'.[16]

Two days later, on 10 June Clayton and J. B. Webb addressed a meeting in the City Hall; the meeting was sponsored by the Methodist and Anglican churches, and the subject was 'The Relation of the Church to the Present Situation in South Africa'. The City Hall was filled to capacity.

It is necessary to remind the reader at this point that the Government was still determined to remove the coloured voters to a separate roll. The first Act – which aimed to do this by simple majority – had been declared *ultra vires* by the Appellate Court on the grounds that a two-thirds majority of both Houses sitting together was required. The Government had then secured the passage of an Act which made Parliament a High Court with powers greater than those of the Appellate Court, but that had also been declared *ultra vires*. In 1953, having increased his majority in the elections Malan had tried to woo the waverers in the Opposition to give him a two-thirds vote, but had failed. Now in 1955 the new Prime Minister, J. G. Strijdom, with a reputation for *kragdadigheid*,* decided to enlarge and reconstruct the Senate in such a way that the two-thirds majority would be assured. There was nothing in the Constitution to prevent enlargement or reconstruction of the Senate, no matter for what purpose it might be used; the makers of the Constitution had not foreseen such a development.[17]

To great applause Clayton condemned the Senate Bill. 'The Coloured people are in a very real sense a sacred trust. And on the extent to which Europeans keep faith with them will the Europeans be judged at the bar of history, and at a higher tribunal than that.'

For the first time Clayton permitted himself a rare and uncomplimentary reference to Verwoerd. 'The Minister of Native Affairs said to me not long ago, "We are not Nazis, you know." A rose by any other name would smell as sweet.'

Clayton addressed himself to the problem which undoubtedly greatly exercised his mind in the closing years of his life. He said that it had recently been suggested that because the powers that be were ordained of God,

**Kragdadigheid* has no real English equivalent. In Afrikaans it indicates an admirable quality. When the Afrikaans word is used in English conversation it may or may not be derogatory. It means the quality of doing deeds of power, but often carries the implication that the doer has more power than sense.

everything that any Government does was divinely inspired and according to God's will. But that was not so. Was Nero divinely inspired in the burning of Christians? Was the Government of the U.S.S.R. divinely inspired? Or nearer home, would the Nationalists say that the Smuts Government had been divinely inspired? It was true that God in his mercy did overrule the failure of men and bring good out of what might be evil, but stupidity and sin are to be found in those who govern as well as in those who are governed. 'It is not our duty to be popular. It is our duty to be faithful and refuse to be silenced. We must obey God rather than man.'

But the Church must not be tied to a party. It must follow its vocation of being a nation's conscience, 'and a conscience is always an inconvenient thing'. Speaking of complete apartheid he said, 'For myself I have the greatest respect for those who put forward this policy, and I believe completely in their sincerity. But I do not believe that it is economically possible. . . . Surely it is a counsel of despair to say that the only way in which we can live in the same country is by an arrangement that we should be completely separated from each other?' What was more, such a notion conflicted with the teaching of the New Testament.[18]

Two days after the City Hall meeting Prime Minister Strijdom, speaking in Johannesburg, poured scorn on the United Party for claiming that its race policies had a moral basis. But with his usual *kragdadigheid* he said that unless the white man remained *baas*, it was all up with him. As a rule Strijdom left it to Verwoerd and others to supply the moral and philosophical patter, but he was as convinced as they that Nationalist race policy was moral perfection. The *Cape Times* preferred Clayton's professional opinion, delivered in the City Hall, as being 'far more weighty'. It approved of Clayton's two tests of the Nationalist claim to represent Christian civilisation. The first was the coloured franchise. The coloured people had no Reserves, land, or cultural identity. Total apartheid, which was the only kind of apartheid that could pretend to have any moral foundation, was impossible for them. Therefore *baasskap* over them must be imposed and rule maintained by force. The second test was that of migrant labour, which must increase under Nationalist policy. It was based on the wreck of African family life, and if the Nationalists could claim this as a moral project, their reasoning was even more supple than had been suspected.[19]

Die Kerkbode said of Clayton and Webb that, although the subject had been 'Christian Witness in South Africa', it could be taken for granted that they had spoken on race relations. In the last few years they had been unable to talk about anything else. *Die Kerkbode* asked why they must discuss this when they had just returned from abroad. It protested against Webb's frequent attempts to bring the N.G.K. under discussion at public meetings. Why could he not go direct to the N.G.K.? The leaders of the N.G.K. could also say a great deal about the English churches. Would that solve the race problem? No good was to be expected from this method. It could destroy all trust. *Die Kerkbode* called on its critics to drop these methods. They were appropriate for agitators, but not for leaders of the Christian churches.[20]

A week after the City Hall meeting Clayton was given his 'welcome back' meeting in the Drill Hall. It was attended by nearly two thousand people of all races. Clayton was given a gift of £1,165 'to do with as you like'. Bishop Lavis told the audience that the *Church Times* in England had described the Archbishop as having 'the rhetoric of Churchill, the depth of Temple, and the eyebrows of George Robey'. Tom Savage, who had been Rector of Springs when Clayton was Bishop of Johannesburg, who had returned to England and had now been called to become the Dean of Cape Town, said that the Archbishop always knew 'when to speak and when to keep silent'. Clayton, who was in tremendous form, told the meeting that he found it difficult to believe that all these generous things could possibly be true. He told his hearers that the S.P.G. had given him a gift of £30,000 to meet the new needs that had arisen after the passing of the Bantu Education Act – an announcement that caused a gasp of surprise and much applause.* Clayton thanked the diocese for its generous gift of £1,165 and said he hardly knew what to do with the money. Speakers had been undeservedly generous about his work, and he warned his hearers that he came of a very long-lived family. He was glad to be back, and above all happy to be with all his people again to face together whatever lay ahead.[21]

Clayton was much moved by his reception, especially from so many of his people whom he never saw except from on high or from afar. He wrote in *Good Hope* of 27 July 1955 to give thanks for the meeting and the gift. 'So strengthened . . . I shall return to my work for what cannot and ought not to be a very long time. How long it is not possible to say. That depends on a number of factors at present unknown.'

He told the story of the nonagenarian English bishop of the last century, who said when it was suggested he should resign, 'What would be the use of my resigning? They would only appoint one of these sickly young men.' Clayton added, 'I do not propose to imitate the bishop, for even in these decadent days there are young men who are not sickly.' He was now 70 but he could still write, 'The speeches that were made are a stimulus to me that I should try to make them come true.'

Not everything was perfect. He felt he must express his opinion of those who were urging the Church of England to show a more active concern for South Africa. 'I understand that a large number of priests of the Province have given their assent to what amounts to an attempt to teach the Convocations of Canterbury and York what is their own business. . . . I do think that the action that has been taken is both impertinent and unwise.'[22]

Many people, including myself, jumped to the conclusion that Huddleston must have been behind it all, but Huddleston told me that he had no knowledge of it. Thus far it remains a mystery. But the rift between Clayton and Huddleston had widened further. As we have seen, Clayton had disapproved of the article 'The Church Sleeps On', but, wrote Huddleston, 'he disapproved even more of my impertinent letters to himself, and he had

*In his charge to Provincial Synod, 12.11.1955, he said he had received £25,000 direct from the S.P.G. I did not investigate further. See Clayton, *Where We Stand*, page 42.

every reason to do so. At the time I really was so deeply involved emotionally that I have no doubt that I wrote too strongly.'[23]

That was true. The destruction of Sophiatown, of the mission and the schools was for Huddleston almost too much to be borne. The school of Christ the King had been closed in obedience to the decision of the diocese of Johannesburg to close its schools. But the anguish of parents was insupportable. Therefore it reopened a month later as a private school without subsidy, and charged a fee of ten shillings a month. That was necessary if the teachers were to be paid, and the parents were willing to pay. So great was the urgency to Huddleston and so great his will to persist that he opened the school having not yet obtained the departmental registration required by the Bantu Education Act. The African National Congress in its turn took the extreme step of urging a total boycott of all schools. Seven thousand children took part in the boycott, and were told that they could not be allowed in any school again. The grave punishment of expulsion is still widely used in South Africa; it is not the career of the child that matters, but the upholding of the law. Private and disguised schools were started; they were called cultural clubs, and did not have and dared not have any blackboards, books, or benches. The disguise was useless. When Huddleston visited the cultural club, they sang a song for him, with the words, 'Down with Bantu Education'. Of such visits, such songs, such boycotts, Clayton totally disapproved.

Meanwhile the Government pushed ahead with its plans to reconstruct the Senate. As part of its strategy it appointed five additional judges to the Appellate Bench, and introduced the Appellate Division Quorum Bill, which made provision for a full quorum for the consideration of constitutional cases. The Minister of Justice did not attempt to hide the intention of the Bill. It was to make it less likely that the Appellate Division would invalidate Acts of Parliament.

It was the Senate Bill that led to the founding in Johannesburg of the women's movement, first known as the Women's Defence of the Constitution League, and later as the Black Sash. It asked the mayor of Johannesburg to call a public meeting, at which 18,000 people were present. It then collected 100,000 signatures on a petition against the Bill, and presented it to the Prime Minister. Two days later the Bill became law.

The Black Sash is still active today. Although it has declined numerically, it has not lost its courage and determination, and its sure grasp of what political measures must be subjected to moral judgement. The uniform of the organisation was a white dress with a black sash a symbol of mourning for the death of the constitution and the rule of law. The members appeared in public in silent protest, carrying placards, and providing unofficial guards for Cabinet Ministers on such occasions as the opening of courts, prisons, and bridges, drawing upon themselves the abuse of white bystanders who thought society was perfect, and evoking from the Ministers varying responses, of politeness, stony-eyed aloofness, or, from Eric Louw, waspish humour. In recent days its public protests have been directed largely against those laws which permit detention, which may be prolonged indefinitely, without charge or trial. The organisation was confined to white women, on the grounds that only they were voters. This was a typically South African reason, and the Minister of the Interior, Dr. Donges, twitted them for defending coloured rights and excluding coloured women. Nevertheless it was very probable that a public stand by white and coloured women together would have led to public violence, if not in Durban and Cape Town, then certainly in Johannesburg and Pretoria.*

Clayton strongly approved of the Black Sash. Although he was always reluctant to call for Days of Prayer, usually on the grounds that church people should pray anyway, he welcomed the decision of the Black Sash to observe a Day of Prayer in the Cape Peninsula. He stated publicly that he was glad to know that so many women were anxious about the future of their country and were prepared to face ridicule and personal hardship to show their disquiet. He suggested that the purpose of the day ought to be the commending of the country to God that He might order all things according to His love and wisdom. 'We must not attempt to use the name of God in order to bring to fruition purposes of our own.' Because Black Sash had been founded by lay people it should remain a lay movement. Prayers would gain in sincerity if with simplicity and spontaneity they carried it through themselves. They must not stop at a Day of Prayer – they must think as clearly as possible about the affairs of their country and say what they thought as clearly and boldly as they could.[24]

Although Clayton had expressed the hope more than once that the diocese of Johannesburg would not ask again for money from the S.P.G., in 1949 the S.P.G. planned to assist theological education in South Africa, and Clayton, then Archbishop, and his brother bishops, accepted the offer. They decided to use the money for increase of staff at St. Bede's, Umtata; the training of African catechists at Estcourt; the training of coloured catechists at Zonnebloem; theological education work of the Community of the Resurrection; and the establishment of a Catechists' School in the Orange Free State.

Again in 1952 the S.P.G. suggested a new method of giving help to the Church of the Province. All diocesan requests to the S.P.G. were to go first to the Archbishop, and it is quite clear that he intended with what wisdom he had at his command to make his own recommendations. He had already in 1951 discussed with the S.P.G. the differences in stipends paid in the different dioceses, and he had hoped that the S.P.G. would bear this in mind when making grants.[25] On 27 March 1953 Clayton suggested to the S.P.G. that the diocese of Bloemfontein might stand a reduction because of the new goldfields in the Orange Free State; also Grahamstown, because of the higher percentage of white Anglicans; while Zululand and Basutoland might receive more because of the higher percentage of black Anglicans. One thing is clear, that the generosity of the Church of England to the Church in South Africa did not seem to have abated as a result of the

*This colour-bar was removed in 1963.

Second World War. And in 1955 it rose to extraordinary heights. The debt of the Anglican Church to the S.P.G. would be hard to overestimate. From the earliest days of Bishop Gray in Cape Town to the last days of Clayton's life, its gifts had been abundant.

One of Clayton's archiepiscopal visits in 1956 was important. That was to the lonely island of Tristan da Cunha, which though then belonging to the diocese of St. Helena, could almost never be visited by its bishop because it was not on any commercial sea-route. It was therefore usually visited by the Archbishop of Cape Town, through the courtesy of the Royal Navy, which was about to send the frigate H.M.S. *Leopard* to call at the island. Now Clayton was no lover of the sea, and had not been so since childhood. Though he was of considerable girth, his legs were thin and his feet small; he was therefore both unsure of his balance and afraid of the coldness of the water. On the frigate he was, according to Cowdry, 'a howling success', and took part in all the entertainments if he was physically able to do so. But descending from the frigate into the waiting boat was for him a big ordeal. The descent was made in a bosun's chair, and although it was handled by experts, Clayton experienced physical fear, of the same kind that he felt when crossing a busy street.

The two days on Tristan were a howling success also, but the difficulty and unpleasantness of the descent, probably less so the ascent, reinforced his feeling that it was time for him to retire. He wrote of his visit, 'I was conscious of the fact that a younger and more agile bishop would have been able to do a great deal more than I could do.'[26] It was more than a year earlier that he had written to Cecil Wood (when recalling him to South Africa) his thoughts on retirement:

'[This] is a dangerous kind of letter to write. But on the whole it seems best to treat you as Samson treated Delilah, and to tell you all that is in my heart. I trust you will not treat me as Delilah treated Samson. You know something of my position in this Diocese. I am in my 70th year and clearly I can't go on for ever. If my health holds I shall go on till the next Provincial Synod at the end of 1955.'

Clayton also wrote: 'It is of course impossible to know who my successor will be. But I doubt whether the Diocese will be willing to import someone from outside South Africa. And as I look round my brother Bishops, it seems to me that there are at least equal chances that my successor will be unmarried.'[27]

November 1955 was his last Provincial Synod. He gave thanks to the S.P.G. for its great generosity. He again stated his view, that he would not feel able to condemn any scheme of *total* separation as unChristian, but it seemed fairly clear that those in authority had no intention of applying it. He was well aware of the difficulties of the stating of an alternative policy, but they must not deceive themselves that the policy as it was put forward was equitable or could be permanent. He condemned again the detention of people without trial, but would not compare the cruelty of such procedure with the cruelty of Hitler's Germany. But he said sternly, 'An atmosphere of suspicion is a bad thing to produce in a country and leads to disaster. But that is what is being produced today.' He respected his condemnation of the altering of the Constitution to make it possible to take away entrenched rights, and concluded with his unfailing words of encouragement.

But before he did that he had something to say about the good name of South Africa.

'We are citizens of South Africa. We have every desire to be good and loyal South Africans. But things are being done here which seem to me to have besmirched the name of South Africa. I say these things here because I believe this is the right place in which to say them. I have had an opportunity of saying them abroad, an opportunity which I did not myself seek; but there, just because the people I was talking to had only heard one side of the case, I did my level best to make clear the point of view of those of whose policy I was speaking. I greatly prefer to say these things in this country where both I and those to whom I am speaking have heard the other side. And I say them to you my fellow churchmen because I believe they are true and I want you to think about them. I do not know whether you agree with them. I am not committing you by what I say. There is no kind of disloyalty in disagreeing with your bishop. But for myself I do care immensely for the good name of South Africa. So, I am sure, do you. And if we think these things are true we must not conceal them but speak of them openly.'[28]

There was no one in the country who could speak quite like that, with such clarity and simplicity. Yet there were some to whom such language was totally incomprehensible; or perhaps one should say, there were those who found it incomprehensible that anyone should utter such thoughts. How could their party and their rulers, who were filled with such love of country, possibly besmirch its name? If their rulers had a fault, it was that they did not clap this sanctimonious agitator into gaol.

On 9 December 1955 Clayton paid his last visit to St. John's College, Johannesburg, and gave them a speech to remember. It was Clarke's last speech day and Clayton paid handsome tribute to him. Huddleston was there too, being a member of the Council. It was their last meeting. Both of them knew that Huddleston was going to be recalled, though it had not yet been made public. Huddleston also knew that Clayton had advised Raynes to recall him. With considerable charity, Huddleston did not ascribe this to any wish on Clayton's part to get rid of him. He was sure that Clayton felt that he had become too heavily involved for his spiritual health, and he thought that Huddleston might be arrested. Huddleston paid a special visit to St. John's to say goodbye to him, and 'received little more than a grunt'. This he found painful, coming from the man to whom he had written in 1948:

'These past six years have been far and away the happiest of my life. Laus Deo! And certainly part of their happiness had been due to the very cordial relationship with you, and to the knowledge that – even in disagreement – I could always count on your wisdom, patience and affection.' Huddleston concluded: 'Of your charity keep a small corner in your prayers for the Community, and for me, that I may not be too foolish or impetuous or impatient. Yours affectionately and obediently, Trevor Huddleston, C.R.'[29]

When Huddleston returned to England, recalled by Raynes to become the Master of Novices, he wrote to say that he had been hurt by Clayton's attitude, to which the Archbishop replied with the observation that they were 'different kinds of person' and that he just could not see or express things as Huddleston did.[30] And that was true, and went to show, one supposes, that we are fearfully and wonderfully made.

They did not communicate again.

29

'No time to be lost'

Although Huddleston had gone, he fired a tremendous volley from England. That was the book *Naught for Your Comfort*. It was just as well that he had gone, because his life might well have been in danger. Minister Louw was outraged by the book, and condemned Huddleston, Reeves, Stanley Uys, Alexander Campbell, John Gunther, Adlai Stevenson, and others. He included me, saying, 'He is supposed to be a South African.'[1]

In discussion of the State Information vote, Louw said that the book was doing 'incalculable harm'. The words 'Christian' and 'Christ' were on almost every second page; people did not know that they were dealing with a religious fanatic. The debate reached its lowest level when Arthur Barlow said it was imperative for a reply to be written. He suggested someone like Mrs. Millin, the well-known South African writer.

Mr. Moore: She is not a front bencher.

Mr. Barlow: No, but she is not a fool like you are.

Barlow was ordered to withdraw this brilliant rejoinder, but appealed again for a writer. Louw assured him that a reply was on the way.[2] This was *You are Wrong, Father Huddleston*, by Alexander Steward of the South African Information Department. It was a poor book, partly because refutation of the statements of another always makes a poor book, partly because it was written by a poor writer. It enjoys a richly deserved obscurity.

The turmoil in Parliament was intensified by the publication of the news that the Department of Native Affairs had ordered Huddleston's school of Christ the King 'to close forthwith'.* Verwoerd being absent from the House, the Minister of Justice stated that this had been done because the application for registration had been turned down. What was more, Huddleston, with the backing of Reeves, had opened the school first and applied for registration afterwards.[3] P. A. Moore, United Party M.P., said that he had not the slightest doubt that the Anglican community – he himself was not an Anglican – was being singled out by the Minister in order that he might vent his spleen on them. Verwoerd, back in the House, repudiated the accusation with the contempt that he said it deserved. He condemned Reeves for expecting parents to pay fees of ten shillings per month.[4] He said, 'Bishop Reeves uses every conceivable opportunity to abuse me, but

*The school was subsequently ordered to close at the end of the term.

that leaves me quite cold; I am not interested in it.' But he objected strongly to any attempt by Reeves to associate him with a struggle against the Anglican Church.[5]

Although those M.P.s who spoke were unanimous in their condemnation of Huddleston, they were divided in their views on the closing of Huddleston's school. Although Verwoerd denied any animus against the Church of the Province, and though he asserted that Reeves's attacks left him cold, it was difficult to believe him. Clayton certainly did not believe him. Whatever distrust Clayton felt over the actions of Reeves and Huddleston, he was angered by Verwoerd's action in ordering the school of Christ the King to close. In February 1956 he opened his presidential address to the biennial meeting of the Christian Council with these strong words about the closing of the school.

'My first inclination was to throw away all that I had prepared to say to you this evening, and to talk about that. The Minister's action seems so petty. It is a dangerous thing to impute motives, but it certainly gives the impression that it is motivated by personal animosity; it shows a complete disregard of the desires of the parents and indifference to the welfare of the children. But I am sure I should be wrong if I were to talk about it at length this evening.'[6]

Clayton also wrote a strong letter to Verwoerd questioning the validity of his arguments in Parliament. He said that it appeared from reports in the press that the Minister had two reasons for refusing registration. One was that Christ the King was a protest school. The evidence for this was that the Anglican school-buildings in the diocese of Johannesburg had not been made available to the Government, and that the bishop had expressed strong disagreement over the removal of Africans from Sophiatown to Meadowlands. Clayton pointed out that there was no legal obligation to hand over the buildings, and that any person had a right to disagree so long as he did not incite people to break the law. 'If evidence could be produced that the teaching in the school were subversive it would be natural that registration should be refused, but I find it hard to believe that the decision of a Minister in such a matter should be dictated by his personal feelings about the Bishop rather than by the evidence before him of what is actually being taught in the school.'

The Minister's second reason for refusing registration was that the parents paid comparatively high fees. Clayton wrote that it was difficult to see why that was an objection. It seemed to involve a refusal to recognise the rights of parents, 'a refusal which is difficult to reconcile with the emphasis which you have laid upon the desirability of African parents taking more responsibility' for the education of their children. It was also important that the school had a long waiting-list, which indicated that 'African parents did not share your views that the fees charged were extortionate'. Clayton concluded by venturing to ask if the Minister would not reconsider his decision.[7]

It was not the kind of letter that Verwoerd would like. Although written with propriety, it suggested that Verwoerd's reasoning was faulty and that he had allowed his personal feelings to affect a ministerial decision. Nor would Verwoerd take kindly to a suggestion that he could be inconsistent. He instructed his private secretary to reply to Clayton's letter, and this action was construed by Clayton and others as either an intended slight, or at best an indication that the Minister was too busy a man to reply personally to archbishops.

Verwoerd's private secretary wrote that it would not be possible to reconsider the decision. He said that Clayton had taken the version of the United Party and its press, and this did not convey correctly the attitude of the Department and the Minister. The so-called long waiting-list 'had also been queried'. 'The Minister and his Department are quite convinced that the action taken is in the best interests of the Bantu parents and children, and that this will be realised in due course just as the attacks on many other worthwhile measures were gradually proved wrong.'[8]

The lack of communication between Clayton and the Government was now to all intents and purposes complete. His presidential address to the Christian Council, the introductory words of which related to the closing of the school of Christ the King, was further proof of this. He indicated that he had some very critical things to say. Again he used strong words: 'The situation in the country is, as I see it, quite lamentable.'

Clayton said that he regarded the scriptural justification of apartheid as being non-existent. It was true that there is Old Testament authority for keeping Jews and Gentiles apart, but the purpose of the coming of Jesus was not separation but unity. Apartheid was a retreat from the New Testament into the Old. 'I believe that, perhaps gradually, but surely, the various races must be associated together in the government of the country. It is only if that happens that each group will cease to think only of what is for the good of their own group, and begin to care for what is in the interests of the country as a whole.'

He said that the giving of dictatorial powers to individual Ministers was a very great evil. The best way to fight Communism was not to imitate the methods of Communism. 'We want some better answer than that. . . . We want Christian answers to Christian questions.'

He wanted the Christian Council to speak with one voice on these matters. He closed his address with grave words, 'My friends, there is no time to be lost.'[9]

It was not surprising that when Clayton was asked to lecture at the University of Cape Town summer school, he chose the subject 'Church and State', nor is it surprising that the lecture was moral rather than philosophical. The theme seemed now always to be present in his mind. If the law of the State commanded something to be done which was believed to be contrary to God's law, then 'people should disobey and take the consequences'. If the laws of the State were not righteous, then it lost its claim on man's obedience. The State did not exist for its own aggrandisement but to make it possible for men to live the good life. There was one joke that illustrated his own peculiar wit. He was asked by a questioner whether politicians should be allowed to quote from the scriptures, and he replied, 'As the devil is allowed to quote from the scriptures, I don't see why a politician should not.'[10] This was greeted with much laughter, in which he joined with gusto.

No one, except the foolish, had ever suggested that Clayton had now become so involved in the discussion of political questions that he was neglecting his duties as shepherd and priest. His charges to ordination candidates were proof that this could not be so. 'You must so exercise your ministry that people think of you first as a man of God, a representative of Christ, and not as a protagonist of this or that policy, whether political or social.'[11] Yet it could not be denied that the questions of Church and State, of race relations, and of civil liberties, were continuously in his mind. He now began more and more to ask himself the questions which are perhaps asked more often in South Africa than in any other country: What is the future? Where are we going? How are we going to solve the problem of the co-existence of so many races, so many languages, so many cultures? He attempted to answer these questions in an address called '*Quo Vadis*?' delivered in 1956.[12] It is as relevant today as it was then.

What is the future? It is unpredictable. Certain things might happen – another world war, or the rise of a great man, 'European or non-European'. One cannot dogmatise. Nor can one make a blueprint. Nor can one see the ultimate effects of certain measures.

Clayton spoke of separate development. It was meant for Europeans too. The English-speaking group have been given an invitation to participate rather like 'the invitation which was permanently extended to the young lady of Riga who went for a ride on a tiger'. Clayton dismissed the contention that an immigrant could not become a good citizen unless he forgot all that he had inherited. Africans were to be strangers and sojourners in the European areas, without the stabilising influences of family life. Industries were to be started in African areas, so that Africans might develop there with the guidance of Europeans.

If there were to be justice in this separation the amount of land must bear some relation to the population. 'Does anyone really suppose that enough land is to be provided at the expense of the European to provide anything like a fair division?' He asked, 'Is there to be Home Rule for coloured people on the Cape Flats?' Factories? Universities? 'A very great man indeed will have to emerge' if he is to persuade the European people to do this.

What would you get? You would get more and more non-Europeans in the European areas, working as serfs – a big, discontented, rightless, dangerous industrial population. You would get homelands, with an increasing amount of Home Rule, economically unsound, overcrowded. Tribalism would be strengthened. Was it really necessary to reproduce the worst features of the Balkan Peninsula in South Africa? 'I have tried very hard to appreciate what I believe to be the really sincere and idealistic attempts to secure a happy future for all races in South Africa on these lines, but I cannot do it.'

Was there an alternative? Clayton felt that he must say that under previous governments there had been no policy at all. 'The present Government at least produced a policy and started along a road, but it seems to me to lead in the wrong direction.'

Was there any other alternative? 'I think there is. But it is not the sort of policy to which we South Africans* are likely to take kindly. . . . Surely Christians ought to want to work towards friendship and association rather than separation?' And here he repeated the argument of his presidential address, that 'perhaps gradually, but surely' the various race groups must be associated together in the government of the country; only so could any common loyalty be achieved.

Clayton said that he believed in the multiracial state. 'What is needed is less ideology and more understanding of human nature and care for human happiness. . . . I do not think that we ought to hurry what is called integration. You can be as tiresomely ideological about that as about apartheid.' Clayton gave his opinion that the whole interracial situation would be transformed by decent housing and reasonable amenities, but he did not mention the gross disparity between black and white income, which today is regarded as the greatest obstacle in the way of achieving any kind of common society. He concluded: '*Quo Vadis*? Perhaps the best answer can be given very shortly. We need to take the road from the City of Fear to the City of Faith.'

It is interesting to reflect that Verwoerd did not think in such categories. As far as he was concerned South Africa was not a City of Fear at all. It was in the hands of a strong, courageous, dedicated government, with a master plan for the future. He knew of course that the master plan was in great measure his own creation, but he did not boast of that. He was in fact not a boastful man; he was simply one with complete confidence in the rightness of what he was doing. When Margaret Ballinger asked a question in Parliament about the development of what were called 'the Reserves', he told her that she, because she was the leader of the Liberal Party, had not the slightest right to ask anything that concerned the principle of the apartheid policy. He further told her that she had the right to make only one request to him, and that was to abolish the Reserves and to introduce racial equality throughout the country. In other words, because the Liberal Party condemned apartheid, she had no right to ask questions about its implementation.[13]

Although Strijdom was the Prime Minister, Verwoerd in fact ruled the country. It was not entirely his own doing. The fact is that politics had become race. So far as one knows, there was no jealousy between Strijdom and himself. Verwoerd had no desire to oust his Prime Minister; he had power enough. He was the man most to be feared.

The tide of legislation came in as fast and strong as ever. The Senate Act

*It is clear that Clayton meant 'white South Africans'. It was a lapse of which he was seldom guilty.

had been passed in 1955 and by its enlargement Strijdom now had a two-thirds majority if the two Houses sat together. The Appellate Court, with one dissentient, decided that the reconstruction of the Senate was constitutionally unexceptionable. The dissentient was Oliver Schreiner, who contended that the Senate had been reconstructed for one reason and one only, and that was to circumvent the entrenched clauses. It should be recorded that he never achieved the honour of becoming Chief Justice, a post for which he was pre-eminently fitted. Strijdom now secured the passage of the Separate Representation of Voters Act, and all coloured voters were removed to a separate roll, and were given representation by white M.P.s in Parliament.*

The events filled many with despair. The sense of powerlessness, the uselessness of making representations, the refusal of the Government to receive deputations, Verwoerd's *fiat* that Margaret Ballinger had no right to ask him questions, made some feel that their kind of world had come to an end. Clayton wrote about the bitterness, unhappiness, selfishness, and cowardice that made one despair. This was the cross of Christ, this was faith facing reality. He wrote: 'Let us bring our own failures and our share in the corporate guilt of our country to the foot of the Cross and ask for strength and courage to share that Cross, and in the power of the Crucified to share in his redemptive work.'[14]

Meanwhile he himself had had a bit of fortune. He had succeeded to a great extent in ending the estrangement which had for so long existed between the diocese on the one hand, and the parishes of St. John, Wynberg, and St. Peter, Mowbray, on the other. The independence of these two parishes had been recognised by the Parliament of the Cape of Good Hope in the nineteenth century. Now they had decided to dissociate themselves from the 'Church of England in South Africa', the Church-in-Limbo which was recognised neither by the Church of England nor by the Church of the Province. They wished now to enter into a 'formal declaration of association with the Church of the Province.' The terms of the declaration still allowed them a certain measure of independence; for example they paid their own stipends, and appointed their own priests, but the Archbishop would license them. Clayton was delighted, and wrote that the Church of the Province 'would be glad of any closer association which might be attained in the future'.[15] The new arrangement was regarded as a feather in his cap.

Although certainly mellowing, he could still show flashes of his old form. S. H. Clarke, having retired from St. John's, was now living in Cape Town, and was licensed by Clayton to celebrate and preach in the diocese. Clarke was visiting 'Bishopscourt' and said to Clayton, 'I see Hickinbotham's

*As might be expected, this representation was also doomed to be abolished, and a Coloured Representative Council was established. It was reconstituted as the Coloured Persons' Representative Council in 1964. It spends money allocated to it by the white Parliament, but its legislative power is precisely zero. It has one advantage: it has given an official platform to some very forthright coloured speakers.

report on the Church of England in South Africa has just come out.' Clayton said, 'If you can't talk about something else, then don't talk at all.' Clarke, who was regarded by many as a formidable man, accepted this rudeness as one of the eccentricities of greatness.

It was in this last year of his life that Clayton gave an address which as far as one knows was unique. The submerged poetic streak was suddenly revealed. He spoke to the Clerical Society on George Herbert.[16]

He told them that few priests became famous. The Curé d'Ars was one, and George Herbert was another. Clayton found Herbert enthralling, and he was going to tell the society why. Herbert wanted the religion of a gentleman and the pleasures of a worldly life. Clayton quoted from him copiously. Herbert's poetry is nothing like the thundering of Amos and nothing like Clayton's own simple, trenchant, mordant, witty speech. It is certainly as magnificent as any Christian poetry that was ever written, but it has as well a delicate, indescribable beauty, and Clayton, who was not palpably a lover of anything delicate or indescribable, was clearly under the spell of it. Did he have to wait to re-read it until he had reached the letter H in his library or would he take it down and read it at any time?

> When first Thou didst entice to Thee my heart,
> I thought the service brave;
> So many joys I writ down for my part,
> Besides what I might have
> Out of my stock of Natural delights,
> Augmented with thy gracious benefits.
> Both heaven and earth
> Paid me my wages in a world of mirth.

'But', said Clayton, 'the Hound of Heaven was on his track.' At first all was 'milk and sweetness', but came sicknesses that cleaved his bones. He decided to become a priest. He also decided to marry and Clayton devoted two of the pages of his script to the subject of Herbert and marriage. Then he who had written down so many joys for his part, became more and more known for his sanctity. He was patient in affliction, chaste, avoided covetousness and luxury especially in drinking, was strict in keeping his word, for otherwise how would his people believe what he preached? He thought that the vicar must be a great student of Scripture, and should know about tillage and pasturage. In spite of the affliction, which was tuberculosis, he insisted on sitting or standing or kneeling in a straight and steady posture.

Clayton said that Herbert had the 'diffident, hesitating attitude inspired by the fundamental reverence and reserve which is perhaps the most characteristic product of Anglicanism at its best'. That is strange, is it not, that this strange man whose own diffident and hesitating attitude was not easy to discover and discern, should feel so drawn to this gentle genius of long ago?

Clayton concluded with a reading of the poem 'Love', one of the most beautiful in the English language, a poem that must be read with care and solicitude, lest the hearer miss a meaning hidden in words of utmost simplicity, or not understand who is talking to whom.

Love made me welcome: yet my soul drew back,
Guilty of dust and sin.
But quick-eyed love, observing me grow slack
From my first entrance in,
Drew nearer to me, sweetly questioning
If I lacked anything.

A guest, I answered, worthy to be here:
Love said, you shall be he.
I, the unkind, ungrateful? Ah, my dear,
I cannot look on thee.
Love took my hand and smiling did reply,
Who made the eyes but I?

Truth, Lord, but I have marred them: let my shame
Go where it doth deserve.
And know you not, saith love, who bore the blame?
My dear, then I will serve.
You must sit down, saith love, and taste my meat.
So I did sit and eat.

Alas, that one was not there.

Two days later he returned to the realities of the present, and lectured on 'The Right of Association' to a meeting of the Law Society. It was in fact a talk on freedom and the State, the subject that was always in his mind. He said his talk would be amateurish, but of course it was not.

He spoke of the manifold associations into which men enter:

'Whether or not a particular country is a home of freedom depends mainly on the attitude of the State towards these associations. The individual citizen does not find his interest and the really effective influences that minister to the development of his character, in direct association with the State. Perhaps he did so in the City States of Greece, provided, of course, that he was a freeman and not a slave. But in the larger modern State he cannot do so. It is the mark of a totalitarian State that it wants him to do so. In so far as it is successful it produces a population of yes-men. That is what the totalitarian State desires.'

But a Christian could not desire it, nor could he be a totalitarian. If the State existed, as he believed, to make it possible for man to lead the good life, then it should encourage the growth of these associations and give them as much freedom as possible. No Christian could accept the State as his ultimate authority. His ultimate authority is and must be Christ. 'But if a man is led by his conscience to break the laws of the State he must be prepared to take the consequences, as the early Christians were.'

Clayton then went on to make a statement of the kind which is utterly incomprehensible to the devout Nationalist. He said that it was true and quite likely that an individual in a multiracial society might belong to some association of which the members did in fact belong to his particular racial group only. 'But as he grows in general culture and his character develops and his interests widen, he desires to associate himself with people who have the same interests whatever be the racial group to which they belong.'

Clayton said he did not want to discuss the rights and wrongs of apartheid. But compulsory apartheid meant a limitation of freedom for all races. The State was in fact trying to rule over at least two, and probably three or four different nations at the same time. On these nations it imposed many laws which were common to them all; but certain laws applied to certain nations and not to others. 'Thus in relation to one nation it is a democracy and in relation to the others it is not. It is all very odd.'

Clayton declared that the only association that could rightly be outlawed as subversive was one which set out to break existing laws, not one which set out to get them changed. He was in fact protesting against the growing authoritarianism of the South African Government. The Communist Party of South Africa had already been outlawed. He did not live to see the outlawing of the African National Congress and the Pan–African Congress, nor the passing of a law which made the continuance of the multiracial Liberal Party impossible. But he could see clearly the direction in which the tide was flowing, and he could see no sign whatever of its ebbing. This lecture, and the presidential address to the Christian Council, and the talk '*Quo Vadis?*', are the utterances of a man whose understanding of South Africa was deep indeed, for all that he had been born an Englishman.[17] As has been pointed out already in this biography, this man, who was thought by some to be insensitive to the feelings of others, never offended South Africans by speaking of England as home. Nor was he capable of putting his hand on his heart and saying with loyal emotion, 'I am now a true South African.' In this very lecture he stated the bald facts, 'I am English by birth. I am South African by nationality.' The truth was that he was interested in neither birth nor nationality.

It was now time for his holiday. For some years Sir Evelyn and Lady Baring had asked him to go to them at Nairobi. Sir Evelyn had been the British High Commissioner when Clayton arrived at 'Bishopscourt' and they had often been his only two guests to dinner. After dinner they would go and sit sedately in the big drawing-room. But if the storytelling mood was on him, great things lay ahead. 'His feet would go up beside him on the sofa, and he would lie on one elbow like a Roman emperor, while he shook all over with laughter till the tears ran down his face . . . in these moods he loved gossip and was not above a little malice.'

The Barings had not seen Clayton for four years, and thought he looked tired and a great deal older. They had a small chapel reached by a very steep attic stair, and thought it would be too much for him. But although handicapped by gout, increasing weight, and his chronic unsureness of balance, he climbed the stairs with grunts and puffing and a great deal of noise to say Mass for them, 'nearly every morning'. Lady Baring wrote to me, 'Once in the Chapel he became a different being.' That was true; that was one of the occasions when one forgot the malice and irritability, or rather when one learned to see them as the excrescences on the oak.

There were young people in the house, but he did not have much to say to them. 'During luncheon he would sit with a detached and abstracted air, taking no part in the give and take of a family party.' In the afternoons he would like to be taken for a drive. He had no eye for either scenery or wild animals, but would like to talk, very often about his early life.

The Barings thought he was a great man. Lady Baring concluded her notes with these words: 'Spiritually, he gave one the feeling of being founded upon a Rock, and a rock of granite with its foundations deep in the sea. When he spoke about God, you felt as if your gaze was being lifted to search the far horizon and you were drawn into his own humility and worship.'

Soon after Clayton's return he set out to visit the diocese of Damaraland, a diocese of vast distances and inferior roads. From that he returned very tired. On 1 October 1956, he wrote to the Dean of the Province, then Bishop Cullen of Grahamstown, sending him his resignation as Archbishop of Cape Town and Metropolitan of the Province. 'I shall be 72 in December, and though my health is quite good, good enough for me to have been able to fulfil all my engagements during the last few years, I am conscious that as I get older I become less capable of assimilating new ideas and of initiating movements, and it seems to me that this is not good for the Province.' Clayton expressed the hope that he would retire after Easter 1957, and asked that his letter should be sent to all the bishops. He added a private letter of his own, saying that he thought a Metropolitan should not continue long after 70 unless there were special circumstances, and he knew of no such special circumstances in his case.

The bishops knew of special circumstances. The crisis in the relations between the Church of the Province and the Nationalist Government was worsening. Who could speak and lead with such authority as the Archbishop? Cullen wrote that the younger bishops would find it 'cause for great alarm' if Clayton were to resign in the immediate or not-quite-so-immediate future. He added his own opinion: 'I should feel great alarm if you went just now.'[18]

That same month Clayton tendered his resignation to the Episcopal Synod. Bishop Vernon Inman of Natal wrote later in *The Vineyard*,[19] 'We were filled with dismay.' Inman believed that Clayton 'was genuinely surprised' that the bishops so valued his leadership. After a frank expression of his misgivings, Clayton withdrew his resignation. One cannot record these events without a certain wonder. The bishops knew all his failings, his irritabilities, his capacity for crushing rebukes. They knew that he could tell to Bishop A a malicious story about Bishop B, and to Bishop B a malicious story about Bishop A. But to them too he gave the feeling that he was founded upon a Rock. One might risk repeating the observation that we are fearfully and wonderfully made.

Inman knew the ambivalence well. Clayton had stayed with him the year before when the Episcopal Synod had met in Pietermaritzburg. At breakfast one morning some hadedahs flew over the roof, uttering their unmistakable cries, which sound like 'ha, ha, hadehah'. The Zulus call them *inkankane*, a name which is also onomatopoeic. Clayton asked, 'What is that?' Young Paul Inman, a boy of 15, said 'That's a hadedah, your Grace.' 'What's a hadedah?' 'A hadehah is an ibis, your Grace.' Clayton said with impatience, 'Nonsense, that's not an ibis. An ibis doesn't make a noise like that.' 'I'm sorry your Grace, but it's an ibis.' Bishop Inman stood up and said, 'Your Grace, there's only one way to settle this. I'll go and get Roberts's book of birds.' In his study Inman looked it up first just to make sure that his son was right. He came back and put down the book at the open page. 'It would appear that Paul is right, your Grace.' Clayton read what Roberts had to say about the hadedah. There it was on the printed page. Reason triumphed over emotion. He put down the book and said to the boy, 'Dear son Paul, forgive an old man for being so stupid. I'm sorry.' Neither father nor son ever forgot it. And why should they have? Such apologies were rarer than any bird.

The last charge to the Diocesan Synod of Cape Town. The date, 5 December 1956. Unknown to Clayton and the congregation, the police had started in the early hours of the morning on the mammoth task of arresting 156 South Africans on charges of treason. Their trial was to last four years, after which the court discharged them all. To most observers the whole trial was something between tragedy and farce. To the Nationalists it was a splendid example of *kragdadigheid*.

Had Clayton known of these events, he would no doubt have considered them in his charge. But he announced that he would devote it to the affairs of the coloured people of his diocese, for it seemed to him that of all the population groups they were suffering most. He himself did not believe that the policy of apartheid held much promise for the African people, but he was prepared to recognise the honesty of some who did. But the policy could hold no promise for the coloured people at all. The entrenched franchise had now gone, replaced by the separate roll. But already there was a move to abolish the separate roll for Africans. Then what security was there?

Clayton then dealt with the Group Areas Act, the law which would move many hundreds of thousands of coloured people to separate residential and trading areas. He believed that the proclamation of Group Areas on a racial basis was wrong.

'I do not believe in compulsory segregation at all. I think there can be too much planning, too much regimentation, and I think it is bad for all of us, but especially bad for those who carry it out. For power over other people's lives brings with it terrible temptations. Don't you all know how easily the boss can become a bully?

'But here in the Cape Peninsula what I believe bad everywhere is especially bad. . . . It involves compulsory moving of thousands from their homes. It involves the dislocation of trade, real chaos about schools, and churches also. Though, with regard to churches, I say without hesitation that the Church is going to follow her people wherever they go. But it will be difficult and expensive.'

Clayton returned to the franchise. The Group Areas Act would bear down harder on those who had no votes, 'or whose votes can be discounted because their names are not on the common roll'.

He said that he did not believe that the Government wanted to cause hardship to the coloured people or any other people. But they were obsessed with the idea of apartheid. Clayton gave two reasons for thinking that the worst would not happen: one was the difficulty of implementation, the other was the uneasiness of the N.G.K. He said, 'I hope this is not mere wishful thinking.'

'And I want to end with a word to my non-European brethren. Don't let yourselves get converted to apartheid. And try to get a Christian sense of proportion. I know it isn't easy. But it is true that what really matters about you is not what you possess, or what others think of you; but what you are yourself in the sight of God. Who steals my purse steals trash. Who steals my vote steals something that is not much better. But if a man impairs your integrity, he has done you real harm. If you grow bitter, if hatred or desire for revenge comes into your heart, then you have let him do you real harm. Don't let that happen.' He ended, as always, with encouragement. 'Easter Day follows Good Friday; but without Good Friday there would be no Easter Day. So lift up your hearts.'

And their hearts were lifted up because of him. He said to them in this same charge that he had tried to make his own motto that which had been laid down for him by an African priest: 'The Bishop has no colour.' Well, there could be no doubt that he had succeeded. He had no colour, he had no pride of race, he had identified himself with the country of his adoption and its people. His heart went out especially to his African and coloured people, in his own controlled way. And they knew it. Though for many of them life was an endless struggle, their hearts were lifted up because of him.

It was Christmas time. He wrote to Foster van der Byl, Rector of Caledon: 'If I shall not be more nuisance than I am worth, I should like to come and help in your parish this Christmas.' He arrived on Christmas Eve, and celebrated in several parts of the parish on Christmas morning, but he would not stay for Mrs. van der Byl's excellent dinner because he wanted his driver to have Christmas dinner with his family at 'Bishopscourt'. Van der Byl had not married until he was in his forties, and Clayton had said to him, 'I think that as you want to be married it would be a good thing if I moved you to another parish. I do not think it would be right for you to ask your wife to come and live in the home which you have already made. If you move into a new home, then she can make it for you, and that is how it should be.'

Van der Byl had what one might call an unusual experience. He had gone to stay at 'Bishopscourt' with some trepidation, having been warned to keep quiet at breakfast. But when he came out of chapel Clayton roared at him, 'Good morning, Reverend.' At the breakfast table Clayton read in the newspaper that an 'Onion Queen' had been crowned at Villiersdorp, and he proceeded with great gusts of laughter to suggest rules for electing a 'Synod Queen'. He also made suggestions as to which ladies of the diocese might be chosen, suggestions which Van der Byl did not think it wise to pass on. One need hardly say that Van der Byl was one of the priests who felt what amounted to a veneration for his bishop.

So the year 1956 came to its end. But before it did so Clayton took an important decision. He decided to join a number of leading South Africans in establishing a Treason Trial Defence Fund, and in appealing for its generous support. The establishing of the Defence Fund was a knife-edge issue. There were many white people – what one might call good sound reasonable people – who could not understand why any decent person should want to defend anyone charged with treason. In 1956 the powers of the Government and the security police were so great, and were used so ruthlessly, that reasonable people became fearful people instead. Collecting in Durban from the city's advocates, I was asked by more than one of them, 'But if you want to defend accused persons, why choose to defend those accused of treason?' That English proverb which is serviceable in fear-ridden countries was on many lips: 'Where there's smoke, there must be fire.' And of course there was fire, of the same kind that burned down the Reichstag.

One can say one thing about Clayton's action. If another man had taken it – for example his successor Joost de Blank – there would have been considerable Anglican dissatisfaction. But Clayton was at the height of his authority. Many Anglicans considered that if he took such an action, it must be justified. And those who disagreed with him would do so privately.

His reasons for supporting the Fund were unimpeachable. A man is innocent until he is proved guilty. Further it was in the interest of the good name of South Africa that every accused person should have and should be seen to have a fair trial. Lastly, he was confident that the Fund would be wisely administered. He showed his confidence by becoming the Honorary President of the Cape Town branch of it.[20]

The S.P.G. wrote to him expressing their appreciation of his action and that of Bishop Reeves in supporting the Fund.[21] He in his turn wrote to the S.P.G. and said that he was wholly in agreement with its decision not to issue any appeal for the Fund, 'I don't think there is anything for you to do in the matter except to say your prayers.'[22]

30

'We cannot obey this law'

The trial now began of the 156 people charged with treason. The Government would not sit idle while people, some dangerous, some foolish, prepared the way for that anarchy which would enable the Red international conspiracy to gain possession of this shining citadel of Christian civilisation. Among the most notable accused were Albert Lutuli, president of the African National Congress, and Professor Z. K. Matthews of Fort Hare, both avowed Christians.

While the Minister of Justice and the security police watched out for plotters, the Minister of Native Affairs moved on with the master plan. He and his colleagues had already made interracial marriage and interracial sex illegal. They had already legislated for the establishment of separate residential and trading areas. They now announced that they would legislate to establish separate universities. But Verwoerd – with the full support of the Cabinet – intended to go further. The association of different races had long been anathema to him. He now announced new legislation to make other forms of association illegal. This was the Native Laws Amendment Bill. Its famous clause 29 (c) was designed to make association in 'church, school, hospital, club or other institution, or place of entertainment', difficult if not impossible. It became known as the 'church clause'.

State and Church (or at least part of the Church) were moving into a confrontation. This particular confrontation has taken different forms, but it has continued until now, and shows no signs of abating. It has been accompanied by increasing estrangement between the English and the Dutch Reformed Churches.

On 9 January 1957, *Die Kerkbode* published an editorial entitled 'Our Church and Its Sister-churches'. It said that the N.G.K. was in an unenviable position in relationship with the English Protestant churches, which were spreading propaganda against South Africa overseas. In the press there were almost daily reports of the extremely unfortunate attitude of most of the English church leaders. 'Educated in England, unacquainted with the history, language and ideals of our nation, and totally lacking in feeling for the circumstances of our country, these men give themselves the right to say precisely *who* and *what* we are. How can they criticise us without even knowing us?'

Die Kerkbode was angry with Cecil Wood, the Rector of Hermanus. He had given a lecture under the aegis of the Black Sash, in which he attributed the silence of the N.G.K. to its support of the Government. He described the N.G.K. as the Nationalist Party at prayer. It was wrong, wrote *Die Kerkbode*, that this silence, which stemmed from the N.G.K. rule of *afsydigheid* (aloofness, non-alignment), could be interpreted in this way. 'We are being driven further into two separate camps which treat each other as opponents instead of co-workers.'

The effect of clause 29 (c) of the Native Laws Amendment Bill was precisely that. It provided *inter alia* that no church established in the 'white' part of a town after the beginning of 1938, and which admitted *an African*, could be conducted without the permission of the Minister of Native Affairs, given with the concurrence of the local authority. Similar permission was required for any meeting, assembly, or gathering attended by *an African* on church premises.

It should be noted that in 1937, under the United Party government of Hertzog and Smuts, an amendment was made to the Natives (Urban Areas) Act that any institution established after the beginning of 1938, which catered *mainly for Africans*, required this same twofold approval, and by 'institution' was meant any church, school, place of entertainment, hospital, club, and so on. But Verwoerd now sought control over any institution that admitted *an African*.[1]

The reasons were simple. There was the usual one of law and order. But one of the two deep underlying reasons was the anger and resentment aroused in many a white breast by the sight and sound of Africans congregating, talking, singing, shouting, dancing, in 'white' streets. This anger and resentment was often related to the emotion of fear: a congregation of Africans in a 'white' area filled many white people with anxiety, more especially if it occurred at night. This is the reason for the often-heard demand that the white suburbs should be 'white by night'. Of all those who clamoured for it, one of the most honest was Verwoerd, who was one of the few white South Africans of means who kept no black servants at all. The other deep underlying reason was the anger aroused by the holding of racially mixed parties in white neighbourhoods by white 'liberalists'.

The publication of the Native Laws Amendment Bill evoked protest from the English churches throughout South Africa. The first church body to react was the Cape Peninsula Church Council, of which the Church of the Province was a member. The action committee of the Christian Council of South Africa asked the Prime Minister to receive a deputation; he referred them to the Minister of Native Affairs. These protests were later to be repeated by the Methodist Church of South Africa, the Presbyterian Church of South Africa, the Baptist Union of South Africa, and the Seventh Day Adventist Church Conference. The Roman Catholic Archbishops of Durban, Pretoria, and Cape Town stated that their churches would remain open to members of all racial groups, regardless of the consequences. The Minister of Native Affairs was later to accuse the churches of using the appeal to freedom of worship as a 'smokescreen for their anti-Government propaganda', and to state that this very propaganda had made the granting of an interview purposeless.[2]

Whether Verwoerd was shaken by this wave of protest, one will probably never know. It is doubtful whether any biographer will ever tell us. He showed a granite face to the world, and he had said that the Afrikaner must be as granite against those who wished to destroy him. He therefore gave the outward impression of complete confidence and complete determination. Yet one may be permitted to question its reality. For the first time in his career he complained, even after the publication of the Bill, that people had protested before they clearly understood the Government's intentions. He publicly thanked those bodies who brought their doubts to him, rather than exert pressure by way of extensive publicity and agitation.[3]

Surely he must have been shaken. The Christian churches have always taken seriously the injunction of Jesus to go and teach all nations. He had told his disciples that all power had been given to him in heaven and in earth. Was Jesus wrong then? Had some special power been given to the Minister of Native Affairs in the Union of South Africa, so that he could say to a Church, 'I order, with the concurrence of the local authority, that you should admit no African to worship'? Was a State, purporting to be Christian, empowered by God to forbid the Christian Church to admit any person, and what was more, on grounds of his race? Or on the grounds that this Christian State had decided that this black Christian should worship only in a black Church? And what were the Government's intentions, if they were not these?

If Verwoerd therefore, in the most private recesses of his self, felt any uncertainty as to the rightness or wisdom of what he was proposing to do, his uncertainty was about to be increased.

In the 73rd year of his life, Clayton contemplated an action which was by no means pleasing to him. For the first time in his life he contemplated, not only defiance of the law but the urging of others to defy the law, the penalties for which were extremely heavy.* Clayton summoned to meet him at 'Bishopscourt' on Shrove Tuesday, 5 March 1957, Archibald Cullen, Bishop of Grahamstown and Dean of the Province, Ambrose Reeves, Bishop of Johannesburg, Robert Selby Taylor, Bishop of Pretoria, and Vernon Inman, Bishop of Natal. This was a committee appointed by Episcopal Synod in 1956 to meet in the case of a crisis of this kind.

Clayton spent a good part of the week ending 2 March in drafting a letter from the bishops of the Church of the Province to the Prime Minister. He had written many letters in his life, but he spent unusual time and care over this one, because it was the most important he had ever written. He had preached many times on the text 'We ought to obey God rather than men', but had not looked with a very favourable eye on those who thought that was what they were doing. Now he was about to do it himself.

Clayton did not adopt this course cheerfully. There was none of the

*See chapter 26, page 224.

rejoicing that had filled Peter and John and all their company when these two had said,'For we cannot but speak the things which we have seen and heard.' He was contemplating the doing of something for which in one way his whole life had prepared him, and for which in another way it had not. He was going to do something that he had never, except in these closing years of his life, thought that he would do.

Well might he have gone about this unsought duty with great gravity, even heaviness of spirit. He was proposing to resist the powers that be, and had not St. Paul written, 'Whosoever therefore resisteth the power, resisteth the ordinance of God; and they that resist shall receive to themselves damnation'? But after all these years Clayton had come to the opposite conclusion, that he was more likely to receive damnation if he did not resist the power.*

There was another reason for his gravity. It seems clear that he believed that the Attorney-General would have him charged with incitement, and that he would go to prison. The idea of going to prison filled him with a revulsion that was almost fear. Cowdry was a prison chaplain, and had often told Clayton of the horrors of prison life, the bucket for urination and defecation, and the prison food, a cold grey mess in a greasy dish. Would he be allowed to celebrate and to receive? Daily, as his custom was? Would the gout be worse in prison? Would they call him 'Your Grace' or 'Clayton' or just 'you'? It was his practice to visit Roeland Street Gaol once a year, and these visits depressed him greatly.

He rang Ted Langmore, Rector of St. Anne's, Maitland, a man very dear to him. He said to him, 'If you haven't anyone better to preach on Quinquagesima Sunday, I'll come,' and he added, 'Could you put up with me for supper?' Langmore was devoted to Clayton. It was he who told me the story of the woman parishioner who, having unsuccessfully reported him to Clayton, went back to Langmore and said, 'I am going to report your Archbishop to the Archbishop of Westminster.' Clayton should have laughed his great laugh, but according to Langmore he was not amused.

Clayton arrived early at St. Anne's, Maitland, but he would not have a drink. According to Langmore he looked as though the whole weight of the world was on his shoulders. He said to Langmore, 'Ted, next Sunday I may be in prison.' Langmore exclaimed, 'Your Grace!' and Clayton said, 'It's true. I have written a letter and it will not be liked by the Government, who might send me to prison.' Langmore said to him, 'If you go to prison, I think that the majority of us would follow.' Clayton said,'I don't want to go to prison. I am much too old. But if I have to go I'll go.' Langmore was near weeping. They had supper, but Clayton would still not have a drink. At evensong he preached an evangelical sermon of the utmost simplicity. Most of the sermons of his last few months were of this kind. Langmore parted with him that evening in great anxiety. He said to me, 'I think he was suffering. It was in his face. He did not like to challenge the powers that be.'

*The *New English Bible* is much less ferocious. It says that those who resist 'have themselves to thank for the punishment they will receive'.

It seems to me extremely unlikely that the Government would have sent Clayton and the bishops to prison. Their *kragdadigheid* was not quite so *kragdadig* as that. Yet as the law stood, they would have had to do it. There was only one thing to do and that was to modify the law. I think Hitler would have sent Clayton to prison or executed him, but not Strijdom and Verwoerd. They would have shrunk from the prospect of sending so many church leaders, not only Anglicans, and undoubtedly very many of their followers to prison. In any case there were practical difficulties. There would not have been enough room for them. The weapon that Clayton proposed to wield proved to be very powerful, but he was never to know it.

On Tuesday the four bishops arrived. The main discussion took place on Ash Wednesday, the first day of Lent. They were at once in agreement that the law as set out in clause 29 (c) could not be obeyed, and that the Prime Minister should be notified. All that was left to do was to approve Clayton's letter. This was done with a few modifications. The letter read thus:

Dear Mr. Prime Minister,

We, Bishops of the Church of the Province of South Africa, are approaching you rather than the Minister of Native Affairs because we believe that the issues raised in Clause 29 (c) of the Native Laws Amendment Bill cannot be regarded merely as Native affairs. It appears to us that as far as the Anglican Church is concerned, churches and congregations in every urban area within the Union, even those mainly attended by Europeans, will be affected by this clause. Further, it is our belief that the Clause raises the issue of religious freedom and more particularly that of freedom of worship, and we venture to submit that this is a wider issue than that of Native Affairs only.

We desire to state that we regard the above-mentioned clause as an infringement of religious freedom in that it makes conditional on the permission of the Minister of Native Affairs

(*a*) The continuance in existence of any church or parish constituted after January 1st 1938 in an urban area except in a location which does not exclude Native Africans from public worship;

(*b*) the holding of any service in any church in an urban area except in a location to which a Native African would be admitted if he presented himself;

(*c*) the attendance of any Native African at any synod or church assembly held in an urban area outside a location.

The Church cannot recognise the right of an official of a secular government to determine whether or where a member of the Church of any race (who is not serving a sentence which restricts his freedom of movement) shall discharge his religious duty of participation in public worship or to give instructions to the minister of any congregation as to whom he shall admit to membership of that congregation.

Further, the Constitution of the Church of the Province of South Africa provides for the synodical government of the Church. In such synods, bishops, priests and laymen are represented without distinction of race or colour. Clause 29 (c) makes the holding of such synods dependent upon the permission of the Minister of Native Affairs.

We recognise the great gravity of disobedience to the law of the land. We believe that obedience to secular authority, even in matters about which we differ in opinion, is a command laid upon us by God. But we are commanded to render unto Caesar the things which be Caesar's, and to God the things that are God's. There are therefore some matters which are God's and not Caesar's, and we believe that the matters dealt with in Clause 29 (c) are among them.

It is because we believe this that we feel bound to state that if the Bill were to become law in its present form we should ourselves be unable to obey it or to counsel our clergy and people to do so.

We therefore appeal to you, Sir, not to put us in a position in which we have to choose between obeying our conscience and obeying the law of the land.

We have the honour to remain, Sir,

Yours faithfully,
(signed on behalf of the Bishops of the
Church of the Province of South Africa)
✠ GEOFFREY CAPETOWN
Archbishop & Metropolitan.[4]

After the bishops had decided on the final draft, Clayton took Reeves aside (by the arm, which was unusual for him) and said, 'Reeves, I don't want to go to prison. I'm an old man. I don't want to end my days in prison. But I'll go if I have to.'

It was therefore a sober and solemn occasion, quite apart from the fact that it was Ash Wednesday. The bishops flew from Cape Town by early planes on the Thursday morning. They had already said goodbye to their archbishop, but to their surprise he came down at six in the morning to see them off, dressed in a towelling-robe over his pyjamas, and black stockings with holes in them. He bade them all farewell very warmly.

After Mass and breakfast Clayton busied himself in his study. One of his tasks was to sign the typed letter for delivery to the Prime Minister. After lunch he dictated letters to Cowdry, from half-past one until about a quarter to three. At about three o'clock Cowdry heard him singing and moving about his study, which he always did very noisily. Down in the garden below the study Mr. Ackerman the head gardener and his assistant saw the Archbishop at the window. His head was out of the window and he was looking down at the ground. This was not unusual. At other times he would stretch out his arms and put his hands on the sides of the window frame. When he did these things Ackerman would say to himself, 'The Archbishop has a lot of work and he is thinking.' On this afternoon of 7 March Ackerman saw the Archbishop leave the window and, soon after, heard the sound of a chair moving, and what seemed to be books falling, followed by a cry. But these things were not unusual, and Ackerman thought nothing of them. At twenty past three Cowdry went to the study, to remind the Archbishop that he must leave at half past three for a committee meeting of the Mission to Moslems. The Archbishop was lying on the floor between his desk and the bookcase. Cowdry thought that he was playing a game, and said, 'Get up, your Grace.' Then with great shock he realised that the Archbishop was dead.

He called Mrs. Shackleford, the housekeeper, and they loosened the clothing at his throat, of course to no avail. Cowdry then telephoned the doctor, and the committee of the Mission to Moslems. Canon Roseveare, a member of the committee, came at once, and they said together the office for the Commendation of the Soul.

> Go forth, O Christian Soul, on your journey from this World.
> In the name of God the Almighty Father who created you. Amen.
> In the name of Jesus Christ who suffered for you. Amen.
> In the name of the Holy Spirit who strengthened you. Amen.
> In communion with the Holy Apostles, Confessors and Martyrs, and all the blessed Saints, and aided by Angels and Archangels, and all the armies of the Heavenly host. Amen.
> May your portion this day be in the new Jerusalem, the abode of peace, and your dwelling in the heavenly Zion. Amen.

By the following morning the whole country knew that the Archbishop was dead. The tributes were warm and numerous. One will be enough. It was contained in a statement issued by the Revd. P. J. van der Westhuyzen on behalf of the N.G.K.:

'The Dutch Reformed Church shares the irreparable loss in the passing of Dr. Geoffrey Clayton.

'Besides [having] contacts with him that were the privilege of individuals, representatives of the whole Church met him on the occasions when he addressed our Synod.

'No one who was present will ever forget it. The impression of humility and greatness, of good humour and piety, remains a lasting memory.

'Naturally he did not share all the views of our Church. Sometimes he said so. But always he was admired for his clearly expressed moderate views, and above all for the way he presented the oneness of Christ that binds together the different nations of the Christian Church.'[5]

The leading Nationalist newspaper, *Die Burger*, did not find itself able to be so generous. After a formal account of Clayton's life and death, it wrote: 'Dr. Clayton caused a sensation when he expressed himself in favour of 'unashamedly English schools'. He also frequently identified himself with liberalist agitation against Apartheid policy.'

The Government of South Africa, unable to ignore Clayton in life, ignored him in death. Nothing spoke more eloquently of the times in which he had lived than the fact that at the funeral of one of the most eminent of all South Africans, and of a man who had been the head of one of the largest churches in South Africa, the Government did not see fit to send anyone to attend. Neither the Government nor the Governor-General was represented.

Of all the tributes that were published, not one said as much as Rouse's few words when Clayton left Johannesburg in 1948, 'My heart is turned to water.' So were the hearts of many turned now. Who would now defend them?

31

Verwoerd Bows to the Wind

Bishop Cullen of Grahamstown, by virtue of his office as Dean of the Province, was now the Acting Metropolitan. He telephoned to Cowdry and instructed him to add the name of the Dean to the Archbishop's letter, so that the Prime Minister might have someone to reply to.

On 8 March Cowdry sent the Archbishop's letter to the Prime Minister, adding the name of the Dean. He himself wrote: 'Since the enclosed letter was dictated and signed by the Archbishop of Cape Town, His Grace has departed this life.'

But the Prime Minister did not answer either of the letters. He referred them to the Minister of Native Affairs. Nor did Verwoerd answer them; he instructed his private secretary to do so. Mr. Barnard wrote:

'The Minister of Native Affairs regrets that the bishops of the Church of the Province of South Africa saw fit to initiate and subscribe to a campaign in the Press, and even to threaten disobedience to the laws of the land, without either awaiting the second reading of the Bill to discover the scope and intent of the clause concerned or first seeking in a spirit of Christian goodwill the opportunity for clarification, and if necessary amendment of the wording.

'The Bishops of the Church of the Province of South Africa are, however, advised to desist from further participation in this most unnecessary agitation and to await the full exposition during the second-reading debate of what was always intended and how the clause is to be redrafted to eliminate all possibility of suspicion and misunderstanding.'[1]

There was much acrimonious press debate over the actions of the Archbishop, the Prime Minister, and the Minister of Native Affairs over the church clause itself. *Die Transvaler* asserted that no inroad on the freedom of worship was intended, and commented:

'As long as liberalistic* bishops and canons, professors, students and politicians can freely attend church and hold meetings and socials together with non-Europeans, apartheid will be infringed in its marrow. It is high time for this to end.'

The debate in Parliament was equally acrimonious. Verwoerd now intro-

*Of all these words, *liberal*, *liberalist*, *liberalistic*, I have never found out which is most odious, and have therefore laid claim to them all. I would even accept *liberalistical*.

duced a second version of the restrictive clause. In doing so he made much of two arguments. The first was that the Churches had raised no objections to the Native Laws Amendment Act in 1937, which said that no person shall conduct, outside a location, Native village, Native hostel, or area approved by the Minister, any church, school, or other institution or any place of entertainment which was not in existence at the commencement of the Native Laws Amendment Act in 1937, mainly for the benefit of Natives, without approval of the Minister given with the concurernce of the local authority concerned. Why did they not object then? He agreed that he had in the first version of clause 29 (c) introduced new provisions into the law, making it apply to clubs and other types of gatherings and to all churches attended by Natives, even though it should be only one Native who attends. It would be seen then that there was no extension of principle, only of scope. He had amended the law so that it would apply to clubs also, 'to ensure that they sin* as little against segregation as the churches'.[2]

Verwoerd's second argument was that people like the late Archbishop of Cape Town persisted in saying that clause 29 (c) made religious freedom 'conditional on the permission of the Minister of Native Affairs'. But the Minister had to have the concurrence of the local authority. If the local authority said No and he said Yes, then the local authority would be the final arbiter. 'It will be clear from this to honourable members how distorted and unreasonable these attacks are because they fail completely to appreciate this type of fact.' This was the kind of argument in which Verwoerd excelled. It left out of account the fact that Clayton and the bishops had not thought that the local authority had any more right to control church attendance than the Minister himself.

Verwoerd condemned the propagandists who were saying that by introducing a new version of the controversial clause, he was trying 'to water down the clause'. All that he had done was to show a 'willingness to draft it in full detail, however long it may become'. He did not criticise the Churches; some church leaders and members agreed with him. He read parts of two letters, written in English, to prove this. He was astonished, however, that the Roman Catholic Church had intervened, when in Spain and Colombia, Protestant worship was subject to the permission of the Roman Catholic governments. If it was a sin that people of different races should worship in different churches, why was it not a sin for people of the same race to worship in different churches? Were the church leaders out for vengeance, 'because they no longer have Bantu education in their hands?' He quoted Vernon Inman, Bishop of Natal, who had used the words 'the devilish device known as apartheid'. Were those the words of a Christian or a politician? Verwoerd praised the Afrikaans churches which 'did not allow themselves to become implicated'.[3]

On 9 March the *Cape Argus* reported that officials of the Native Affairs

*I have also read the Afrikaans version of *Hansard*. The Minister used the word *sondig*, which means 'sin' or 'offend'. One would not therefore know if the Minister meant to use the extremely strong expression, to 'sin' against apartheid.

Department were re-examining the controversial clause to see 'whether it expressed precisely the intentions of the Minister of Native Affairs'. The fact is that the clause had expressed precisely those intentions, but the Bishops' letter had introduced a doubt as to whether those intentions could safely be carried out. Accordingly Verwoerd on 21 March tabled an amended clause, which differed from the original in these ways. First, the Church concerned would be given a stated, reasonable time to make representations. Secondly, the Minister would consider the availability or otherwise of alternative facilities. Thirdly, the Minister would not direct that no African might attend any church service or function in a 'white' area unless in his opinion Africans were creating a nuisance, or that it was undesirable that Africans should be present in the numbers in which they ordinarily attend. Then came the most important amendment of all. *If the Minister's notice were disobeyed, it would be the African worshipper, not the church, that would be guilty of an offence.*[4]

Verwoerd went on to reveal his hatred of interracial association. He condemned those people in Pietermaritzburg and Durban who were trying to develop multiracial clubs. He said that in view of the attitude of the Liberal Party towards race questions, 'it is not at all unnecessary for Parliament to take steps timeously to curb these activities of theirs'.*

'We find that there are Whites who take pleasure in arranging special social gatherings where Whites and non-Whites mix freely, not because they feel the need for contact but because they like to demonstrate.... They even throw open the doors and windows so that everyone can see what is going on. They allow Whites and non-Whites to lean out of the windows to annoy the neighbours. That is what has been happening.... There are, for instance, areas where nobody in the whole neighbourhood would think of doing such things, except for one liberalist who does them deliberately.'[5]

Towards the end of March a Commission appointed by the Federal Council of the N.G.K. (that is the Council of the N.G. churches of the Cape, the Transvaal, the Orange Free State, and Natal) drew up an eight-point statement setting out its views on the original clause 29 (c). The statement was sound and forthright.

1. The Gospel of Jesus Christ emanates from God to all mankind and is subject to no human limitations.

2. The task is laid on the Church of Christ, in obedience to the Head of the Church, to proclaim the Gospel throughout the world and to all peoples.

3. The right to determine who, when, *where*† and to whom the Gospel shall be proclaimed is exclusively in the competence of the Church.

4. It is the duty of the State, as the servant of God, to allow *full*† freedom to the Church in the execution of its divine calling and to

*Nevertheless the Government allowed the Liberal Party to continue for eleven more years before making the interracial political parties illegal.

†These two words are italicised for reasons which will appear later.

respect the sovereignty of the Church in its own sphere.

5. When the State lays down provisions which limit the attendance of services or *bona fide* religious gatherings arranged by the Church, it affects the freedom of religion and the sovereignty of the Church.

6. Therefore it is to the benefit of the Church and the State that each should confine itself strictly to the task which through the Word of God is entrusted to it, and the Church is called upon to warn the State of possible obstruction of the execution of the task of the Church.

7. For that reason we regret that we and, as far as we know, other Christian Churches originally did not devote the necessary attention to all the implications of the original Act which already in principle imposed limitations on specific church gatherings.

8. The Church acknowledges the fact that the State is called upon to act against the propagation of sedition and incitement under the cloak of religion; but nevertheless the Federal Council feels that as far as this legislation is concerned it cannot agree with the width of impact of the proposed provisions of the Bill.

The Federal Council appointed a delegation to interview the Minister of Native Affairs, who assured its members that the Bill was not intended to interfere with freedom of worship so long as the freedom was not misused. To remove all possible misunderstanding he would re-word the clause, framing it in a positive rather than a negative form.

One can only suppose that Verwoerd asked for something in return. Be that as it may, the delegation published an account of the discussion, omitting all mention of points 5, 6, 7, and 8, and omitting the word *where* in point 3, and the word *full* in point 4. By omitting the word *where* the delegation virtually capitulated to the Minister. It was the *where* that all the controversy had been about.

The Minister's second re-wording did not alter the intention of the clause in any way. Instead of directing that no African shall attend a church service in a 'white' area, he now took the power to direct that the attendance of Africans should cease as from a date specified. Why that should have satisfied any delegation is beyond one's powers to explain.

The Bill became law on 24 April 1957. It was passed by 78 votes to 47 in the Lower House, the 78 in favour being Nationalists, the 47 being members of the United and Labour Parties, and the Native Representatives.

On 14 July pastoral letters were read in all Anglican churches in South Africa, calling upon clergy and people to ignore the new clause, and to disobey any notice that might be issued by the Minister. The letters contained these words: 'Before God and with you as my witnesses, I solemnly state that not only shall I not obey any direction of the Minister of Native Affairs in this regard, but I solemnly counsel you, both clergy and people, to do likewise.'

The Acting Metropolitan wrote in *The Forum* of August 1957: 'Even though their pastoral letters only hypothetically call for disregard of directives which have not yet been signed, I know that it is with a heavy heart that each one has signed and issued his pastoral. It seems almost fantastic that such a situation should have arisen in a Christian country.'

What made the hearts of the bishops heavier was the fact that the new clause made the African and not the church the offender. Yet even then the bishops were laying themselves open to the charge that they were inciting others to break the law. And if the court should decide that the law was being broken *by way of protest*, the punishment, as we have seen, could be heavy indeed.

A week later the Catholic bishops declared that 'Catholic churches must, and shall remain open to all without regard to their racial origin'. Earlier still than this, when the second version of clause 29 (c) had been published, the Christian Council of South Africa had declared, 'We shall be forced to disregard the law.' The Methodist Church sent a telegram to the Prime Minister expressing the same sentiments, and the Joint Committee of Christian laymen of the Cape Peninsula were refused an audience by the Minister when they wished to protest in person against the clause. These protests which had been made earlier by other churches still stood, in spite of the amendments to the clause.

The so-called 'church clause' also affected schools, hospitals, clubs, and 'similar institutions'. The Group Areas Act (which did not fall under the Department of Native Affairs) was also amended to make illegal the 'occupation' by any person of any land or premises not zoned for his racial group, and 'occupation' was defined to include the presence of any person who attended any place of entertainment or partook of refreshments, in any land or premises not zoned for his racial group. The penalty for unlawful occupation was heavy, up to a fine of £200 or imprisonment for two years. It was clearly the intention of the Government to prevent social mixing whenever and wherever possible.

The Pietermaritzburg and Durban International Clubs closed down rather than seek permission to continue. The South African Institute of Race Relations decided to continue as before. The Liberal Party stated its complete opposition to the Bill; it did not intend to seek any permission to hold its meetings, and recognised further that there were members of the party who on grounds of conscience would be unable to obey the law. The National Union of Students stated that it would in no way seek the permission of the Minister to carry out its activities; it did not recognise the right of the Government to ban multiracial gatherings. Private organisations of all kinds protested against the Act. Meetings of protest were held throughout South Africa. Professor L. J. du Plessis, head of the Department of Law at the University of Potchefstroom, said that in view of the newly gained independence of Ghana and the possibility that black diplomats might be posted to South Africa, there was a need for multiracial clubs in every major city and town.[6]

It remains to be said that the editorial attitude of *Die Kerkbode* was on the whole compliant. It regretted that neither in 1937 nor in 1957 had the

Government approached the churches before legislating on church attendance. It was a riddle that 'our English brothers' had accepted the law of 1937 without a word of protest. It was satisfied that the Minister meant well. It quoted the four points which had been published by the N.G.K. delegation, but did not mention the omission of *where* in point 3 or *full* in point 4. It concluded, 'Here, as elsewhere, only good is in store when Church and State find each other in mutual respect and gracious co-operation.'[7] In its next issue *Die Kerkbode* assured its readers that the appearance of an African minister in the white N.G.K. pulpit at Pinelands was not a demonstration against the clause. 'It is an *exception* that will occur very *seldom* in our Church, but which however is also again completely *natural* in the light of the spiritual bonds that exist between us and Bantu Christians. Our church policy is not *undermined* by this, nor *renounced*, nor even *changed*, but rather *refined* to stand out in its spiritual light and clarity.' The whole editorial will repay the study of churchmen, historians, and psychologists.[8] Clayton would have read it with wonderment.

It must also be recorded that *Die Kerkbode* gave space to readers who did not share its view of the clause, the most notable of these being Dr. B. B. Keet of the N.G.K. Seminary at Stellenbosch.

The great storm finally blew itself out. The clause as it affects the churches has hardly been heard of from that day to this. On Synod Sundays in Johannesburg, Pretoria, Grahamstown, and indeed every cathedral city, crowds, sometimes very large, of Africans flock into the 'white' areas. It is not in the big cities and towns, but rather in the small towns and villages, that the white citizens would be affronted and would complain to the Minister or the local authority, of 'nuisance and excessive numbers', and so set the law in majestic operation. But the phenomenon of mixed congregations is one of the big cities and towns rather than of the small towns and villages. There is another thing to be said. The behaviour of African worshippers attending a church in a 'white 'area is invariably so modest, so courteous, and often so humble, that it would be only a mean-natured person who would lodge such a complaint, and he would earn the disapproval of many of his fellow-citizens who, while not objecting to the law in principle, would have hesitated to see it come into operation.

Whatever the cause, the letter of the bishops must be regarded as a considerable event in South African history. Verwoerd made it abundantly clear that he had not re-worded the clause because of the letter, but because of the decorous and Christian representations made to him by those who would never stoop to deliver attacks 'distorted and unreasonable'. They gave him a way out to do something which he would otherwise have found unspeakably humiliating. One thing is certain, he had no conception of the stature of the man who had written the Bishops' letter. Of Clayton's world he understood almost nothing.

On 25 October 1957, the Right Revd. Joost de Blank was enthroned as Archbishop and Metropolitan in St. George's Cathedral, Cape Town.

So the Clayton age came to its end.

32

'Let us be thankful'

There is a question often asked in South Africa. Similar questions are no doubt asked in every country by those who believe that they have some kind of duty to make their society more just, more tolerant, more merciful, that they have some kind of duty to influence or oppose or even capture the Government, so that their aims, which they believe to be just and proper, may be realised.

In South Africa this question seems – to us at least – to have a special relevance and poignancy. Were the efforts made before 1948, by people like Hoernlé and the Rheinallt Joneses, Z. K. Matthews, and A. B. Xuma and Selope Thema, Hofmeyr and Margaret Ballinger, Clayton and other leaders of the churches – were they worth making? And the efforts made between 1948 and 1957, by people like Lutuli and Mandela and Naicker, by Winifred Hoernlé and again Margaret Ballinger, by members of many organisations, by Huddleston and Reeves and again Clayton and other leaders of the churches – were they worth making?*

The asking of this question is by no means limited to people of little courage, or cynics, or the disillusioned. It is sometimes – in moments of despair – asked by people of courage also. Was it all worth while? Would it not have been better, more useful, if all these people had left South Africa, and either given their loyalty to some new country or tried to work for change in South Africa from abroad?

Some of those who read this biography might ask, of what use was Clayton's life? Did his actions or his speeches ever bring about any change in the law, except for the one occasion when Verwoerd was compelled to veer slightly from his course, and to amend a clause before he could get it enacted, and then virtually to make no use of it? Indeed it must be said with shame that the profound racial questions which now face the older churches, black power and black consciousness and black theology and black rejec-

*There are many other names. It would be impossible and uncraftsmanlike to mention them all. South Africa may well be described as a country of fear, but it is a country of courage also. I choose as a representative of men and women of courage, Mr. Peter Brown, one-time chairman of the Liberal Party of South Africa, and now in 1973 in his tenth year of banning. For over nine years his calm, clear, sensible voice has not been allowed to be heard. His offence? Unknown, locked in the breast of the Minister.

tion, are not those which are created by any government. They come from within society and from within the churches themselves, and are a consequence of the fact that the South African churches have been too much conformed to the world in which they were set, and have, many of them, for all their disapproval of the colour-bar, had one of their own.

Would not Clayton have done better if he had stayed in England, not only for the Church but for himself? Might he not have become Archbishop of Canterbury? Might he not perhaps have succeeded Temple, and given to the Church of England a primate of equal stature? Why come and waste twenty-three years of his life in South Africa, during which years he achieved nothing?

If some devout inquirer had asked Clayton this question, he would have answered it patiently. He would not have said, 'You call yourself a Christian but you do not understand the meaning of the Christian life, nor the meaning of the Cross.' He was impatient of specious argument, but patient with devout inquiry. He might have quoted the prayer of St. Ignatius de Loyola: 'Teach us . . . to labour and not to ask for any reward, save that of knowing that we do Thy will.' Roy Cowdry, using this very prayer as his text, said in a sermon preached after Clayton's death: 'The consuming passion of the late Archbishop was to be the servant of God and the servant of God's Church.'

If a man like Clayton could be said to have had a consuming passion, this was certainly it. Cowdry could say on the occasion that he had delayed in taking Synge back to 'Bishopscourt' for dinner, 'I've had enough of the old man. He's been having a tantrum and stamping his feet at me.' But Cowdry knew the old man in his role of a servant. And when one had known the old man in his role of a servant, one would have gone back to him tomorrow.

Had not Clayton thundered at the Johannesburg Synod: 'The Church is not here primarily to serve society. Its prime duty is to worship God and obey Him. . . . Let us therefore be very careful that it is God's will we are trying to obey, and that we are not merely trying to make the Church do something that we want to be done.'

Had he not said these words to the Cape Town Diocesan Synod: 'My brethren of the clergy. You set out with high ideals. You have often been disappointed. The things you wanted have not happened. Well, there was no promise that they would. There are two great commandments, the love of God and the love of neighbour. Don't try to live on the love of neighbour. . . . It is only the love of God that will save you from growing sour and cynical, or content with secular compensations. You can't live on the love of neighbour. You can live on the love of God.'

The best-known photograph of Clayton was published on the front cover of *Church News* on 20 March 1957.* It does not look like the portrait of a man whose life has been wasted, or who thought that it had been. Nor did it look like the portrait of a man who could scare the life out of priests and servers, who in solemn procession could deliver a kick at a cushion made

*See plate 12.

with piety but which was in a place where he did not want it to be. He looks the picture of benignity. There is the great bald head that contained those subtle mechanisms of genius which enabled him to speak words of such wisdom with utmost simplicity, and to recognise any form of deception or pretension. And under that the George Robey eyebrows, and the far-seeing and deep-seeing eyes. And under them the great quivering mouth that could explode into such laughter, even at his own jokes, as when he said, 'When I was ordained I made up my mind that no one should ever say, "What a nice young man." ' And then the pause. 'And no one ever did.'

Of course he was a sinner, as we all are. It would have been impossible to call him a saint. But that he was a great, strange, extraordinary man, who had chosen the task of holding up the weak and binding up the broken, and who had devoted himself faithfully to the performance of it all the days of his life, there can be no doubt. He was not noted for humility, but that he was humble was known to those who knew him. He may at times have been arrogant towards men, but in the presence of God he humbled himself as surely as those old men and women in Johannesburg who entered the churches on their hands and knees.

Let us be thankful.

Appendix

When Dr. N. M. Wells arrived at 'Bishopscourt' he described the cause of the Archbishop's death as a heart seizure. There were in the Archbishop's medical history some indications that such a thing might happen.* But it was reasonable to surmise, as many did, that his decision to defy the powers that be had played a great part in this sudden death.

The undertakers arrived to take away the Archbishop's body to prepare it for the lying-in-state in his cathedral. Cowdry had made his own decision; after preparation the body would be brought back to lie at 'Bishopscourt' that night, which it did, uncoffined, on a bed in the study. On the morning of Friday, 8 March, the coffin was brought, and the body lay in state in the 'Bishopscourt' chapel until nine o'clock that evening. A steady stream of people visited the chapel, most of them being coloured residents of the nearby village of Protea. There was no sound except for the subdued weeping of the women.

At nine o'clock the body was taken to the Cathedral, where there was an all-night vigil. Again many hundreds of people of all races filed past the coffin to pay their last respects to the great Archbishop. The funeral service was to take place at half-past ten on the Saturday, to be preceded by a Requiem Mass said by Cowdry, and to be followed by a cremation service at Maitland.

As part of his will Clayton had written instructions to be carried out after his death. These were entitled 'To Whom It May Concern', 20 August 1949.

'I desire to express my strong wish that, after my decease, no memorial be erected to me, no appeal be made for money for any such memorial, either in St. George's Cathedral, Cape Town, or anywhere else.

'As to my funeral, I desire that no hymn be sung at it which is suitable for a Saint's Day, but that the note of the service should be one of penitence.

'I should prefer to be cremated, and that my ashes should be interred somewhere where there is no Colour Bar, not in a cemetery reserved for Europeans.'

These wishes were not all observed. On 24 April of this year, 1957, his ashes were buried in the Cathedral under a flagstone bearing his name, though it might have been argued that such a memorial could not be said to have been erected. The stone bore the simple words, 'Geoffrey Hare Clayton, Archbishop of Cape Town, 1948–1957'. The ashes were interred during a service lasting only a few minutes in the presence of the bishops and the members of the Elective Assembly who had gathered to choose a new Metropolitan. The closing prayer of the service was this:

*On the advice of his doctor, Clayton gave up smoking in January 1957, because of vascular obstruction'.

'O God of the spirits of all flesh, we praise and magnify thy holy name for this his servant who has finished his course in thy faith and fear. We thank thee that thou didst not give him the spirit of fear, but of power and of love and of a sound mind; and we beseech thee to grant that we, following the good example of him who has loved and served thee here, and is now at rest, may at the last enter with him into the fullness of thine unending joy, through Christ our Lord. Amen.'

A brass was also placed in the floor of the parish church of Chesterfield, showing Clayton with folded hands. His left arm holds the primatial cross to his body, and in the top left-hand corner is the coat-of-arms of Cape Town. Round the brass run the words: 'Pray for the soul of Geoffrey Hare Clayton, Vicar of this Parish 1924–34, and latterly Archdeacon of Chesterfield, Bishop of Johannesburg 1934–48, Archbishop of Capetown 1948–57. Jesu mercy.'

His wishes in regard to his funeral and his cremation were strictly observed. It is very often the custom at funeral services, usually at the wish of relatives, for a triumphal and thankful note to be sounded. Clayton ensured that this would not happen. He had from the pulpit called himself a shop-soiled sinner, and he took seriously the words, 'The remembrance of them is grievous unto us; the burden of them is intolerable'.

After the Requiem Mass at which the celebrant was Roy Cowdry, the choir and clergy, the Dean of Cape Town Thomas Savage, Coadjutor-Bishop Sidney Lavis, and Bishop Hunter of George representing the bishops of the Province, re-entered the packed Cathedral for the office of the Burial of the Dead. The choir sang '*Domine, refugium*', the ninetieth psalm, containing those words: 'The days of our age are threescore years and ten, and though men be so strong that they come to fourscore years: yet is their strength then but labour and sorrow; so soon passeth it away, and we are gone.'

Bishop Lavis announced that there would be no address, but time would be given to the congregation to give thanks for the life of the Archbishop. The lesson was read by the Bishop of George, and was taken from the fifteenth chapter of the epistle to the Corinthians, containing these well-known words:

'Behold, I shew you a mystery; We shall not all sleep but we shall all be changed, in a moment, in the twinkling of an eye, at the last trump! for the trumpet shall sound, and the dead shall be raised incorruptible, and we shall be changed. For this corruptible must put on incorruption, and this mortal must put on immortality . . . then shall be brought to pass the saying that is written, Death is swallowed up in victory.'

Dean Savage closed the service with prayers, but the most moving moment came after them, when the choir, led by a boy's pure soprano voice, sang the Russian Kontakion of the Departed.

'Give rest, O Christ, to thy servant with thy saints, where sorrow and pain are no more, neither sighing, but life everlasting. Thou only art immortal, the Creator and Maker of man: and we are mortal formed of the earth, and unto earth shall we return, for so thou didst ordain when thou createdest me, saying, Dust thou art, and unto dust shalt thou return. All we go down to the dust; and weeping o'er the grave, we make our song, alleluya, alleluya.

'Give rest, O Christ, to thy servant with thy saints: where sorrow and pain are no more, neither sighing, but life everlasting.'

Then the funeral procession left for the Maitland crematorium, thousands of people standing in silence as the hearse passed down Wale Street and Adderley Street.

Notes to Sources

Pages 5–13

CHAPTER 2

1. According to Sir Francis Clayton, author of *The Claytons*, she was awarded the O.B.E. According to Mr. H. Savory, registrar of the archdeaconries of Northampton and Oakham in the diocese of Peterborough, she was awarded the C.B.E. The Town Clerk's department in Peterborough confirmed this.
2. Told to Dr. Horton Davies by Clayton. See *The Outspan*, 20.4.51.
3. 13.7.67, to the author.
4. Told by Clayton himself, when Archbishop of Cape Town, preaching in Johannesburg on the occasion of the diamond jubilee of the Community of the Resurrection, 26.4.52.
5. A favourite story of the Revd. Philip Jourdaan.
6. To the author, 27.4.67.
7. Told to the author by the Revd. Canon K. A. Chaffey, Rector of Muizenberg, Cape.

Pages 14–21

CHAPTER 3

1. The information about his B.A. of 1908 is contained in a letter date 29.6.68 from Mr. N. C. Kittermaster, librarian of Rugby School, to the late Dr. A. W. Blaxall. It says 'B.A. 1908' and nothing more.
2. *Church News*, Cape Town, xxiii, 1957.
3. I am indebted for the material dealing with St. Mary's the Less to Dr. Arthur L. Peck of Cambridge; also to the Revd. and Mrs. A. F. Royston, then Sunday-school teachers at Little St. Mary's.
4. The Revd. Dr. Horton Davies was told this by Clayton, who regarded it as a 'perfect epigram'. See *The Outspan*, 20.4.51.
5. To the author, 27.4.67.
6. Told by Canon Rosevcarc of Cape Town to Arthur Calder Marshall.
7. *The Doctrine of the Church and Christian Reunion*, John Murray, London, 1920.
8. Mrs. A. F. Royston, Sunday-school teacher, Guide Captain and Assistant Sacristan, in notes dated 8.8.68. See also *Cambridge Daily News*, 8.9.24.

Pages 22–35

CHAPTER 4

1. It is to the Revd. Claude Handford that I am indebted for much of the material used in this chapter. He died in 1972.
2. Letter dated 12.11.24, to be found in the Chesterfield parish magazine, December 1924.

3. Harris to me, 27.4.67. To him too I am indebted for much of the material used in this chapter.

4. As related to Handford by an elderly churchwarden.

5. Clayton to the Revd. T. W. Hugall, 26.9.49.

6. Horton Davies, *The Outspan*, 20.4.51.

7. To the author, 27.4.67.

8. The letter was signed by D. Chitty, on behalf of G. W. Dymond, S. G. Chance, F. Thatcher, G. A. B. Newenham, C. E. Tomkinson, G. E. Martineau, E. P. Hindley, R. P. R. Carpenter, C. W. Handford, R. F. Yates, M. H. R. Synge, A. L. Brightman, D. B. Harris, and himself.

9. Written 10.5.43, when Dymond was Rector of Boksburg, and Clayton was Bishop of Johannesburg. 10. 1.10.33.

11. From notes taken at an informal meeting in the Chesterfield Vicarage, on 21.7.68, by Betty Foster.

12. Chesterfield parish magazine, January 1928.

13. 31.3.34, Clayton papers, AB 191, personal documents, Library of the University of the Witwatersrand.

14. 2.5.34, ibid.

15. Chesterfield parish magazine, March 1934. 16. Ibid.

17. Clayton papers, Library of the University of the Witwatersrand.

18. This scroll is nowhere to be found.

19. Horton Davies, *The Outspan*, 20.4.51.

20. Ibid. 21. Ibid. 22. *Yea and Nay*, 1938 edition, p. 32.

Pages 36–42

CHAPTER 5

1. Acts viii.17–19.

2. Much of the diverting material that follows is from Canon Redvers Rouse of Johannesburg.

3. *Rand Daily Mail*, 25.5.34. 4. *The Outspan*, 20.4.51.

5. Told to me by the Revd. W.F. Rea of Hilton, Natal.

Pages 43–8

CHAPTER 6

1. Such sexual intercourse was prohibited in 1950. Such intermarriage was prohibited in 1949. I remind readers that the Nationalist Party came to power in 1948.

2. Huddleston, p. 74.

3. Sundkler, *Bantu Prophets in South Africa*, p. 17.

Pages 49–54

CHAPTER 7

1. *The Watchman*, December 1934.

2. This story I found in 'The Vicar's Letter', taken from an English parish magazine. The cutting not only bears no date, but gives no clue as to the parish. But the vicar obviously knew Clayton in his younger days. He refers to the fact that Clayton was consecrated 'over thirty years ago'.

Pages 55–63

CHAPTER 8

1. Told to me (1970) by Father Pierce-Jones of Cape Town. Clayton's father, then Canon of Peterborough, was present when Pierce-Jones was ordained deacon in 1913.

2. Lewis and Edwards, *Historical Records of the Church of the Province of South Africa*.
3. When Canon Rouse told me this story, he said the hymn was 'Oft in danger, oft in woe'. When he read the typescript, he said, and insisted, that it was 'Fight the good fight'. With regret I changed the script.
4. *The Watchman*, April 1935.
5. This, and the following material, are from *The Watchman*, November 1935.

Pages 64–73

CHAPTER 9

1. *The Watchman*, November 1934.
2 *The Watchman*, February 1936.
3. Revd. Philip Makgalemele, Priest in Charge, Lichtenburg, to the Revd. Donald Bailey, December 1948, on hearing that the bishop had been elected Archbishop of Cape Town.
4. *The Sword*, Bloemfontein Diocesan Magazine, April 1957.
5. Quoted by Eric Walker, *A History of Southern Africa*, p. 647.
6. *The Watchman*, November 1937.
7. *The Watchman*, March 1937.
8. Hellmann (ed.), *Handbook on Race Relations in South Africa*, pp. 362 f.
9. All the following material and quotations are from the Report of the Interdepartmental Committee on Native Education, 1935–1936, U.G. 29/1936.
10. H. Jowitt, Director of Education, Uganda.
11. *The Watchman*, November 1936.
12. *The Watchman*, August 1937.
13. *The Watchman*, November 1937.
14. *The Watchman*, December 1937.
15. Paton, *Hofmeyr*, p. 230; abridged ed., p. 180.
16. *The Watchman*, November 1936.

Pages 74–82

CHAPTER 10

1. I cannot give the name of my informants, but I have no reason to doubt them.
2. Told to me by the Revd. Basil Berthold, Cape Town.

Pages 83–9

CHAPTER 11

1. Told to me by Mrs. A. J. van Ryneveld.
2. *The Watchman*, August 1936. The quotation comes from Cowper's *Olney Hymns*.
3. *The Watchman*, January 1938.
4. U.S.P.G. Papers, 1937.
5. *The Watchman*, November 1937.
6. All these extracts from Clayton papers, AB 191, cutting.
7. Dr. Horton Davies in *The Outspan*, 10.4.51. The address is now lost or destroyed.

Pages 90–9

CHAPTER 12

1. All the foregoing material is from *The Watchman*, October 1939.
2. *The Watchman*, November 1939
3. *Die Kerkbode*, 30.8.39.
4. *Die Kerkbode*, 28.6.39.
5. Paton, *Hofmeyr*, chapters 27 and 28 (10, 11 and 12 of abridged edition), give an account of the extraordinary events of this period.

6. Issue of 1.5.40. 7. Issue of 14.8.40.
8. Issue of 16.10.40. 9. Issue of 24.7.40.
10. Told to me by the Right Revd. Patrick Barron, Bishop of George.
11. S.P.G. files for 1939, letter dated 13.5.40.
12. Clayton papers, AB 191, personal documents, folder 1.
13. S.P.G. files, 1935. 14. S.P.G. files, 1940.
15. S.P.G. files, 1941. 16. S.P.G. files, 1941.
17. *The Watchman*, June 1941. 18. *The Watchman*, January 1942.
19. *The Watchman*, Bishop's Charge, November 1941.
20. This brief account was written with the help of Canon R. P. Y. Rouse.

Pages 100–5

CHAPTER 13

1. *The Watchman*, Bishop's Charge, October 1940.
2. *The Watchman*, January 1941.
3. Africans were asked to join the army, but out of regard for a very deep white prejudice and fear they were not to be armed. On some critical occasions these regulations were ignored by commanding officers.
4. The material for the last few pages is from *The Watchman*, November 1941.
5. Paton, *Hofmeyr*, p. 334; abridged ed., p. 265.

Pages 106–12

CHAPTER 14

1. *Race Relations*, first quarter 1941.
2. The foregoing material is from *Common Sense*, January 1941, February 1941.
3. Hoernlé to Clayton, 21.10.41. This, and the other letters used in this chapter, are in the D. L. Smit Collection in the Library of Rhodes University. Although I knew of the Clayton–Hoernlé discussion, I would not have known of the correspondence but for the interest of Dr. Rodney Davenport of the University.
4. *Star*, 24.10.41.
5. Clayton to Hoernlé, 25.10.41. 6. Hoernlé to Clayton, 28.10.41.
7. Smit to Hoernlé, 21.11.41. 8. Hoernlé to Smit, 27.11.41

Pages 113–22

CHAPTER 15

1. The material for this first portion of chapter 15 comes from *The Watchman*, August 1942.
2. *The Watchman*, July 1942.
3. *The Watchman*, August 1942.
4. The foregoing material is from *The Watchman*, November 1942.
5. These words are written down from memory. But others who were present agree that they contain the substance.

Pages 123–8

CHAPTER 16

1. This is the account of Dorothy Maud herself. The account given by Nicholas Mosley, in *The Life of Raymond Raynes*, differs slightly.
2. This is splendidly recorded in chapters 9–16 of Mosley's *The Life of Raymond Raynes*. The most intimate story of Sophiatown itself is found in Trevor Huddleston's *Naught for Your Comfort*. I have drawn a great deal on both these books.

3. Mosley, p. 72. The next paragraph is also largely quotation from Mosley.
4. Mosley, p. 92.
5. Mosley, p. 125.
6. Mosley, p. 122.
7. Mosley, p. 126.
8. *The Watchman*, December 1943.

Pages 129–39

CHAPTER 17

1. *The Watchman*, February 1944.
2. *A Time to Speak*, p. 103.
3. *A Time to Speak*, p. 121.
4. According to the *Oxford Dictionary of Quotations*, this was said by some unknown person, probably a scholar of Rugby, of the headmaster Dr. Frederick Temple, father of Archbishop William Temple.
5. Clayton papers, AB 191, personal documents, folder 1.
6. To Florence Blaxall, 17.7.68.

Pages 140–50

CHAPTER 18

1. *The Watchman*, November 1944.
2. *The Watchman*, October 1944.
3. *The Watchman*, December 1944.
4. Ffrench-Beytagh to Calder Marshall, August 1960.
5. *The Watchman*, July 1945.
6. Paton, *Hofmeyr*, p. 392; abridged ed., p. 309.
7. Said to me.
8. *The Watchman*, February 1945.
9. This material is taken from the twelfth charge, *The Watchman*, November 1945.
10. D. F. Malan, *Afrikaner-volkseenheid*, p. 229.
11. *The Watchman*, November 1945.
12. The fourteenth charge, *The Watchman*, December 1947.
13. *The Watchman*, September 1947.
14. Romans viii.24–5.
15. Clayton papers, AB 191, folder 5.
16. *Good Hope*, December 1950.

Pages 151–60

CHAPTER 19

1. Arthur Blaxall, writing from memory of a conversation with Clayton.
2. Michael Scott, notes written for me, 30.8.68.
3. All the preceding scriptural quotations are from Romans xiii.
4. *A Time to Speak*, p. 168.
5. *Naught for Your Comfort*, p. 55.
6. Clayton papers, AB 191, folder 1.
7. Huddleston in *The Watchman*, April 1946.
8. For a fuller account of these events, see Paton, *Hofmeyr*, chapter 35; abridged ed., chapter 14.
9. Walker, *A History of Southern Africa*, p. 764.
10. *The Watchman*, November 1946.
11. This was first suggested to me by Bishop Vernon Inman, and later confirmed by Mr. Leif Egeland, who was in 1948 South African High Commissioner in London, and was also one of Smuts's nominations for an honorary degree at the same ceremony.
12. Clayton papers, AB 191, folder 1.
13. *The Watchman*, October 1947.
14. Clayton to S.P.G., 13.5.40, 22.7.44, 4.1.45.
15. *The Watchman*, October 1947.
16. *The Watchman*, December 1947. The text is from James i.5.

Pages 161–70

CHAPTER 20

1. Said by Dr. Langley, Archbishop of Canterbury, when opening the first Conference. Lambeth Palace is the London home of the Archbishop.
2. *The Watchman*, January 1948.
3. January, February and March.
4. Matthew xix.3–9.
5. Mark x.2–12; Luke xvi.18.
6. I Corinthians vii.1–16.
7. In the first of his three articles in *The Watchman*, January 1948.
8. *The Watchman*, June 1948.
9. Clayton papers, AB 191, sermons and addresses – typescripts and manuscripts, box 1; sermon delivered 9.5.48.
10. For an account of these days, see Paton, *Hofmeyr*, chapters 38 and 39; abridged ed., chapters 15 and 16.
11. Margaret Ballinger, *From Union to Apartheid*, p. 246.
12. All the foregoing material is from Clayton papers, AB 191, personal documents, folder 1, and AB 191, letters 1949–1954, plus undated folder 2. The Garbett anecdote was told me by Dick Yates.
13. Clayton papers, AB 191, personal documents, folder 1, letters of congratulation.
14. Quoted in *The Watchman*, July 1948.
15. *Daily News*, Durban, 4.5.72.
16. See page 33.
17. Wilson and Thompson, *Oxford History of South Africa*, vol. 1, p. 39.
18. A handwritten sermon as usual undated, Clayton papers, AB 191, sermons and addresses, box 1.
19. 16.6.48.

Pages 171–7

CHAPTER 21

1. *The Watchman*, December 1948.
2. *Church News*, 8.12.48.
3. F. W. S. Aldridge, Rector of Heidelberg.
4. Told to me by the Revd. S. H. Clarke, living in Eastbourne, England.
5. See Joshua viii.5.
6. This story was told to the writer by Canon Rouse.
7. Told to the writer by Canon K. A. Chaffey, Cape Town.
8. All the foregoing material, except where otherwise stated, is to be found in Clayton papers, AB 191, personal documents, folder 1.

Pages 178–86

CHAPTER 22

1. A story told to the writer by the Revd. Horace Willson and his friend the Revd. Basil Berthold.
2. Copy given to the writer by Donald Bailey. The secular clergy are those not belonging to the monastic orders.
3. *Transvaal Methodist*, January 1949.
4. Matthew v.22.
5. All the foregoing material from the *Cape Times*, 3.2.1949.

Pages 187–200

CHAPTER 23

1. I remind readers that Native Representatives were white persons elected by Africans. This representation was finally abolished in 1960. Its history from 1936–60 can be read in Mrs. Ballinger's book *From Union to Apartheid*.
2. Clayton papers, AB 191, sermons and addresses, box 1.

3. e.g. 13.4.1949 and 1.6.1949, respectively. 4. 20.10.1948.
5. G. M. C. Wassenaar, 1.12.1948.
6. 8.3.1950. 'Uit die Vrystaat' means 'Out of the Orange Free State'.
7. 18.1.1956. 8. 12.1.1949. 9. 13.4.1949. 10. *Cape Argus*, 21.5.1949.
11. *Hansard*, vols. 66–9, col. 6440, 24.5.1949. All *Hansard* column numbers are taken from the files in the Natal Society Library. For some reason unknown to me the column numbers in the University of Natal Library, Durban, are often different.
12. 28.12.1949.
13. Clayton papers, AB 191, sermons and addresses, box 1. 14. See page 87.
15. Clayton papers, AB 191, folder 2, letters 1949–54 plus undated papers. The lecture was also published and circulated. 16. *Church News*, 16.11.1949.
17. So writes Margaret Ballinger, *From Union to Apartheid*, p. 391.
18. All the foregoing material is from 'Opening Address Delivered by the Most Revd. Lord Archbishop of Cape Town, to the Conference of Headmasters and Headmistresses of Private Schools, December 1950'.
19. *Cape Times*, *Cape Argus*, 6.3.1954.
20. *Cape Argus*, 6.3.1954. 21. *Die Burger*, 9.3.1954.
22. *Die Kerkbode*, 13.12.1950. 23. *Good Hope*, 17.1.1951.

Pages 201–10

CHAPTER 24

1 *The Cape to the Zambesi*, vol. xvi, no. 1. 2. Ibid., vol. xvii, no. 3.
3. Archdeacon King wrote this account for me. 4. *Good Hope*, July 1951.

Pages 211–23

CHAPTER 25

1. *A History of Southern Africa*, p. 823. 2. *Cape Times*, 26.4.1951.
3. Ballinger, *From Union to Apartheid*, pp. 268–9.
4. Estimated by Major Piet van der Byl, Smuts's Minister of Native Affairs, *Hansard*, vols. 74–6, 18.6.1951.
5. All the foregoing material is to be found in Clayton, *Where We Stand*, pp. 16–21.
6. *Good Hope*, 21.11.1951. And more strongly, *Good Hope*, 19.3.1952.
7. All the foregoing from *Cape Times*, 31.3.1952. 8. 16.4.1952.
9. *Good Hope*, 21.5.1952. 10. *Good Hope*, 20.8.1952.
11. Told to the writer by Archdeacon Foster van der Byl.
12. Told to me by Canon Synge. 13. *Good Hope*, 19.11.1952.

Pages 224–31

CHAPTER 26

1. Walker, *A History of Southern Africa*, p. 838.
2. *A Survey of Race Relations, 1952–3*, p. 37.
3. *Good Hope*, 18.2.1953. 4. *Good Hope*, 25.3.1953. 5. *Good Hope*, 24.6.1953.
6. *Die Kerkbode*, 19 & 26.1.1955, 2, 9, 16 & 23.2.1955, 9 & 16.3.1955.
7. *Die Kerkbode*, 15.7.1953. 8. *Die Kerkbode*, 9.9.1953. 9. 9.12.1953.
10. See Walker, *A History of Southern Africa*, p. 855. Also *A Survey of Race Relations, 1953–4*, p. 16. 11. *Good Hope*, November 1953.
12. *A Survey of Race Relations, 1952–3*, p. 38.
13. The foregoing material from the *Cape Times*, 27.10.1953.
14. *Cape Times*, 28.10.1953.
15. Foregoing material from *A Survey of Race Relations, 1952–3*, p. 66.
16. This is the title of chapter 9 of *Naught for Your Comfort*.
17. The fifth charge is to be found in Clayton, *Where We Stand*, p. 24.

Pages 232–45

CHAPTER 27

1. All the foregoing from *A Survey of Race Relations, 1953–4*, pp. 93 f.
2. *Hansard*, vol. 84, col. 2629, 24.3.1954.
3. *Hansard*, vol. 86, col. 6211, 3.6.1954.
4. Col. 6216, 3.6.1954.
5. Ibid.
6. *Hansard*, vol. 86, col. 6216, 3.6.1954.
7. Col. 6217, 3.6.1954.
8. Col. 6219, 3.6.1954.
9. Col. 6221, 3.6.1954.
10. *Cape Times*, 19.5.1954.
11. *A Survey of Race Relations, 1953–4*, p. 96.
12. Told to me by Bishop Reeves.
13. *Forum*, December 1954.
14. *Hansard*, vol. 84, col. 2518 f, 23.3.1954.
15. Col. 2710, 24.3.1954.
16. Col. 2879, 26.3.1954.
17. Col. 2884, 26.3.1954.
18. *Hansard*, vol. 85, col. 3120 f, 31.3.1954.
19. Paton, *Hofmeyr*, p. 399.
20. Ibid., p. 497.
21. *Hansard*, vol. 85, col. 4079, 27.4.1954.
22. *Good Hope*, 18.4.1954.
23. 10.10.1954.
24. *Cape Times* and *Cape Argus*, 30.10.1954.
25. *Good Hope*, 15.12.1954, the Archbishop's charge.
26. See 'Time, Gentlemen, Time', *Forum*, February 1955.
27. 19.5.1954.
28. *Cape Times*, 8.12.1954.

Pages 246–61

CHAPTER 28

1. *Hansard*, vol. 87, col. 883 f., 9.2.1955.
2. *Naught for Your Comfort*, chapter 10.
3. Huddleston to Paton, 26.6.1967.
4. *Good Hope*, 20.4.1955.
5. 28.4.1955.
6. 28.4.1955.
7. A. W. Wells in the *Cape Argus*, 5.5.1955, also *Good Hope*, 25.5.1955.
8. *Good Hope* supplement, 25.5.1955.
9. *Cape Times*, 30.4.1955.
10. *Cape Argus*, 18.6.1955.
11. Clayton papers, AB 191, sermons and addresses, box 1.
12. Clayton, *Where We Stand*, page 42.
13. *Church News*, 15.6.1955.
14. Huddleston to Paton, 30.9.1970.
15. Much of the foregoing told to the biographer by the Most Revd. Robert Selby Taylor, Archbishop of Cape Town.
16. *Good Hope*, 22.6.1955.
17. See Ballinger, *From Union to Apartheid*, p. 304, for the astonishing details.
18. Foregoing material from *Cape Times*, 11.6.1955.
19. *Cape Times*, 13.6.1955.
20. 22.6.1955.
21. *Good Hope*, 22.6.1955, *Cape Times*, 18.6.1955.
22. *Good Hope*, 22.6.1955.
23. Huddleston to Paton, 30.9.1970.
24. *Cape Times*, 18.6.1955.
25. 15.10.1951.
26. *Good Hope*, 26.10.1955.
27. Clayton to Wood, 22.7.1954.
28. The foregoing material from Clayton, *Where We Stand*, pp. 41 f.

29. Clayton papers, AB 191, cuttings.
30. Huddleston to Paton, 30.9.1970.

Pages 262–74

CHAPTER 29

1. *Hansard*, vol. 90, col. 993, 3.2.1956.
2. *Hansard*, vol. 91, col. 4554, 27.4.1956.
3. *Hansard*, vol. 90, col. 1347, 10.2.1956.
4. Col. 1999, 6.3.1956.
5. Col. 2027, 6.3.1956.
6. *Rand Daily Mail*, 7.2.1956. Also Clayton papers, AB 191, sermons and addresses.
7. Clayton to Verwoerd, 10.3.1956, published in *Church News*, 18.4.1956.
8. Fred Barnard to Clayton, published in *Church News*, 18.4.1956.
9. *Cape Times*, *Cape Argus*, 9.2.1956. Also Clayton papers, AB 191, sermons and addresses, typed sermons, 1952–57.
10. *Cape Times*, 16.2.1956.
11. Clayton papers, AB 191, folder 3, written sermons.
12. This address is to be found in Clayton papers, AB 191, folder 3, written sermons. It is not dated, but Clayton says he has been in South Africa for twenty-five years. This makes it 1956. It could possibly be the address he gave to the Christian Council, because some of the thoughts in the two documents are identical. Yet it appears rather to be a purely political discussion, except for the conclusion. I decided to treat it as an address given to some body other than the Christian Council.
13. Ballinger, *From Union to Apartheid*, p. 370.
14. *Good Hope*, 22.2.1956.
15. *Good Hope*, 23.11.1955, 23.5.1956.
16. Clayton papers, AB 191, sermons and addresses, typed sermons.
17. The lecture was published in Butterworth's *South African Review*, 1957.
18. This correspondence is to be found in the file 'Clayton, Geoffrey, Most Reverend, Deceased', in the records of the diocese of Cape Town.
19. Of April 1957.
20. *Good Hope*, 20.2.1957.
21. Sulston to Clayton, 21.12.1956, U.S.P.G. papers, London.
22. Clayton to Roberts, 27.12.1956, ibid.

Pages 275–82

CHAPTER 30

1. See *A Survey of Race Relations, 1956–7*, pp. 17 f.
2. *A Survey of Race Relations, 1956–7*, pp. 18 f.
3. *Hansard*, vol. 94, col. 3217, 21.3.1957.
4. Clayton, *Where We Stand*, p. 54.
5. *Cape Times*, 8.3.1957.

Pages 283–8

CHAPTER 31

1. *Cape Argus*, 13.3.1957.
2. *Hansard*, vol. 94, col. 3227, 21.3.1957.
3. All the foregoing material from *Hansard*, vol. 94, cols. 3235 f., 21.3.1957.
4. *A Survey of Race Relations, 1956–7*, p. 19.
5. *Hansard*, vol. 94, cols. 3238–9, 21.3.1957.
6. Most of the foregoing material comes from *A Survey of Race Relations, 1956–7*, pp. 21 f.
7. 17.4.1957.
8. 24.4.1957. The italics appear in the original.

Index

Abernethy, Gerald, 75, 181
Ackerman, Charles, 181, 280
activism and pietism, 12–13, 51–2, 54, 72, 121, 137, 158, 204, 208, 251, 277
African Children's Feeding Scheme, 142
African Clergy and Laymen Association, 138
African clergy, status of, 46, 65-6; Clayton's reforms, 67, 138
African Mine Workers Union, 134, 134–5n, 156
African National Congress, 134, 134n, 204, 233, 240, 246, 257, 270
Afrikaans, Clayton and, 41, 48, 87, 243
Afrikaner Party, Havenga's, 93, 163
Alexandra bus boycott, 143
All Saints' Mission, Engcobo, Clayton's visit to, 206–7
All-African Native Convention, 62
Anderson, Ronald, 77
Anglo–Boer War, 88
Anglo–Catholicism, 18-19
antisemitism, 83–4, 189
apartheid, 44, 45-6, 46-7, 59, 61-2, 117, 228; Bishop's Commission Report, 118; Malan's promise, 145; Nationalist victory plans, 164; parliamentary representation, 179; traditions in Cape Province, 217; *Die Transvaler*, 283; Clayton: 'The Apartheid Issue', 242-3; total separation, 259; scriptural justification, 264; the future, 256-6; an alternative, 266; 'The Right of Association', 269-70
'Apartheid Issue, The' (Clayton's B.B.C. talk), 242-3
Appellate Court, Bloemfontein, 219, 220
Appellate Division Quorum Bill, 257
Archbishop of Cape Town, Clayton elected, 172-3; tributes, 174-6; farewell gifts from Johannesburg, 180; enthroned in St. George's Cathedral, 183-5; meeting in Cape Town City Hall, 185
archiepiscopal visits: Southern Rhodesia, 205-6; St. John's diocese, 206-7; Basutoland, 207; St. Helena, 207; Tristan da Cunha, 259; Damaraland, 271
Army Education Service, 104
arrival in South Africa, Clayton's, 38
Asiatic Land Tenure and Indian Representation Act, 151
Athlone, Princess Alice of, 124
Atlantic Charter, 99, 104

baasskap, see white supremacy
Bachelor of Arts, Clayton graduates as, 14
Bailey, Donald, 138, 177, 179
Ballenden, Graham, 144
Ballinger, Mrs. Margaret, 183, 187, 191–2, 213, 238, 266
Bantu Authorities Bill, 213–14
Bantu Education Act, 217, 229, 232–7
Baring, Sir Evelyn and Lady, 30, 183, 270
Barlow, Arthur, 238–9, 262
Basutoland, Clayton's visit to diocese of, 207
beerhall profits, see Native Revenue Account
Bell, George, Bishop of Chichester, 174
Bethal, 153
bishop, Clayton consecrated, 37
Bishop of Johannesburg, Clayton elected, 31; enthroned in St. Mary's Cathedral, 38–40
Bishop's Commission, 101, 103, 105, 114; Report *The Church and the Nation*, 116–19, 129, 141; Continuation Committee, 129, 145
Bishop's Fund, 85
'Bishop's House' rebuilt, 98
'Bishopscourt', Clayton moves to, 180–2
Black Consciousness, 89n, 289–90
Black Power, 89n, 289–90
Black Sash, 257–8, 276
Blaxall, Arthur, 30, 120, 138, 173
Blaxall, Florence, 30, 98
Bloemhof, 57
Bradfield, William, Bishop of Bath and Wells, 174
Brink, C. B., 239, 243–4
Broederbond, 135
Brookes, Edgar, 183, 187, 213
Brown, Peter, 289n
Bull, Father, 8
Burger, 198, 281

Caledon, 203, 273
Calvinism and Catholicism (or non-Calvinism), 47, 113–14, 131, 170, 197, 198–9

Cambridge and Clayton: at Pembroke, 8–14; Chaplain and Fellow of Peterhouse, 14; Dean of Peterhouse, 15; Vicar of St. Mary's the Less, 16–21; honorary doctorate, 165–6; preached at Pembroke, 251
Cambridge Inter-Collegiate Christian Union, 9
Campaign for Right and Justice, 134–6
Cape Argus, 173
Cape Native Voters' Convention, 62
Cape Times, 250, 255
Cape Town, diocese of: coloured staff, 200; 'welcome back' gift to Clayton, 256
Carinus, Mrs. J. G., 183
Carpenter, R. P. R., 22, 29
Carter, Stephen, C.R., 128
Central Africa, Province of, 209; inauguration of Archbishop, 252
Central African Federation, 252
Chamber of Mines, 156
Chaplain to the Forces, Clayton appointed, 15–16
charges, Clayton's: as Bishop of Johannesburg, 50–2, 62, 68, 71, 72, 74, 85, 91, 101, 106, 115, 140, 144, 147, 156, 159 171; as Archbishop, 198–9, 210, 214–15, 229–30, 235–6, 272
Chesterfield, 7; Clayton's ministry, ch. 4 *passim*; induction as vicar, 23; Archdeacon, 24; introduces Sung Eucharist, 26; Rural Dean, 28; Examining Chaplain to Bishop of Derby, 28; four-day bazaar, 28–9; shyness, 30; farewell gifts and tributes, 33; revisit, 169; memorial brass, 294
Chignell, Nan, 30, 139
Christ the King, Church of, Sophiatown, 55, 125–6, 128; school, 257, 262–4
Christian Council of South Africa, 113, 224, 226, 234, 263, 276
Christian Institute, 131n
'Christian Reconstruction' conference, 113–14
Christian Social Front, 137
'Christian Unity—An Anglican View' (Clayton's address), 193–4
Christian–Nationalism, 97; Christian–National Education, 190, 197
'Christianity and Race' (Clayton's address to S.A.I.R.R.), 188
Church and State: Bishop's Commission, 116, 117; 122, 152, 180, 187, 222, 225 255, 264–5, 269; letter to P.M., 277–80; N.G.K., 285–6
'Church and State' (Clayton's lecture at U.C.T.), 264–5
Church and the Nation, The, see Bishop's Commission
'church clause', see Native Laws Amendment Act
Church Extension Fund, 85
Church News, 191, 290
Church of England in South Africa, 267, 268
Church of Sweden, 39
Church of the Province of South Africa, ch. 1 *passim*; election of Metropolitan, 74, 172; joint evangelism, 87; centenary, 157; theoretical structure, 160; fourteen dioceses, 205; parishes of St. John, Wynberg, and St. Peter, Mowbray, 267; Dean of the Province, 271, 283
'Church Sleeps On, The', by Huddleston, 240–2
Church Women's Society, 98, 139
Churchill, Winston, 96, 99, 165
Citizens' Housing League, 246
civil obedience, see Church and State
Clack, Maurice, 134, 181
Clarke, S. H., 8–9, 55, 96, 175–6, 260, 267–8
Clayton, Sir Francis Hare, *The Claytons*, 6, 175
Clayton, Geoffrey Hare, and: activism and pietism,12–13, 51–2, 54, 72, 121, 137, 158, 204, 208, 251, 277; alternative to apartheid, 264, 266; beauty 32–3, 38, 181–2; British tradition, 197, 215; boycott, 217–18, 241, 251, 257; Christian morality, 10–11; despair, 267; divorce, 161, 169; drink, 76, 226; George Herbert, 268–9; hope, 106–12, 148, 150; irritability, 10–11, 13, 18, 61, 79, 98, 166, 204; keeping of papers, 15–16, 32, 173; love, 149, 163; music, 23–4, 188; new order, 100–5, 108, 140; relationship with Dutch Reformed churches, 87, 192–3, 195, 198, 243–5 281; sexual morality, 11, 18; sexual 'nature', 11, 208; snobbery, 16, 41–2; telephone, 98; totalitarian state, 85, 91, 220, 233, 269; trusteeship, 102, 108; women, 6, 11, 30, 116, 139, 166, 182
Clayton, Harold, (G. H. C.'s brother), 5, 6, 169, 175
Clayton, Katherine, (G. H. C.'s mother), 5, 6, 9, 11, 15, 16, 31–2
Clayton, Katherine, (G. H. C.'s sister), 5, 6, and see Mrs. Katherine Roberts
Clayton, Lewis, (G. H. C.'s father), 5, 9, 15, 16
Clayton, Lewis Hare, (G. H. C.'s brother), 5, 6
Claytons, The, 6
Clegg, A. S., 39
clergy, Clayton's relationship with his, 10, 18, 23, 25, 29, 32 75, 76, 178, 202–4, 208; particular relationship with African and Coloured clergy, 43–4, 57, 63, 66–7, 82, 88, 155, 176, 273
Collins, Canon John, 239–40
Coloured Representative Council (later Coloured Persons' Representative Council), 267n
Comber, Tom, 120, 120n
Commission on Coloured Education, 229, 230
Commission on Native Education, 215–16
Communism and Communists, 91–2, 117, 133, 135–6, 167, 171, 185, 190, 204, 213–14, 215, 233, 264, 270, 275; and see Suppression of Communism Act
Community of the Resurrection: Mission to Undergraduates, 8; Mission to the

University, March 1913, 9; in diocese of Johannesburg, 44, 47; Priory of St. Peter, Rosettenville, 55; St. Peter's School, 80; parish of Sophiatown, 124; Superior of World Community, 126; *C.R.*, quarterly review, 126; Salisbury, 205; diamond jubilee and Clayton's sermon, 220; Bantu Education Act, 236; 247; Penhalonga, 253
Conference of Headmasters and Headmistresses of Private Schools, Clayton's address to, 196–8
Congregational Church, 48, 62
Congress of Democrats, 204, 233
Corlett, Councillor, 109
Cowdry, Roy, 6, 15, 77, 77n, 208–9, 221–2, 259, 278, 280–1, 283, 290
Criminal Laws Amendment Act, 224
Cry, the Beloved Country, 112
Cuddesdon, Clayton at, 14
Cullen, H. A., Bishop of Grahamstown, 14, 205, 271, 277, 283
Currey, Ronald, 58, 80
Cutten, J. R., 86

Dadoo, Dr. Yusuf, 135
Damaraland, Clayton's visit to diocese of, 271
Dankes, Francis Whitfield, Bishop-Suffragan of Plymouth, 37
Darbyshire, John Russell, Archbishop of Cape Town, 74–6, 95, 113, 166
Darbyshire, Miss, 74, 180–1
Davies, Dr. Horton, 'The Most Reverend Geoffrey Clayton', 41
de Blank, Joost, 274; Archbishop of Cape Town, 288
de la Rey, Dolf, 211
deacon, Clayton's ordination as, 14
Deane, Frederic, Bishop of Aberdeen, 174
death of Archbishop Clayton, 281; tributes and reactions, 281–2, 293; instructions in will, 293; funeral, 294; Government ignores funeral, 281–2; interment of ashes, 293–4; memorials: in St. George's Cathedral, 293, in Chesterfield, 294; estate, 181
Defiance Campaign (or Resistance Campaign), 219–20, 222, 224
Devonshire, Duke and Duchess of, 28
Dilworth-Harrison, T., 33, 169
Diocesan College, Rondebosch, 200
Diocesan Commission, see Bishop's Commission
dispatches, Clayton mentioned by Allenby in, 16
Doctor of Divinity, Clayton's honorary degree, 158, 165–6
du Plessis, Prof. L. J., 287
Duncan, Mr. and Mrs. Graeme, 181
Dutch Reformed churches (including Nederduitse Gereformeerde Kerk), 4, 47; view of race and goal of separate racial destinies, 47, 180, 188, 189–91, 199, 214, 223, 226, 227–8; relationship to Nationalist Government, 47, 276; relationship with other churches, 47–8, 87, 226, 275; relationship with Clayton, 87, 192–3, 195, 198, 243, 281; Second World War, 91; at Fort Hare conference, 114n; Clayton addresses N.G.K. Synod, 192; request for Board of Censors, 226; Christian Council, 226; national interracial conference, 226–7, 234, 243–5; 275–6; tribute to Clayton, 281; 'church clause', 284, 285–8
Dymond, George, 22, 29, 77, 77n

Eaton, A. W., 101, 103, 105, 113, 119, 129, 147
ecumenism, 19, 20–1, 87, 167–8 193–5, 243–4, 245
Edmunds, Alderman W. H., 33
education, African (and see schools, African mission), 69–70, 69n; Report of the Interdepartmental Committee on Native Education (1936), 70; 72, 89, 102n; school-feeding, 142, 192; 156, 213, 215–17; Eiselen Report, 216; Bantu Education Act, 229, 232–7
Education, Christian-National, 190, 197
education and the Church, see schools, white Anglican private, and schools, African mission
Egeland, Leif, 165
Eiselen, Dr. W. W. M., 215
Eiselen's Commission, see Commission on Native Education
'Ekutuleni', 55, 124
Elective Assembly: of diocese of Johannesburg, 3, 4; of diocese of Cape Town, 172
Ely Cathedral, Clayton priested in, 15
England, Clayton's visits to: in 1948: 162–9, and see under Lambeth conference; in 1955: problem of how to behave, 248–9; speech to S.P.G. in Church House, 249–50; Nationalist reaction, 250; *Cape Times* defence, 250; speech to S.P.G. in Albert Hall, 250–1; S.P.G.'s gift, 251; 'welcome back' meeting, 256
Episcopal Synod, 179, 183, 192, 227–8, 271
Establishment, 31
Ethiopia, Order of, 48, 177
evangelism, 129, 142, 146–7, 148–9, 234
Evening Post, 214

Federal Council of the N.G.K.: statement of the Commission on 'church clause', 285–6; delegation to Minister, 286
ffrench-Beytagh, Gonville Aubie, 77–9, 77n, 141, 144, 149, 202
Figgis, John Neville, C.R., 7, 11–13, 20 96
financial resources, Clayton's, 181
Fisher, Geoffrey, Archbishop of Canterbury, 174, 247
Fisher, Leonard, Bishop of Natal, 172, 205
Forbes, Percy, 4, 119–20, 121
Fort Hare, University College of, 57, 113–14
Forum, 236
Fouche, J. J., 198

franchise, 44–5, 53, 53n, 61–2 88n; Bishop's Commission Report, 118–19, 118n; 130, 142, 156, 179, 180, 211, 267, 273
Frere, Father, 8
Friends of Diocesan Missions, 95
funeral, Clayton's, 281–2, 293–4
Furse, Michael, Bishop of St. Albans, 4

Garbett, Cyril, Archbishop of York, 165
Gardiner, J. Bruce, 39, 159
Gawe, James, 46n
Gearing, H. E., 183, 185
George Williams Prize for Theology, Clayton awarded, 14
George VI and royal family, visit of, 158
Gerdener, Dr. G. B. A., 190, 192, 226
Germiston, 79
Gibbs, Michael, Dean of Cape Town, 172, 181, 183, 208–9
Good Hope, 212, 221, 222, 225, 231, 256
Goodall, Eric, C.R., 128
Gore, Bishop Charles, 4
Government, Clayton voices criticism of: 179, 214–15, 220, 221, 224, 233, 239, 254–5, 260, 263–4, 272–3, 277–80
Government, Coalition, 53
Government, Nationalist: 'black spots', 44; Immorality Act, 45–6; domestic servants, 115; parliamentary representation, 179, 211; racial separation, 187, 191–2; church schools, 199–200; sensitivity to criticism, 248–9; ignores Clayton's funeral, 281–2; and see under: Separate Representation of Voters Act; High Court of Parliament; Public Safety Act; Criminal Laws Amendment Act; Reservation of Separate Amenities Act; Bantu Authorities Bill; Bantu Education Act; Group Areas Act; Natives Resettlement Act; Senate Act; Appellate Division Quorum Bill; Mixed Marriages Bill; Native Laws Amendment Act
Government, United Party, 72, 83, 88, 143–4, 156, 276; and see under: Native Land Bill; Representation of Natives Bill; Asiatic Land Tenure and Indian Representation Act
Grahamstown, 136, 149–50, 221
Gray, James, 39
Gray, Prof. J. L., 100, 108
Great St. Mary's, Cambridge, 9
Gregorowski, William Victor, and Mrs., 203, 218
Group Areas Act, 192, 196, 272–3; amended, 287

hadedah, 272
Handford, Claude, 7, 22
Hanray, Thomas, Bishop of Argyll and the Isles, 174
Harris, Donald, 10–11, 17, 24, 29, 33; sister, 30
Havenga, N. C., 163
Hepworth, Bernard, (Father Thomas), 9
Herbert, George, 268–9
Herero people, 154
Hermanus, 247
Hertzog, Gen. J. B. M., 1, 45, 48, 53, 53n, 67, 70, 83, 85, 88, 93, 97, 100
Higgs, H. R., 38, 130, 157–8
High Court of Parliament, 220
Hill, Francis, C.R., 39, 66
Hoernlé, Alfred, 83–4, 100, 106–12
Hofmeyr, Anna, 94–5
Hofmeyr, J. H., 71, 83, 85; White supremacy, 100; trusteeship, 73, 102; the new order, 104; and Hoernlé, 107; African schools, 142, 217; miners' strike, 156; death, 164, 187
Hofmeyr, J. M., 114n
Hofmeyr, Senator Willie, 94
holidays, Clayton's: alphabetical, 17; with ffrench-Beytagh, 79, 149; in war-time, 115; with Yates and ffrench-Beytagh, 141–2; to England and Lambeth Conference; 162–9; 221; with Selby Taylor, 252; with Barings, 270–1
Holt, Basil, 244
Holy Orders, Clayton's decision to take, 8
Holy Orthodox Eastern Church, 39
'home' to England from South Africa, 1–2, 41, 238–9, 270
'homelands', see Reserves
Hopefield, 203
Hoskyns, Bishop, 23
How, John, Bishop of Glasgow and Galloway, 8, 29
Huddleston, Trevor, C.R., 43; *Naught for Your Comfort*, 47, 237, 262; activism, 54; Bishop's Commission Report, 120; relationship with Clayton, 121, 142–3, 157, 176, 236–7, 241–2, 247–8, 253, 256–7, 260–1; Prior of Christ the King, 128, 131–3, 142–3, 152, 154, 157, 229; Bantu Education Act, 236–7; Resettlement Bill, 237–9; 'The Church Sleeps On', 240–2; destruction of Sophiatown, 246; school of Christ the King, 257, 262–4; recalled to England, 260–1; *You are Wrong, Father Huddleston*, by Alexander Steward, 262
'Huddleston Jazz Band', 142
Hudson, Bishop, 95
Hugo, J. F., 48
Hunter, John, Bishop of George, 294
Hurst Court Preparatory School, 6

Immink, Councillor, 110
Immorality Act, 44–5, 196
independent churches, African, 48
Indian Congress, 134, 134n, 151, 204, 233, 246
Inman, Mrs. Vernon, 183
Inman, Paul, 272
Inman, Vernon, Bishop of Natal, 271–2, 277, 284
International Clubs, Pietermaritzburg and Durban, 287
Isidore, Dr., Chief Rabbi, 39

James, A. H. Jeffree, 234
James, H. A., 7
Jewish Board of Deputies, 135–6

Johannesburg, city, 3
Johannesburg, diocese of, 1, 3; staff, 46; Synod, 53–4; during the war, 95, 114; 'Friends of Diocesan Missions', 95; grant from S.P.G., 96; shortage of man-power, 96; church-building during war, 97–8; financial position (1947), 159; Bantu Education Act, 236
Johannesburg City Council, 40, 109–10, 115, 132–3, 143, 144

Karney, Arthur Baillie Lumsdaine, Bishop of Johannesburg, 1, 2, 39, 46, 58, 66, 123
Keet, Dr. B. B., 93, 226, 227, 288
Keppel-Jones, Arthur, *When Smuts Goes*, 196
Kerkbode, 47; official periodical of the N.G.K., 91; outbreak of war, 91–2; policy during war, 92–3; 'Church and Parliament', 170; 189–91, 199; tercentenary festival, 218; 223, 226, 227; Canon Collins, 239; 245, 255; 'church clause', 287–8; 'Our Church and Its Sister-churches', 275–6
Killick, Father, 17–18
King, Edward, 202–3
King, John Alexander, 206–7
Kirby, Mrs. Dorothy, 30, 139
Kliptown, 97n, 98
Kontakion of the Departed, 294
Koster, 98
Krugersdorp, 94–5

Lambeth Conference, 161, 166–9, 171
Lang, Cosmo Gordon, Archbishop of Canterbury, 37
Langmore, Edward, 76, 278
Lavis, Sidney, Coadjutor-Bishop of Cape Town, 172, 183, 184, 185, 199, 221, 248, 294
Lawrence, Clare, 124
Leake, Margaret, 124
'Leseling', House of Light, 127
letter from Bishops to Prime Minister: drafted, 279–80; Dean's name added, 283; answer from Verwoerd's secretary, 283
letters, pastoral, on 'church clause', 286–7
Liberal Party, 196, 204, 266, 270, 285, 285n, 287, 289n
liberalism and liberals, 84; Hoernlé's address to S.A.I.R.R., 106–7; 135, 170, 283n, 285
Lichtenburg, 48
Linley, Ernest, 22, 23
locations, African, see townships
London Missionary Society, 64
Louw, Eric, 225, 228, 262
Lovedale, mission school, 114
Lutuli, Albert, 275

Mabuto, A., 176
McBride, Clive, 200
McCarthy, E. D. B., 183
Madras Conference of the International Missionary Council, 87
Makhetha, Fortescue, Suffragan-Bishop of Lesotho, 46n
Malan, Dr. D. F., 67, 70, 85, 93; and new order, 104, 145; Prime Minister, 191, 212, 214, 224, 234
Malan, F. J. Berning, 114
Malan, 'Sailor', 211
Malherbe, E. G., 104
Malvern Conference, 103, 129, 129n
Margaret Teresa, Sister, 175
Marie Louise, Princess, 28
'Mark, The', 78
Markham, Violet, 28, 30
Marquard, Leo, 104
Martineau, George, 29
Matthews, Prof. Z. K., 275
Mataboge, Alpheus, 154–5
Maud, Dorothy, 43, 55, 95, 123–7; and Clayton, 126–7
Meadowlands, 237
memorials to Clayton: his wishes in will, 293; St. George's Cathedral, 293; Chesterfield, 294
Methodist Church, 39, 48, 62, 91, 254, 276, 287
Mguli, R. E. M., 176
Michaelhouse, 58, 80
migratory labour, 45, 121–2, 255
Millington, Christopher, C.R., 164
Milner-White, of King's, later Dean of York, 8
miners' strike, African, 156
Minns, Violet, 32
Missionary Conferences, diocesan, 66, 72
missionary work, 64, 68, 69, 69n, 95, 138, 213
Mixed Marriages Bill, 191–2
Moederkerk (Mother Church), 192
Molefe, Christian, 138
Moroka, 222
Mothobi, Lucas, 57
Mountain Inn, 141, 253
Munton, Winifred, 124
Murray, G. de C., 193

National Union of Students, 104, 116, 287
Nationalism and Nationalists, Afrikaner, 1; mission schools, 69, 71–2, 89, 213; black Englishmen, 71, 164, 216; Hitler and Nazism, 83, 92; anti-semitism, 83; Second World War, 91, 97; reunion of anti-Smuts and anti-war Afrikaners, 92; *broedertwis*, 93; 145; election won, 164; communism, 171, 213–14; goal of separate racial destinies, 179–80, 189; resentment of Clayton abroad, 250
Nationalist Party: under Hertzog, 1, 45, 70; under Malan, 67, 70, 83; reconciliation, 92, 135, 145, 163; election won (1948), 164; increased majority (1952), 225
Native, 3n
Native Affairs Commission, 72–3
Native Land Bill, 62
Native Laws Amendment Act, 275, 276, 283–8; protest of non-Calvinist churches, 276, 277–80, 286–7; reaction of Dutch Reformed churches, 285–6, 287–8; other protest, 287
Native Mission Fund, 65, 159

Native Representatives, 187, 213
Native Revenue Account, 102, 109, 115
Natives Representative Council, 62, 156, 191, 213
Natives Resettlement Act, 237–9
Naught for Your Comfort, 47, 237, 262
Nederduitse Gereformeerde Kerk (N.G.K.), see Dutch Reformed churches
New Brighton, Port Elizabeth, 222
new order, social, 99, 100–5 *passim*; Hoernlé, 108; 'Christian Reconstruction' conference, 113–14; post-war reconstruction, 140–1
New Order (Oswald Pirow's), 93, 100
Newclare, 43, 132
Nicholl, W. G., 7
Nicholls, Heaton, 72
Nicol, William, 190
non-white, 3n
Nyovane, C. H. P., 176

Orlando, 40, 127
Ossewabrandwag ('Ox-wagon Watch'), 93
Owl Club, 185–6

Paget, Edward, Archbishop of Central Africa, 4, 11, 37, 182, 205–6, 209, 252
Paget, Mrs. Rosemary, 11, 182
Palmer, William, Dean of Johannesburg, 3, 4, 30, 53, 56, 95, 112, 161, 166, 169, 231
Pan-African Congress, 270
Parker, Wilfrid, Bishop of Pretoria, 39, 123
Pass, H. L., 8
pass system, 3n
Passive Resistance Campaign, see Defiance Campaign
Paterson, Ned, 38
Paton, Alan, 75n, 77, 78, 97n, 100n, 112, 116–17, 117n, 162, 176, 214, 246
Peacey, Bishop Basil, 94–5, 201
Pearce, Edmund, Bishop of Derby, 32
Peck, Dr. Arthur L., 17
Pembroke College, Cambridge: Clayton at, 8, 14; made Honorary Fellow, 231; preached, 251
pensions of clergy, 139
Peter, Clayton's dog, 75
Peter Ainslie Memorial Lecture, 193 4
Peterborough, Clayton family at, 5, 9
Peterhouse, Cambridge: Clayton Chaplain and Fellow of, 14; Dean, 15; Honorary Fellow, 158
Peterhouse School, 252
Phelps, Francis, Archbishop of Cape Town, 36–7, 74, 74n
Philip, Dr. John, 64
physical appearance, Clayton's, 17–18
pietism, see activism and pietism
Pirow, Oswald, 93, 100
Plettenberg Bay, 79
politics and religion, 41, 51–2, 63, 147–8, 215, 224–5, 230, 234, 265
Potchefstroom, 38, 57, 86, 97
Presbyterian Church, 39, 62, 245, 245n, 276
Pretoria, administrative capital, 3
priest, Clayton ordained, 15
Public Safety Act, 224

'*Quo Vadis?*' (address by Clayton), 265–6

race and the churches, 46–7, 48; Clayton's first charge, 50–1; Bishop's Senate and second Senate, 59–60; Report *The Church and the Nation*, 117, 130; status of African clergy, 138–9; 157–8, 160, 179–80, 187–8, 189–91, 199–200; Clayton on nature and duty of Church of the Province, 210; 226–9; N.G.K. national interracial conference, 243–5; 255, 273; and see Native Laws Amendment Act
Raikes, H. R., 39
Rakale, Canon Andreas, 46, 79–80, 81
Rakale, David, 138
Rakale, Leo, C.R., 79–82, 175
Raynes, Raymond, C.R., 55, 81, 110; priest-in-charge, Sophiatown, 124–6; relationship with Clayton, 125–6; appointed Superior, C.R., 126; return to Mirfield, 127; 247
Read, John, 64
reading, Clayton's gift of, 7–8
Reeves, Ambrose, 54, 149, 154; Bishop of Johannesburg, 204, 207; relationship with Clayton, 204, 208, 236, 253; and Sharpeville, 207–8; Bantu Education Act, 236–7; Resettlement Bill, 237; destruction of Sophiatown, 246; 262–3, 274, 277, 280
'Relation of the Church to the Present Situation in South Africa, The', Methodist and Anglican public meeting, 254
Report of the Interdepartmental Committee on Native Education, 70–1
representation, parliamentary: African, 179; Coloured, 179, 211–12, 219–20, 267, 267n; Indian, 191
Representation of Natives Bill, 61–2
Reserves (now 'homelands'), 3n, 44, 45, 213–14
retirement, Clayton's thoughts on, 245, 256, 259; resignation, 271; resignation withdrawn, 271
Revision of Prayer Book, 31, 31n
Reynecke, Johan, 114, 244
rhinoceros, 178
Rhodes University College, 193
Rhodesia, Southern, visit to diocese of, 205–6
'Right of Association, The' (Clayton's address to the Law Society), 269–70
Roberts, Mrs. Katherine (Kitty), 98–9, 169, see also Katherine Clayton
Roberts, Robert, 6
Roman Catholic Church, 47–8, 91, 113, 276, 287
'Roman danger', 190, 197, 226
Rose Innes, Sir James, 62
Rouse, Redvers, 38, 57; Archdeacon of Native Missions, 60; journey to Makwassi with Clayton, 60–1; and

black stipends, 65; 138–9, 76, 96, 105, 119, 129, 177
Rugby, Clayton at, 6–7, 8n; Old Rugbeian, 42
Runge, Father, C.R., 43
Russell, David, 46n

Sabi River bungalows, 253–4
St. Alban's Coloured Mission, 134
St. Andrew's College, Grahamstown, 221
St. Anne's, Maitland, 278
St. Augustine, parish of, 28–9
St. George's Cathedral, Cape Town, 183
St. Helena, Clayton's visit to diocese of, 207
St. Helena Bay, 76, 203–4
St. John's, visit to diocese of, 206–7
St. John's College, 39, 43, 55, 124, 175–6
St. Margaret's, Leicester, 5
St. Mary's and All Saints, Chesterfield, 22; crooked spire, 22, 24, 28, 32
St. Mary's Cathedral, Johannesburg, 38–9
St. Mary's the Less (Little St. Mary's), Cambridge: 7; Clayton as Vicar, 16–21
St. Paul's College, Grahamstown, 78, 136; golden jubilee, 221
Salisbury, Rhodesia, 205, 252
Savage, Tom, Dean of Cape Town, 77, 77n, 78, 256, 294
schools, African mission, 43, 44, 62, 69, 69n, 70–1, 73, 89, 89n, 115, 213, 216, 217, 229, 232–7, 257, 262; threat to mission schools, 62, 69–70, 213, 215–16, 232, 234–5
schools, white Anglican private, 43, 196–8, 199, 225–6
Schreiner, Oliver, 267
Scott, Michael, 8, 54; Bishop's Commission Report, 120, 120n; relationship with Clayton, 121, 136–8, 152, 253; *A Time to Speak*, 133; Campaign for Right and Justice, 134–6; passive-resistance 151–2; 'Tobruk', 153; Bethal, 153; Herero people, 154; return to London, 154; 248
See of Cape Town Endowment Fund, 181
Selwyn, E. G., later Dean of Winchester, 8
Senate, Bishop's, 59; second Senate, 60
Senate Act, 254
separate development, see apartheid
Separate Representation of Voters Act, 211, 212, 219, 220, 267
sermons and addresses, Clayton's: 'The Prodigal Son', 25–6; 40; 'War and the Christian', 90–1; 'The Church and the New Order', 100–1; 149–50; first sermon as Archbishop, 183–5; 'Christianity and Race', 188; private schools conference, 196–7; 193–4, 218–19, 220, 221, 234, 242–3; S.P.G., Church Hall, 249–50; Albert Hall, 250–1; Pembroke College, 251; Central Africa, 252; last Provincial Synod, 260; Christian Council, 263, 264; U.C.T., 264–5, '*Quo Vadis?*' 265–6; on George Herbert, 268–9; Law Society, 269–70
Shackleford, Mrs., 281
Sharpeville, 207
Shaw, Canon Francis L., 22, 23
simple language, Clayton's mastery of, 14–15, 25, 34–5, 174, 205
simplicity in Clayton's life, 209
Sinton, A., 185
Skey, C. W. L., 233, 234
Smit, D. L., Secretary for Native Affairs, 109, 112
Smith, Mr., benefactor, 125
Smuts, Gen. J. C., 45, 48, 53; tolerance of criticism, 54; 67, 70, 83, 88; Battle of Britain, 97; white supremacy, 100; new order, 104; 136; African housing, 143–4; African miners' strike, 156; Chancellor of Cambridge, 159, 165; election lost, 163–4; death, 196
Snell, Mr. and Mrs. F., 252
Sobukwe, E. A., Suffragan-Bishop of St. John's, 46n
Social and Economic Council, 104
Society for the Propagation of the Gospel, 95, 123, 159, 247; Clayton's addresses, 249–50, 250–1; South African Emergency Fund's gift of £30,000, 251; grants to aid the Church of the Province, 258; 274
Society of Jews and Christians, 84, 100, 108
Society of the Sacred Mission, 236
Sophiatown, 43, 55, 123–8, 132–3, 134, 142, 237, 246–7
South Africa Act (1909), 211, 219
South African Institute of Race Relations, 3n, 45, 84, 106, 188, 204, 232, 287
Spens, Sir Will, 4n, 8, 8n
Stanley, Sir Herbert, 180–1, 183 185, 186, 208, 254
Star, 109, 142, 237
Steward, Alexander, *You are Wrong, Father Huddleston*, 262
stipends of priests, 46, 65–6, 138–9, 140
Strauss, J. G. N., 212, 219
Strijdom, J. G., 227, 234; Prime Minister: Senate Act, 254, 255; 266–7, 283
Sudbury, Stanley, 185
Sundkler, Dr. Bengt, 48
Suppression of Communism Act, 196; Suppression of Communism Amendment Act, 213; 220, 240
Swart, C. R., 196
Swartz, George, Suffragan-Bishop of Cape Town, 46n, 76, 181, 200, 203–4
Syfret, Doris, 30
Sylvester, George and Mrs., 203
Synge, Canon, 221–2
Synge, M. H. R., 32, 37

Tambo, Oliver, 240
Taylor, Robert Selby, Bishop of Pretoria, 252–4, 277
Temple, William, Archbishop of Canterbury, 8n, 141, 149, 150
Ten Points Peace Plan, 103
tercentenary festival, 217–19
Theology, 8
Thomas, Father, (Bernard Hepworth), 9
Time to Speak, A, 133
Times, The, 141

Tobiansky, Mr., 132
'Tobruk', shanty town, 153
Toc H, 77–8
Tomkinson, Cyril, 167
Torch Commando, 211, 219, 225
townships, African, (or locations), 3n, 43, 55, 67, 132, 237
Toynbee, Arnold, *Civilization on Trial*, 174
Transvaler, 283
treason charges and trial, 272
Treason Trial Defence Fund, Clayton supports, 274
Tristan da Cunha, Clayton's visit to, 259
trusteeship, 102, 107
Tugman, Dr. Mary, 123

Union of South Africa, Constitution of, 179
United Party, 45, 53n, 85, 135, 145, 187; as Opposition, 212, 225
University Church Society, Cambridge, 8–9, 11
University of Cape Town, 264
University of the Witwatersrand, 39, 243
Unlawful Organisations Bill, see Suppression of Communism Act
Urquhart, Robert, 39
Ussher, Adv. D'Arcy, 105, 114

van der Byl, Foster, 273–4
van der Kemp, Johannes, 64
van der Merwe, Dr. A. J., 192, 226
van der Westhuyzen, P. J., 281
van Rensburg, Hans, 93
van Schoor, J. J. F., 212
van Wyk, F. J., 239–40
van Zyl, Gov. Gen. and Mrs. Brand, 183
Vereeniging, police raids on location, 67–8
Verwoerd, Dr. Hendrik Frensch: appointed Minister of Native Affairs, 209–10; 215, 216, 229, 232–4, 236; and Clayton, 216–17, 254, 263–4, 288; Resettlement Bill, 237–8; Sophiatown, 246; closing of school of Christ the King, 262–4; 266; Native Laws Amendment Act, 275–6, 283–5, 288; hatred of interracial association, 285
Vicar of Chesterfield, Clayton, 22–35
Vicar of St. Mary's the Less, Clayton, 16–21
Victor, Osmund, C.R., 123

Volksblad, 197–8
Voortrekker centenary celebrations, 86
Voortrekker Monument, 196

Waddy, Canon, 95
Walker, Eric, 212
Wand, John William Charles, Archbishop of Brisbane, 37
War, Second World: declared, 88; catastrophic 1940, 96, 99; invasion of Russia, and Pearl Harbour, 99; Mussolini fallen, 128; and Clayton: 84–5, 88; 'War and the Christian', 90–1; 96–7, 140; VJ Day celebration, 144
'War and the Christian' (Clayton's sermon), 90–1
War Veteran's Action Group, see Torch Commando
Watchman, 2, 4, 36, 65, 112, 113, 129, 130, 138, 158, 169
Watson, A. S., 138
Watson, Spencer, 38
Webb, Dr. J. B., 180, 195, 238, 254
Wells, A. W., 249, 250
Wells, Dr. N. M., 293
Western Areas Protest Committee, 246
Western Native Township, 43, 132
Westlake, Prof. John, Q.C., (Clayton's great-uncle), 14
When Smuts Goes, 196
white supremacy, 100, 116–17, 131n, 212, 213, 227, 255
Whitelaw Robert, 7, 22
Wilkie, A. W., 114
will, Clayton's 293
Willson, Horace, 178
Winter, Tom, 182
Winter, Mrs., 182
Women's Defence of the Constitution League, see Black Sash
Wood, Cecil, 247, 276
World Council of Churches, 190
Wurts, T. M., 147
Wynn, later Bishop of Ely, 8

Yates, Dick, 15, 18, 37, 77, 77n, 138, 141, 144, 152, 208
Yea and Nay, by Clayton, 34
You are Wrong, Father Huddleston, 262

Zulu, Alpheus, Bishop of Zululand, 46